SHAKESPEA

Volume 1

ROMEO AND JULIET

ROMEO AND JULIET
Critical Essays

Edited by
JOHN F. ANDREWS

Routledge
Taylor & Francis Group

LONDON AND NEW YORK

First published in 1993

This edition first published in 2015
by Routledge
2 Park Square, Milton Park, Abingdon, Oxon, OX14 4RN

and by Routledge
711 Third Avenue, New York, NY 10017

Routledge is an imprint of the Taylor & Francis Group, an informa business

© 1993 John F. Andrews

British Library Cataloguing in Publication Data
A catalogue record for this book is available from the British Library

ISBN: 978-1-138-84955-6 (Set)
eISBN: 978-1-315-72488-1 (Set)
ISBN: 978-1-138-84975-4 (Volume 1)
eISBN: 978-1-315-72492-8 (Volume 1)
Pb ISBN: 978-1-138-85271-6 (Volume 1)

Publisher's Note
The publisher has gone to great lengths to ensure the quality of this book but points out that some imperfections from the original may be apparent.

Disclaimer
The publisher has made every effort to trace copyright holders and would welcome correspondence from those they have been unable to trace.

ROMEO AND JULIET
Critical Essays

John F. Andrews

GARLAND PUBLISHING, INC. • NEW YORK & LONDON
1993

Library of Congress Cataloging-in-Publication Data

Romeo and Juliet : critical essays / [edited by] John F. Andrews.
      p.   cm. — (Shakespearean criticism ; vol. 10) (Garland
reference library of the humanities ; vol. 910)
   Includes bibliographical references (p.   )
   ISBN 0-8240-4795-8 (alk. paper)
   1. Shakespeare, William, 1564–1616. Romeo and Juliet.
I. Andrews, John F. (John Frank), 1942– . II. Series.
III. Series: Garland reference library of the humanities; vol. 910.
PR2831.R65 1993
822.3'3—dc20   93-16203
                                         CIP

Printed on acid-free, 250-year-life paper
Manufactured in the United States of America

Contents

Part II. *Romeo and Juliet* in Performance

Part III. *Romeo and Juliet* as a Product of Elizabethan Culture

Contents vii

Introduction

Romeo and Juliet was the first drama in English to confer full tragic dignity on the pangs and perils of youthful ardor. Its protagonists are now enshrined on the high altar of love's sanctuary, and the lyricism that seals their death-marked union has made their vows legendary in every language that possesses a literature.

Shakespeare evidently completed his portrayal of Verona's pride in the mid-1590s.[1] From all indications their story moved audiences in the playwright's own day, and it has maintained a secure position in the repertory from the author's theater to our own. For more than a century it has been a staple of the school curriculum. Speeches from it have been recited by teenagers the world over, and it has probably occasioned more amateur performances than any other play. Not surprisingly, it has also spawned a prolific progeny of offshoots, among them evocative scene-paintings by William Blake and Henry Fuseli, a stately opera by Hector Berlioz, soul-stirring ballets by Peter Ilyich Tchaikovsky and Sergei Prokofiev, a pulsating Broadway musical by Leonard Bernstein, Arthur Laurents, Jerome Robbins, and Stephen Sondheim, an affecting 60s film by Franco Zeffirelli, and a lacrimose best-seller (later made into a 70s movie) by Erich Segal. Meanwhile, as might be expected, it has provided an irresistible target for parodists. People who have never read the work or witnessed a staging of it can repeat puerile jests about the Balcony Scene. As a consequence the heroine's initial utterance in a setting that has been petrified into a cliché is arguably the most frequently cited—and undoubtedly the most widely misunderstood—query in the lexicon of popular culture.[2]

Today *Romeo and Juliet* is a title that everyone is expected to know, or at least know something about. Its central figures are household names. But distorted impressions of them, and of their tragedy, are now so indelibly fixed in our memories that many of us are inclined either to disregard the drama entirely or to regard it too lightly to register its capacity to touch a modern theatergoer's deepest sympathies.

ix

And that is the reason behind the present anthology: to reintroduce contemporary readers to a masterpiece that is considerably more resonant, complex, and problematical than it is usually assumed to be.

The volume commences with eight articles on the aesthetic qualities of *Romeo and Juliet*, the impact its structure has upon the way we experience the play. Mark Van Doren opens the collection with some remarks about the imagistic brilliance of an early work that he describes as "furiously literary." Then D. A. Traversi contemplates the "'metaphysical' balance" of a plot that oscillates between the "twin realities, at once separate and identical, of love and death." Harry Levin reflects on what he classifies as a technical paradox: a dramatic "form" that both employs and supersedes the "formality" it subjects to critical inquiry. M. M. Mahood scrutinizes the tragedy's verbal medium and shows that *Romeo and Juliet*'s incessant wordplay is integral to the suspension of judgment it solicits from the audience as the action unfolds. Susan Snyder then demonstrates that this suspension is generic as well as semantic: she notes that *Romeo and Juliet* depends for many of its effects upon the arousal and frustration of expectations that derive from comic conventions. In an analysis of what he diagnoses as a tendency toward "nominalism" in the protagonists, James L. Calderwood suggests that both the lovers and the play itself are involved in an ontological and experiential quest for "everlasting rest." Marjorie Garber calls attention to the repetitive patterns and scenic juxtapositions that organize the events of the drama and guide our responses to them. And Ralph Berry argues that in both formal and thematic respects "the sonnet is the channel through which the play flows."

From a concern with structure the anthology moves in the second section to nine articles on the text of *Romeo and Juliet* as a score for performance. James Black points to some of the stage pictures, the "reduplicated groupings" an audience sees while watching the tragedy evolve in the playhouse. Jack Jorgens emphasizes the visual aspects of Zeffirelli's cinematic interpretation of the drama. Then three actresses comment on the plot from their viewpoints as erstwhile participants in it: Dame Peggy Ashcroft and Julie Harris approach the play from the perspective of Juliet, and Brenda Bruce looks at the lovers and their situation through the eyes of Juliet's Nurse. Approaching the same character from an external observer's coign of vantage,

Stanley Wells assesses the theatrical potential in the Nurses's apparent "inconsequentiality." Philip McGuire outlines the role that dance plays in the action. In an effort to discern what America's most ambitious musical illustrates about the twentieth-century appeal of Shakespeare's most famous couple, Robert Hapgood compares the tragedy to *West Side Story*. Then Barbara Hodgdon draws on recent productions and adaptations of *Romeo and Juliet* to raise some radical questions about what constitutes a dramatic script.

To conclude we turn to eight attempts to assay *Romeo and Juliet* with touchstones from the age that gave rise to it and conditioned its inaugural reception. Franklin M. Dickey situates the protagonists of Shakespeare's work against their counterparts in the playwright's primary source, the 1562 poem on *Romeus and Juliet* by Arthur Brooke. John W. Draper and Douglas L. Peterson relate the principles of Renaissance astrology to the psychology of the drama's characters. And James C. Bryant offers evidence that Elizabethans might have brought a less trusting attitude to the Friar than do most of today's viewers. From here the investigation proceeds to three articles on the part that gender has in what happens on the Shakespearean stage. Coppélia Kahn explores the difficulties of "Coming of Age" in the Renaissance, with special focus on the maturation process for young men. Marianne Novy links male role-modeling to the nexus of love and violence in the supercharged atmosphere of an early modern city-state. And Edward Snow shows that "Sexual Difference" is inscribed in the very discourse of the hero and heroine. The collection then draws to a close with the editor's own speculations about what a sixteenth-century London playgoer might have made of the ethical and theological issues implicit in Shakespeare's earliest love tragedy.

It goes without saying that the twenty-five essays in these pages are but a sample of the vast commentary *Romeo and Juliet* has elicited over the centuries. Many a valuable study is referred to in the notes accompanying the articles assembled here, and the person who puts such information to its fullest use will heed the counsel of a pinstriped Yankee diamond expert and "look it up."

xii   Romeo and Juliet

NOTES

1. The range of dates usually assigned the play is 1594–96, with most scholars leaning toward late 1595 or early 1596. A few have tried to push the date back to 1591, and a handful have urged an even earlier period of composition.

2. The situation was not helped when a 1984 "translation" of the play by A. L. Rowse rendered the line "O Romeo, Romeo, wherefore are you, Romeo?" Shortly after Rowse was interrogated about this reading on "The MacNeil/Lehrer NewsHour" (April 23, 1984), Russell Baker wrote a *New York Times Magazine* column ("The Romeo Riddle," May 20, 1984) in which he confessed that, like most of his acquaintances, he had gone through life thinking that Juliet's question meant "Where are you, Romeo?" rather than "Why do you have to be named Romeo?"

Romeo and Juliet

Part I

The Language and Structure
of *Romeo and Juliet*

Mark Van Doren

From *Shakespeare*

When Juliet learns that Romeo has killed Tybalt she cries out that he is a beautiful tyrant, a fiend angelical, a dove-feathered raven, a wolfish lamb, a damned saint, an honorable villain. This echoes Romeo's outcry upon the occasion of Tybalt's first brawl in the streets of Verona: brawling love, loving hate, heavy lightness, serious vanity, chaos of forms, feather of lead, bright smoke, cold fire, sick health, still-waking sleep—Romeo had feasted his tongue upon such opposites, much in the manner of Lucrece when wanton modesty, lifeless life, and cold fire were the only terms that could express her mind's disorder. Of Romeo's lines, says Dr. Johnson, "neither the sense nor the occasion is very evident. He is not yet in love with an enemy, and to love one and hate another is no such uncommon state as can deserve all this toil of antithesis." And of the pathetic strains in "Romeo and Juliet" generally Dr. Johnson adds that they "are always polluted with some unexpected depravations. His persons, however distressed, have a conceit left them in their misery, a miserable conceit."

"Romeo and Juliet," in other words, is still a youthful play; its author, no less than its hero and heroine, is furiously literary. He has written at last a tragedy which is crowded with life, and which will become one of the best-known stories in the world; but it is crowded at the same time with clevernesses, it keeps the odor of ink. Images of poison and the grave are common throughout the dialogue, and they fit the fable. The frame of the author's mind is equally fitted, however, by a literary imagery.

There is much about words, books, and reading; as indeed there
is in "Hamlet," but with a difference. The servant who delivers
Capulet's invitations to the feast cannot distinguish the names
on his list, and must have Romeo's help (I, ii). Lady Capulet
commands Juliet to

> Read o'er the volume of young Paris' face
> And find delight writ there with beauty's pen; . . .
> This precious book of love, this unbound lover,
> To beautify him, only lacks a cover.   (I, iii, 81–8)

Romeo's first kiss to Juliet, she remarks, is given "by the book" (I,
v, 112). Love can suggest to Romeo (II, ii, 157–8) the way of
schoolboys with their books. Mercutio with his last breath accuses
Tybalt of fighting by "the book of arithmetic" (III, i, 106). Juliet,
continuing in her rage against Romeo because he has killed her
cousin, demands to know:

> Was ever book containing such vile matter
> So fairly bound?   (III, ii, 83–4)

And words seem to be tangible things. Romeo wishes his name
were written down so that he could tear it (II, ii, 57); when the
Nurse tells him how Juliet has cried out upon his name it is to
him

>   As if that name,
> Shot from the deadly level of a gun,
> Did murder her.   (III, iii, 102–4)

And the lovers take eloquent turns (III, ii, iii) at playing variations
on "that word 'banished,'" which can "mangle" them and is
indeed but "death mis-term'd."

Even the wit of Romeo and his friends—or, as Dr. Johnson
puts it, "the airy sprightliness" of their "juvenile elegance"—has
a somewhat printed sound. When Romeo, going to the ball, wants
to say that the burden of his passion for Rosaline weighs him
down and makes him less wanton than his friends he resorts
once again to the literary idiom:

> For I am proverb'd with a grandsire phrase.   (I, iv, 37)

Not that the wit of these young gentlemen is poor. It is
Shakespeare's best thus far, and it is as brisk as early morning;

the playful youths are very knowing and proud, and speak always—until the sudden moment when lightness goes out of the play like a lamp—as if there were no language but that of sunrise and spring wind.

Lightness goes out suddenly with the death of Mercutio. Yet everything is sudden in this play. Its speed is as great as that of "Macbeth," though it carries no such weight of tragedy. The impatience of the lovers for each other and the brevity of their love are answered everywhere: by Juliet's complaint at the unwieldly slowness with which the Nurse returns from Romeo, by Capulet's testiness as he rushes the preparations for the wedding, by the celerity of the catastrophe once its fuse has been laid.

It is a tragedy in which the catastrophe is everything and so must be both sudden and surprising. Death is not anticipated by as much as anticipates the ends of Shakespeare's major tragedies: that is to say, by all that has been said or done. A few premonitions are planted. The Prologue warns us that the lovers are star-cross'd, misadventur'd, and death-mark'd. Romeo's mind misgives him as he arrives at Capulet's feast, and he imagines

Some consequence yet hanging in the stars.   (I, iv, 107)

Juliet's couplet when she learns her lover's name,

My only love sprung from my only hate!
Too early seen unknown, and known too late!   (I, v, 140–1)

and her experience of second sight as Romeo descends from her chamber:

O God, I have an ill-divining soul!
Methinks I see thee, now thou art below,
As one dead in the bottom of a tomb   (III, v, 54–6)

are there to light the way towards a woeful conclusion. And Friar Laurence's moral is clearly underlined:

These violent delights have violent ends,
And in their triumph die, like fire and powder,
Which as they kiss consume.   (II, vi, 9–11)

But such things are significantly few, and they are external to the principal tragic effect, which is that of a lightning flash against the night.

Night is the medium through which the play is felt and in which the lovers are most at home—night, together with certain fires that blaze in its depths for contrast and romance. "Romeo and Juliet" maintains a brilliant shutter-movement of black and white, of cloud and lightning, of midnight and morning. We first hear of Romeo as one who cherishes the torch of his love for Rosaline in "an artificial night" of his own making; he pens himself in his chamber, "locks fair daylight out," and is for having the world "black and portentous" (I, i). If day is life, as Friar Laurence says it is, then life is for Romeo the enemy of love, which can exist in its purity only by itself, in the little death of a private darkness. Hidden in that darkness it can shine for the knowing lover with a brightness unknown to comets, stars, and suns. When he first sees Juliet he exclaims:

> O, she doth teach the torches to burn bright!
> It seems she hangs upon the cheek of night
> As a rich jewel in an Ethiop's ear.   (I, v, 46–8)

"Blind is his love and best befits the dark," jests Benvolio (II, i, 32) as he searches with Mercutio for Romeo in Capulet's garden; but Benvolio does not understand the power that illuminates his friend's progress. In the next scene, standing with Romeo under the balcony, we reach the lighted goal.

> It is the east, and Juliet is the sun. . . .
> Two of the fairest stars in all the heaven,
> Having some business, do entreat her eyes
> To twinkle in their spheres till they return.
> What if her eyes were there, they in her head?
> The brightness of her cheek would shame those stars,
> As daylight doth a lamp; her eyes in heaven
> Would through the airy region stream so bright
> That birds would sing and think it were not night.

Juliet and love are Romeo's life, and there is no light but they. Juliet may be disquieted by the thought of so much haste:

> It is too rash, too unadvis'd, too sudden,
> Too like the lightning, which doth cease to be
> Ere one can say it lightens.

But Romeo can only cry, "O blessed, blessed night!" There follows a scene in which Friar Laurence salutes and blesses the morning.

Yet his voice does not obliterate our memory of many good-nights the lovers had called to each other, and it is soon (III, v) Juliet's turn to bless the night that she and Romeo have had with each other. She cannot admit that day is coming. Dawn is some mistake, "some meteor." Day, if it is indeed here, will be as death. And when the Nurse convinces her that darkness is done she sighs:

> Then, window, let day in, and let life out.

For her too love has become the only light; something that shines with its own strength and from its own source, and needs night that it may be known. "O comfort-killing Night, image of hell!" Lucrece had wailed (764). But night is comfort here, and day—when kinsmen fight, when unwelcome weddings are celebrated, when families wake up to find their daughters dead—is the image of distress. "O day! O day! O day! O hateful day!" howls the Nurse when she finds Juliet stretched out on her bed. She means a particular day, but she has described all days for the death-mark'd lovers. It is perhaps their tragedy that they have been moved to detest day, life, and sun.

At any rate their career derives its brilliance from the contrast we are made to feel between their notion of day and night and the normal thought about such things. Normality is their foe, as it is at last their nemesis; the artificial night of Juliet's feigned death becomes the long night of common death in which no private planets shine. The word normality carries here no moral meaning. It has to do merely with notions about love and life; the lovers' notion being pathetically distinguished from those of other persons who are not in love and so consider themselves realistic or practical. One of the reasons for the fame of "Romeo and Juliet" is that it has so completely and clearly isolated the experience of romantic love. It has let such love speak for itself; and not alone in the celebrated wooing scenes, where the hero and heroine express themselves with a piercing directness, but indirectly also, and possibly with still greater power, in the whole play in so far as the whole play is built to be their foil. Their deep interest for us lies in their being alone in a world which does not understand them; and Shakespeare has devoted much attention to that world.

Its inhabitants talk only of love. The play is saturated with the subject. Yet there is always a wide difference between what the protagonists intend by the term and what is intended by others. The beginning dialogue by Sampson and Gregory, servants, is pornographic on the low level of puns about maidenheads, of horse-humor and hired-man wit. Mercutio will be more indecent (II, i, iv) on the higher level of a gentleman's cynicism. Mercutio does not believe in love, as perhaps the servants clumsily do; he believes only in sex, and his excellent mind has sharpened the distinction to a very dirty point. He drives hard against the sentiment that has softened his friend and rendered him unfit for the society of young men who really know the world. When Romeo with an effort matches one of his witticisms he is delighted:

> Now art thou sociable, now art thou Romeo, now art thou
> what thou art, by art as well as by nature.   (II, iv, 93–5)

He thinks that Romeo has returned to the world of artful wit, by which he means cynical wit; he does not know that Romeo is still "dead" and "fishified," and that he himself will soon be mortally wounded under the arm of his friend—who, because love has stupefied him, will be capable of speaking the inane line, "I thought all for the best" (III, i, 109). Romeo so far remembers the code of his class as to admit for a moment that love has made him "effeminate." Mercutio would have applauded this, but he has been carried out to become worms' meat and Romeo will have the rest of the play to himself as far as his friends and contemporaries are concerned. There will be no one about him henceforth who can crack sentences like whips or set the hound of his fancy on the magic scent of Queen Mab.

The older generation is another matter. Romeo and Juliet will have them with them to the end, and will be sadly misunderstood by them. The Capulets hold still another view of love. Their interest is in "good" marriages, in sensible choices. They are matchmakers, and believe they know best how their daughter should be put to bed. This also is cynicism, though it be without pornography; at least the young heart of Juliet sees it so. Her father finds her sighs and tears merely ridiculous: "Evermore show'ring?" She is "a wretched puling fool, a whinning mammet," a silly girl who does not know what is good for her. Capulet is Shakespeare's first portrait in a long gallery of fussy, tetchy, stubborn, unteachable old men: the Duke of York in "Richard II," Polonius, Lafeu, Menenius. He is tart-

tongued, breathy, wordy, pungent, and speaks with a naturalness
unknown in Shakespeare's plays before this, a naturalness
consisting in a perfect harmony between his phrasing and its
rhythm:

> How how, how how, chop-logic! What is this?
> "Proud," and "I thank you," and "I thank you not;"
> And yet "not proud." Mistress minion, you,
> Thank me no thankings, nor proud me no prouds,
> But fettle your fine joints 'gainst Thursday next,
> To go with Paris to Saint Peter's Church,
> Or I will drag thee on a hurdle thither.   (III, v, 150–6)

We hear his voice in everything he says, as when for instance the
Nurse has told him to go to bed lest he be sick tomorrow from so
much worry about the wedding, and he argues:

> No, not a whit! What! I have watch'd ere now
> All night for lesser cause, and ne'er been sick.   (IV, iv, 9–10)

His speaking role has great reality, along with an abrasive force
which takes the temper out of Juliet's tongue.

The Nurse, a member of the same generation, and in Juliet's
crisis as much her enemy as either parent is, for she too urges the
marriage with Paris (III, v, 214–27), adds to practicality a certain
prurient interest in love-business, the details of which she
mumbles toothlessly, reminiscently, with the indecency of age.
Her famous speech concerning Juliet's age (I, iii, 12–57), which
still exceeds the speeches of Capulet in the virtue of dramatic
naturalness, runs on so long in spite of Lady Capulet's attempts
to stop it because she has become fascinated with the memory of
her husband's broad jest:

> *Nurse.* And since that time it is eleven years;
> For then she could stand high-lone; nay, by the rood,
> She could have run and waddled all about;
> For even the day before, she broke her brow;
> And then my husband—God be with his soul!
> 'A was a merry man—took up the child.
> "Yea," quoth he, "dost thou fall upon thy face?
> Thou wilt fall backward when thou hast more wit;
> Wilt thou not, Jule?" and, by my holidame,
> The pretty wretch left crying and said, "Ay."
> To see, now, how a jest shall come about!
> I warrant, an I should live a thousand years,

I never should forget it. "Wilt thou not, Jule?" quoth he;
And, pretty fool, it stinted and said, "Ay."
Lady Capulet. Enough of this; I pray thee, hold they peace.
Nurse. Yes, madam; yet I cannot choose but laugh,
To think it should leave crying and say, "Ay."
And yet, I warrant, it had upon it brow
A bump as big as a young cockerel's stone;
A perilous knock; and it cried bitterly.
"Yea," quoth my husband, "fall'st upon thy face?
Thou wilt fall backward when thou comest to age;
Wilt thou not, Jule?" It stinted and said, "Ay."

The Nurse's delight in the reminiscence is among other things
lickerish, which the delight of Romeo and Juliet in their love
never is, any more than it is prudent like the Capulets, or
pornographic like Mercutio. Their delight is solemn, their behavior
holy, and nothing is more natural than that in their first dialogue
(i, v) there should be talk of palmers, pilgrims, saints, and prayers.

It is of course another kind of holiness than that which appears
in Friar Laurence, who nevertheless takes his own part in the
endless conversation which the play weaves about the theme of
love. The imagery of his first speech is by no accident erotic:

I must up-fill this osier cage of ours
With baleful weeds and precious-juiced flowers.
The earth, that's nature's mother, is her tomb;
What is her burying grave, that is her womb;
And from her womb children of divers kind
We sucking on her natural bosom find.   (ii, iii, 7–12)

The Friar is closer to the lovers in sympathy than any other
person of the play. Yet this language is as alien to their mood as
that of Capulet or the Nurse; or as Romeo's recent agitation over
Rosaline is to his ecstasy with Juliet. The lovers are alone. Their
condition is unique. Only by the audience is it understood.

Few other plays, even by Shakespeare, engage the audience
so intimately. The hearts of the hearers, surrendered early, are
handled with the greatest care until the end, and with the greatest
human respect. No distinction of Shakespeare is so hard to define
as this distinction of his which consists of knowing the spectator
through and through, and of valuing what is there. The author of
"Romeo and Juliet" watches us as affectionately as he watches
his hero and heroine; no sooner has he hurt our feelings than he
has saved them, no sooner are we outraged than we are healed.

The author of "King Lear" will work to the same end on a grander scale. Here he works lyrically, through our sentiments, which he keeps in trust. Capulet is an old fool, but we can pity him when the false death of Juliet strikes him dumb at last. As for that false death, our being in on the secret does not prevent us from being touched by it, or from needing the relief which the musicians stand by to give. Five short words at Juliet's bier—"O my love! my wife!" make up for all of Romeo's young errors. Juliet's appeal after her father has stormed out of the room:

> Is there no pity sitting in the clouds,
> That sees into the bottom of my grief?   (III, v, 198–9)

is not to the outer world, it is to us. The tension of the entire play, while we await the kiss of fire and powder which will consume its most precious persons, is maintained at an endurable point by the simplicity with which sorrow is made lyric. Even the conceits of Romeo and Juliet sound like things that they and they alone would say, for we know their fancies to be on fire, and we have been close to the flame. Tolstoy, wishing to deny Shakespeare's supposed "talent for depicting character," said it was nothing but a knack with the emotions. "However unnatural the positions may be in which he places his characters, however improper to them the language which he makes them speak, however featureless they are, the very play of emotion, its increase, and alteration, and the combination of many contrary feelings, as expressed correctly and powerfully in some of Shakespeare's scenes, and in the play of good actors, evokes even, if only for a time, sympathy with the persons represented." Shakespeare, in other words, was merely a great poet with a correct and powerful understanding of the surrendered heart, the listening mind; it is the audience, whom he spares nothing yet handles gently, that he makes over in his own image. Which of the two things he does, creates characters or creates comprehenders of character, may not ultimately matter. At least it is clear that one who has witnessed "Romeo and Juliet" has been taken apart and put together again; has been strangely yet normally moved; has learned a variety of good things about himself; and has been steadily happy in the knowledge.

D. A. Traversi

From *An Approach to Shakespeare*

Romeo and Juliet, Shakespeare's first youthful tragedy—if we exclude for the present purpose *Titus Andronicus*—has a number of clear points of contact with the sonnets. These are most obviously apparent in the style of the play, which here and there incorporates actual sonnets into the dramatic structure and makes at all times a considerable use of sonnet imagery; but the theme too turns, as in some of the sonnets we have just considered, upon the relation of love to the action of time and adverse circumstance. At least one of the questions that the tragedy poses is, indeed, familiar from the sonnets. To what degree can youthful love be regarded as its own justification—"bears it out even to the edge of doom,"[1] as the sonnet has it—or, alternatively, to what extent do the lovers share the conviction that this is simply an empty, rhetorical affirmation? The answer the play gives lies not in any simple assertion, whether affirmative or otherwise, but rather in a balance of contrasted realities. The Prologue strikes a sinister note from the outset by telling us that we are about to witness "the *fearful* passage of a *death-marked* love"; but it is necessary to add that the disaster to which this love will be brought is in great part a result of the hatred of the older generations, in which the young participate, if at all, as victims involved in a situation not of their choosing. Though the young lovers are indeed "star-crossed," destined to die, their response to experience, and the contrast with those around them who only *believe* that they are reasonable and mature, gives the relationship to which they have pledged their generosity a proper measure of validity. Their love must indeed accept the reality of death, which its very origin and nature demand; but once this had been accepted, it remains true that a sense of incommensurate worth, of *true* value, survives to color their tragedy.

The Prologue has no sooner been spoken when the circumstances that will lead fatally to the destruction of love are introduced in the shape of the irrational vanity of the Capulet-Montague feud. The servingmen who so touchily eye one another in the streets of Verona are at once lecherous and self-important, uneasily conscious of breaking what they know to be the law even as they insult their opposites. The masters, on this first showing, are little or no better than their men, combining touchiness and senility in a particularly distasteful way. Their wives know them better than themselves; when Capulet testily calls for his sword to join in the melee, his wife says ironically: "A crutch, a crutch! why call you for a sword?" (I. i), and Lady Montague is equally at pains to hold back her husband from "seeking a foe." On the more active side, reason is habitually overruled by brute instinct, Benvolio's sensible attitude—"I do but keep the peace"—balanced by Tybalt's irrational spoiling for a fight: "I hate hell, all Montagues, and thee!" (I. i). The fair comment on so much obstinate and "canker'd hate" is left, here as it will be throughout the play, to Prince Escalus, who shows himself conscious, as an impartial ruler, of the ruin to which these senseless attitudes will lead, and who does what he can to hold them in check. We may conclude by the end of this opening that, if this is a fair picture of "experience," there is likely to be something to be said in favor of the romantic idealism of youth.

Romeo himself, however, is by no means romantically presented on his first appearance: not, at any rate, if "romanticism" means an acceptance of him at his own estimate. Benvolio tells us of having seen him stealing furtively, almost as a man ashamed, "into the covert of the wood," and Montague speaks of him locking out "fair daylight," making "himself an artificial night" (I. i). Even in the conventional idiom of *The Two Gentlemen of Verona*, we should recognize these as unfavorable signs. They prepare us for a Romeo who is at this stage in love with himself as Rosaline's unrequited lover, a Romeo

> to himself so *secret* and so *close*, . . .
> As is the bud bit with *an envious worm;*   (I. i)

a creature, in other words, "doting" rather than loving, perversely enamored of his own self-centered and melancholy reflections. The distance he will cover in his progress through the play needs to be measured against the deliberate conventionality of this beginning. All this is amply confirmed when Romeo himself appears and utters his first elaborate "complaints":

> O brawling love! O loving hate!
> O anything of nothing first create!
> O heavy lightness! serious vanity!—

to which, shortly after, he adds further considerations on a more sententious level:

> Love is a smoke raised with the fume of sighs;
> Being purged, a fire sparkling in lovers' eyes;
> Being vex'd, a sea nourish'd with lovers' tears:
> What is it else? a madness most discreet,
> A choking gall and a preserving sweet.   (I. i)

This is a Romeo who can indeed say of himself, a good deal more truly than he yet knows, "This is not Romeo; he's some other where," even as he complains from a point of view still naïvely limited to the self that his mistress has no share in love's generosity, that she will not *give* herself in fulfillment of its essential law. To Benvolio's question, "Then she hath sworn that she will still live chaste?" Romeo replies:

> She hath, and in that sparing makes huge waste;
> For beauty, starved with her severity,
> Cuts beauty off from all posterity.   (I. i)

This is, of course, an argument familiar from the sonnets, and one which this play will in due course turn to serious ends. Romeo is still speaking within the limits of convention, urging upon the object of his desire that generosity which he has not yet had occasion to show in himself. He is soon to find a love that is ready to give for what is, in the eyes of the world, folly; but, until this is so, his character cannot begin to develop to its true tragic stature.

At this point, and after some talk of Capulet's forthcoming feast, we turn from Romeo to Juliet, who is urged by her mother to think of marriage and who replies, in her still unawakened simplicity: "It is an honour that I dream not of" (I. iii). Juliet, indeed, is surrounded here, as she will be almost to the end of the play, by the "experienced," by those who are always ready to give their advice on the proper conduct of her life. Such is the Nurse, with her combination of easy sentiment and deep-rooted cynicism, her belief, at once normal and senile in its discursive presentation, that love is a prompting of the flesh which is destined to find its social fulfillment in a suitably contrived marriage; such too is her own mother, who looks back complacently on the destiny which at some remote moment in the past gave her to Capulet and which she is ready to elevate, for her daughter's benefit, into a universal pattern:

> By my count,
> I was your mother much upon these years
> That you are now a maid.   (I. iii)

As Lady Capulet goes on to refer to Paris' suit in language deliberately and appropriately contrived—

> This precious book of love, this unbound lover,
> To beautify him, only lacks a cover—   (I. iii)

Juliet, the moment of whose awakening is still to come, can only reply in the simple terms of filial obedience.

As Romeo moves toward the fatal meeting with Juliet, his attitude is set in contrast to that of Mercutio, who offers him advice in terms of an essentially worldly common sense, which is not on that account less relevant to his state of sentiment. Mercutio is convinced that the supposed tribulations of love have an easy remedy which he and his friends propose to apply:

> we'll draw thee from the mire
> Of this sir-reverence love, wherein thou stick'st
> Up to the ears.   (I. iv)

The famous "Queen Mab" speech, to which these exchanges lead, is a brilliant exercise in poetic bravura, of the type to which Shakespeare, in the first flush of his creative powers, was especially attracted. It is, however, also more than that, insomuch as it emphasizes, against Romeo's superficially settled attitudes, the inconstancy of human impulses in the state of love, the lively unpredictability of love itself:

> This is that very Mab
> That plats the manes of horses in the night,
> And bakes the elf-locks in foul, sluttish hairs,
> Which once untangled much misfortune bodes:
> This is the hag, when maids lie on their backs,
> That presses them and learns them first to bear.   (I. iv)

The similarity between this and the habitual language of Puck, in *A Midsummer Night's Dream*, is surely not accidental; there is the same sense of the mischievous and the incongruous, even the same faintly sinister delight in the upsetting of fixed sentimental attitudes and unalterable moral categories. This is essentially a *comic* attitude to love, as different from Romeo's self-absorbed devotion to Rosaline as it will prove to be from his dedication to Juliet. Romeo moves at this point, as he will continue to do, in a sphere entirely remote from Mercutio's comic exhortations; but it is notable that he answers his friend's exuberance with a first obscure intimation of fear. When Mercutio has confessed that his talk has been of "nothing but vain fantasy," "thin of substance as the air," and "more inconstant than the wind," Romeo recognizes his foreboding in the face of the still unknown future:

> my mind misgives
> Some consequence, yet hanging in the stars,
> Shall bitterly begin his fearful date
> With this night's revels, and expire the term
> Of a despised life closed in my breast,
> By some vile forfeit of untimely death.   (I. iv)

Romeo's concern for his "despised life" still answers to his early sentimental state, which finds in pessimism an intimate, finally self-indulging necessity; but it remains true that it is at this point that the play's persistent association of love and death enters the hero's mind for the first time.

In this way we are brought to the fatal ball in the house of the Capulets. Old Capulet, most typically, plays his part as host to the accompaniment of jests about "corns" and memories of his lost youth:

> I have seen the day
> That I have worn a visor, and could tell
> A whispering tale in a fair lady's ear,   (I. v)

and so forth for as long as his relations and friends will bear with him; but, as he goes on to confess to his cousin, "you and I are past our dancing days," and the present lies with Romeo as he forms his fatal question:

> What lady's that, which doth *enrich* the hand
> Of yonder knight?

It is typical of Romeo that his first reference to Juliet should speak of her in terms of "enrichment," the enhancing effect proper to beauty; significant too that his first reaction to the sight of her should give him the force to break through all former artifice, to rise to what, though still romantic in inspiration, is in effect a new intensity:

> O, she doth teach the torches to burn bright!
> It seems she hangs upon the cheek of night
> Like a rich jewel in an Ethiop's ear;   (I. v)

a beauty capable, indeed, of transforming life, but which he can also, with what is already a sense of foreboding, hail immediately afterward as "Beauty too rich for use, for earth too dear." Already, moreover, the world is ominously present at the birth of this new vision, and answers to the lover's rapt confession of his transformed state—"I ne'er saw true beauty till this night"— with Tybalt's harsh recognition—"This, by his voice, should be a Montague"—even as he calls for his sword. The sinister note has been struck once and for all, briefly but not on that account less powerfully, in spite of Capulet's determination that his feast shall not be interrupted, and in spite of the confrontation of Romeo's unruly enemy with the old man's stubborn "will." Yet again, as will occur so often in this play, age and youth, authority and passion meet, as Capulet's angry assertion of his right to command—"Am I the master here? or you? go to"—meets the younger man's grudging aside;

> Patience perforce with wilful choler meeting,
> Makes my flesh tremble in their different greeting,   (I. v)

and as this in turn leads to the threatening conclusion:

> this intrusion shall,
> Now seeming sweet, convert to bitterest gall.

The spare, tense economy of these exchanges is the sign of a dramatist working at the height of his newly discovered and continually expanding powers.

The first exchange between Romeo and Juliet, which follows immediately on this clash of contrary and headstrong wills, is carried on, by a most effective contrast, in artificial sonnet form, which makes it a matter of "saints" and "pilgrims," the expression of a still strained and tense devotion. As the lovers exchange their first kiss, however, it is already to a play upon "sin" which carries threatening overtones:

> —Thus from my lips by thine my sin is purg'd.
> —Then have my lips the sin that they have took.
> —Sin from my lips? O trespass sweetly urged!
> Give me my sin again.   (I. v)

At this point, if ever, we may feel familiar poetic conventions in the process of being brought to what is finally a dangerous, a precarious life. Indeed, when Juliet, after Romeo has left her, says:

> If he be married,
> My grave is like to be my wedding-bed,   (I. v)

the play's characteristic note of ominous splendor is being firmly struck; we may already sense, however obscurely, that this love is destined to end in death, but that death itself may be ennobled by the dedication which love can bring to its acceptance. For the immediate moment, moreover, we should note that the new situation is conveyed through a corresponding development in character; for Juliet, who has hitherto shown herself submissive to parental authority, being now newly born to love learns at once to disguise her true feelings. Already she has shown enough presence of mind to preface her question about Romeo's identity by enquiries about two other guests, whose identity in no way concerns her; and when she has been betrayed by the intensity of her own feeling into crying, incautiously,

> Prodigious birth of love it is to me,
> That I must love a loathed enemy,   (I. v)

and is challenged by the Nurse to explain her outburst, she turns aside the threatened revelation with a beautifully off-hand reference to

A rhyme I learn'd even now
Of one I danced withal.

By the end of this admirably contrived scene, a situation as tensely actual, as ominously poised over contradiction, as any briefly conveyed in the sonnets is being endowed with dramatic life. In the episode which follows, after the Chorus has further underlined the elements of foreboding which accompany the birth of this love, Mercutio proceeds with his taunting of Romeo for his infatuated devotion to Rosaline. "Speak but one rhyme, and I am satisfied," he urges, continuing his comic attack upon the romantic excess to which he still believes his friend is subject; but he fails, of course, to obtain the response of his victim, whose heart and mind are fully engaged elsewhere. Romeo's true answer, indeed, is uttered before Juliet:

But soft! what light through yonder window breaks?
It is the east, and Juliet is the sun!   (II. ii)

In the invocation which follows, the expression is, of course, still conventional in form, still a reflection of some of the most familiar motives of the poetry of courtly love:

her eyes in heaven
Would through the airy region stream so bright
That birds would sing and think it were not night.

Beyond this deliberate play with words and conceits, however, we can respond also to a process by which true sentiment, not necessarily of a mature or admirable kind, is engaged upon the task of filling out convention, endowing it with life. The young lover, as he contemplates the object of his desire, projects his sensuous imagination into the celebration of her person:

See, how she leans her cheek upon her hand!
O, that I were a glove upon that hand,
That I might touch that cheek!   (II. ii)

The urgency of the expression, in fact, though still extreme and precarious in its quality, is being made to answer to the reality of intense emotion: "Call me but love, and I'll be new baptized"; "dear saint." We are not being invited here to any easy identification with the lover's new states of feeling. The language which prevails in this speech, and through the greater part of the

entire episode, is at once plainly excessive, even an indulgence of
sentiment, and, in terms of romantic love, expressive of a true
devotion, entirely different from the superficial, self-centered
attitudes which have prevailed, almost up to this moment, in
Romeo's declarations of his love for Rosaline. The new situation
is far more complex, a far more intricate compound of conflicting
realities. Because this new love bears within itself an element of
excess, a neglect of all realities except those which its own
consummation involves, it will end in death; but because it is
also a true emotion (and true not least in relation to the aged
experience that sets itself up so consistently to thwart it, to deny
its truth), because its intensity answers, when all has been said,
to love's *value*, it will be felt to achieve, even in its inevitable
frustration, a certain measure of triumph over circumstance.

The element of contradiction makes its presence felt
throughout this famous scene. Juliet, here as nearly always a
good deal more realistic than Romeo, knows from the first that
their love is surrounded by a sinister reality which its material
circumstances confirm:

> The orchard walls are high and hard to climb,
> And the place death, considering who thou art;

to which his passionate reply is at once, when viewed in terms of
worldly common sense, a further expression of excess, and, in
relation to the new vision which has taken possession of him, a
sign of the nature of true love:

> With love's light wings did I o'erperch these walls,
> For stony limits cannot hold love out:
> And what love can do, that dares love attempt.

The Romeo who speaks after this fashion, and who goes on to
say:

> wert thou as far
> As that vast shore wash'd with the farthest sea,
> I would adventure for such merchandise,

is clearly a new person in relation to the conventional lover whom
Mercutio and his friends could justly ridicule in the opening
scenes. His eyes have been opened to the reality of love as an
"adventure," involving the total commitment of self, the

willingness to risk all to obtain the rich "merchandise," the prize of great value which love—if in fact it is a central reality in human experience—implies. This gesture of the gift of self, however, is at once necessary and dangerous, balanced over a void. This is recognized again, and in a new way, by Juliet when she answers Romeo's entranced declarations with a direct simplicity of her own and calls for an answering directness and simplicity from her lover:

> O gentle Romeo,
> If thou dost love, pronounce it faithfully.

Romeo's far-flung declarations of the value and intensity of love call, as their natural counterpart, for plainer, more naturally human decisions, and it is these which Juliet is here emphasizing. By so doing, she does not, of course, call in question the truth and validity of the emotions which have transported Romeo to what is in effect a new life; but she is saying that these transports call for translation into a more intimate key, demand incorporation into a more common, but not on that account a less precious or valid reality.

The following duet, as we may properly call it, carries on this balance of intensity and artifice, idealism and reality:

> —Lady, by yonder blessed moon I swear,
> That tips with silver all these fruit-tree tops,—
> —O, swear not by the moon, th' inconstant moon,
> That monthly changes in her circled orb,
> Lest that thy love prove likewise variable.
> —What shall I swear by?
> —Do not swear at all;
> Or, if thou wilt, swear by thy gracious self,
> Which is the god of my idolatry,
> And I'll believe thee.   (II. ii)

Juliet prefers plain statement to Romeo's elaborate declarations of faith; declarations, moreover, made in the name of the "inconstant" moon, and so ominously suggesting impermanence. "Do not swear at all," she pleads, or swear, if at all, by the plain object of her love, his "gracious self"; but she too strikes the note of impermanence in her confession of "idolatry," which at once answers to a true intensity and places it in the expression whilst leading to her final confession of misgiving:

> I have no joy of this contract to-night;
> It is too rash, too unadvised, too sudden,
> Too like the lightning, which doth cease to be
> Ere one can say, "it lightens."   (II. ii)

Throughout this exchange, the imagery of night which provides the appropriate conditions for the romanticism that unites these lovers is also the background, finally embracing a sinister element, against which love shines out in real but precarious and transitory splendor. Having thus expressed the misgivings which already shadow her love, and which she is more ready at this stage to grasp than Romeo, Juliet counters them with her affirmation, equally splendid and more positive in its implications, of love's inherent generosity:

> My bounty is as boundless as the sea,
> My love as deep; the more I give to thee,
> The more I have, for both are infinite.   (II. ii)

This is the central Shakespearean affirmation that love asserts itself through giving, and that its gift is of the kind which enriches and is an indication of value, of "infinity." In the light of this, her repeated returns to the casement to salute Romeo yet again are, dramatically speaking, profoundly true to life. They serve to rouse Romeo from the misgivings to which he has been subjected, and which in his case are associated with night and the illusion of dreams—

> I am *afeard*,
> Being in night, all this is but a dream,
> Too flattering-sweet to be substantial—

until his doubts are finally dispelled in the positive affirmation of his outburst: "It is my soul that calls upon my name," and in the final blended dedication:

> —I have forgot why I did call thee back.
> —Let me stand here till thou remember it.
> —I shall forget, to have thee still stand there,
> Remembering how I love thy company.
> —And I'll still stay, to have thee still forget,
> Forgetting any other home but this.   (II. ii)

Poised against a background of night and impermanence love
asserts briefly, for the duration of this scene, its anticipation of
life and permanence to come. As this statement of dedication draws to a close, we are
brought back once more in contrast to the world of experience,
which returns this time in the shape of Friar Lawrence, who—
unlike the other old men in this play—is aware that the young
have feelings of their own, but who, being himself old, is debarred
from sharing the reality of their feelings. It is within the limits of
his understanding of life that he should see birth and death as
related processes of nature:

> The earth that's nature's mother is her tomb;
> What is her burying grave, that is her womb;

it is also within his capacity to make allowances, theoretically
and as an observer, for the contradictory principles that he sees,
not without a certain subtlety of vision, as exercising their
dominating and opposite action upon human nature:

> Two such opposed kings encamp them still
> In man as well as herbs, grace and rude will.   (II. iii)

Yet, whilst recognizing in the Friar this true moralizing vision,
we must also feel that the entry at this point of Romeo,
"wounded" and seeking the remedy for ills which are beyond all
abstract cure, represents in most vivid form the impact of real
life upon theory and remote moralizing. The Friar contemplates
the lover's predicament from his own point of view, which Romeo
must find irrelevant; for him Juliet is one more "young woman"
among many, with whom a young man has fallen in love. The
Friar, moreover, is interested in this love, not in itself but as an
instrument for ending, as he hopes, the family feud by which
Verona is so intolerably divided; to this worthy end he will set
his own typically old man's contrivances into action, only to
discover for himself the truth that so many others will experience,
mainly to their own undoing, in this play, that life will always
tend to move, beyond the attempted control of those who seek to
direct it in accordance with ends of their own, to its own
conclusions.

It is in this spirit that the Friar agrees, although with
foreboding, to perform the marriage that Romeo demands of

him. He accedes, in fact, whilst Romeo, again prophetically, brings together love and death as he asserts the *value* of his devotion:

> come what sorrow can,
> It cannot countervail the exchange of joy
> That one short minute gives me in her sight:
> Do thou but close our hands with holy words,
> Then *love-devouring death* do what he dare,
> It is enough I may but call her mine.(II. vi)

This, with its desire to crowd the unique intensity of love into "one short minute," and to set the achievement of this union against the devouring action of time, is close in spirit to the great sonnets on mutability. It amounts to a renewed and intensified bringing together of the contrary sensations which make up what we can properly call the "metaphysical" heart of this play. The Friar, speaking as ever in terms of experience, utters his contrasted warning against the perils which these one-sided ecstasies imply: "These violent delights have violent ends," he says, and, going on to speak, in terms which again touch upon a central contradiction of the tragedy, of "immoderate appetite," he urges the pair to "love moderately." This, of course, he is able to do precisely because he is a spectator, separated by age and outlook from the imperious claims of passion. His attempts to understand the situation of the lovers are, indeed, rather conscientiously painstaking than successful. "O, so light a foot," he says feelingly of Juliet,

> Will ne'er wear out the everlasting flint;

and this, if it is true, as seen from one point of view, is from another—that of the lovers themselves—besides the point. It is a view spoken from the standpoint of "experience," knowledge of the ways of the world, which ignores, however, the reality of that engagement in their emotion which is, in this same scene, the substance of Juliet's reply to Romeo:

> They are but beggars that can count their worth;
> But my true love is grown to such excess,
> I cannot sum up sum of half my wealth.   (II. vi)

Here we have a familiar cluster of ideas associated with love and indicating its essential value. The refusal to consider emotion in terms of mere accountancy, to "count their wealth," saves lovers, in the moment of their mutual engagement, from being "beggars," gives to their "true" emotion such "excess"—and here the elements of truth and exaggeration are deliberately balanced one against the other—that it escapes all temporal estimates of value and asserts, however dangerously and precariously, its own valuation. In phrases such as these, which the estimate of "reason" represented by such as Friar Lawrence finds finally incomprehensible, but in which love's generosity imposes, whilst the mutual commitment lasts, its own conviction, the conventional poetic idea of "love's wealth" points beyond any limit of mere convention to the heart of the tragedy which here concerns us.

The outside world, however, though the lovers can succeed at certain moments in ignoring it, is still there, ready to strike; as Benvolio says, immediately after Juliet has spoken in this way, "The day is hot, the Capulets abroad" (III. i). Mercutio, reasonable after his own fashion to the last, exposes in no uncertain terms to his friend the essential vanity of all the family quarrels by which Verona is divided. "Thou wilt quarrel," he points out, "with a man that hath a hair more, or a hair less, in his beard than thou hast"; but as soon as Tybalt appears, dangerously on the warpath, he is as obstinate in refusing to give way as any of the others:

—By my head, here comes the Capulets.
—By my heel, I care not;   (III. i)

and again, still more stubbornly, "I will not budge for no man's pleasure, I." The double stress on "I" is proof that, in despite of his qualities of human and reasonable detachment, Mercutio is as subject as any other man to the irrational folly which prevails in both parties, and therefore as incapable as any of the rest of escaping the doom that awaits them all. It is striking to note that, in the midst of so much unreason, it is only Romeo, in his new situation, who expresses himself with realism to the man who insists in regarding himself as his mortal enemy:

I do protest, I never injured thee,
But love thee better than thou canst devise;   (III.i)

in view of these words there is supreme irony in the fact that when Romeo, immediately after, intervenes to separate Mercutio and Tybalt, the only result is that his enemy is able to stab his friend under his arm. Once again, death makes his entry, but this time not in words alone, but in its irreparable reality, to be saluted by the dying Mercutio in phrases which contrast to magnificent effect, by their very sobriety, with all the alternately exuberant and fevered poetry which has decorated its impact to such varying effect in the preceding course of the play. "The hurt cannot be much," says Romeo, at once expressing a friend's irrational hope and, we may feel, seeking to hide from himself the appalling consequences of his well-meant gesture. Mercutio's reply transposes the whole incident to a new level of tragedy. "No," he says, with a rueful gravity to which the survival of his old humorous tone lends a further dimension, "'tis not so deep as a well, nor so wide as a church-door; but 'tis enough, 'twill serve"; and again: "ask for me to-morrow, and you shall find me a grave man" (III. i). In this way, and to the accompaniment of Mercutio's last pun, the whole emotional quality of the play undergoes, in effect, a transformation. Nothing even in romantic and youthful love will be the same after Mercutio's departure as it was before it. The dying man's last judgment upon the events which have led to his death is indeed clear and final. "A plague o' both your houses"; in the light of the unanswerable truth which this represents, Romeo's hesitant plea—"I thought all for the best"— may strike us as a pathetic illusion, finally something less than adequate. Romeo, indeed, is driven to feel his own responsibility for what has happened, and to fall in reaction, when Tybalt returns, into something very like the revenger's base rant. "Fire-eyed fury be my conduct now," are the words he utters, just after he has said of himself, dwelling upon his love:

> O sweet Juliet,
> Thy beauty hath made me effeminate.   (III. i)

We need not necessarily feel that the new mood of "fury" is more manly—though Romeo may wish, as he speaks, to believe it so—than the "effeminacy" which inspired him to behave reasonably toward the man he is now about to kill. At all events, it is the facts, rather than his attempt to react to them, that seriously count at this stage. As Romeo, in his new desperate mood, dispatches Tybalt and accepts Benvolio's advice to flee, the action has passed beyond human control to fall under the influence of the "stars" as the Prince pronounces, in stern justice and for the public peace, the sentence of banishment upon the latest murderer.

It is significant that it is precisely at this moment, when the course of events can clearly be seen passing beyond the lovers' possible control, that Juliet shows more clearly than ever before that she has become a good deal more than the unawakened adolescent of the opening scenes. If she now calls upon "love-performing night," it is in no mere prolongation of the earlier romantic exchanges—and, indeed, in this sense it has always been Romeo, rather than herself, who has felt so intensely the attractions of the extinction of light—but in search of the full physical consummation of her love. Her words are in this sense precise and firm:

> O, I have bought the mansion of a love,
> But not possess'd it, and, though I am sold,
> Not yet enjoy'd; so tedious is this day
> As is the night before some festival
> To an impatient child that hath new robes
> And may not wear them.   (III. ii)

Her new intensity, however, is not unrelated to a note of hysteria, and there is indeed something surprising in the presence, in the passage just quoted, of imagery that actually carries a hint of the brothel ("possess'd . . . sold . . . enjoy'd"); we should not suggest that Juliet's love is affected, in its quality, by these undertones, but that they answer to a new complexity, a shift toward darkness in the moral tone, that is making itself felt elsewhere. Similarly, when the Nurse enters, bringing, as she fears, news of Romeo's death, it is indeed hysteria that plays a major part in the conceptual impression of her contrary emotions:

> Hath Romeo slain himself? say thou but "I,"
> And that bare vowel "I" shall poison more
> Than the death-darting eye of cockatrice:
> I am not I, if there be such an I,
> Or those eyes shut, that make thee answer "I."
> If he be slain, say "I" . . .   (III. ii)

The expressions of contradiction are prolonged through this speech to remarkable effect:

> O serpent heart, hid with a flowering face! . . .
> O nature, what hadst thou to do in hell,
> When thou didst bower the spirit of a fiend
> In mortal paradise of such sweet flesh?

Was ever book containing such vile matter
So fairly bound? O, that deceit should dwell
In such a gorgeous palace!   (III. ii)

The last phrase is, in its intensity of contradiction, almost worthy
of *Othello*. There is about all this a new sense of tragic complexity,
and with it a new depth of psychological penetration, which is
the result of balancing against one another the splendors and the
impossibilities of romantic love. Juliet, awakened from
adolescence into maturity, is discovering that "deceit" can dwell
in the "gorgeous palace" of her dedication, seeing beneath the
"mortal paradise," at once sublimated and subject to decay, of
the "sweet flesh" in which the perfections of her lover are
dangerously "bowered," a "spirit" indeed but—disconcertingly,
opposed to the original simplicity of her youthful idealism—one
which reveals itself under the external manifestations of a "fiend."
The contradictions which the knot of human passion bears within
itself are affirming themselves to this young but rapidly maturing
imagination with almost intolerable intensity.

Meanwhile, and at her side in the moment of stress, the voice
of "experience" continues to assert itself in the observations of
the Nurse. Hers, wrapt in kindly forms, is the voice of a universal
cynicism about the possibilities of love itself:

There's no trust,
No faith, no honesty in men: all perjured,
All forsworn, all naught, all dissemblers.   (III. ii)

It is finally, beneath its appearance of wisdom and detachment, a
self-centered, an impotent voice—"These griefs, these woes, these
sorrows, make me old"—one concerned only with its own
situation. To Juliet it can bring no comfort, and she surrenders to
the unique, impossible reality of her love as she affirms, at once
naturally and against all reason, that

My husband lives, that Tybalt would have slain;
And Tybalt's dead, that would have slain my husband:
All this is comfort.   (III. ii)

The stressing of the fact that Romeo is now not merely her lover,
the object of her romantic devotion, but her married "husband"
is designed to give to this assertion of "comfort" in disaster an
element of the natural; but Juliet herself must know, even as she

speaks, that her situation, and that of Romeo, are not so simple, and indeed she follows this expression of an impossible hope with a recognition of the opposite reality:

"Romeo is banished": to speak that word,
Is father, mother, Tybalt, Romeo, Juliet,
All slain, all dead.   (III. ii)

The premonition of death, once uttered, inevitably affirms itself in her thought. The end of all this tragic excess lies, most typically, in her own prayer: "death, not Romeo, take my maidenhead." It is left to the Nurse to maintain, in her own way and against the direction of her young mistress' mood, the ends of life as she declares her readiness to seek out Romeo for Juliet's "comfort"; and to this proposal Juliet—who has, in the last analysis, no alternative—at the end accedes.

It is appropriately left to the Friar to keep up the note of foreboding. Romeo, he says, is "wedded to calamity," as he brings him the news that he has been banished. Romeo's reply, affirming the love-centeredness of all his thought—

There is no world without Verona walls,
But purgatory, torture, hell itself—   (III. iii)

is from his point of view, outside both the excesses and the transforming effect of love, nothing less than a blasphemy; for Romeo's reactions are based upon the exclusive element of obsession in his passion—

heaven is here,
Where Juliet lives—

and find issue in the fevered contradictions of his high-flown, conceited utterance: "This may flies do, but I from this must fly" (III. iii). Once more, the element of artifice in these words is deliberate, answers to a distraught and finally—as far as it goes— a corrupting emotional state; but though the Friar can reasonably urge "philosophy" upon his penitent, his words remain those of an observer, outside both the splendor and the peril of the lover's state, and Romeo can tell him with natural indignation:

Hang up philosophy!
Unless philosophy can make a Juliet,

and point out, with bitter truth, that his mentor is in no position to feel the valid, the essential truth of his situation: "Thou canst not speak of that thou dost not feel." As though to support the pressure of experience upon him, the Nurse also enters, to report that Juliet is in like case; but her reproach to Romeo for what she sees as his excessive despair —"stand, an you be a man"—is, like the Friar's, at once objectively true and, from the victim's point of view, an irrelevance.

The truth is that Friar Lawrence, representing a common sense which is second nature to him, speaks at this moment of what he does not understand. An onlooker from the outside, he sees in Romeo's transports of frustration and grief only "the unreasonable fury of a beast," and finds it natural to reprove the young man for his betrayal of true manliness:

> Thy noble shape is but a form of wax,
> Digressing from the valour of a man, . . .
> And thou dismember'd with thine own defence.   (III. iii)

It is important, at this point, to see that this judgment, which is the type of many others made in the course of the play, is at once true, needing to be said, and—as seen from the standpoint of the victim—besides the point, uttered by one who cannot, by his very nature, understand what is really at stake. In the same way, the Friar's attempts to console Romeo, combining encouragement with reproach—

> thy Juliet is alive,
> For whose dear sake thou wast but lately dead . . .
> Happiness courts thee in her best array;
> But, like a misbehaved and sullen wench,
> Thou pout'st upon thy fortune and thy love:
> Take heed, take heed, for such die miserable—(III. iii)

constitute at once a valid warning, which the final tragedy will terribly confirm, and amount—seen from the standpoint of Romeo's absorbing and consuming passion—to so much irrelevant and facile moralizing. Before the play ends the Friar's faith in "experience" as a guide in life will lead him to conclude that everything has its remedy, is susceptible to a little rational manipulation; and it is in this spirit, well-meaning but shortsighted, finally complacent, that he plans the stratagem that will only serve to hasten the concluding disaster. For he and the

Nurse who so admires him— "O, what learning is!"—are, in the last analysis, essentially of the same kind.

"Experience," meanwhile, in the grosser and more insensitive form represented by old Capulet, is busy about its own shortsighted plans. "Well, we were born to die" is his characteristic comment on Tybalt's death, and it is decided that Juliet, in order to shake her from her supposed grief for the dead man, will be bundled as quickly as possible into marriage with Paris. Once again, facile good intentions serve only to hasten disaster. It is against this ominous background that Romeo and Juliet achieve (III. v) the brief consummation of their mutual love. It is a consummation, as we now have reason to expect, which is at once intense, contradictory, and finally poised over fear: fear, above all, for the future, whilst life is being plucked, in intense and breathless haste, from the insubstantial present. The nightingale signs in "the *fearful* hollow" of her lover's ear, and Romeo, exultant as he is in the moment of achievement—

> Night's candles are burnt out, and *jocund* day
> Stands tip-toe on the misty mountain tops—

can only precariously maintain his happiness. "I must be gone and live, or stay and die." Life is, for him, with Juliet, and absence from her means death; so that, when Juliet—as ever more realistic at heart—clings desperately to what she knows to be an illusion— "thou needst not to be gone"—he is ready to deny truth in the name of his love: "I'll say yon grey is not the morning's eye." Once again, however, the end of love is foreseen to lie in death: "Come, death, and welcome! Juliet wills it so." Even, however, as Romeo accepts the illusion upon which his life now rests, it is Juliet who returns to daily reality—"It is the lark that sings so out of tune"—and who foresees that they must separate. Truth, in other words, stands most delicately balanced against illusion; to decide which is which, and to what end they are interwoven, could be described as precisely the crux of this tragedy. As Juliet admits that "more light and light it grows," it is left to Romeo to make his comment of tragic foreboding: "More light and light: more dark and dark our woes."

At this point reality intervenes in yet another form, as the Nurse interrupts the lovers to bring news, with daybreak, of the approach of Lady Capulet. There is once again an ominous note in Juliet's last question, "thinkst thou we shall ever meet again?" and though Romeo's reply seems to suggest confidence—

> I doubt it not; and all these woes shall serve
> For sweet discourses in our time to come—

the sinister death note reaffirms itself in the last words which, in the event, Juliet will speak to her lover alive:

> O God! I have an ill-divining soul.
> Methinks I see thee, now thou art below,
> As one dead in the bottom of a tomb.   (III.v)

At the last she is left to rely upon fortune—that deity "fickle" in the eyes of the world, tending at all times to impose separation—to send Romeo back to her arms. The world beyond the lovers proceeds, meanwhile, on its own paths of misunderstanding. Lady Capulet believes that her daughter weeps for Tybalt and offers, in typically "experienced" terms, her moralizing consolation:

> some grief shows much of love,
> But much of grief shows still some want of wit.

As always, "experience" seeks the solution to all problems in "moderation": seeks it precisely where love, of its very nature, is unable to find it. It is noteworthy, however, as a sign of the way in which the complexities of maturity are imposing themselves, that when Romeo is mentioned, Juliet shows herself old enough to dissemble to her mother. "Indeed," she says,

> I never shall be satisfied
> With Romeo, till I behold him—dead;

what she does not know, and what constitutes, of course, the irony of this situation, is that this "satisfaction" is very shortly to be granted her. Her mother, meanwhile, has come to bring her news of the "wedding" which has been arranged by the elderly and the "experienced" for what they have decided is her own good; and her more formidable father now enters to confirm his "decree." At this point, we are clearly shown the fundamental insensibility of those who claim to be versed in the ways of the world: shown it nowhere more obviously than in Capulet's unreasoning rage at Juliet's timid attempts to cross him—"My fingers itch!"—and scarcely less evidently in her own mother's callous remark: "I would the fool were married to her grave." And so, indeed, she shall be, sooner than Lady Capulet knows;

but meanwhile the Nurse is allowed to utter her protest in the name of a certain human feeling—"You are to blame, my lord, to rate her so"—only to evoke the father's egoistic stressing of what he believes to be his own unrewarded care and toil:

> Day, night, hour, tide, time, work, play,
> Alone, in company, still my care hath been
> To have her match'd.   (III. v)

It is, in fact, his own self-esteem which feels itself affronted by his daughter's obstinacy, and which prompts him to turn her away unless she is docile to his will. Juliet, indeed, faced by a situation slipping beyond all possible control, feels herself caught in a trap:

> Alack, alack, that heaven should practise stratagems
> Upon so soft a subject as myself;

but when she seeks advice from the Nurse, who has so recently shown her some measure of understanding, it is only to be told that Romeo is a "dishclout" in comparison with Paris; there is point indeed in her own final disenchanted comment: "Well, thou hast comforted me marvellous much."

Thus abandoned by those from whom she might have expected help, Juliet decides to turn to the Friar, only—by yet another ironic mischance—to find Paris, her discreet and honorable suitor, in advance of her at his cell. Even as she asks for counsel, she already sees her ultimate "solution" in the death which is pressing itself upon her intimate reflections. Rather than be forced to marry Paris, she says,

>   shut me nightly in a charnel-house,
> O'ercovered quite with dead men's rattling bones,
> With reeking shanks and yellow chapless skulls;
> Or bid me go into a new-made grave,
> And hide me with a dead man in his shroud;
> Things that to hear them told, have made me tremble. (IV. i)

Her thoughts are full of the charnel-house, the obsessive presence which will from now on live in her mind side by side with love. Precisely these things, which she now regards with horror, she is fated to do; but we should recognize too that these forebodings, excessive as they are, are spoken in the name of loving faith:

> I will do it without fear or doubt,
> To live an unstain'd wife to my sweet love.

Strong in the love which this determination reflects, Juliet is able at this crisis to dissemble beyond her years. Her deception of her father, in the very act of professing filial obedience (IV. ii), is no doubt a sin, but a sin conceived in the name of natural love and in the face of an egoistic and unimaginative opposition; once more, we find ourselves faced with the play's central tragic contradiction. To affirm the rights of love, Juliet finds herself driven to dissemble; her situation is one which can, of its nature, have no happy solution, but we cannot—unless we are ready to share the egoism and incomprehension of her parents—simply leave her condemned of deception.

Alone with her resolution, Juliet is not surprisingly given over to fear. She confesses to feeling "a faint cold fear" which "thrills through her veins" (IV. iii) as she, who has found her elders so lacking in understanding, contemplates the possibility that even the Friar may be ready to betray her. The thought drives her back upon her increasing obsession with mortal decay, as she contemplates in her imagination the tomb

> Where bloody Tybalt, yet but green in earth,
> Lies festering in his shroud,

and thinks of the dreadful possibility of her awakening by his side:

> Alack, alack, is it not like that I
> So early waking, what with loathsome smells
> And shrieks like mandrakes torn out of the earth,
> That living mortals hearing them run mad:
> Or, if I wake, shall I not be distraught,
> Environed with all these hideous fears? (IV. iii)

Meanwhile, in the scene which at once follows these somber premonitions (IV. iv), the preparations for life and festivity are afoot, and the Nurse, foreseeing an imminent marriage, is in her element; just before she discovers Juliet's "death," and in the presence of her "body," she jests broadly over the coming consummation of her wedding:

> Sleep for a week; for the next night, I warrant,
> The County Paris will set up his rest
> That you shall rest but little. (IV. v)

Gross and insensitive as they no doubt are, these are after all words of life; and it answers to the play's intention that they are the prelude to the Nurse's own discovery of what she thinks to be, not life, but its opposite, the image of death. Capulet too, in his lament, equally joins love and death as he reveals the "truth" to Paris:

> O son, the night before thy wedding-day,
> Hath death lain with thy wife; see, where she lies,
> Flower as she was, deflowered by him.   (IV. v)

The Friar, for his part, adds his appropriate note to the whole by stressing another kind of life:

>   confusion's cure lives not
> In these confusions. Heaven and yourself
> Had part in this fair maid; now heaven hath all . . .
> Your part in her you could not keep from death,
> But heaven keeps his part in eternal life.(IV. v)

We need neither reject this simply as so much abstract moralizing, nor accept it as the last word on the tragedy which is now approaching its final stages. It represents the voice of "experience," which belongs to but does not exhaust the total impact of life. "She's best married that dies married young"; "Nature's tears are reason's merriment"; it is hard not to feel, as we hear these hard things so easily said, that from this sententious "wisdom" something—which is, perhaps, finally life itself—has been excluded.

The illusion of life, indeed,—if illusion it be—is precisely what Romeo expresses in the very next scene:

> My bosom's lord sits lightly in his throne,
> And all this day an unaccustom'd spirit
> Lifts me above the ground with cheerful thoughts.

It affirms itself even against the contrary sensations which have taken possession of his sleep:

> I dreamt my lady came and found me dead—
> Strange dream, that gives a dead man leave to think!—
> And breathed such life with kisses in my lips,
> That I revived and was an emperor.
> Ah me! how sweet is love itself possess'd,
> When but love's shadows are so rich in joy!   (V. i)

Here the central contrast which we have followed through the whole course of the play presents itself from yet another standpoint. The force of love affirms itself, momentarily, in and through an illusion that yet partakes of life; but Romeo has no sooner spoken than Balthazar enters with news of Juliet's "death," and her lover's answer corresponds to yet another change of mood: "Is it e'en so? then I defy you, stars!" (V. i). Where Juliet visited the Friar in search of advice and consolation, Romeo in the madness of his desperate resolve now seeks out the sinister apothecary—sinister by his own account (V. i)—to obtain poison for the ending of his life. Meanwhile, to emphasize the operations of a malignant fortune beyond human control, Friar John's mission has gone astray, undoing all Lawrence's previsions, and Juliet is left, in his own words, as "Poor living corse, closed in a dead man's tomb!" (V. ii).

The last scene of the tragedy opens with Paris at the monument, uttering over Juliet's "tomb" his own decent lament in sonneteering terms. He is interrupted by Romeo in his new mood of desperate, essentially death-directed resolution:

> I will tear thee joint by joint
> And strew this hungry churchyard with thy limbs:
> The time and my intents are savage-wild,
> More fierce and inexorable by far
> Than empty tigers or the roaring sea.   (V. iii)

The lover's thoughts revolve characteristically in his mad excess of grief—a fitting pendant to the almost equally mad excess which formerly marked one extreme of his love—round the obsession of the charnel—"Thou detestable maw, thou womb of death"—but it is worth noting that, even as he declares himself to Paris as "a desperate man," he can still address his rival as "Good gentle youth." As he goes on to say, still to Paris, and with profound truth: "By heaven, I love thee better than myself"; the mood is one which, as has often been pointed out, reminds us of Hamlet, whom he also now resembles in being driven unwillingly to kill. Awakening almost at once to the desperate reality of his deed, he sees his victim as joined obscurely to himself in a common adverse fate—"one writ with me in sour misfortune's book"—in an attitude which combines a measure of true nobility with a touch of self-compassion.

These events lead to their culmination in the moment at which Romeo looks on Juliet as she lies on her "tomb" as on a marriage bed, and sees in his grim surroundings, which the radiance of her presence in his imagination transforms into "a feasting presence full of light." We may legitimately ask ourselves whether this represents reality, of an imaginative kind, or illusion in the eyes of common sense; and the answer is surely both. There follows Romeo's noble hymn to death or rather to beauty as transfigured by love and thereby rendered triumphant over circumstance and the grave:

> Thou art not conquer'd; beauty's ensign yet
> Is crimson in thy lips and in thy cheeks,
> And death's pale flag is not advanced there;   (V. iii)

but, of course, in reacting to and accepting the beauty of this, we shall not forget that the point lies, though Romeo is unaware of it, in the fact that Juliet is *alive*. Meanwhile, love and the desire to die are romantically (or shall we say, pathetically? or even self-indulgently? or, possibly, both?) fused in Romeo's words:

> shall I believe
> That unsubstantial death is amorous,
> And that the lean abhorred monster keeps
> Thee here in dark to be his paramour?   (V. iii)

The truth is that "the palace of dim night" exercises upon Romeo here, as it had done to less extreme effect earlier in the play, a profound attraction, which persuades him to seek his repose, "here, here," "with worms that are thy chambermaids"; the slightly sententious tone is surely part, though we may agree that it is not all, of the complete effect. Romeo's final nostalgia is, at all events, for "everlasting rest," for the opportunity to

> shake the yoke of inauspicious stars
> From this world-wearied flesh;   (V. iii)

and we should perhaps be chary of either accepting this mood at its declared value or of exclusively condemning it. Whilst giving its full worth to the romantic power which inspires Romeo's words, we need not take him at this moment entirely at his own self-estimate; for the speaker is moved, on his own confession, by a "desperate pilot," the end of whose guidance will be to lead him to run on "the dashing rocks" his "sea-sick weary bark." Never in Shakespeare, surely, is suicide accepted quite simply at its own essentially self-dramatizing estimate; though we must add, to do justice to the complete effect, that here it is given its full value, in terms of the poetry, as an element in romantic love. Romeo's final words before he kills himself sum up precisely this vital contrast, as they join life and death in a reflection of the play's complex mood: "Thy drugs are *quick*" (*quick* in the double sense of *rapid* and *alive*), "Thus with a *kiss* I die." There could be no more fitting conclusion than this "metaphysical" balance of contrasted emotions for a play which has turned from the first upon the twin realities, at once separate and identical, of love and death.

Immediately after this last gesture the world returns, in the shape of a Friar Lawrence now moved, most significantly, by fear. The limitations of "experienced" detachment, even when joined to recognized virtue and good intention, have by now been thoroughly exposed. As Juliet, too late, awakens, he can only call her from

> that nest
> Of death, contagion, and unnatural sleep;

only confess at the last his own human limitations:

> A greater power than we can contradict
> Hath thwarted our intents.

In a last effort to remedy what is in fact beyond mending, the Friar proposes to direct Juliet to a monastery, but here once more his measure of understanding and his desire to contrive for the best are powerless before the unanswerable vehemence of her retort: "Go, get thee hence, for *I will not away*" (V. iii). For her imagination, centered on love as the source of life to the exclusion of all other realities, the "poison" on Romeo's lips may yet be a "restorative." None other, indeed, is logically available to her; for she is ready to die where she has been awakened to life, to seek in death the only remedy for her tragic situation.

To the aged survivors, now belatedly chastened by the tragedy that they have helped to bring about, the spectacle before them of the youthful dead comes as a reminder of their own approaching end; as Lady Capulet puts it,

> this sight of death is as a bell
> That warns my old age to a sepulchre.

The Prince, as representative of law and civilization in a city where both have been set aside to tragic effect, is left to denounce a feud that has been the cause of so much death and loss, where life and unity might have resulted from the consummation of love in marriage:

> See, what a scourge is laid upon your hate,
> That heaven finds means to kill your joys with love.

Or, as he puts it in the act of winding up this tragic action, "A glooming peace this morning with it brings."

NOTE

1. Sonnet CXVI.

Harry Levin

Form and Formality in
Romeo and Juliet

"Fain would I dwell on form—", says Juliet from her window to
Romeo in the moonlit orchard below,

> Fain would I dwell on form—fain, fain deny
> What I have spoke; but farewell compliment!   (II.ii.88–89)[1]

Romeo has just violated convention, dramatic and otherwise,
by overhearing what Juliet intended to be a soliloquy. Her cousin,
Tybalt, had already committed a similar breach of social and
theatrical decorum in the scene at the Capulets' feast, where he
had also recognized Romeo's voice to be that of a Montague.
There, when the lovers first met, the dialogue of their meeting
had been formalized into a sonnet, acting out the conceit of his
lips as pilgrims, her hand as a shrine, and his kiss as a culminating
piece of stage-business, with an encore after an additional
quatrain: "You kiss by th' book" (I.v.112). Neither had known
the identity of the other; and each, upon finding it out, responded
with an ominous exclamation coupling love and death (120, 140).
The formality of their encounter was framed by the ceremonious
character of the scene, with its dancers, its masquers, and—except
for Tybalt's stifled outburst—its air of old-fashioned hospitality.
"We'll measure them a measure", Benvolio had proposed; but
Romeo, unwilling to join the dance, had resolved to be an onlooker
and carry a torch (I.iv.10). That torch may have burned
symbolically, but not for Juliet; indeed, as we are inclined to
forget with Romeo, he attended the feast in order to see the

Reprinted from *Shakespeare Quarterly* 4(1960), 3–11, with permission of
the author and the Folger Shakespeare Library.

dazzling but soon eclipsed Rosaline. Rosaline's prior effect upon him is all that we ever learn about her; yet it has been enough to make Romeo, when he was presented to us, a virtual stereotype of the romantic lover. As such, he has protested a good deal too much in his preliminary speeches, utilizing the conventional phrases and standardized images of Elizabethan eroticism, bandying generalizations, paradoxes, and sestets with Benvolio, and taking a quasi-religious vow which his introduction to Juliet would ironically break (I.ii.92–97). Afterward this role has been reduced to absurdity by the humorous man, Mercutio, in a mock-conjuration evoking Venus and Cupid and the inevitable jingle of "love" and "dove" (II.i.10). The scene that follows is actually a continuation, marked in neither the Folios nor the Quartos, and linked with what has gone before by a somewhat eroded rhyme.

> 'Tis in vain
> To seek him here that means not to be found,

Benvolio concludes in the absence of Romeo (41, 42). Whereupon the latter, on the other side of the wall, chimes in:

> He jests at scars that never felt a wound.   (II.ii.1)

Thus we stay behind, with Romeo, when the masquers depart. Juliet, appearing at the window, does not hear his descriptive invocation. Her first utterance is the very sigh that Mercutio burlesqued in the foregoing scene: "Ay, me!" (II.ii.25). Then, believing herself to be alone and masked by the darkness, she speaks her mind in sincerity and simplicity. She calls into question not merely Romeo's name but—by implication—all names, forms, conventions, sophistications, and arbitrary dictates of society, as opposed to the appeal of instinct directly conveyed in the odor of a rose. When Romeo takes her at her word and answers, she is startled and even alarmed for his sake; but she does not revert to courtly language.

> I would not for the world they saw thee here,

she tells him, and her monosyllabic directness inspires the matching cadence of his response:

> And but thou love me, let them find me here. (77, 79)

She pays incidental tribute to the proprieties with her passing suggestion that, had he not overheard her, she would have dwelt on form, pretended to be more distant, and played the not impossible part of the captious beloved. But farewell compliment! Romeo's love for Juliet will have an immediacy which cuts straight through the verbal embellishment that has obscured his infatuation with Rosaline. That shadowy creature, having served her Dulcinea-like purpose, may well be forgotten. On the other hand, Romeo has his more tangible foil in the person of the County Paris, who is cast in that ungrateful part which the Italians call *terzo incòmodo*, the inconvenient third party, the unwelcome member of an amorous triangle. As the official suitor of Juliet, his speeches are always formal, and often sound stilted or priggish by contrast with Romeo's. Long after Romeo has abandoned his sonneteering, Paris will pronounce a sestet at Juliet's tomb (V.iii.11–16). During their only colloquy, which occurs in Friar Laurence's cell, Juliet takes on the sophisticated tone of Paris, denying his claims and disclaiming his compliments in brisk stichomythy. As soon as he leaves, she turns to the Friar, and again—as so often in intimate moments—her lines fall into monosyllables:

> O, shut the door! and when thou hast done so,
> Come weep with me—past hope, past cure, past help!
>
> (IV.i.44–45)

Since the suit of Paris is the main subject of her conversations with her parents, she can hardly be sincere with them. Even before she met Romeo, her consent was hedged in prim phraseology:

> I'll look to like, if looking liking move.   (I.iii.97)

And after her involvement she becomes adept in the strategems of mental reservation, giving her mother equivocal rejoinders and rousing her father's anger by chopping logic (III.v.69-205). Despite the intervention of the Nurse on her behalf, her one straightforward plea is disregarded. Significantly Lady Capulet, broaching the theme of Paris in stiffly appropriate couplets, has compared his face to a volume:[2]

> This precious book of love, this unbound lover,
> To beautify him only lacks a cover.

> The fish lives in the sea, and 'tis much pride
> The fair without the fair within to hide.   (I.iii.89–90)

That bookish comparison, by emphasizing the letter at the expense of the spirit, helps to lend Paris an aspect of unreality; to the Nurse, more ingenuously, he is "a man of wax" (76). Later Juliet will echo Lady Capulet's metaphor, transferring it from Paris to Romeo:

> Was ever book containing such vile matter
> So fairly bound?   (III.ii.83–84)

Here, on having learned that Romeo has just slain Tybalt, she is undergoing a crisis of doubt, a typically Shakespearian recognition of the difference between appearance and reality. The fair without may not cover a fair within after all. Her unjustified accusations, leading up to her rhetorical question, form a sequence of oxymoronic epithets: "Beautiful tyrant, fiend angelical, . . . honorable villain!" (75–79). W. H. Auden, in a recent comment on these lines,[3] cannot believe they would come from a heroine who had been exclaiming shortly before: "Gallop apace, you fiery-footed steeds . . . !" Yet Shakespeare has been perfectly consistent in suiting changes of style to changes of mood. When Juliet feels at one with Romeo, her intonations are genuine; when she feels at odds with him, they should be unconvincing. The attraction of love is played off against the revulsion from books, and coupled with the closely related themes of youth and haste, in one of Romeo's long-drawn-out leavetakings:

> Love goes toward love as schoolboys from their books;
> But love from love, towards school with heavy looks.
>   (II.ii.157–158)

The school for these young lovers will be tragic experience. When Romeo, assuming that Juliet is dead and contemplating his own death, recognizes the corpse of Paris, he will extend the image to cover them both:

> O give me the hand,
> One writ with me in sour misfortune's book!   (V.iii.82)

It was this recoil from bookishness, together with the farewell to compliment, that animated *Love's Labour's Lost*, where literary artifice was so ingeniously deployed against itself, and Berowne

was taught—by an actual heroine named Rosaline—that the best
books were women's eyes. Some of Shakespeare's other early
comedies came even closer to adumbrating certain features of
Romeo and Juliet: notably, *The Two Gentlemen of Verona*, with its
locale, its window scene, its friar and rope, its betrothal and
banishment, its emphasis upon the vagaries of love. Shakespeare's
sonnets and erotic poems had won for him the reputation of an
English Ovid. *Romeo and Juliet*, the most elaborate product of his
so-called lyrical period, was his first successful experiment in
tragedy.[4] Because of that very success, it is hard for us to realize
the full extent of its novelty, though scholarship has lately been
reminding us of how it must have struck contemporaries.[5] They
would have been surprised, and possibly shocked, at seeing lovers
taken so seriously. Legend, it had been heretofore taken for
granted, was the proper matter for serious drama; romance was
the stuff of the comic stage. Romantic tragedy—*"an excellent
conceited Tragedie of Romeo and Juliet"*, to cite the title-page of the
First Quarto—was one of those contradictions in terms which
Shakespeare seems to have delighted in resolving. His innovation
might be described as transcending the usages of romantic
comedy, which are therefore very much in evidence, particularly
at the beginning. Subsequently, the leading characters acquire
together a deeper dimension of feeling by expressly repudiating
the artificial language they have talked and the superficial code
they have lived by. Their formula might be that of the anti-
Petrarchan sonnet:

Foole said My muse to mee, looke in thy heart and write.[6]

An index of this development is the incidence of rhyme, heavily
concentrated in the First Act, and its gradual replacement by a
blank verse which is realistic or didactic with other speakers and
unprecedentedly limpid and passionate with the lovers. "Love
has no need of euphony", the eminent Russian translator of the
play, Boris Pasternak, has commented. "Truth, not sound, dwells
in its heart."[7]

Comedy set the pattern of courtship, as formally embodied
in a dance. The other *genre* of Shakespeare's earlier stagecraft,
history, set the pattern of conflict, as formally embodied in a
duel. *Romeo and Juliet* might also be characterized as an anti-
revenge play, in which hostile emotions are finally pacified by
the interplay of kindlier ones. Romeo sums it up in his prophetic
oxymorons:

> Here's much to do with hate, but more with love.
> Why then, O brawling love! O loving hate!
> O anything, of nothing first create!   (I.i.162–164)

And Paris, true to type, waxes grandiose in lamenting Juliet:

> O love! O life! not life, but love in death!   (IV.v.58)

Here, if we catch the echo from Hieronimo's lament in *The Spanish Tragedy,*

> O life! no life, but lively form of death,

we may well note that the use of antithesis, which is purely decorative with Kyd, is functional with Shakespeare. The contrarieties of his plot are reinforced on the plane of imagery by omnipresent reminders of light and darkness,[8] youth and age, and many other antitheses subsumed by the all-embracing one of Eros and Thanatos, the *leitmotif* of the *Liebestod,* the myth of the tryst in the tomb. This attraction of ultimate opposites—which is succinctly implicit in the Elizabethan ambiguity of the verb *to die*—is generalized when the Friar rhymes "womb" with "tomb", and particularized when Romeo hails the latter place as "thou womb of death" (I.iii.9, 10; V.iii.45). Hence the "extremities" of the situation, as the Prologue to the Second Act announces, are tempered "with extreme sweet" (14). Those extremes begin to meet as soon as the initial prologue, in a sonnet disarmingly smooth, has set forth the feud between the two households, "Where civil blood makes civil hands unclean" (4). Elegant verse yields to vulgar prose, and to an immediate riot, as the servants precipitate a renewal—for the third time—of their masters' quarrel. The brawl of Act I is renewed again in the *contretemps* of Act III and completed by the swordplay of Act V. Between the street-scenes, with their clashing welter of citizens and officers, we shuttle through a series of interiors, in a flurry of domestic arrangements and family relationships. The house of the Capulets is the logical center of action, and Juliet's chamber its central sanctum. Consequently, the sphere of privacy encloses Acts II and IV, in contradistinction to the public issues raised by the alternating episodes. The temporal alternation of the play, in its accelerating continuity, is aptly recapitulated by the impatient rhythm of Capulet's speech:

> Day, night, late, early,
> At home, abroad, alone, in company,
> Waking or sleeping . . .(III.v.177–179)

The alignment of the *dramatis personae* is as symmetrical as
the antagonism they personify. It is not without relevance that
the names of the feuding families, like the Christian names of the
hero and heroine, are metrically interchangeable (though "Juliet"
is more frequently a trochee than an amphimacer). Tybalt the
Capulet is pitted against Benvolio the Montague in the first street-
fight, which brings out—with parallel stage-directions—the heads
of both houses restrained by respective wives. Both the hero and
heroine are paired with others, Rosaline and Paris, and
admonished by elderly confidants, the Friar and the Nurse.
Escalus, as Prince of Verona, occupies a superior and neutral
position; yet, in the interchange of blood for blood, he loses "a
brace of kinsman", Paris and Mercutio (V.iii.295). Three times he
must quell and sentence the rioters before he can pronounce the
final sestet, restoring order to the city-state through the lovers'
sacrifice. He effects the resolution by summoning the patriarchal
enemies, from their opposite sides, to be reconciled. "Capulet,
Montague," he sternly arraigns them, and the polysyllables are
brought home by monosyllabics:

> See what a scourge is laid upon your hate
> That heaven finds means to kill your joys with love. (291–293)

The two-sided counterpoise of the dramatic structure is well
matched by the dynamic symmetry of the antithetical style. One
of its peculiarities, which surprisingly seems to have escaped the
attention of commentators, is a habit of stressing a word by
repeating it within a line, a figure which may be classified in
rhetoric as a kind of *ploce*. I have cited a few examples incidentally;
let me now underline the device by pointing out a few more.
Thus Montague and Capulet are accused of forcing their parties

> To wield old partisans in hands as old,
> Cank'red with peace, to part your cank'red hate. (I.i.100, 102)

This double instance, along with the wordplay on "cank'red,"
suggests the embattled atmosphere of partisanship through the
halberds; and it is further emphasized in Benvolio's account of
the fray:

Came more and more, and fought on part and part.   (122)

The key-words are not only doubled but affectionately intertwined, when Romeo confides to the Friar:

As mine on hers, so hers is set on mine.   (II.iii.59)

Again, he conveys the idea of reciprocity by declaring that Juliet returns "grace for grace and love for love" (86). The Friar's warning hints at poetic justice:

These violent delights have violent ends.   (II.vi.9)

Similarly Mercutio, challenged by Tybalt, turns "point to point", and the Nurse finds Juliet—in *antimetabole*—"Blubb'ring and weeping, weeping and blubbering" (III.ii.165; iii.87). Statistics would prove illusory, because some repetitions are simply idiomatic, grammatical, or—in the case of old Capulet or the Nurse—colloquial. But it is significant that the play contains well over a hundred such lines, the largest number being in the First Act and scarcely any left over for the Fifth.

The significance of this tendency toward reduplication, both stylistic and structural, can perhaps be best understood in the light of Bergson's well-known theory of the comic: the imposition of geometrical form upon the living data of formless consciousness. The stylization of love, the constant pairing and counterbalancing, the *quid pro quo* of Capulet and Montague, seem mechanical and unnatural. Nature has other proponents besides the lovers, especially Mercutio their fellow victim, who bequeathes his curse to both their houses. His is likewise an ironic end, since he has been as much a satirist of "the new form" and Tybalt's punctilio in duelling "by the book of arithmetic" as of "the numbers that Petrarch flowed in" and Romeo's affectations of gallantry (II.iv.34, 38; III.i.104). Mercutio's interpretation of dreams, running counter to Romeo's premonitions, is naturalistic, not to say Freudian; Queen Mab operates through fantasies of wish-fulfillment, bringing love to lovers, fees to lawyers, and tithe-pigs to parsons; the moral is that desires can be mischievous. In his repartee with Romeo, Mercutio looks forward to their fencing with Tybalt; furthermore he charges the air with bawdy suggestions that—in spite of the limitations of Shakespeare's theatre, its lack of actresses and absence of close-ups—love may have something to do with sex, if not with lust, with the physical complementarity of male and female.[9] He is abetted, in that respect, by the malapropistic garrulity of the Nurse, Angelica, who is naturally bound to Juliet through having been her wet-nurse, and who has lost the infant daughter that might have been Juliet's age. None the less, her crotchety hesitations are contrasted with Juliet's youthful ardors when the Nurse acts as go-between for Romeo. His counsellor, Friar Laurence, makes a measured entrance with his sententious couplets on the uses and abuses of natural properties, the medicinal and poisonous effects of plants:

> For this, being smelt, with that part cheers each part;
> Being tasted, slays all senses with the heart. (II.iii.25, 26)

His watchword is "Wisely and slow", yet he contributes to the grief at the sepulcher by ignoring his own advice, "They stumble that run fast" (94).[10] When Romeo upbraids him monosyllabically,

> Thou canst not speak of that thou doest not feel,

it is the age-old dilemma that separates the generations: *Si jeunesse savait, si vieillesse pouvait* (III.iii.64). Banished to Mantua, Romeo has illicit recourse to the Apothecary, whose shop—envisaged with Flemish precision—unhappily replaces the Friar's cell, and whose poison is the sinister counterpart of Laurence's potion.

Against this insistence upon polarity, at every level, the mutuality of the lovers stands out, the one organic relation amid an overplus of stylized expressions and attitudes. The naturalness of their diction is artfully gained, as we have noticed, through a running critique of artificiality. In drawing a curtain over the consummation of their love, Shakespeare heralds it with a prothalamium and follows it with an epithalamium. Juliet's "Gallop apace, you fiery-footed steeds", reversing the Ovidian *"lente currite, noctis equi"*, is spoken "alone" but in breathless anticipation of a companion (III.ii.1). After having besought the day to end, the sequel to her solo is the duet in which she begs the night to continue. In the ensuing *débat* of the nightingale and the lark, a refinement upon the antiphonal song of the owl and the cuckoo in *Love's Labour's Lost*, Romeo more realistically discerns "the herald of the morn" (III.v.6). When Juliet reluctantly agrees, "More light and light it grows", he completes the paradox with a doubly reduplicating line:

More light and light—more dark and dark our woes!   (35, 36)

The precariousness of their union, formulated arithmetically by
the Friar as "two in one" (II.vi.37), is brought out by the terrible
loneliness of Juliet's monologue upon taking the potion:

> My dismal scene I needs must act alone.   (IV.ii.19)

Her utter singleness, as an only child, is stressed by her father
and mourned by her mother:

> But one, poor one, one poor and loving child.   (v.46)

Tragedy tends to isolate where comedy brings together, to reveal
the uniqueness of individuals rather than what they have in
common with others. Asking for Romeo's profession of love,
Juliet anticipates: "I know thou wilt say 'Ay'" (II.ii.90). That
monoysllable of glad assent was the first she ever spoke, as we
know from the Nurse's childish anecdote (I.iii.48). Later, asking
the Nurse whether Romeo has been killed, Juliet pauses self-
consciously over the pun between "Ay" and "I" or "eye":

> Say thou but 'I,'
> And that bare vowel 'I' shall poison more
> Than the death-darting eye of cockatrice.
> I am not I, if there be such an 'I';
> Or those eyes shut that make thee answer 'I.'
> If he be slain, say 'I'; or if not, 'no.'
> Brief sounds determine of my weal or woe.   (III.ii.45–51)

Her identification with him is negated by death, conceived as a
shut or poisoning eye, which throws the pair back upon their
single selves. Each of them dies alone—or, at all events, in the
belief that the other lies dead, and without the benefit of a
recognition-scene. Juliet, of course, is still alive; but she has already
voiced her death-speech in the potion scene. With the dagger,
her last words, though richly symbolic, are brief and monosyllabic:

> This is thy sheath; there rest, and let me die.   (V.iii.170)

The sense of vicissitude is re-enacted through various gestures
of staging; Romeo and Juliet experience their exaltation "aloft"
on the upper stage; his descent via the rope is, as she fears,
toward the tomb (III.v.56).[11] The antonymous adverbs *up* and

down figure, with increasing prominence, among the brief sounds that determine Juliet's woe (e.g., V.ii.209–210). The overriding pattern through which she and Romeo have been trying to break—call it Fortune, the stars, or what you will—ends by closing in and breaking them; their private world disappears, and we are left in the social ambiance again. Capulet's house has been bustling with preparations for a wedding, the happy ending of comedy. The news of Juliet's death is not yet tragic because it is premature; but it introduces a peripety which will become the starting point for *Hamlet*.

> All things that we ordained festival
> Turn from their office to black funeral—

the old man cries, and his litany of contraries is not less poignant because he has been so fond of playing the genial host:

> Our instruments to melancholy bells,
> Our wedding cheer to a sad burial feast;
> Our solemn hymns to sullen dirges change;
> Our bridal flowers serve for a buried corse;
> And all things change them to the contrary. (IV.v.84–90)

His lamentation, in which he is joined by his wife, the Nurse, and Paris, reasserts the formalities by means of what is virtually an operatic quartet. Thereupon the music becomes explicit, when they leave the stage to the Musicians, who have walked on with the County Paris. Normally these three might play during the *entr'acte*, but Shakespeare has woven them into the dialogue terminating the Fourth Act.[12] Though their art has the power of soothing the passions and thereby redressing grief, as the comic servant Peter reminds them with a quotation from Richard Edward's lyric *In Commendacion of Musicke*, he persists in his query: "Why 'silver sound'?" (131) Their answers are those of mere hirelings, who can indifferently change their tune from a merry dump to a doleful one, so long as they are paid with coin of the realm. Yet Peter's riddle touches a deeper chord of correspondence, the interconnection between discord and harmony, between impulse and discipline. "Consort", which can denote a concert or a companionship, can become the fighting word that motivates the unharmonious pricksong of the duellists (III.i.48). The "sweet division" of the lark sounds harsh and out

of tune to Juliet, since it proclaims that the lovers must be divided
(v.29). Why "silver sound"? Because Romeo, in the orchard, has
sworn by the moon

> That tips with silver all these fruit-tree tops.   (II.i.108)

Because Shakespeare, transposing sights and sounds into words,
has made us imagine

> How silver-sweet sound lovers' tongues by night,
> Like softest music to attending ears!   (167–168)

NOTES

1. Line-references are to the separate edition of G. L. Kittredge's
   text (Boston, 1940).

2. On the long and rich history of this trope, see the sixteenth chapter
   of E. R. Curtius, *European Literature and the Latin Middle Ages*, tr.
   W. R. Trask (New York, 1953).

3. In the paper-bound Laurel Shakespeare, ed. Francis Fergusson
   (New York, 1958), p. 26.

4. H. B. Charlton, in his British Academy lecture for 1939, *"Romeo
   and Juliet" as an Experimental Tragedy*, has considered the
   experiment in the light of Renaissance critical theory.

5. Especially F. M. Dickey, *Not Wisely But Too Well: Shakespeare's
   Love Tragedies* (San Marino, 1957), pp. 63–88.

6. Sir Philip Sidney, *Astrophel and Stella*, ed. Albert Feuillerat
   (Cambridge, 1922), p. 243.

7. Boris Pasternak, "Translating Shakespeare", tr. Manya Harari, *The
   Twentieth Century*, CLXIV, 979 (September 1958), p. 217.

8. Caroline Spurgeon, *Shakespeare's Imagery and What It Tells Us* (New
   York, 1936), pp. 310–316.

9. Coleridge's persistent defense of Shakespeare against the charge
   of gross language does more credit to that critic's high-mindedness
   than to his discernment. The concentrated ribaldry of the gallants
   in the street (II.iv) is deliberately contrasted with the previous
   exchange between the lovers in the orchard.

10. This is the leading theme of the play, in the interpretation of Brents Stirling, *Unity in Shakespearean Tragedy: The Interplay of Themes and Characters* (New York, 1956), pp. 10–25.

11. One of the more recent and pertinent discussions of staging is that of Richard Hosley, "The Use of the Upper Stage in *Romeo and Juliet*", *Shakespeare Quarterly*, V, 4 (Autumn 1954), 371–379.

12. Professor F. T. Bowers reminds me that inter-act music was probably not a regular feature of public performance when *Romeo and Juliet* was first performed. Some early evidence for it has been gathered by T. S. Graves in "The Act-Time in Elizabethan Theatres", *Studies in Philology*, XII, 3 (July 1915), 120–124—notably contemporary sound cues, written into a copy of the Second Quarto and cited by Malone. But if—as seems likely—such practices were exceptional, then Shakespeare was innovating all the farther.

M. M. Mahood

From *Shakespeare's Wordplay*

1

Romeo and Juliet is one of Shakespeare's most punning plays; even a really conservative count yields a hundred and seventy-five quibbles. Critics who find this levity unseemly excuse it by murmuring, with the Bad Quarto Capulet, that 'youth's a jolly thing' even in a tragedy. Yet Shakespeare was over thirty, with a good deal of dramatic writing already to his credit, when *Romeo and Juliet* was first performed. He knew what he was about in his wordplay, which is as functional here as in any of his later tragedies. It holds together the play's imagery in a rich pattern and gives an outlet to the tumultuous feelings of the central characters. By its proleptic second and third meanings it serves to sharpen the play's dramatic irony. Above all, it clarifies the conflict of incompatible truths and helps to establish their final equipoise.

Shakespeare's sonnet-prologue offers us a tale of star-crossed lovers and 'The *fearfull passage* of their *death-markt* loue'.[1] *Death-marked* can mean 'marked out for (or by) death; foredoomed'. If, however, we take *passage* in the sense of a voyage (and this submeaning prompts *trafficque* in the twelfth line) as well as a course of events, *death-marked* recalls the 'euer fixed marke' of Sonnet 116 and the sea-mark of Othello's utmost sail, and suggests the meaning 'With death as their objective'. The two meanings of *fearful* increase the line's oscillation; the meaning 'frightened' makes the lovers helpless, but they are not necessarily so if the

Reprint of "Romeo and Juliet" from *Shakespeare's Wordplay*, by M. M. Mahood. London: Methuen & Co., 1957, pp. 56–72, with permission.

word means 'fearsome' and so suggests that we, the audience, are awe-struck by their undertaking. These ambiguities pose the play's fundamental question at the outset: is its ending frustration or fulfilment? Does Death choose the lovers or do they elect to die? This question emerges from the language of the play itself and thus differs from the conventional, superimposed problem: is *Romeo and Juliet* a tragedy of Character or of Fate? which can be answered only by a neglect or distortion of the play as a dramatic experience. To blame or excuse the lovers' impetuosity and the connivance of others is to return to Arthur Broke's disapproval of unhonest desire, stolen contracts, drunken gossips and auricular confession. Recent critics have, I believe, come nearer to defining the play's experience when they have stressed the *Liebestod* of the ending and suggested that the love of Romeo and Juliet is the tragic passion that seeks its own destruction. Certainly nearly all the elements of the *amour-passion* myth as it has been defined by Denis de Rougemont[2] are present in the play. The love of Romeo and Juliet is immediate, violent and final. In the voyage imagery of the play[3] they abandon themselves to a rudderless course that must end in shipwreck:

> Thou desperate Pilot, now at once run on
> The dashing Rocks, thy seasick weary barke:
> Heeres to my Loue.   (V.iii.117–19)

The obstacle which is a feature of the *amour-passion* legend is partly external, the family feud; but it is partly a sword of the lovers' own tempering since, unlike earlier tellers of the story, Shakespeare leaves us with no explanation of why Romeo did not put Juliet on his horse and make for Mantua. A *leitmotiv* of the play is Death as Juliet's bridegroom; it first appears when Juliet sends to find Romeo's name: 'if he be married, My graue is like to be my wedding bed'. At the news of Romeo's banishment Juliet cries 'And death not Romeo, take my maiden head', and she begs her mother, rather than compel her to marry Paris, to 'make the Bridall bed In that dim Monument where Tibalt lies'. The theme grows too persistent to be mere dramatic irony:

> O sonne, the night before thy wedding day
> Hath death laine with thy wife, there she lies,
> Flower as she was, deflowred by him,
> Death is my sonne in law, death is my heire.
> My daughter he hath wedded.   (IV.v.35–9)

Romeo, gazing at the supposedly dead Juliet, could well believe

> that vnsubstantiall death is amorous,
> And that the leane abhorred monster keepes
> Thee here in darke to be his parramour.   (V.iii.103–5)

Most significant of all, there is Juliet's final cry:

> O *happy* dagger
> This is thy sheath, there rust and let me *dye*.   (V.iii.169–70)

where *happy* implies not only 'fortunate to me in being ready to my hand' but also 'successful, fortunate in itself' and so suggests a further quibble on *die*. Death has long been Romeo's rival and enjoys Juliet at the last.

In all these aspects *Romeo and Juliet* appears the classic literary statement of the *Liebestod* myth in which (we are told) we seek the satisfaction of our forbidden desires; forbidden, according to Freud, because *amour-passion* is inimical to the Race, according to de Rougemont because it is contrary to the Faith. Shakespeare's story conflicts, however, with the traditional myth at several points. Tragic love is always adulterous. Romeo and Juliet marry, and Juliet's agony of mind at the prospect of being married to Paris is in part a concern for her marriage vow: 'My husband is on earth, my faith in heauen'. Again, Romeo faces capture and death, Juliet the horror of being entombed alive, not because they want to die but because they want to live together. These woes are to serve them for sweet discourses in their time to come. In contrast to this, the wish-fulfilment of the *Liebestod* is accomplished only by the story of a suicide pact. Drama has furnished many such plots since the middle of the last century. Deirdre and her lover deliberately return to Ireland and the wrath of Conchubar because it is 'a better thing to be following on to a near death, than to be bending the head down, and dragging with the feet, and seeing one day a blight showing upon love where it is sweet and tender'. What makes Synge's play a tragedy is that the blight does show before the lovers are killed. By itself, the suicide pact offers the audience wish-fulfilment not *katharsis*. The good cry we enjoy over the worn reels of *Meyerling* bears only a remote relationship to the tragic experience of *Romeo and Juliet*.

The real objection to reading *Romeo and Juliet* as the *Liebestod* myth in dramatic form is that it is anachronistic to align the play with pure myths like that of Orpheus and Eurydice or with the modern restatement of such myths by Anouilh and Cocteau. Shakespeare's intention in writing the play was not that of the post-Freud playwright who finds in a high tale of love and death the objective correlative to his own emotions and those of his audience. We may guess that the story afforded Shakespeare an excited pleasure of recognition because it made explicit a psychological experience; but he did not, on the strength of that recognition, decide to write a play about the death wish. Like Girolamo de la Corte, whose *History of Venise* appeared about the time *Romeo and Juliet* was first acted, Shakespeare believed his lovers to be historical people. He read and retold their adventures with the detached judgment we accord history as well as with the implicated excitement we feel for myth. The story is both near and remote; it goes on all the time in ourselves, but its events belong also to distant Verona in the dog days when the mad blood is stirred to passion and violence. The resultant friction between history and myth, between the story and the fable, kindles the play into great drama. When we explore the language of *Romeo and Juliet* we find that both its wordplay and its imagery abound in those concepts of love as a war, a religion, a malady, which de Rougemont has suggested as the essence of *amour-passion*. If the play were pure myth, the fictionalising of a psychological event, all these elements would combine in a single statement of our desire for a tragic love. But because the play is also an exciting story about people whose objective existence we accept during the two hours' traffic of the stage, these images and quibbles are dramatically 'placed'; to ascertain Shakespeare's intentions in using them we need to see which characters are made to speak them and how they are distributed over the course of the action.

2

Act I begins with some heavy-witted punning from Sampson and Gregory—a kind of verbal tuning-up which quickens our ear for the great music to come. The jests soon broaden. This is one of Shakepeare's most bawdy plays, but the bawdy has always a dramatic function. Here its purpose is to make explicit, at the beginning of this love tragedy, one possible relationship between man and woman: a brutal male dominance expressed in sadistic quibbles. After the brawl has been quelled, the mood of the scene alters 'like a change from wood wind, brass and tympani to an andante on the strings'[4] in Benvolio's tale of Romeo's melancholia; and Romeo himself appears and expresses, in the numbers that Petrarch flowed in, the contrary relationship of the sexes: man's courtly subjection to women's tyranny. Rosaline is a saint, and by his quibbles upon theological terms Romeo shows himself a devotee of the Religion of Love:

> She is too faire, too wise, wisely too faire,
> To merit blisse by making me *dispaire*.   (227–8)

Love is a sickness as well as a cult, and Romeo twists Benvolio's request to tell in sadness (that is, seriously) whom he loves, to an expression of *amour-maladie*:

> A sicke man in *sadnesse* makes his will:
> A word ill vrgd to one that is so ill.   (208–9)

It is characteristic of this love learnt by rote from the sonnet writers that Romeo should combine images and puns which suggest this slave-like devotion to his mistress with others that imply a masterful attack on her chastity.[5] Love is a man of war in such phrases as 'th' incounter of assailing eies' which, added to the aggressive wordplay of Sampson and Gregory and to the paradox of 'ô brawling loue, ô louing hate', reinforce the theme of ambivalence, the *odi-et-amo* duality of passion.

All the Petrarchan and anti-Petrarchan conventions are thus presented to us in this first scene: love as malady, as worship, as war, as conquest. They are presented, however, with an exaggeration that suggests Romeo is already aware of his own absurdity and is 'posing at posing'. 'Where shall we dine?' is a most unlover-like question which gives the show away; and Benvolio's use of 'in sadnesse' implies that he knows Romeo's infatuation to be nine parts show. Romeo is in fact ready to be weaned from Rosaline, and the scene ends with a proleptic pun that threatens the overthrow of this textbook language of love. 'Examine other bewties', Benvolio urges, but for Romeo, 'Tis the way to call hers (exquisit) in question more'. By *question* he means, with a play upon the etymology of *exquisite*, 'consideration and conversation'; but we guess, if we do not know, that Rosaline's charms will be called into question in another sense when set beside the beauty of Juliet.

Love in Verona may be a cult, a quest or a madness. Marriage is a business arrangement. Old Capulet's insistence to Paris, in the next scene, that Juliet must make her own choice, is belied by later events. Juliet is an heiress, and her father does not intend to enrich any but a husband of his own choosing:

> *Earth* hath swallowed all my hopes but she,
> Shees the hopefull Lady of my *earth*.   (I.ii.14–15)

This quibbling distinction between *earth* as the grave and *earth* as lands (as Steevens points out, *fille de terre* means an heiress) is confounded when Juliet's hopes of happiness end in the Capulets' tomb. We recall the dramatic irony of this pun when Old Capulet speaks his last, moving quibble:

> O brother Mountague, giue me thy hand,
> This is my daughters *ioynture*, for no more
> Can I demaund.   (V.iii.296–8)

The ball scene at Capulet's house is prolonged by a revealing punning-match between Romeo and Mercutio. Romeo's lumbering puns are the wordplay of courtly love: the other masquers have nimble soles, he has a soul of lead: he is too bound to earth to bound, too sore from Cupid's darts to soar in the dance. Mercutio's levity, on the other hand, is heightened by his bawdy quibbles. Mercutio appears in early versions of the tale as what is significantly known as a ladykiller, and his dramatic purpose at this moment of the play is to oppose a cynical and aggressive idea of sex to Romeo's love-idolatry and so sharpen the contrast already made in the opening scene. Yet just as Romeo's touch of self-parody then showed him to be ready for a more adult love, so Mercutio's Queen Mab speech implies that his cynicism does not express the whole of his temperament. The falsity of both cynicism and idolatry, already felt to be inadequate by those who hold these concepts, is to be exposed by the love between Romeo and Juliet. Like Chaucer two centuries previously, Shakespeare weighed the ideas of the masterful man and the tyrannical mistress and wisely concluded that 'Love wol nat be constreyned by maistrie'.

For the ball scene, Shakespeare deploys his resources of stagecraft and poetry in a passage of brilliant dramatic counterpoint. Our attention is divided, during the dance, between the reminiscences of the two old Capulets (sketches for Silence and Shallow) and the rapt figure of Romeo who is watching Juliet. Nothing is lost by this, since the talk of the two pantaloons is mere inanity. We are only aware that it has to do with the passage of years too uneventful to be numbered, so that twenty-five is confused with thirty; simultaneously we share with Romeo a timeless minute that cannot be reckoned by the clock. Yet the old men's presence is a threat as well as a dramatic contrast. They have masqued and loved in their day, but ' 'tis gone, 'tis gone'.

Romeo's first appraisal of Juliet's beauty is rich not only in its unforgettable images but also in the subtlety of its wordplay. Hers is a 'Bewtie too rich for vse, for earth too deare'. When we recall that *use* means 'employment', 'interest' and 'wear and tear', that *earth* means both 'mortal life' and 'the grave', that *dear* can be either 'cherished' or 'costly' and that there is possibly a play upon *beauty* and *booty* (as there is in *Henry IV* part 1, I.ii.28), the line's range of meanings becomes very wide indeed. Over and above the contrast between her family's valuation of her as sound stock in the marriage market and Romeo's estimate that she is beyond all price, the words contain a self-contradictory dramatic irony. Juliet's beauty is too rich for use in the sense that it will be laid in the tomb after a brief enjoyment; but for that very reason it will never be faded and worn. And if she is *not* too dear for earth since Romeo's love is powerless to keep her out of the tomb, it is true that she is too rare a creature for mortal life. Not all these meanings are consciously present to the audience, but beneath the conscious level they connect with later images and quibbles and are thus brought into play before the tragedy is over.

The counterpoint of these scene is sustained as Romeo moves towards his new love against the discordant hate and rage of her cousin. Tybalt rushes from the room, threatening to convert seeming sweet to bitter gall, at the moment Romeo touches Juliet's hand. The lovers meet and salute each other in a sonnet full of conceits and quibbles on the Religion of Love—'palme to palme is holy Palmers kis'; 'grant thou least faith turne to dispaire'; 'Saints do not moue'—for the place is public and they must disguise their feelings beneath a social persiflage. The real strength of those feelings erupts in Romeo's pun—'O *deare* account!'— and in Juliet's paradox—'My onely loue sprung from my onely hate'—when each learns the other's identity, and the elements of youth and experience, love and hate, which have been kept apart throughout the scene, are abruptly juxtaposed. Then the torches are extinguished and the scene ends with a phrase of exquisite irony, when the Nurse speaks to Juliet as to a tired child after a party: 'Come lets away, the strangers all are gone.' Romeo is no longer a stranger and Juliet no longer a child.

A quibbling sonnet on love between enemies and some of Mercutio's ribald jests separate this scene from that in Capulet's orchard.[6] It is as if we must be reminded of the social and sexual strife before we hear Romeo and Juliet declare the perfect harmony of their feelings for each other. At first Romeo seems still to speak the language of idolatry, but the 'winged messenger of heauen' belongs to a different order of imagination from the faded conceits of his devotion to Rosaline. The worn commonplaces of courtship are swept aside by Juliet's frankness. One of the few quibbles in the scene is on *frank* in the meanings of 'generous' and 'candid, open', and it introduces Juliet's boldest and most beautiful avowal of her feelings:

> *Rom.* O wilt thou leaue me so vnsatisfied?
> *Iul.* What satisfaction canst thou haue to night?
> *Rom.* Th'exchange of thy loues faithful vow for mine.
> *Iul.* I gaue thee mine before thou didst request it:
> And yet I would it were to giue againe.
> *Rom.* Woldst thou withdraw it, for what purpose loue?
> *Iul.* But to be franke and giue it thee againe,
> And yet I wish but for the thing I haue,
> My bountie is an boundlesse as the sea,
> My loue as deepe, the more I giue to thee
> The more I haue, for both are infinite.   (II.ii.125–35)

Thus the distribution of wordplay upon the concepts of love-war, love-idolatry, love-sickness, serves to show that the feelings of Romeo and Juliet for each other are something quite different from the *amour-passion* in which de Rougemont finds all these disorders. For Romeo doting upon Rosaline, love was a malady and a religion; for Mercutio it is sheer lunacy ('a great naturall that runs lolling vp and downe') or a brutal conquest with no quarter given. All these notions are incomplete and immature compared to the reality. When Romeo meets Mercutio the next morning a second quibbling-match ensues in which the bawdy expressive of love-war and love-madness is all Mercutio's.

Romeo's puns, if silly, are gay and spontaneous in comparison
with his laboured conceits on the previous evening. Then, as he
explained to Benvolio, he was not himself, not Romeo. Now
Mercutio cries: 'now art thou sociable, now art thou Romeo'. In
fact Romeo and Juliet have experienced a self-discovery. Like
Donne's happy lovers, they 'possess one world, each hath one
and is one'; a world poles apart from the Nirvana quested by
romantic love. The play is a tragedy, not because the love of
Romeo for Juliet is in its nature tragic, but because the ending
achieves the equilibrium of great tragedy. The final victory of
time and society over the lovers is counterpoised by the
knowledge that it is, in a sense, *their* victory; a victory not only
over time and society which would have made them old and
worldly in the end (whereas their deaths heal the social wound),
but over the most insidious enemy of love, the inner hostility
that 'builds a Hell in Heaven's despite' and which threatens in
the broad jests of Mercutio. For we believe in the uniqueness of
Romeo's and Juliet's experience at the same time as we know it
to be, like other sublunary things, neither perfect nor permanent.
If our distress and satisfaction are caught up in the fine balance
of great tragedy at the end of the play, it is because, throughout,
the wordplay and imagery, the conduct of the action and the
grouping of characters contribute to that balance. The lovers'
confidence is both heightened and menaced by a worldly wisdom,
cynicism and resignation which, for the reason that candleholders
see more of the game, we are not able to repudiate as easily as
they can do.

3

The play's central paradox of love's strength and fragility is
most clearly expressed in the short marriage scene (II.vi). On the
one hand there is Romeo's triumphant boast:

>   come what sorrow can,
> It cannot counteruaile the exchange of joy
> That one short minute giues me in her sight:
> Do thou but close our hands with holy words,
> Then loue deuouring death do what he dare,
> It is inough I may but call her mine.   (3–8)

On the other hand there are the forebodings of Friar Laurence:

> These violent delights haue violent endes,
> And in their triumph die like fier and powder:
> Which as they kisse *consume*,   (9–11)

where *consume* means both 'reach a consummation' (*N.E.D.*v.2)
and 'burn away, be destroyed'. These conflicting themes of
satisfaction and frustration coalesce in the Friar's words on Juliet's
entry:

> Here comes the Lady, Oh so *light* a foote
> Will *nere weare out* the euerlasting flint.   (16–17)

An ambiguity of pronunciation between 'near' and 'ne'er' and
another of meaning in *wear out*[7] enable us to distinguish four
possible readings here before, with cormorant delight, we swallow
the lot. Juliet's foot is so light that

    (i)   it will never wear away the everlasting flint;
   (ii) it will never last it out;
  (iii) it will nearly outlast it;
  (iv) it will nearly wear it away.

The first of these is the obvious meaning, platitudinously suited
to the speaker. The second anticipates our fear that the lovers are
too beset with enemies on the hard of road of life to be able to
last the course, whereas the third contradicts this by saying that
Juliet's love and beauty, because time will not have the chance to
wear them away, will last in their fame nearly as long as the
rocks of earth. And this contradiction is heightened by (iv) in
which *light* has a suggestion of Juliet's luminous beauty,[8] and the
flint is that of a flintlock; so that the line is connected with the
sequence of paradoxical light images running through the play.
Love is spoken of as a sudden spark or a flash of lighting. Juliet's
forebodings in the balcony scene—

> I haue no ioy of this contract to night,
> It is too rash, too vnaduisd, too sudden,
> Too like the lightning which doth cease to bee,
> Ere one can say, it lightens   (II.ii.117–20)

—are deepened here by the Friar's talk of fire and powder and
again in the next act by his reproaches to Romeo:

Thy wit, that ornament, to shape and loue,
Mishapen in the conduct of them both:
Like powder in a skillesse souldiers flaske,
Is set a fier by thine owne ignorance.   (III.iii.129–32)

In sum, love is as easily extinguishable as it appears to Lysander
in *A Midsummer Night's Dream*:

Briefe as the lightning in the collied night,
That (in a spleene) vnfolds both heauen and earth;
And ere a man hath power to say, behold,
The iawes of darknesse do deuoure it vp:
So quicke bright things come to confusion.   (I.i.145–9)

Yet Romeo, when he experiences 'a *lighting* before death', uses
the pun not only to imply that he has enjoyed a lightning brief
happiness before being

    dischargd of breath,
As violently, as hastie powder fierd
Doth hurry from the fatall Canons wombe,   (V.i.63–5)

but also to sustain the image of Juliet's luminous beauty which
makes 'This Vault a feasting presence full of light'. For alongside
the images of sparks, torches, lightning, are others which associate
Romeo and Juliet with the unquenchable heavenly lights.
Mercutio's 'We waste our lights in vaine, light lights by day' is
ironically apposite to Romeo's love of Rosaline, who is a mere
candle before the sun that breaks from Juliet's window. Two
passages which have been slighted as conceits are an essential
part of this theme:

Two of the fairest starres in all the heauen,
Hauing some busines do[9] entreate her eyes,
To twinckle in their spheres till they returne.
What if her eyes were there, they in her head,
The brightnesse of her cheek wold shame those stars,
As day-light doth a lampe, her eye in heauen,
Would through the ayrie region streame so bright,
That birds would sing, and thinke it were not night. (II.ii.15–22)

Giue me my Romeo, and when I shall die,
Take him and cut him out in little starres,
And he will make the face of heauen so fine,
That all the world will be in loue with night,
And pay no worship to the garish Sun.   (III.ii.21–5)

Romeo and Juliet stellify each other, the love which appears to be quenched as easily as a spark is extinguished is, in fact, made as permanent as the sun and stars when it is set out of the range of time. The same paradox is sustained by the flower images which are closely associated with those of light. The 'gather the rose' theme was of course inevitable in a love tragedy of the High Renaissance. Shakespeare's rose imagery, however, is more than rhetorical, and serves to stress the central themes of the play.[10] The rose was dramatically appropriate as a love symbol because it was so often a prey to the invisible worm: 'Loathesome canker liues in sweetest bud.' Romeo is devoured by his infatuation for Rosaline 'as is the bud bit with a enuious worme' and the Friar, gathering herbs, moralises over the adulteration of the good in a life by its evil until 'the Canker death eates vp that Plant'. Romeo and Juliet are spared this. Death lies on Juliet just as its earlier semblance had done

> like an vntimely frost,
> Vpon the sweetest flower of all the field.   (IV.v.28–9)

This early frost forestalls the heat of the sun as well as the blight in the bud, since a further fitness of the image consists in the speed with which both roses and 'fresh female buds'[11] bloom and wither in the south. Although Lady Capulet seems never to have been young she tells Juliet

> I was your mother, much vpon these yeares
> That you are now a maide,   (I.iii.72–3)

and the cruelty of Verona's summers is implicit in Old Capulet's words:

> Let two more Sommers wither in their pride,
> Ere we may thinke her ripe to be a bride.   (I.ii.10–11)

The marriage scene, after its strong statement of love as the victor-victim of time, closes with a quibbling passage already discussed in which Romeo and Juliet defy time's most powerful allies. Romeo, in an image of music, challenges the notion that passion is discordant by nature, Juliet rejects the prudence of social considerations in her declaration of love's richness—'I cannot sum vp sum of halfe my wealth'. This last image is a foretaste of *Antony and Cleopatra*, and it would be interesting to compare the success of love's three enemies in Shakespeare's three double-titled tragedies. In *Troilus and Cressida* they win hands down. Society, in the shape of the Trojan War, again compels secrecy and again separates the lovers; the inner corruption of love itself makes Cressida unfaithful; and the burden of the play is that 'Loue, friendship, charity, are subjects all To enuious and calumniating time'. By contrast, *Antony and Cleopatra* is a clear victory for the lovers. Society, seen as the pomp of Rome, is a world well lost; the dismal drunken party we witness on Pompey's barge contrasts poorly with the revels of Antony and Cleopatra—which are left to our imagination. The lovers are old and wise enough to be reconciled to the ambivalence of their feelings, which is implicit in the play's imagery. Finally, time cannot harm them when they have eternity in their lips and eyes; at the end of the play Cleopatra is again for Cydnus to meet Mark Antony.

In *Romeo and Juliet* love's enemies have a Pyrrhic victory which begins with the slaying of Mercutio at the beginning of Act III. Like many of Shakespeare's characters, Mercutio dies with a quibble that asserts his vitality in the teeth of death. He jests as long as he has breath; only if we ask for him *tomorrow* shall we find him a grave man. But it is a grim joke, to accompany a dying curse. The Elizabethans, who believed in the power of curses, would have seen in the play's subsequent events the working-out of Mercutio's cynical knowledge that love is inseparably commingled with hate in human affairs. Romeo kills Tybalt, the cousin whose name he now tenders as dearly as his own. Juliet responds to the news with an outburst—'O serpent heart hid with a flowring face . . .' which, by recalling the loving hate of Romeo's infatuation with Rosaline, threatens the harmony and permanence of the love between Romeo and Juliet. She recovers her balance, but we have felt the tremor and know that even these lovers cannot sustain many such shocks.

Some of the most notorious puns in Shakespeare occur in this scene between Juliet and her Nurse, when the Nurse's confusion misleads Juliet into thinking Romeo has killed himself:

Hath Romeo slaine himselfe? say thou but *I*,
And that bare vowell *I* shall poyson more
Then the death darting[12] *eye* of Cockatrice,
I am not *I*, if there be such an *I*.

Or those *eyes* shut[12], that makes thee answere *I*:
If he be slaine say *I*, or if not, no.   (III.ii.45–50)

Excuses might be made for this. It does achieve a remarkable
sound-effect by setting Juliet's high-pitched keening of 'I' against
the Nurse's moans of 'O Romeo, Romeo'. It also sustains the eye
imagery of Juliet's great speech at the opening of this scene: the
runaways' eyes, the blindness of love, Juliet hooded like a hawk,
Romeo as the eye of heaven. But excuses are scarcely needed
since this is one of Shakespeare's first attempts to reveal a
profound disturbance of mind by the use of quibbles.[13] Romeo's
puns in the next scene at Friar Laurence's cell are of the same
kind: flies may kiss Juliet, but he must fly from her; the Friar,
though a friend *professed*, will offer him no sudden mean of death,
though ne'er so mean; he longs to know what his concealed lady
says to their cancelled love. This is technically crude, and perhaps
we do well to omit it in modern productions; but it represents a
psychological discovery that Shakespeare was to put to masterly
use in later plays. Against this feverish language of Romeo's,
Shakespeare sets the Friar's sober knowledge that lovers have
suffered and survived these calamities since the beginning of
time. For the Friar, 'the world is broad and wide', for Romeo,
'there is no world without Verona wall'. When the Friar tries to
dispute with him of his 'estate', the generalised, prayer-bookish
word suggests that Romeo's distress is the common human lot,
and we believe as much even while we join with Romeo in his
protest: 'Thou canst not speak of that thou dost not feele.' Tragedy
continually restates the paradox that 'all cases are unique and
very similar to others'.

The lovers' parting at dawn sustains this contradiction.
Lovers' hours may be full eternity, but the sun must still rise.
Their happiness has placed them out of the reach of fate; but
from now on, an accelerating series of misfortunes is to confound
their triumph in disaster without making it any less of a triumph.
With Lady Capulet's arrival to announce the match with Paris,
love's enemies begin to close in. Juliet meets her mother with
equivocations which suggest that Romeo's 'snowie Doue' has
grown wise as serpents since the story began, and which prepare
us for her resolution in feigning death to remain loyal to Romeo:

Indeed I neuer shall be satisfied
With Romeo, till I behold him. Dead
Is my poore heart so for a kinsman vext.[14]   (III.v.94–6)

This is a triple ambiguity, with one meaning for Juliet, another for her mother and a third for us, the audience: Juliet will never in fact see Romeo again until she wakes and finds him dead beside her.

A pun which has escaped most editors is made by Paris at the beginning of Act IV. He tells the Friar he has talked little of love with Juliet because 'Venus smiles not in a house of teares'. Here *house of tears* means, beside the bereaved Capulet household, an inauspicious section of the heavens—perhaps the eighth house or 'house of death'. Spenser's line 'When oblique Saturne sate in the house of agonyes'[15] shows that the image was familiar to the Elizabethans, and here it adds its weight to the lovers' yoke of inauspicious stars. But this is one of very few quibbles in the last two acts. The wordplay which, in the first part of the play, served to point up the meaning of the action is no longer required. What quibbles there are in the final scenes have, however, extraordinary force. Those spoken by Romeo after he has drunk the poison reaffirm the paradox of the play's experience at its most dramatic moment:

> O *true* Appothecary:
> Thy drugs are *quicke*. Thus with a kisse I die.   (V.iii.119–20)

Like the Friar's herbs, the apothecary's poison both heals and destroys. He is *true* not only because he has spoken the truth to Romeo in describing the poison's potency, but because he has been true to his calling in finding the salve for Romeo's ills. His drugs are not only speedy, but also *quick* in the sense of 'life-giving'. Romeo and Juliet 'cease to die, by dying'.

It is the prerogative of poetry to give effect and value to incompatible meanings. In *Romeo and Juliet*, several poetic means contribute to this end: the paradox, the recurrent image, the juxtaposition of old and young in such a way that we are both absorbed by and aloof from the lovers' feelings, and the sparkling wordplay. By such means Shakespeare ensures that our final emotion is neither the satisfaction we should feel in the lovers' death if the play were a simple expression of the *Liebestod* theme, nor the dismay of seeing two lives thwarted and destroyed by vicious fates, but a tragic equilibrium which includes and transcends both these feelings.

NOTES

1. L. 9. The prologue is not given in the Folio, but is found in the second, third and fourth Quartos. My quotations in this chapter are all from the Shakespeare Association facsimile of the Second Quarto.

2. *L'Amour et l'Occident* (Paris, 1939).

3. See Kenneth Muir and Sean O'Loughlin, *The Voyage to Illyria* (1937), p. 72

4. Harley Granville-Barker, *Prefaces to Shakespeare*, series II (1930), p. 6.

5. See G. E. Matthews, 'Sex and the Sonnet', *Essays in Criticism* II (1952), pp. 119–37.

6. Mercutio's 'This field-bed is too cold for me to sleepe' seems to be an echo of the Nurse's words to the lovers in Broke's poem:

   Loe here a fielde, (she shewd a fieldbed ready dight)
   Where you may, if you list, in armes, revenge your selfe
      by fight.

   As often with Shakespeare, a piece of rhetorical decoration in the source has become an integral part of the play's imagery, by prompting its quibbles on love as war.

7. As in the shoe polish advertisement: 'They're well-worn but they've worn well.' For discussion of the *Romeo and Juliet* passage see the correspondence in the *T.L.S.* for April 3, 17 and 24 and May 1, 1943.

8. There are previous puns on *light*:

   Away from light steales home my heauie sonne (I.i.142);
   Being but heauie I will beare the light (I.iv.12); And not
   impute this yeelding to light loue, Which the darke night
   hath so discouered (II.ii.105–6).

9. For the Second Quarto's *to*.

10. As the author of *2 Henry VI*, Shakespeare must almost unconsciously have connected rose images with the rivalry of two great houses. For the light-flowers cluster see I.i.139–45 and 156–8; I.ii.24–30; II.ii.117–22.

11. I borrow the phrase from the Bad Quarto. The accepted texts have 'fresh fennell buds'.

12. For the Second Quarto's *arting* and *shot*.

13. He had already done so in *Two Gentlemen of Verona* but the device is less startling in a comedy.

14. The Arden editor, following Theobald's reading, prints it thus:

> Indeed, I never shall be satisfied
> With Romeo, till I behold him—dead—
> Is my poor heart so for a kinsman vex'd.

15. *The Faerie Queene*, II.ix.52.

Susan Snyder

Romeo and Juliet:
Comedy into Tragedy

Romeo and Juliet is different from Shakespeare's other tragedies in that it becomes, rather than is, tragic. Other tragedies have reversals, but in *Romeo and Juliet* the reversal is so radical as to constitute a change of genre: the action and the characters begin in familiar comic patterns, and are then transformed—or discarded—to compose the pattern of tragedy.

Comedy and tragedy, being opposed ways of apprehending the real world, project their own opposing worlds. The tragic world is governed by inevitability, and its highest value is personal integrity. In the comic world 'evitability' is assumed; instead of heroic or obstinate adherence to a single course, comedy endorses opportunistic shifts and realistic accommodations as means to an end of new social health. The differing laws of comedy and tragedy point to opposed concepts of law itself. Law in the comic world is extrinsic, imposed on society *en masse*. Its source there is usually human, so that law may either be stretched ingeniously to suit the characters' ends, or flouted, or even annulled by benevolent rulers. Portia plays tricks with the letter and spirit of Venetian law to save Antonio. The Dukes in *The Comedy of Errors* and *A Midsummer Night's Dream*, when the objects are family reunions and happily paired lovers, simply brush aside legal obstacles. Even deep-rooted social laws, like the obedience owed to parents by their children, are constantly overturned. But in the tragic world law is inherent: imposed by the individual's own nature, it may direct him to a conflict with

Reprinted from *Essays in Criticism* 20 (1970), 391–402, with permission of the author and the journal.

the larger patterns of law inherent in his universe. The large pattern may be divine, as it generally is in Greek tragedy, or it may be natural and social, as in *Macbeth* and *King Lear*. Tragic law cannot be altered; it does no good to stop breeding destruction, or to tell destruction to tell gods or human individuals to stop being themselves.

In these opposed worlds our sense of time and its value also differs. The action of comedy may be quickly paced, but we know that it is moving towards a conclusion of 'all the time in the world'. The events of tragedy, on the other hand, acquire urgency in their uniqueness and their irrevocability: they will never happen again, and one by one they move the hero closer to the end of his own time in death. In comedy short-term urgencies are played against a dominant expansiveness, while in tragedy a sense that time is limited and precious grows with our perception of an inevitable outcome.

In its inexorable movement and the gulf it fixes between the central figure and the others, tragedy has been compared to ritual sacrifice. The protagonist is both hero and victim, separated from the ordinary, all-important in his own being, but destined for destruction. That is the point of the ritual. Comedy is organized like a game. The ascendancy goes to the clever ones who can take advantage of sudden openings, plot strategies, and adapt flexibly to an unexpected move. But luck and instinct win games as well as skill, and comedy takes account of the erratic laws of chance that bring a Dogberry out on top of a Don John and, more basically, of the instinctive attunement to underlying pattern that crowns lovers, however unaware and inflexible, with final success.

Romeo and Juliet, young and in love and defiant of obstacles, are attuned to the basic movement of the comic game toward social regeneration. But they are not successful: the game turns into a sacrifice, and the favoured lovers become its marked victims. This shift is illuminated by a study of the play's two worlds and some secondary characters who help to define them.

If we divide the play at Mercutio's death, the death that generates all those that follow, it becomes apparent that the play's movement up to this point is essentially comic. With the usual intrigues and go-betweens, the lovers overcome obstacles in a move toward marriage. This personal action is set in a broader social context, so that the marriage promises not only private satisfaction but renewed social unity:

For this alliance may so happy prove
To turn your households' rancour to pure love.[1]

The state that requires this cure is set out in the first scene. The Verona of the Montague-Capulet feud is like the typical starting point of the kind of comedy described by Northrop Frye: 'a society controlled by habit, ritual bondage, arbitrary law and the older characters.'[2] Even the scene's formal balletic structure, a series of matched representatives of the warring families entering on cue, conveys the inflexibility of this society, the arbitrary division that limits freedom of action.

The feud itself seems more a matter of mechanical reflex than of deeply felt hatred. As H. B. Charlton has noted, its presentation here has a comic aspect.[3] The 'parents' rage' that sounds so ominous in the Prologue becomes in representation an irascible humour: two old men claw at one another only to be dragged back by their wives and scolded by their Prince. Charlton found the play flawed by this failure to plant the seeds of tragedy, but the treatment of the feud makes good sense if Shakespeare is playing on *comic* expectations.

Other aspects of this initial world of *Romeo and Juliet* suggest comedy. Its characters are the minor aristocracy and servants familiar in comedies, concerned not with wars and the fate of kingdoms but with arranging marriages and managing the kitchen. More important, it is a world of possibilities, with Capulet's feast represented to the young men as a field of choice. 'Hear all, all see', says Capulet to Paris, 'And like her most whose merit most shall be' (I. ii. 30–31). 'Go thither', Benvolio tells Romeo, 'and with unattainted eye/Compare her face with some that I shall show . . .'[4] and Rosaline will be forgotten for some more approachable beauty. Romeo rejects the words, of course, but in action he soon displays a classic comic adaptability, switching from the impossible love to the possible just as Proteus, Demetrius, Phoebe, and Olivia do in their respective comedies.

Violence and disaster are not absent, of course, but they are unrealized threats. The feast yields a kind of comic emblem when Tybalt's potential violence is rendered harmless by Capulet's festive accommodation.

Therefore be patient, take no note of him.
It is my will; the which if thou respect,
Show a fair presence and put off these frowns,
An ill-beseeming semblance for a feast.   (I. v. 73–76)

This overruling of Tybalt is significant, for Tybalt is a recognizably tragic character, the only one in this part of the play. He alone takes the feud seriously: It is his inner law, the propeller of his fiery nature. He speaks habitually in the tragic rhetoric of honour and death:

> What, dares the slave
> Come hither, cover'd with an antic face,
> To fleer and scorn at our solemnity?
> Now by the stock and honour of my kin,
> To strike him dead I hold it not a sin.   (I. v. 57–61)

Tybalt's single set of absolutes cuts him off from a whole rhetorical range available to the other young men of the play: lyric love, witty fooling, friendly conversation. Ironically, his imperatives come to dominate the play's world only when he himself departs from it. While he is alive, Tybalt is an alien.

In a similar manner, the passing fears of calamity voiced by Romeo, Juliet, and Friar Laurence are not allowed to dominate this atmosphere. If the love of Romeo and Juliet is already imaged as a flash of light swallowed by darkness (an image invoking inexorable natural law), it is also expressed as a sea venture, which suggests luck and skill set against natural hazards, chance seized joyously as an opportunity for action. 'Direct my sail', Romeo tells his captain Fortune,[5] but soon he feels himself in command:

> I am no pilot; yet, wert thou as far
> As that vast shore wash'd with the farthest sea,
> I would adventure for such merchandise.   (II. ii. 82–84)

The spirit is Bassanio's as he adventures for Portia, a Jason voyaging in quest of the Golden Fleece.[6] Romeo is ready for difficulties with a traditional lovers' stratagem, one that Shakespeare had used before in *Two Gentlemen of Verona*: a rope ladder 'which to the high topgallant of my joy/Must be my convoy in the secret night' (II. iv. 201–202).

But before the ladder can be used, Mercutio's death intervenes to transform this world of exhilarating venture. Mercutio has been almost the incarnation of comic atmosphere. He is the best of game-players, endlessly inventive, full of quick moves and counter-moves. Speech for him is a constant play on multiple possibilities: puns abound because two or three meanings are

more fun than one, and Queen Mab brings dreams not only to
lovers like Romeo but to courtiers, lawyers, parsons, soldiers,
maids. These have nothing to do with the case at hand—Romeo's
premonition—but Mercutio is not bound by events. They are
merely points of departure for his expansive wit. In Mercutio's
sudden, violent end, Shakespeare makes the birth of a tragedy
coincide exactly with the symbolic death of comedy. The element
of freedom and play dies with him, and where many courses
were open before, now there seems only one. Romeo sees at once
that an irreversible process has begun:

> This day's black fate on moe days doth depend [hang over],
> This but begins the woe others must end.   (III. i. 124–125)

It is the first sign in the play's dialogue pointing unambiguously
to tragic causation. Romeo's future action is now determined: he
must kill Tybalt, he *must* run away, he is fortune's fool.

This helplessness is the most striking quality of the second,
tragic world of *Romeo and Juliet*. That is, the temper of the new
world is largely a function of onrushing events. Under pressure
of events, the feud turns from farce to fate, from tit for tat to
blood for blood. Lawless as it is in the Prince's eyes, the feud is
dramatically the law in *Romeo and Juliet*. Previously external and
avoidable, it has now moved inside Romeo to become his personal
law. Fittingly, he takes over Tybalt's rhetoric of honour and death:

> Alive in triumph, and Mercutio slain?
> Away to heaven respective lenity,
> And fire-ey'd fury be my conduct now!
> Now, Tybalt, take thy 'villain' back again
> That late thou gavest me.   (III. i. 127–131)

Even outside the main chain of vengeance, the world is suddenly
full of imperatives: against his will Friar John is detained at the
monastery, and against his will the Apothecary sells poison to
Romeo. Urgency becomes the norm as nights run into mornings
in continuous action and the characters seem never to sleep. The
new world finds its emblem not in the aborted attack but in the
aborted feast. As Tybalt's violence was out of tune with the
Capulet feast in Act II, so in Acts III and IV the projected wedding
is made grotesque when Shakespeare insistently links it with
death.[7] Preparations for the feast parallel those of the first part,
so as to underline the contrast when

All things that we ordained festival
Turn from their office to black funeral—
Our instruments to melancholy bells,
Our wedding cheer to a sad burial feast.   (IV. v. 84–87)

I have been treating these two worlds as consistent wholes in
order to bring out their opposition, but I do not wish to deny
dramatic unity to *Romeo and Juliet*. Shakespeare was writing one
play, not two, and in spite of the prominence of the turning point
we are aware that premonitions of disaster precede the death of
Mercutio and that hopes for avoiding it continue until near the
play's conclusion. The world-shift that converts Romeo and Juliet
from instinctive winners into sacrificial victims is thus a gradual
one. In this connection the careers of two secondary characters,
Friar Laurence and the Nurse, are instructive.

In being and action these two belong to the comic vision.
Friar Laurence is one of a whole series of Shakespearean
manipulators and stage-managers, those wise and benevolent
figures who direct the action of others, arrange edifying tableaux,
and resolve intricate public and private problems. Notable in the
list are Oberon, Friar Francis in *Much Ado*, Helena in the latter
part of *All's Well*, Duke Vincentio and Prospero. Friar Laurence
shares the religious dress of three of this quintet and participates
to some extent, by his knowledge of herbs and drugs, in the
magical powers of Oberon and Prospero. Such figures are frequent
in comedy but not in tragedy, where the future is not manipulable.
The Friar's aims are those implicit in the play's comic movement,
an inviolable union for Romeo and Juliet and an end to the
families' feud.

The Nurse's goal is less lofty, but equally appropriate to
comedy. She wants Juliet married—to anyone. Her preoccupation
with marriage and breeding is as indiscriminate as the life force
itself. But she conveys no sense of urgency in all this. Rather, her
garrulity assumes that limitless time that frames the comic world
but not the tragic. In this sense her circumlocutions and
digressions are analogous to Mercutio's witty flights and to Friar
Laurence's counsels of patience. The leisurely time assumptions
of the Friar and the Nurse contrast with the lovers' impatience,
creating at first the normal counterpoint of comedy[8] and later a
radical split that points us, with the lovers, directly to tragedy.

For what place can these two have in the new world brought
into being by Mercutio's death, the world of limited time, no

effective choice, no escape? In a sense, though, they define and sharpen the tragedy by their very failure to find a place in the dramatic progress, by their growing estrangement from the true springs of the action. 'Be patient', Friar Laurence tells the banished Romeo, 'for the world is broad and wide' (III. iii. 16). But the roominess he assumes in both time and space simply does not exist for Romeo. His time has been constricted into a chain of days working out a 'black fate', and he sees no world outside the walls of Verona (III. iii. 17).

Comic adaptability again confronts tragic integrity when Juliet is faced with a similarly intolerable situation—she is ordered to marry Paris—and turns to her Nurse for counsel as Romeo does to the Friar. The Nurse replies with the traditional worldly wisdom of comedy. Romeo has been banished and Paris is very presentable. Adjust yourself to the new situation.

> Then, since the case so stands as now it doth,
> I think it best you married with the County.
> O, he's a lovely gentleman!   (III. v. 218–220)

She still speaks for the life force. Even if Paris is an inferior husband, he is better than no husband at all.

> Your first is dead—or 'twere as good he were
> As living here and you no use of him.   (226–227)

But such advice has become irrelevant, even shocking, in this context. There was no sense of jar when Benvolio, a spokesman for accommodation like the Nurse and the Friar, earlier advised Romeo to substitute a possible for an impossible love. True, the Nurse is urging violation of the marriage vows; but Romeo was also sworn to Rosaline, and for Juliet the marriage vow is a seal on the integrity of her love for Romeo, not a separate issue. The parallel points up the progress of tragedy, for while Benvolio's advice sounded sensible and was in fact unintentionally carried out by Romeo, the course of action outlined by the Nurse is unthinkable to the audience as well as Juliet. The memory of the lovers' dawn parting that began this scene is too strong. Juliet and the Nurse no longer speak the same language, and estrangement is inevitable. 'Thou and my bosom henceforth shall be twain', Juliet vows privately.[9] Like the death of Mercutio, Juliet's rejection of her old confidante has symbolic overtones.

The possibilities of comedy have again been presented only to be discarded.

Both Romeo and Juliet have now cast off their comic companions and the alternate modes of being that they represented. But there is one last hope for comedy. If the lovers will not adjust to the situation, perhaps the situation can be adjusted to the lovers. This is the usual comic solution, and we have at hand the usual manipulator to engineer it. The Friar's failure to bring off that solution is the final definition of the tragic world of the play. Time is the villain. Time in comedy generally works for regeneration and reconciliation, but in tragedy it propels the protagonists to destruction; there is not enough of it, or it goes wrong somehow. The Friar does his best: he makes more than one plan to avert catastrophe. The first, typically, is patience and a broader field of action. Romeo must go to Mantua and wait

> till we can find a time
> To blaze your marriage, reconcile your friends,
> Beg pardon of the Prince, and call thee back . . .(III. iii. 150–152)

It is a good enough plan, for life if not for drama, but it depends on 'finding a time'. As it turns out, events move too quickly for the Friar, and the hasty preparations for Juliet's marriage to Paris leave no time for cooling tempers and reconciliations.

His second plan is an attempt to *gain* time, to create the necessary freedom through a faked death. This is, of course, another comic formula; Shakespeare's later uses of it are all in comedies. It is interesting that the contrived 'deaths' of Hero in *Much Ado*, Helena in *All's Well*, Claudio in *Measure for Measure*, and Hermione in *The Winter's Tale*, unlike Juliet's, are designed to produce a change of heart in other characters.[10] Time may be important, as it is in *The Winter's Tale*, but only as it promotes repentance. Friar Laurence, less ambitious and more desperate than his fellow manipulators, does not hope that Juliet's death will dissolve the families' hatreds but only that it will give Romeo a chance to come and carry her off. Time in the comic world of *The Winter's Tale* co-operates benevolently with Paulina's schemes for Leontes' regeneration; but for Friar Laurence it is both prize and adversary. Romeo's man is quicker with the news of Juliet's death than poor Friar John with the news of the deception. Romeo himself beats Friar Laurence to the Capulets' tomb. The onrushing tragic action quite literally outstrips the slower steps of accommodation before our eyes. The Friar arrives too late to prevent one half of the tragic conclusion, and his essential estrangement is only emphasised when he seeks to avert the other half by sending Juliet to a nunnery. It is the last alternative to be suggested. Juliet quietly rejects the possibility of adjustment and continuing life: 'Go, get thee hence, for I will not away' (v. iii. 160).

The Nurse and the Friar illustrate a basic principle of the operation of comedy in tragedy, which might be called the principle of irrelevance. In tragedy we are tuned to the extraordinary. *Romeo and Juliet* gives us this extraordinary centre not so much in the two individuals as in the love itself, its intensity and integrity. Our apprehension of this intensity and integrity comes gradually, through the cumulative effect of the lovers' lyric encounters and the increasing urgency of events, but also through the growing irrelevance of the comic characters.

De Quincey perceived in the knocking at the gate in *Macbeth* the resumption of normality after nightmare: 'the re-establishment of the going-on of the world in which we live, which first makes us profoundly sensible of the awful parenthesis that has suspended them.'[11] I would say rather that the normal atmosphere of *Macbeth* has been and goes on being nightmarish, and that it is the knocking at the gate that turns out to be the contrasting parenthesis, but the notion of a sharpened sensitivity is valid. As the presence of alternate paths makes us more conscious of the road we are in fact travelling, so the Nurse and the Friar make us more 'profoundly sensible' of Romeo's and Juliet's love and its true direction.

After *Romeo and Juliet* Shakespeare never returned to the comedy-into-tragedy formula, although the canon has several examples of potential tragedy converted into comedy. There is a kind of short comic movement in *Othello*, encompassing the successful love of Othello and Desdemona and their safe arrival in Cyprus, but comedy is not in control even in the first act. Iago's malevolence has begun the play, and our sense of obstacles overcome (Desdemona's father, the perils of the sea) is shadowed by his insistent presence. The act ends with the birth of his next plot.

It is not only the shift from comedy to tragedy that sets *Romeo and Juliet* apart from the other Shakespeare tragedies. Critics have often noted, sometimes disapprovingly, that external fate rather than character is the principal determiner of the tragic outcome. For Shakespeare, tragedy is usually a matter of both character and circumstance, a fatal interaction of man and moment. But in this play, although the central characters have their weaknesses, their destruction does not really stem from these weaknesses. One may agree with Friar Laurence that Romeo is rash, but it is not his rashness that propels him into the tragic chain of events but an opposite quality. In the crucial duel between Mercutio and Tybalt, Romeo tries to make peace. Ironically, this very intervention contributes to Mercutio's death.

> *Mer*: Why the devil came you between us? I was hurt under
> your arm.
> *Rom*: I thought all for the best.   (III. i. 108–109)

If Shakespeare wanted to implicate Romeo's rashness in his fate, this scene is handled with unbelievable ineptness. Judging from the resultant effect, what he wanted to convey was an ironic dissociation between character and the direction of events.

Perhaps this same purpose dictated the elaborate introduction of comic elements before the characters are pushed into the opposed conditions of tragedy. Stress on milieu tends to downgrade the importance of individual temperament and motivation. For this once in Shakesperean tragedy, it is not what you are that counts, but the world you live in.

NOTES

1. II. iii. 91–92. All Shakespeare references are to *The Complete Works*, ed. G. L. Kittredge (Boston, 1936).

2. *Anatomy of Criticism* (Princeton, 1957), p. 169. Although the younger generation participates in the feud, they have not created it; it is a legacy from the past.

3. *Shakespearian Tragedy* (Cambridge, 1948), pp. 56–57.

4. I. ii. 89–90.

5. I. iv. 113.

6. *Merchant of Venice* I. i. 166–174.

7. III. iv. 23–28; III. v. 202–203; IV. i. 6–8; IV. i. 77–86; IV. i. 107–108; IV. v. 35–39; V. iii. 12.

8. Clowns and cynics are usually available to comment on romantic lovers in Shakespeare's comedies, providing qualification and a widened perspective without real disharmony. A single character, like Rosalind in *As You Like It*, may incorporate much of the counterpoint in her own comprehensive view.

9. III. v. 242. Later, in the potion scene, Juliet's resolve weakens temporarily, but she at once rejects the idea of companionship. The effect is to call attention to her aloneness:

> I'll call them back again to comfort me.
> Nurse!—What should she do here?
> My dismal scene I needs must act alone. (IV. iii. 17–19)

10. The same effect, if not the plan, is apparent in Imogen's reported death in *Cymbeline*.

11. 'On the Knocking at the Gate in *Macbeth*,' *Shakespeare Criticism: A Selection*, ed. D. Nichol Smith (Oxford, 1916), p. 378.

James L. Calderwood

Romeo and Juliet: A Formal Dwelling

As an indirect entry to *Romeo and Juliet* let me dwell for a moment on Shakespeare's management of vows, since vows are especially good indices of a dramatist's conception of language in addition to having a strong bearing on character, motive, even dramatic form. In *Titus Andronicus* Shakespeare saw in the vow a formal principle of Senecan revenge tragedy. Out of the chaos of his material the dramatist contrives a teleology in which the vow serves as a structural promise to be redeemed by a culminating act of vengeance. The strangest vow in that strange play, however, is not Titus's vow of vengeance but Lucius's vow of mercy (in 5.1), which results from Aaron's insistence that unless his child goes free he like his descendant Iago "never will speak word." Shakespeare makes much of this contract between Lucius and Aaron partly because it introduces an element of mercy into a drama whose zestful cruelty makes Antonin Artaud's pronouncements on that subject seem saccharine by comparison but partly too because like so many other bizarre encounters in the play it figures his dramatic problem of uniting words and actions. The contract involves the exchange of Lucius's "word" for Aaron's "plot," and that is precisely the kind of contract Shakespeare has himself been trying without success to negotiate in *Titus Andronicus*. By spinning out the implications of Lucius's vow one might arrive at a fairly good notion of the central dramatic problem of the play.

Vows are equally significant in *Love's Labour's Lost*. In vowing themselves to the life of Academe the scholars rely on the autonomy of words, not as they function in society but as defined,

Reprinted from *Shakespearean Metadrama*. Minneapolis: University of Minnesota Press, 1971, pp. 85–119, with permission.

purified, and sworn to by themselves. So constituted, words will suppress nature in the form of the scholars' own "affections" and "the huge army of the world's desires" (primarily women). Since a purely private verbal world is impossible, their fragile fortress of words collapses before the assaulting army of the world's desires marching in petticoats from France. The scholars then scatter a second set of vows during their Muscovite wooing scene, each to the wrong lady, the disastrous effect of which suggests that if words may be overvalued through private hoarding they may also be undervalued through promiscuous spending. Behind the surface plight of laboring lovers hiding behind words and then distributing them wildly in all directions stands the poet's metadramatic plight as he tries to arbitrate between the individual and private needs of his art on the one hand and the all-too-public and debased nature of the language in which his art must be cast. No solution to that problem is arrived at in *Love's Labour's Lost*. Neither by trying to virginize the universal whore language nor by trailing her about the streets and risking contamination himself can the playwright achieve the elusive and mysterious marriage of language and art that will make him whole.

It is generally supposed that *Titus Andronicus* preceded *Love's Labour's Lost*, and if so then the comedy may be seen as a reaction to the would-be tragedy, a recoiling from violent action, contrived plots, and stage sensationalism. The result is a purely verbal, plotless, essentially nondramatic work. Since it is also generally supposed that *Lover's Labour's Lost* preceded *Romeo and Juliet* perhaps the latter can be considered in some degree at least as a response to the issues dealt with in the comic play. The marriage of the hero and heroine for instance would seem to acquire special significance in view of the conspicuous non-marriage of the lovers in the earlier play. In *Love's Labour's Lost* marriage was conceived of as the proper terminus of dramatic form, where the play ought to but perversely refuses to end, and as the product of a true language. Neither form nor language is discovered, however, and we are left with a mannered, courtly play of words illustrating its author's astonishing virtuosity but also, as he himself underscores by thrusting Mercade into the nonaction, a certain glib and glittering superficiality. The truth of the feelings is first suppressed by words and later distorted and obscured by them. As the purgative punishments of the scholars imply, the poet's language must somehow incorporate inner truth and outer reality, the mystery of love and such bleak facts of nature as time, suffering, death.

II

These then are the major metadramatic issues, at least on the side of language, confronting Shakespeare as he turns to *Romeo and Juliet*. From the problem of language he moves on in this play to the problem of dramatic form. But first let us focus on language and particularly on the balcony scene of 2.2 where vows again come into prominence. The place to begin is of course Juliet's famous complaint against the tyranny of names:

> 'Tis but thy name that is my enemy;
> Thou art thy thyself though not a Montague.
> What's Montague? It is nor hand nor foot
> Nor arm nor face nor any other part
> Belonging to a man. O be some other name!
> What's in a name? That which we call a rose
> By any other word would smell as sweet.
> So Romeo would, were he not Romeo called,
> Retain that dear perfection which he owes
> Without that title. Romeo, doff thy name,
> And for thy name, which is no part of thee,
> Take all myself.   (2.2.38–49)

Here and more widely throughout the play, brilliantly figured in the implicit metaphor of family and relatives, verbal nominalism is equated with a kind of social personalism. That is, in her anxiety to circumvent the opposition of their relatives Juliet would reject all relations and find ultimate truth in the haecceity, thisness, or as she puts it "dear perfection" of a totally unaffiliated Romeo. In the same way nominalism rejects the family or tribal relations of words in their more universal and abstract forms and situates verbal truth in the concrete and particular terms that seem most closely tied to the unique, unrelated, and hence true objects of which reality is composed. Juliet's nominalism here is a position with which the poet can readily sympathize,[1] because words come to the poet as Romeo comes to Juliet, trailing dark clouds of a prior public identity. Romeo comes to Juliet not merely from the streets of Verona and the house of Montague but from the shallows of Petrarchan love dotage as well, since he begins this play as Berowne ended his, an unrequited wooer of "Rosaline" (who is appropriately no more than a "name" in *Romeo and Juliet*). Juliet's verbal program is roughly analogous to that of the scholars of Navarre when they sought to establish their Academe. Where they tried to seal themselves off from the outside world by founding an elite society on a private language, Juliet seeks to go even further, to rename or even "de-name" in the interests of purifying a Romeo who has been abroad with his pseudo-love.[2] (Of course Juliet does not know about Rosaline, but Shakespeare does, and thus has Juliet repudiate Petrarchan "form," "strangeness," and "cunning" a bit further on.)

Romeo is more than willing to be renamed—

> Call me but love and I'll be new baptized;
> Henceforth I never will be Romeo   (2.2.50–51)

—but his language throughout the scene betrays him. Like Berowne, who prematurely thought himself cured of the Petrarchan style, Romeo still has "a trick/Of the old rage" (*Love's Labour's Lost*, 5.2.416–417). It reveals itself most obviously when he begins keening vows:

> Lady, by yonder blessed moon I vow
> That tips with silver all these fruit-tree tops—
> JULIET. O swear not by the moon, the inconstant moon
> That monthly changes in her circled orb,
> Lest that thy love prove likewise variable.
> ROMEO.   What shall I swear by?
> JULIET.   Do not swear at all.
> Or, if thou wilt, swear by the gracious self,
> Which is the god of my idolatry,
> And I'll believe thee.
> ROMEO.   If my heart's dear love—
> JULIET.   Well, do not swear. Although I joy in thee,
> I have no joy of this contract tonight.
> It is too rash, too unadvised, too sudden,
> Too like the lightning, which doth cease to be
> Ere one can say it lightens. Sweet, goodnight.
> This bud of love, by summer's ripening breath,
> May prove a beauteous flower when next we meet.
> Goodnight, goodnight! As sweet repose and rest
> Come to thy heart as that within my breast.
> ROMEO.   O wilt thou leave me so unsatisfied?

JULIET. What satisfaction canst thou have tonight?
ROMEO. The exchange of thy love's faithful vow for
mine.   (2.2.107–127)

Like the scholars of Navarre in their wooing phase ("O who can give an oath?") Romeo is a ready spender of words and, also like them, naively trustful that vows can trace around lovers a magic circle to hold the devilish world at bay. But like the French ladies Juliet has a maturer conception of the laws of verbal contract and the power of their magic. Her rejection of the "inconstant moon" as a third party to the contract and her apprehensions about the rash, unadvised, and oversudden enlarge the more immediate threat of the feuding families to include all that is dangerously unstable beyond the periphery of private feeling. But she is also unsure of Romeo's love, which is available to her only as it is given shape in his language. Instinctively she distrusts his *style*, as Shakespeare forces us to notice by having her twice interrupt him as he cranks up his rhetorical engines in preparation for Petrarchan flights. Throughout this scene, and the play for that matter, it is Romeo's speech that soars airily and often vacuously. Juliet's, though hardly leaden, is more earthbound. She is not opposed to vows entirely—though her nominalism inevitably tends in that direction—but seeks a true language in which they may be expressed. Thus when Romeo selects the moon as a symbol of purity to swear by, she, recognizing the pseudo-purity of his own Petrarchan style, reminds him that the moon is also a symbol of inconstancy. Not the purling phrases rising easily to the lips of a thousand dandies with well-hinged knees but the genuine custom-made article is what she seeks:

> O gentle Romeo,
> If thou dost love, pronounce it faithfully.
> Or if thou think'st I am too quickly won
> I'll frown and be perverse and say thee nay—
> So thou wilt woo; but else, not for the world.
> In truth, fair Montague, I am too fond,
> And therefore thou mayst think my 'haviour light.
> But trust me, gentleman, I'll prove more true
> Than those that have more cunning to be strange.   (2.2.93–101)

"Pronounce it faithfully"—unfortunately Romeo, who would forge a binding verbal contract, is himself bound to the book of form. Like Paris, whom Lady Capulet lengthily describes as a "fair volume" (1.3.79ff), and Tybalt, whom Mercutio despises as an "antic, lisping, affecting fantastico" who stands "much on the new form" (2.4.29–37) and "fights by the book of arithmetic" (3.1.105), Romeo not only kisses "by the book" (1.5.112) but trumpets vows by the book of Petrarchan form. Juliet admits that she *could* play at Petrarchanism and that to do so might even invest her behavior with an appearance of mature reserve that her forthrightness of feeling makes her seem without. But even if a bit fondly, she specializes in truth, not form, and so concludes "but farewell compliment!/Dost thou love me?" (2.2.89–90). Truly virginal, she recoils from the potential contamination of vows loosely and grandiloquently untethered: "Well, do not swear." Do not swear, do not even speak—that is the end of the nominalistic line because even at their best words cannot perfectly reflect the autonomous individuality of objects, or in this case of genuine love. Seeking an ideal communion of love at a level beyond idle breath, Juliet would purify words quite out of existence and reduce dialogue to an exchange of intuition and sheer feeling—a marriage of true minds accomplished without the connective medium of language.

III

If we set Juliet's remarks on the names in a literary perspective instead of a general nominalistic one they might be taken to suggest an extreme toward which the lyric impulse sometimes tends, that is, an ineffable purity. Here it is an ineffable purity of love, but its counterparts elsewhere would include the "unexpressive nuptial song" mentioned by Milton in "Lycidas," that etherealized music in Keats's "Ode on a Grecian Urn"—

> Heard melodies are sweet, but those unheard
> Are sweeter; therefore, ye soft pipes, play on;
> Not to the sensual ear, but, more endeared,
> Pipe to the spirit ditties of no tone

—and the dumb eloquence of lips in Hopkins's "The Habit of Perfection":

> Shape nothing, lips; be lovely-dumb:
> It is the shut, the curfew sent

From there where all surrenders come
Which only makes you eloquent.

Such scattered examples remind us of how its recurrent attraction to the pure and ideal leads lyric toward seclusion from the ruck and reel of time, action, and the world. Etymologically, though not always in practice, lyric aspires to the condition of music, seeking to purify noise into melody and sometimes even, as expressed in the examples above, to a point beyond sound, to stillness. Similarly as regards time and motion, lyric would discover a terminal rest, a retreat from the hurly-burly of action and consequences where thought and feeling crystallize in an expressive stasis. Murray Krieger has demonstrated the apt ambiguity of the word "still" to express in terms of motion the ever-moving fixity of poetry as it sets progressive experience within a transfixing form or, in Yeatsian language, unites the dancer with the dance.[3] In talking about *Romeo and Juliet*, however, we need to enlarge on the ambiguities of stillness by adding silence to the ever-neverness of motion since Juliet, as we have seen, would reduce love's dialogue to a silent communion of unique, inexpressible feeling.

Shakespeare, it is time to say, is abundantly aware how foolish such a *reductio ad silentium* must be from the standpoint of the poet. However intense his own longing to attain a purity out of the swing of speech—and it seems to me considerably so—he knows with Mallarmé that poetry is written with words, not ideas, and especially not ideas before which the poet must become breathless with adoration. If Juliet's view were to prevail the play would turn mute and time stand still, or at least slow down to the point where nine o'clock tomorrow takes twenty years to arrive (2.2.168–170). Drama would dissolve into lyric and lyric would dissolve into a silent center of inexpressible love surrounded by the cacophony of the street scenes, the nurse's babble and Mercutio's bawdry, the expostulations of Capulet, and the intoned *sententia* of Friar Laurence.

The plight of the poet who would retreat within lyric to a purer wordlessness is humorously illustrated when Juliet, after appropriately hearing "some noise within" and retiring briefly to investigate, returns to the balcony and cannot momentarily locate Romeo:

JULIET. Hist! Romeo, hist! O for a falconer's voice
To lure this tassel-gentle back again!
Bondage is hoarse, and may not speak aloud,
Else would I tear the cave where Echo lies
And make her airy tongue more hoarse than mine
With repetition of my Romeo's name.
Romeo!   (2.2.159–165)

If "Necessity" as Berowne said could make the scholars "all
forsworn/Three thousand times within this three years' space"
(*Love's Labour's Lost*, 1.1.150–151), it can also make a sorely
frustrated Juliet acknowledge the indispensability of names within
a little more than a hundred lines of her great protest against
them. In that brief space the tyrannous "bondage" of verbal
categories (locking the free spirit of reality into claustrophobic
linguistic cells) metamorphoses into its opposite, the "bondage"
that prevents Juliet from giving full free voice to that most useful
category "Romeo." For the lovers and for the poet Shakespeare
the notion of establishing communion on a plane of feeling
transcending the imperfections of speech is "but a dream/Too
flattering-sweet to be substantial" (2.2.140–141). Not only must
the lovers rely on names for the rudiments of communication,
but their love itself becomes a great name-singing celebration:

ROMEO. It is my soul that calls upon my name.
How silver-sweet sound lovers' tongues by night,
Like softest music to attending ears!   (2.2.165–167)

JULIET.   . . . and every tongue that speaks
But Romeo's name speaks heavenly eloquence.   (3.2.32–33)

That Juliet somewhat humorously belies herself in this last
quotation, finding a "heavenly eloquence" in the name she earlier
thought inimical to their love, is in keeping with a play that
seems founded on the principle of the oxymoron: she wants, it
seems, a "nameless naming." The paradox metadramatically
reflects the difficulty of Shakespeare's own situation as he wrestles
in this play with the slipperiest of antagonists, verbal purity,
against whom even he may be overmatched. It is a contest waged
between every poet and language, and it ends for better or worse
in a compromise somewhere between the private dream and the
public fact. The contest is the more arduous for being conducted
within the ring of drama where the impulse to verbal purity

takes the form of lyric, which retards, as opposed to action, which impels. I'll get back to this particular issue later; for the moment I need to isolate the linguistic problem from the more embracing dramatic one.

If one charted the private/public range of language in *Romeo and Juliet*, at the furthest private extreme would come "silence," a nominalistic tendency so rigorous as to still speech entirely. Obviously since we do have a script for the play this extreme does not become manifest, except at those moments during performances when the lovers exchange prolonged glances and wordless sighs. Still at this end of the chart would appear the lovers' language within the orchard—self-cherishing, insular, answerable only to private feeling. At the extreme public end of the chart opposite silence is noise, disturbance, disquiet—the "airy world" of the opening scene which the Prince says has "thrice disturbed the quiet of our streets" with civil brawls. (The Prince is significantly more concerned with "peace" as quiet than as cessation of hostilities; the greatest threat to the play is sheer noise, its consistent goal harmonic sound.) Also at this end of the scale despite its affectation of privacy and purity is Romeo's Petrarchan language, full of sighs, show, and manner, and far too "airy" in its own way, as Juliet instantly perceives, to substantialize love in any genuine form. Here too, though antagonistic to Romeo's Petrarchanism, is Mercutio's ribald wordplay, as amusingly impure verbally as the sensuality it dotes on is in comparison to Romeo and Juliet's love.

One would also expect to place Friar Laurence's "holy words" within the public sphere since it is through the public institutions of church and marriage, by having "Holy Church incorporate two in one," that the friar hopes to reunite the oppugnant families. That would seem an ideal union, the private bond of love becoming a public bond of marriage sealing the families, because although love itself may be a fine and private thing marriage is by nature public. Its function is to translate private feeling into the received language of society and so give public residence to what may otherwise be simply emotional vagrancy— unpropertied, subjective, and strange. This love, we know, transcends all that. But nonetheless the wedding *is* private, and the marriage it begets remains so. Consecrated by holy words, the lovers' vows bind them to one another (suggesting that the language of love's communion so absent from *Love's Labour's Lost* has been discovered) but in this private union they remain divorced from the wider social context into which genuine marriage would incorporate them.

Their love then is translated into a language that goes unheard beyond the narrow circle formed by themselves, the friar, and later the nurse. Alone in the privacy of his cell Friar Laurence can celebrate the sacrament of Communion, can give quiet voice to *the* Word (Logos), and have its spiritual benefits circulate among all men. But he cannot do so with the sacrament of marriage. If marriage is to be the medium of a secular, familial communion, its sacramental language must be heard by the fallen families it would save, and in that regard the friar's words are as inaudible as those of the lovers. The most obvious symbol of the friar's inability to give public circulation to his own and the lovers' language is his short-circuited letter to Romeo in Mantua. Like Romeo when he leaves the orchard haven for the brawling streets, the friar's words—surrogates for the lovers' words—run afoul of the "infectious pestilence" of the outside world (5.2.10). (Mercutio's curse "A plague o' both your houses" is thus most literally fulfilled by the plague that detains Friar John.) Despite his intentions then Friar Laurence is less a mediator between private and public spheres than a religious version of the private— his rather monastic celibacy suggesting an analogue to the withdrawn lyric adoration of the lovers. Only when the lovers are dead and he Horatio-like tells their story does the friar finally marry them to the social order and bind the families as he had hoped.

Through neither family nor church can love make its way into the social context, nor through a third major institution, the state. As a political entity the Veronese state is elusive to the vanishing point; its dramatic form is simply the voice of the Prince, quite literally his sentences. In the opening scene ("hear the sentence of your moved prince") he decrees death to anyone who breaks the peace, and in 3.1 he pronounces sentence on Romeo ("A gentler judgment vanished from his lips," the friar reports, "Not body's death but body's banishment"—3.3.10–11). From one standpoint the princely word is not good since the peace it ordained is subsequently broken and the banished body returns; from another it is, since Mercutio and Tybalt die for their offense and Romeo for his (the Prince had said "when [Romeo's] found that hour is his last," and so it is—3.1.200). The political word clearly has its limits—as when the citizen, unaware that Tybalt is dead, cries "Up, sir, go with me./I charge thee in the Prince's name, obey" (3.1.144–145)[4]—but it also has its sovereignty, as Juliet laments:

"Romeo is banished!" To speak that word
Is father, mother, Tybalt, Romeo, Juliet,
All slain, all dead. "Romeo is banished!"
There is no end, no limit, measure, bound,
In that word's death; no words can that woe sound.

(3.2.122–126)

If the Prince's word cannot spring the dead to life and duty as the citizen demanded, it can afflict the living with death.

The major emphasis in 3.2 and 3.3, in which the word "banished" is repeated nineteen times, is to force on the lovers the anti-nominalist realization that although as Juliet said a name is "nor hand nor foot/Nor arm nor face nor any other part/ Belonging to a man," even so airily universal a verb as "banished" can permanently still all those moving parts:

JULIET. That "banished," that one word "banished,"
Hath slain ten thousands Tybalts.   (3.2.113–114)

JULIET.   To speak that word
Is father, mother, Tybalt, Romeo, Juliet,
All slain, all dead.   (3.2.122–124)

ROMEO.   Calling death "banishment"
Thou cut'st my head off with a golden axe.   (3.3.21–22)

If the language of love is inaudible to society, the language of society is deafening to the lovers. From such clangor the only final escape is to the quiet of the grave.

IV

"Banished" is the severing word that immediately threatens and finally destroys the communion of love since because of it the lovers are forced to communicate through society by means of the friar's message, and that is precisely what they cannot do. Only in a state of lyric seclusion hermetically sealed off from the plague-stricken world outside can their language retain its expressive purity. But the lovers cannot remain forever in the orchard, much as they would like to, and the poet cannot escape the fact that whereas his art is private, wrought in his own stylistic image and even given that personal signature that Shakespeare laments in Sonnet 76, his linguistic medium itself is intransigently public. As part of the vulgar tongue the words he would adopt are contaminated by ill usage, by an ever-present epidemic of imprecision, banality, lies, false rhetoric, jargon, true rhetoric, sentimentality, and solecisms, and by more localized historical plagues such as Petrarchanism, Euphuism, inkhorn neologisms, television commercials, social scientese, and beat or hippie nonspeak. Like Juliet on first confronting Romeo, the poet wants to compel words to abandon their corrupt public identities and submit to his cleansing rebaptism. Or again, to use another of the play's metaphors, like Romeo words as public identities must die ("He heareth not, he stirreth not, he moveth not" Mercutio says of Romeo; "The ape is dead"—2.1.15–16) so that they may be reborn within the context of the poem ("Call me but love and I'll be new baptized;/Henceforth I never will be Romeo"—2.2.50–51).

This account of things is perhaps unduly metaphoric and a bit confusing as regards Romeo, whose verbal status is rather ambiguous. His Petrarchan style is impure, as underscored by Juliet's stylistic objections, because in the context of the play it comes from that extramural world outside the orchard. That is not to say that the sonnets of Wyatt, Sidney, Spenser, or Petrarch himself exhibit corrupt language. It is to say that the Petrarchan *style* has a public existence outside individual Petrarchan poems and that in Shakespeare's time—and certainly in his own view, as Sonnet 130 makes clear—it stood for a debased literary currency. Paradoxically at least some of this impurity derives from the fact that the Petrarchan style aspires to pure poetry and in so aspiring becomes an airy, hyperbolic, mechanically artificial expression of unfelt and undiscriminating feelings. In this sense it is too pure ("Virtue itself turns vice, being misapplied"—2.3.21), and when the too pure becomes too popular it turns impure, an infectious blight on the literary landscape.

From this excessive purity excessively available, Juliet recoils, seeking like Shakespeare a more individual style, a more genuine purity. But neither Juliet nor Shakespeare fully succeeds in the attempt to forge a new and authentic idiom. We are clearly asked to regard the movement from Romeo-Rosaline to Romeo-Juliet as an advance from Petrarchan dotage to true romantic love.

And surely in large degree it is—after all, this love seals its bond in marriage and bears it out even to and beyond the edge of doom. Granted, and yet I doubt that either we or Shakespeare can rest fully at ease with the lovers' style. The trouble is that the old Romeo is imperfectly killed off; the ape is not really dead— too much of his Petrarchan manner and language live on in him; and Juliet, despite her anti-Petrarchan bias, too readily quickens to the invitations of his style. Her better speeches are resistance pieces that gain eloquence in the process of denying the power of speech itself, most notably in the balcony scene. She scores well off Romeo's verbal extravagance:

ROMEO. Ah Juliet, if the measure of thy joy
Be heaped like mine, and that thy skill be more
To blazon it, then sweeten with thy breath
This neighbour air and let rich music's tongue
Unfold the imagined happiness that both
Receive in either by this dear encounter.
JULIET. Conceit, more rich in matter than in words,
Brags of his substance, not of ornament.
They are but beggars that can count their worth,
But my true love is grown to such excess
I cannot sum up sum of half my wealth.   (2.6.25–34)

But if the worth of private feeling cannot be assessed in the crude countinghouse of language, Juliet seems not always aware of it. This is most noticeable when on learning that Romeo has killed Tybalt her feelings swing from love to dismay:

O serpent heart hid with a flowering face!
Did ever dragon keep so fair a cave?
Beautiful tyrant! Fiend angelical!
Dove-feathered raven! Wolvish ravening lamb!
Despised substance of divinest show!   (3.2.73–77)

The distinction in the last line between substance and show invites our recollection of the distinction between substance and ornament in her speech just quoted (2.6.30–31) and urges on us the stylistic reversal that has occurred. It is wonderfully fitting that Juliet should register the shock to private feeling by adopting Romeo's Petrarchan oxymorons (cf. 1.1.181–188) at the exact moment when her loyalties turn in the antinominalist direction of "family" (she grieves not for Tybalt the unique but for Tybalt the cousin). She quickly recovers from this style and feeling, as does their love in general, but in the remainder of the scene her style (like Romeo's in 3.3) keeps shrilling upward into a mannered hysteria in which conceit, less rich in matter than in words, brags of its ornmanent, not its substance. Bathos is now their medium, and their verbal excesses are defended on the authority of unique feeling:

> ROMEO. Thou canst not speak of that thou dost not feel.
> Wert thou as young as I, Juliet thy love,
> An hour but married, Tybalt murdered,
> Doting like me and like me banished,
> Then mightst thou speak, then mightst thou tear thy hair
> And fall upon the ground as I do now,
> Taking the measure of an unmade grave.   (3.3.64–70)

Such claims disarm criticism—ours I suppose as well as that of the friar, who must be wincing at the amount of hypothesis required to put him in the position of youth and love. No one denies the validity and intensity of the feeling, but of course a riot of feeling need not necessitate a riot of language and premature measurements of graves that look suspiciously like cribs. Romeo rejects all discipline that originates beyond self, whether moral, social, or stylistic. In effect he repudiates the world, and so hastens logically on to the notion of suicide. When Friar Laurence, harried back and forth across the room by the banging of the world at his door and the blubbering of a Romeo who would dissolve all connections with the world, cries in exasperation "What simpleness is this!" (3.3.77) his choice of the noun is perfect, for in the unblended simpleness of Romeo the man of unique feelings there is indeed at this point great silliness. However, Romeo is not altogether as pure in his simpleness as he would like, and radical purgation is called for:

> O tell me, friar, tell me
> In what vile part of this anatomy
> Doth my name lodge? Tell me, that I may sack
> The hateful mansion.   (3.3.105–108)

To become pure "Romeo" and extirpate his connections with everything beyond self he would destroy "Montague," the "vile part" of him in which the world has staked its claim. But as the friar points out, the dagger that pierces Montague pierces Romeo as well:

Why rail'st thou on thy birth, the heaven, and earth?
Since birth and heaven and earth all three do meet
In thee at once, which thou at once wouldst lose.   (3.3.119–121)

So far as I can see there is small evidence that Romeo absorbs much of the friar's lesson. For him there remains no world beyond the walls of Juliet's garden, where the lovers still strive to meet with all the nominalistic singularity of their Edenic forebears. Their lamentations in 3.2 and 3.3 are only a more strident stylistic version of their speech in 3.5. In this the last scene in which they engage in genuine dialogue before the destructive force of the word "banished" takes its full toll, we see the lyric imagination desperately seeking to impose its own truth on the world of fact and sunrise:

JULIET. Wilt thou be gone? It is not yet near day.
It was the nightingale and not the lark
That pierced the fearful hollow of thine ear.
Nightly she sings on yond pomegranate tree.
Believe me, love, it was the nightingale.   (3.5.1–5)

And again:

JULIET. Yond light is not daylight, I know it, I —
It is some meteor that the sun exhales
To be to thee this night a torchbearer
And light thee on thy way to Mantua.   (3.5.12–15)

In line with her nominalistic "A rose by any other word" Juliet would rebaptize Nature, transforming lark and daylight into nightingale and meteor to the end that time stand still. Romeo allows himself to be persuaded that "it is not day," but as soon as he does so Juliet's lyric preoccupation is gone: "It is, it is! Hie hence, be gone, away!" (3.5.25–26). As it operates in the wide world, language may be less pure than the lovers would wish, but it stands for a view of reality that neither lover nor poet can safely ignore. Time, light, larks, and the usual terms for them remain intransigently themselves, answerable to their public definitions. The lover who withdraws entirely from the world into an autistic domain of feeling must pay for his pleasure with his life, as Romeo would were he to remain in the orchard. By the same token the poet who reshapes language in the exclusive light of his own designs, turning his back on his audience and creating not a truly individual but merely a unique style, must pay for his eccentric pleasures with his poetic life. There is no great danger of that here since the trouble with the lovers' style is not eccentricity but conventionality. The purity it aspires to, like that of the Petrarchanism to which it is uncomfortably akin, is too easily come by. And judging their language this way, I should be quick to add—that is, grading it down for poetic diction and a superabundance of rhetorical figures—is not to impose on the play a modern bias against rhetoric but to accept the implications of the play itself and to honor Shakespeare's own standards, which are implicit in his gradual estrangement over the years from an enameled, repetitive, lyrical style in favor of one that is concentrated, complex, and dramatic.

V

It would seem then that in *Romeo and Juliet* Shakespeare has encountered but by no means resolved the poet's dilemma. No doubt he must often have known perfectly well where he wanted poetically to go and yet could not get there, and knew that too. On the authority of the play's structure we can assume that he wanted to get from Rosaline to Juliet, from pure poetry to a viable poetic purity, but that he did not complete the journey in satisfactory style. That he realized this seems evident from the care he has taken to protectively enclose the lovers' poetic purity. Robert Penn Warren has shrewdly argued that the "impure poetry" of Mercutio and the nurse—poetry, that is, that reflects the impurity of life itself by means of wit, irony, logical contradictions, jagged rhythms, unpoetic diction, and so forth—provides a stylistic context in which we can more readily accept the too pure poetry of the lovers.[5] Warren assumes in other words that the impure poetry in the play functions much as William Empson claims comics subplots function, as lightning rods to divert the audience's potentially dyslogistic reactions away from the vulnerable high seriousness of the main plot (main style).[6] The implication is that Shakespeare is trying to have it both ways at once, that like Juliet asking for an "unnamed naming" in the balcony scene he asks us to accept the authenticity of a style that he himself knows is too pure and therefore needful of protection. From this perspective one sees that in stacking the literary deck against the lovers—by providing the stylistic opposition of

Mercutio and the nurse and the environmental opposition of the feuding families, of fate, coincidences, and mistimings— Shakespeare has actually stacked it in their favor. The obvious contrast is with *Antony and Cleopatra*, and we might note that whereas the impure poetry of Enobarbus functions like that of Mercutio and the nurse, by that time Shakespeare has mastered his own stylistic problems and can imbue those lovers' language with an impurity of its own. If the later technique risks more, it stands to gain more too, and as we all know does.

The argument made here in terms of style can be extended to character and genre also, for the lovers themselves, no less than their style, are too pure and they acquire in the minds of too many readers an unearned tragic stature. Even though the play rejects uniqueness Shakespeare has nominalistically bleached from Romeo and Juliet most of the impurities that rub off on man by virtue of his public contacts. They simply have no public contacts. Despite the importance of family, they are essentially unrelated, meeting as isolated individuals rather than (like Antony and Cleopatra) as complex human beings with social, political, religious, and even national allegiances and responsibilities to contend with. Insufficiently endowed with complexity, with the self-division that complexity makes possible, and with the self-perceptiveness that such division makes possible, they become a study in victimage and sacrifice, not tragedy. Their experience portrays not the erosion within but the clash without, and the plot harries them toward lamentation instead of vision. One of the major ironies of the final scene in the tomb is that for all its imagery of radiance the illumination is entirely outside Romeo, kindled by torches and Juliet's beauty, not by a self-reflective consciousness. On the stylistic failure as it relates to tragedy Maynard Mack says "Comic overstatement aims at being preposterous. Until it becomes so, it remains flat. Tragic overstatement, on the other hand, aspires to be believed, and unless in some sense it is so, remains bombast."[7]

In Shakespeare's protection of the lovers Mercutio plays a crucial role, for although Juliet rejects the false purity of Romeo's Petrarchan style she never has to encounter the rich impurity of Mercutio's speech. And it is Mercutio who seems the genuine threat. The nurse's style is abundantly impure, but that is all it is, whereas Mercutio can deliver pure poetry impurely. In his much-admired, much-maligned Queen Mab speech, which looks so suspiciously and conspicuously irrelevant to the main issues of the play, Mercutio turns pure poetry back on itself. Even while presenting a lengthy illustration of pure poetry he defines it as a product of fancy and foolishness airily roaming like Queen Mab herself through dreaming minds, to which it offers substitute gratifications that have no direct bearing on reality—on real courtier's real curtsies and suits, on lawyers' stunning fees, ladies' kisses, parsons' benefices, soldiers' battles. "Peace, Mercutio, peace!" Romeo cries. "Thou talks'st of nothing." But because Mercutio can talk of something as well as nothing, because he can deal in both pure and impure styles, he is given a tough and enduring eloquence that makes the nurse, mired in the language of sensual expedience, seem gross and Romeo callow. (Romeo to be sure can vie with Mercutio in the lubricities of street speech, but Romeo-with-Juliet is another man altogether; Shakespeare keeps the two scrupulously discrete.)

Entering the orchard where felt experience is soveriegn, Romeo can dismiss Mercutio's extramural ribaldry about Rosaline with a famous line—"He jests at scars that never felt a wound" (2.2.1). When the wound is in the other chest though, Romeo must play straight man to more famous lines:

ROMEO. Courage, man, the hurt cannot be much.
MERCUTIO. No. 'tis not so deep as a well nor so wide as a
church door, but 'tis enough, 'twill serve.   (3.1.98–100)

This asks to be compared to the lovers' style. They repeatedly claim that language is too shallow a thing to reach into the deeps of private feeling, but their own verbal practice is hardly consistent with such a claim. Whenever their feelings are touched, torrents follow. Hence the bristling oxymorons of the stricken Romeo in 1.1—

Why then O brawling love! O loving hate!
O anything, of nothing first create!
O heavy lightness, serious vanity,
Misshapen chaos of well-seeming forms!
Feather of lead, bright smoke, cold fire, sick health!
Still-walking sleep that is not what it is!
This love feel I, that feel no love in this.   (1.1.182–188)

Hence the same oxymorons from Juliet's lips in 3.2 ("Beautiful tyrant! fiend angelical!" etc.) and the bathos of Romeo in 3.3, for example —

> Heaven is here
> Where Juliet lives, and every cat and dog
> And little mouse, every unworthy thing,
> Live here in heaven and may look on her,
> But Romeo may not.   (3.3.29–33)

It is in this context of grotesque verbal posturing, where convulsions of speech coalesce with tantrums of feeling, that Mercutio's words on death acquire a quiet and sustained eloquence. It is those words ironically that best fulfill the stylistic requirements of Juliet's early nominalism. The uniquely felt inner "hurt" Mercutio does not try directly to define, thus avoiding the risks of hyperbole and general verbal inflation that prey on the speech of the lovers when they reflect on *their* wounds. The private feeling that's past the size of speech is suggested only obliquely, in terms of the size of the physical "hurt," and even then by saying not what it is but what it is not. Here in the plain style is functional language, language that like the wound itself is content to be "enough," to "serve" rather than run riot. In general then it is the mixed tones of Mercutio's speech that the lovers most need to incorporate into their own style. But Shakespeare has kept Mercutio permanently stationed on the outer side of the orchard wall, as oblivious to the existence of their love as they are to him.

The public world is too crass and bellicose to assimilate the private truth of love, and Mercutio is a good instance of the fact that there are public truths that the lovers cannot assimilate. Given two such disjunctive languages, only mutual injury remains possible. The lovers' language fails when it seeks to make its way by means of Father John through the plague-ridden world beyond the orchard. Love's feelings hold constant, but during the reunion in the tomb the dialogue of love dissolves into lyric monologues heard only by the speaker. One further step remains. The purity of their love (figured after Romeo's departure in Juliet's resistance to marrying Paris) is reasserted in a second marriage ceremony that is even more private than the first:

> ROMEO. Arms, take your last embrace. And lips, O you
> The doors of breath, seal with a righteous kiss
> A dateless bargain to engrossing death!   (5.3.113–115)

In this final contract the breath of lyric speech and the breath of life are simultaneously expended to seal an endless bond with silence. So too with Juliet, who retreats into a remoter stillness as the noise of the outside world rushes toward her:

Yea, noise? Then I'll be brief. O happy dagger!
This is thy sheath. There rest and let me die.   (5.3.169–170)

As the *Liebestod* stressed by Denis de Rougemont and others,
Romeo and Juliet's love has been a flight from the frustations of
life toward the consummations of the grave. Similary, as *Liebestille*
their linguistic style has been a flight from noise toward a silence
beyond speech. The silence is at last achieved and with it an
expressiveness that extends their own bond of feeling outward.
For embraced in and by death their still figures bespeak the truth
of their love to the wondering representatives of the social order
gathered in the tomb, and do so with such persuasiveness that it
transforms those random and rancorous individuals into a
genuine community united in sorrow and sympathy. The cost,
however, runs high. What is purchased is in the Prince's apt
phrase a "glooming peace"—peace as public amity has been
bought by the sacrifice of the lovers to the peace of an enduring
but eloquent stillness.

VI

Neither in life nor through language then do the lovers make
connections with their social order or the wide world beyond the
orchard. Self-engrossed to the end, their speech admits no
impediments, not even death. Death in fact is less an impediment
than a goal, a terminal value whose stillness, privacy, and
endlessness sum up the character of their love. In this final
marriage to death they divorce the world.

It goes without saying that there is a sentimentality about
the ending of the play that goes down hard—the bravura notes
of Romeo's final speeches, the pathetic suicides, the stagy
recognition scene that seems framed to fulfill the child's morbidly
gratifying wish to be present at his own imagined funeral. But
Shakespeare is not merely pumping up the pathos in order to
celebrate the absoluteness of a fine and constant love done in by
a crass society; he is also attempting to negotiate between private
and public values. In comedy such negotiations are fulfilled in
weddings that incorporate private love into the larger social
context. In tragedy the division between private and public values
is normally bridged by sacrifice: the hero's alienating uniqueness

becomes through his sacrificial death the instrument that binds his survivors to one another and to his now lost and lamented value. So it is with Romeo and Juliet. Though divorced from the world, as "poor sacrifices" they bring about the marriage of the divided society they leave behind. With this wider social marriage the play finds its formal resolution, and so it is ultimately to Shakespeare's maturing concept of dramatic form that the lovers are sacrificed.

Before turning to the question of dramatic form, though, let me note briefly how the statues to be erected by the bereaved fathers confirm the success of sacrifice in bringing about fulfillment in both private and public spheres:

> MONTAGUE.   But I can give thee more.
> For I will raise her statue in pure gold,
> That whiles Verona by that name is known
> There shall no figure at such rate be set
> As that of true and faithful Juliet.
> CAPULET. As rich shall Romeo's by his lady's lie,
> Poor sacrifices of our enmity.   (5.3.298–304)

The statues become the final emblem of the expressive stillness to which the lovers' language has been implicitly devoted since the balcony scene. However, the nominalistic purity to which they had aspired is now transcended since the private meaning and value of their love, as given expression in the silent gold figures, will be made permanently public.

The verbal recoil of the play from noise toward expressive stillness is the more apparent if we analyze the play in terms of an economic or commercial motif that also culminates in the statues. Briefly, the lovers' self-valuation stresses pricelessness, the impossibility of "selling" their love to the two families or the public—especially to Juliet's father, who feudalistically regards marriage as a business transaction. To Romeo Juliet is a "jewel" precious beyond price (the nurse at one point, incidentally, calls her "Jule"): "Beauty too rich for use, for earth too dear" (1.5.48–49). To Capulet she is "the hopeful lady of my earth" (1.2.15)—his *fille de terre*, or "heiress"—who, however, because she is an unmarketable commodity by virtue of prior commitment to Romeo will finally inherit only enough of his land to make a grave (5.3.297). And Juliet says of herself:

They are but beggars that can count their worth;
But my true love is grown to such excess
I cannot sum up sum of half my wealth.   (2.6.32–34)

Paradoxically then Montague "will raise her statue in pure gold"
(5.3.299). The effect of doing so will be on the one hand to reduce
Juliet to the base metal of public commerce but on the other
hand to cast that metal in an unnegotiable form. As pure gold
statuary the lovers retain a pricelessness that transcends
commercial distribution even while their value is "sold" in the
sense of its being publicly shared. This selling of a priceless
commodity is an exact equivalent in commercial terms to the
"expressive stillness" we spoke of on the linguistic plane.

So much for the verbal-commercial aspects of the statues'
nonverbal expressiveness—though their very nonverbalness is
an issue to which we will return in the next section. I have so far
dealt with the stillness of the statues as "silence," but to give the
analysis a turn toward dramatic form I need to stress the
motionlessness of stillness. The gold that was so much the object
of commercial voyages in Shakespeare's time and that once
discovered and minted went its endless voyage from pocket to
pocket finds in the shape of the statues a permanent rest. So does
Romeo, who says more than he knows when he prepares for his
suicide:

> O here
> Will I set up my everlasting rest
> And shake the yoke of inauspicious stars
> From this world-wearied flesh.   (5.3.109–112)

Romeo's experience in the play is depicted among other things
as a voyage.[8] Setting off for what will become his first meeting
with Juliet he says

> But He that hath the steerage of my course
> Direct my sail!   (1.4.112–113)

Again in the balcony scene:

> I am no pilot, yet wert thou as far
> As that vast shore washed with the farthest sea
> I should adventure for such merchandise.   (2.2.82–85)

And finally after his "O here/Will I set up my everlasting rest":

> Come, bitter conduct, come, unsavoury guide!
> Thou desperate pilot, now at once run on
> The dashing rocks thy sea-sick weary bark.   (5.3.116–118)

Thus Romeo voyages through the play to the final port of everlasting rest, which is both the grave and the gold statue commissioned by Capulet. In the form of the statue he embodies the paradox of motionless movement, a dynamic illusion of life artistically arrested—always moving and never moving in the same sense that an "everlasting rest" is both intransitive and ceaseless, a restless rest.[9]

However, motion is more pervasive in the play than this. There is the violent motion or commotion, the street fighting, with which everything begins; there is the balcony scene contract that Juliet calls

> too rash, too unadvised, too sudden,
> Too like the lightning which doth cease to be
> Ere one can say it lightens   (2.2.118–120)

and the quick clandestine wedding that Romeo ("O let us hence; I stand on sudden haste") forces against the friar's counsels of moderation ("Wisely and slow—they stumble that run fast"— 2.3.93–94). There are also Mercutio itching for action, and the pell-mell Tybalt anxious for a grave; the immediacy of Romeo's banishment by the Prince ("Let Romeo hence in haste,/Else when he's found that hour is his last"); the relentless rush of time as the Thursday of Juliet's enforced marriage to Paris is tolled on by Capulet the perpetual-motion matchmaker—

> Day, night, hour, tide, time, work, play,
> Alone, in company, still my care hath been
> To have her matched;   (3.5.178–180)

the speed of Romeo's return from Mantua; and finally the death-dealing liveliness of the poisons ("O true apothecary!/Thy drugs are quick"—5.3.119–120).[10]

The world at large rushes and the lovers haste toward one another, but when they are united, especially within the orchard, time and motion cease. Given the contrasting principles of movement and stasis, the form of the play might be diagrammed as a horizontal line interrupted by several circles indicating the times (in 1.5, 2.2, 2.6, 3.5, and 5.3) when Romeo and Juliet are together. For in each of these five scenes the primary tension is

between staying and departing, and in each scene the lovers are
called out of stillness by the exigencies of time and motion. In 1.5
they have been stilled in a kiss ("Then move not while my prayer's
effect I take"—108) but are interrupted by the nurse calling Juliet
to her mother. In 2.2 Romeo starts to leave but is called back by
Juliet, who then forgets why she did so; their next lines play on
stillness in time and space:

> ROMEO. Let me stand here till thou remember it.
> JULIET. I shall forget, to have thee still stand there,
> Remembering how I love thy company.
> ROMEO. And I'll still stay, to have thee still forget,
> Forgetting any other home but this.   (2.2.172–176)

But at their backs they always hear the nurse's voice clucking
Juliet in and Romeo away (2.2.136, 149, 151). In 2.6 they are so
transfixed by one another that the friar must pun heavily on
leaving and staying even to get them to their own wedding:

> Come, come with me, and we will make short work,
> For, by your leaves, you shall not stay alone
> Till Holy Church incorporate two in one.   (2.6.35–37)

And in 3.5 a world of clocks and irreversible sunrises tolls for
Romeo, who "must be gone and live or stay and die"(11).

Staying a moment ourselves, we should observe that
Shakespeare has here reversed the situation in *Love's Labour's
Lost* in which the faint linear thrust of dramatic action was
constantly diverted and absorbed into the circular eddies of lyric.
If one of the things Shakespeare learned in that play is the inability
of lyric speech to substitute for dramatic action, the effects of
that lesson on *Romeo and Juliet* are apparent in the way the linear
current of action repeatedly overcomes lyric retardations. Though
enraptured by a stillness beyond time and motion, the lovers,
particularly Romeo, have larger obligations to fulfill outside the
orchard walls where Mercutio and Tybalt are impatient to die,
the Prince to deliver his banishment speech, the apothecary to
lay out his quick drugs. With all the play and players waiting for
Romeo (and metadramatically for Shakespeare) he can hardly
linger forever with Juliet.

Though all the scenes mentioned earlier are lyric in their
attempts to set up self-sustaining moments of expressive feeling,
the surrender of lyric to drama is especially evident in 3.5. We

considered this scene earlier as an instance of the lyric style desperately seeking and failing to impose love's longings on nature and time. In the present connection I would stress the lyric *form* of this lovers' parting since in it Shakespeare scrupulously observes all the conventions of the aubade.[11] Thus when the lovers are compelled to part, a traditional lyric form is "parted" also—in the sense both of being interrupted and more important of being relegated from a lyric whole to a dramatic part. The clear implication is that lyric cannot remain sufficient unto itself in drama but like the lovers themselves must be sacrificed to a larger conception of form.

VII

Yet there is a sense in which Shakespeare has tried to give with one hand and take with the other, which after all is the nature of a sacrifice, something won through losing. What he loses, it would appear, is the permanence, fixity, and stillness of lyric; but what he gains is perhaps a greater stillness, that of dramatic form. This is the rushing stasis, the ever-never species of stillness. For all the rush and bustle of action, the hasty mistimings, the voyaging to eternity are locked perpetually in what is at this stage of his career Shakespeare's most carefully plotted and symmetrically patterned play. As if in reaction to the formlessness of *Love's Labour's Lost*, where he invented a plot that was little more than a series of verbal events brought to an abrupt and frustrate conclusion, he next turned to the preestablished plot of Arthur Brooke's *Tragical Historye of Romeus and Juliet*. Though he trimmed most of the suet from Brooke's plump poem of some 6000 lines, compressing the action and tightening the time scheme, he nonetheless followed the main course of its plot with considerable fidelity.

In *Romeo and Juliet* then Shakespeare knew exactly where he was going. No doubt he did so in other plays too—but here he takes pains to announce his formal mastery of his materials and sense of direction, as for instance in the unusual (at this stage of his career) device of the sonnet prologues to Acts 1 and 2, both of which sum up and forecast action. Take the opening prologue:

Two households, both alike in dignity,
  In fair Verona where we lay our scene,
From ancient grudge break to new mutiny
  Where civil blood makes civil hands unclean.
From forth the fatal loins of these two foes
  A pair of star-crossed lovers take their life,
Whose misadventured piteous overthrows
  Doth with their death bury their parents' strife.
The fearful passage of their death-marked love
  And the continuance of their parents' rage
Which, but their children's end, nought could remove,
  Is now the two hours' traffic of our stage;
The which if you with patient ears attend,
  What here shall miss, our toil shall strive to mend.

The journey metaphor later to be associated primarily with Romeo is here assigned to both lovers in "misadventured," perhaps in "children's end," early in "the fearful passage of their death-marked love." Some of that metaphor's linear movement carries over into the following line—"And the continuance of their parents' rage"—so that "continuance" evokes spatial motion as well as temporal duration. Children's love and parental hate both voyage through the play toward the terminal port of death. Then finally the metaphor expands to encompass the presentation of the play itself, fusing temporal and spatial progress in the "two hours' traffic of our stage" figure. For two hours audience and actors are stationed in one theatrical place, and yet as the prologue to Act 3 of *Henry V* puts it —

  our swift scene flies
In motion of no less celerity
Than that of thought.

More important than this kind of stationary movement in theater are the implications of Shakespeare's metadramatic merger of the play's internal fiction, the voyage of the lovers, and the play itself, the traffic of drama ("traffic" appropriately smuggling a commercial connotation into the concept of voyaging). The lovers' voyage occurs under the stars (it is most fittingly a disaster, *dés + astre*), which may be considered as both astrological and astronomical influences. Astrologically the stars are equivalent to fate, the fore-plotted journey of star-crossed lovers. And indeed the course of the lovers' voyage and of Shakespeare's play (dramatic traffic) has been pre-plotted in Arthur Brooke's tragical historye. Appropriately, since *fatum* means the "sentences" of the gods, fate has here a literary dimension, and Romeo is quite right to address the dead Paris as "One writ with me in sour misfortune's book" (5.3.82). His journey and that of all the other characters are fated not merely by "inauspicious stars" (5.3.111) but by their literary analogue, an inauspicious plot adopted from Brooke.

From a metadramatic as opposed to thematic standpoint then the repeated references throughout the play to stars, fate, fortune, the curse of birth, the charted journey, all the deterministic forces bearing on the lovers, testify to the sovereignty not merely of cosmic design in human affairs but of plot and form in the construction of *Romeo and Juliet*.[12] And here too is stationary movement. The great haste of the play, the fractious encounters, the stumbling of those who run fast, the recurrent thrusting of the lovers out of the still stasis of lyric, the ramrodding of time— all this activity is necessitated by a plot that demands movement to perfect its design, to complete the voyage of which it is the chart. As chart or plot the dramatic voyage is still, yet nevertheless contains sequences of evolving actions. Its correlative in the fictional world within the play is the fixed pattern of stars that astrologically "moves" the lovers whose unalterable destiny is to advance to the destination of death.[13]

Not only does Shakespeare forecast his control of dramatic form in the sonnet prologues; he reaffirms it at the end of the play when Friar Laurence, a major manipulator of plot, recapitulates all that has happened (5.3.229–269). At the corresponding point in *Love's Labour's Lost* Shakespeare advertised a failure of dramatic form by allowing Mercade his destructive entrance. Now, however, the friar presents us with a scrupulously detailed forty-line synopsis that accounts for each phase of the action in terms of a governing literary design. In effect the friar pleads his case on the grounds of a coherent plot—not of course his own plot, which failed, but Shakespeare's plot, which succeeds by means of the friar's failure and the lovers' misfortune.

VIII

Shakespeare's success in *Romeo and Juliet* is impressive by comparison with past failures but by no means total. His concentration on, almost celebration of, dramatic form imparts to the play a highly rigid structure based on the division between Montagues and Capulets and between lovers and society. As Sigurd Burckhardt has observed, the play has "a symmetry which, even though it is a symmetry of conflict, is comforting."[14] For despite the family feud the social order is in no real danger of collapse. What turbulence there is gets expressed within a stabilizing framework formed by the Prince and the friar, the one devoted to civil order, the other all reason and moderation. The virulence of the conflict between families is mitigated by the principals themselves, the spindle-shanked and slippered old men who allow the feud to continue less from rancor than from apathy. And the lovers are themselves untainted by the enmities abroad; they are not at odds with an antagonistic society so much as they are simply apart from it—hurt by ricochet rather than direct intent, by a secret that always could be made public but never is. Hence there is a strong sense of the arbitrary about the play and the lovers' fate, which with all its dependence on accident, coincidence, and sheer mistiming seems imposed and gratuitous. Finally at the end there is a too easy resolution both of the social problem of uniting the families and of the dramatic dilemma of finding a style in which the private and public dimensions of language are happily joined.

For the dramatic or more precisely linguistic dilemma is resolved at the end not stylistically but symbolically, by means of the emblematic statues in which Shakespeare has sought to comprise both private and public values. If the lovers' nominalistic conception of speech implies a verbal purity bordering on nonspeech, here in the silence of the statues is that stillness; and if their love has aspired to a lyric stasis, here too in the fixity of plastic form is that stillness. But by being publicly available— representing the lovers and their value but representing them for the Veronese audience—the statues surpass the aspirations and expressive aims of the lovers. The communicative gap between the private secret love and the social order oblivious to the existence of that love is bridged—and this seems the major significance of the statues—by *artistic form*. Cast in such form, the worth of unique experience is popularized without being cheapened. By shifting from a verbal to a visually symbolic plane Shakespeare ingeniously makes the most of his stylistic liabilities while acknowledging silently that the too pure language of the lovers could not in itself effect such a union.[15] For the dual stillness of the statues, their silence and motionlessness, reflects not merely the poetic tendencies of the lovers but in a large sense the formal properties of Shakespeare's play. The statues materialize at the conclusion, that is, precisely at the point at which the play as temporal experience materializes into spatial form for its audience, the point at which form completes itself on stage and crystallizes in our memories. If language has not linked the public and private world, then form does. And seen in the perspective of dramatic form, the division between lovers and social order is not divisive because the principle of division itself, the playing off of the two worlds in opposition, gives rise to the form of *Romeo and Juliet*. The paradox of form is like that of love in "The Phoenix and the Turtle":

> Two distincts, division none:
> Number there in love was slain.

So the most fruitful coalescence of divided worlds is not to be found in the verbal paradoxes of the oxymoron but in the dramatic paradoxes of the play as shaped entity. As symbols of that shaping the statues of the closing scene reflexively comment on Romeo's oxymorons of the opening scene (1.1.181ff). Those oxymorons clashingly connect the two divided spheres of the opening scene, the public quarrel in the streets and Romeo's private dotage on Rosaline. Hence they are uttered just at the moment when Romeo and Benvolio, who have been talking of Romeo's private problems in love, arrive at the place where the street violence occurred. The "airy word" that bred the "civil brawls" (1.1.96) now expresses in the discordance of Romeo's oxymorons the inner brawling of Petrarchan dotage and unites the two spheres of experience, public and private, as versions of a kind of linguistic noise. In both areas the word has gone bad. Though somewhat redeemed by the speech of the lovers later on, the word never gets placed in public circulation. It is left for the statues to symbolize in form an ideal but dramatically unrealized social and verbal union. "Fain would I dwell on form" Juliet told Romeo; but it is really Shakespeare who had dwelt on form in this play, and by doing so has enabled Romeo and Juliet to dwell permanently *in* form.

One final point. I spoke earlier about the nominalistic impulse behind Shakespeare's creation of lovers from whom all family or universal relationships have been deleted—nominalistic because we are asked to confront the lovers as unique particulars. The fact, however, that the lovers are less singular in language and character than we might wish suggests that this deletion of universals is actually antinominalistic, less Aristotelean or Scotist than Platonic. Uniqueness, Shakespeare seems to have realized by the end of this play, is not the condition of being free from universal ties and tendencies; it is not a kind of pure essence left behind after we have burned off all accidental impurities. Distillation of that sort, in fact, leaves us with something very like Platonic universals themselves. But this seems to have been the process by which the lovers were created—a purification by dramatic fiat, giving us a Platonic conception of pure love cast in the role of particulars. At the end of the play, however, Shakespeare seems to sense that with men as with poems uniqueness resides in the form or contextual organization of non-unique qualities—a form sufficiently complex in its internal relations to defy reductive abstraction. Is this not part of the meaning of the statues also? Only by destroying the formal context of the statues can one commercialize the gold of which they are made. Detached though they are from their fictional surroundings, Romeo and Juliet, like the gold in the statues, are permanently embedded in the context of *Romeo and Juliet*, where presumably not even the critic's chisels can get at their priceless worth.

NOTES

1. It is a position with which we can all sympathize, for that matter, since it reflects a recurrent human urge to scour our modes of apprehending experience, to brighten up a world that has been sicklied over by the pale cast of thought and drab expression. Anxious to purify Romeo of his family connections and meet him in all his shining individuality, Juliet might well approve of Husserl's desire for philosophy to return to things themselves, to let phenomena speak for themselves without the mediating and therefore presumably falsifying intervention of the mind with all its presuppositions (of which genus, or family, is surely a major meddler). However, the Hopkinsean "inscape" of man—the unique Romeo freed of his Montague associations—was less attractive to Renaissance moral philosophers, usually registered Platonists, who distinguished between two aspects of human

nature—general and specific, genus and differentia—and felt that although the differentia made men interesting it was the genus that kept them civilized (see for instance Cicero's *Offices*, chapters 30 and 31). Juliet might want Romeo to be able to say "I am myself alone," but the man who actually says it is Richard Crookback at a major moment in a long and uniquely inhuman career (*3 Henry VI*, 5.6.83). In "The King's Language: Shakespeare's Drama as Social Discovery," *Antioch Review*, 21 (1961), 369–387, Sigurd Burckhardt has some brief but shrewd remarks about Juliet's nominalism; and for an excellent equation of nominalism and personalism see Murray Krieger's "The Existential Basis of Contextual Criticism" in *The Play and Place of Criticism* (Baltimore, 1967), pp. 239–251. In his interesting article "The Rose and Its Name: On Denomination in *Othello, Romeo and Juliet, Julius Caesar,*" *Texas Studies in Literature and Language* II (1969), 671–686, Manfred Weidhorn discusses the bondage of verbal categories from which the lovers are liberated by virtue of their meeting without introductions.

2. The walled orchard that isolates the lovers from the harsh realities of Veronese life is very much akin to the park of the scholars in *Love's Labour's Lost*, which was so rigorously declared off limits to foreign speech and female bodies.

3. See "The Ekphrastic Principle and the Still Movement of Poetry; or *Laokoön* Revisited" in *The Play and Place of Criticism*, pp. 105–128.

4. In performances of the play it is sometimes assumed that the citizen addresses a kneeling Benvolio rather than a dead Tybalt. But Benvolio has just said "There lies that Tybalt," not "here" as he would if he were kneeling over him. The citizen, greatly concerned to take Tybalt in, is inattentive to matters such as death, Hamlet's "fell sergeant" who is more "strict in his arrest" even than vigilante citizens.

5. In his famous article "Pure and Impure Poetry" originally printed in the *Kenyon Review* 5 (Spring 1943), 228–254, and since reprinted in many collections of critical essays.

6. Empson's remarks on subplots appear in *Some Versions of Pastoral*, pp. 25–84 of the New Directions paperback edition (New York, 1960).

7. Maynard Mack, "The Jacobean Shakespeare: Some Observations on the Construction of the Tragedies," in *Jacobean Theatre*, vol. 1 of Stratford-upon-Avon Studies, ed. John Russell Brown and Bernard Harris (New York, 1960), p. 15.

8. Moody Prior was the first, I think, to point out the pattern of this voyaging imagery, in *The Language of Tragedy* (New York, 1947), pp. 69–70.

9. "Stillness" as figured in the statues thus takes on the oxymoronic ever-neverness of Keats's urn and the other instances of literary ekphrasis analyzed by Murray Krieger in "The Ekphrastic Principle and the Still Movement of Poetry; or *Laokoön* Revisited."

10. This generalized haste of time and action has been frequently noted, perhaps most significantly in Brents Stirling's chapter "They Stumble That Run Fast" in *Unity in Shakespearean Tragedy* (New York, 1956).

11. These conventions are conveniently listed by R. E. Kaske in "The Aube in Chaucer's *Troilus,*" which appears in *Chaucer Criticism: Troilus and Criseyde and the Minor Poems,* ed. Richard J. Schoeck and Jerome Taylor (South Bend, Ind., 1961), pp. 167–179. However, the conventions are perfectly exemplified in the first sixty-five lines of the present scene, to which I therefore refer the curious reader insufficiently up on his aubes.

12. Stressing the metadramatic implications of fate is in line with the last paragraph of chapter 9 of *The Poetics* where Aristotle (as Kenneth Burke notes in *Language as Symbolic Action,* Berkeley, Calif., 1966, p. 30) "seems to be saying in effect: The way to make a plot effective is to make it seem inevitable, and the way to make it seem wonderful is to make its imitation of inevitability seem fate-driven." Fate, free will, necessity, and other crucial matters of belief about reality are from the standpoint of poetics merely so much grist for the dramatist's mill.

13. In the ambiguousness of these astrological/astronomical stars we may also see figured the paradox of fatality and free will in dramatic characters. Astrologically the lovers are fated to do what they indeed do, to make their dramatic voyage from *a* to *z*, as any literary character is fated to comply with the dictates of the plot in which he finds himself. But if on the other hand we think of the stars as astronomical guides to navigation, they point up the appearance of self-determination in the characters since as navigator man uses stars instead of being astrologically used by them. Combining the two concepts in one symbol as Shakespeare has done gives us man the navigator using the stars to maintain a pre-charted course from which he cannot deviate. Metadramatically the playwright seeks to maintain the appearance of freedom in his characters, to present them to us as free agents who choose the plot (character issuing in action, as A. C. Bradley put it) that has in literary fact chosen them. "Is it even so?" Romeo says on hearing of Juliet's supposed death, "Then I defy you,

stars!" And then on the authority of private feeling and personal volition he rushes back to Verona to keep an appointment in the tomb that Shakespeare's plot had long ago "prescribed" for him.

14. In "The King's Language: Shakespeare's Drama as Social Discovery."

15. In Brooke's poem there are no statues and no gold, only a tomb raised aloft on every side of which in memory of the lovers "were set and eke beneath/Great store of cunning epitaphs." That Shakespeare has eliminated mention of the epitaphs further emphasizes the nonverbal expressiveness of the statues and hence aligns them with the plastic or spatial aspects of Shakespeare's dramatic art. Brooke's poem incidentally appears in volume I of Geoffrey Bullough's *Narrative and Dramatic Sources of Shakespeare* (London and New York, 1957) and somewhat abridged in Alice Griffin's *The Sources of Ten Shakespearean Plays* (New York, 1966).

Marjorie Garber

Romeo and Juliet:
Patterns and Paradigms

Romeo and Juliet, long celebrated as one of the world's great love stories, is also one of Shakespeare's liveliest and most appealing plays. Its tragic tale of "star-crossed lovers" is set against a vivid background of civil strife and domestic controversy in the Italian city of Verona, and its cast includes at least two characters— Juliet's Nurse and Mercutio—who threaten to steal the show. The Nurse, at once bawdy and sentimental, earthy of tongue and soft of heart, has an immediacy about her that cuts across the ages; she is modern and timeless. As for Mercutio, tradition tells us that Shakespeare felt obliged to kill him off in the third act, so that his play would not be usurped—or upstaged—by his own dramatic character. One of Shakespeare's early editors, the poet and critic Samuel Johnson, wrote that "Mercutio's wit, gaiety and courage, will always procure him friends that wish him a longer life," and generations of audiences have borne this out.

But *Romeo and Juliet* has more to offer its viewers than a touching plot and engaging characters. A closer look will show that Shakespeare designed his play in such a way as to guide us skillfully toward a fuller understanding of its complexities, both in structure and in language. To observe this dramatic design, let us begin with the turning point we have already mentioned: the death of Mercutio.

The duel in which Mercutio and Tybalt are slain is central to the play not only in its placement at the beginning of Act III but also in its effect upon the populace of Verona. Mercutio is a

Reprinted from *The Shakespeare Plays: A Study Guide*. La Jolla: University of California, San Diego, 1979, pp. 50–63, with permission of the author.

pivotal figure for many reasons, including his own remarkable poetic imagination—so unlike that of others in the play—and the fact that he is a kinsman to the Prince, rather than to either the Montagues or the Capulets. It is no exaggeration to say that when he dies the world of *Romeo and Juliet* turns from comedy to tragedy. Elements of dramatic comedy abound in the early acts: masques, balls and dances, bawdy jokes, low folkloric characters like the Nurse, even the happy phenomenon of love at first sight. But at the time of the duel the play undergoes a radical alteration. As John Milton laments in *Paradise Lost* when he comes to describe the fall of man, the poet "now must change/Those Notes to Tragic." The second half of the play provides a spectacle of revenge, banishment, and poisoning, with a dénouement at the site of an open tomb—all elements which were already common in Elizabethan tragedy and many of which would reappear a few years later in Shakespeare's *Hamlet*.

In light of this dramatic division within *Romeo and Juliet* it is extremely interesting to see what happens to some of its characters as a result of the duel and the deaths. At the beginning of the play there is a striking symmetry within the cast of characters. Old Montague is balanced by Old Capulet, Lady Montague by Lady Capulet—even their names have the same metrical stress and could be interchanged in any line of verse. There are, as well, two preliminary romantic interests: Rosaline for Romeo, Paris for Juliet, both of them highly conventional figures. Although she may appear at the ball, Rosaline never speaks and seems to be made up entirely of Renaissance love clichés, while Paris appears in general to deserve Lady Capulet's comparison of him to a well-bound book (emphatically *not* the book by which Romeo kisses Juliet at I,v,110). The playwright's dramatic purpose would seem to be to show us how much Romeo and Juliet grow and change once they encounter one another, and for this purpose such relatively stereotyped figures are extremely successful.

In addition to Paris and Rosaline we are offered another symmetrical pair in the Nurse and the Friar, each an adviser and confidant to one of the lovers. They are both old, but otherwise they are opposites. Friar Lawrence may be said to represent authority without experience, since all his maxims about life and love come from books—even if they are holy books. Juliet's Nurse, on the other hand, plainly embodies experience without authority. Swearing by her maidenhead (as it was when she was twelve years old) she quickly lets us know that she has much first-hand knowledge of love, or at least of sex. While the Friar's language is sententious and balanced, often in rhymed couplets, the Nurse's voice is headlong, breathless (like its owner), lewd, and colloquial. She speaks in prose rather than in verse, and, in the early scenes at least, she is probably the most delightful character in the play.

But let us look at what happens to these advisers and authorities, once they are faced with tragedy. The Friar, who has violated his own counsel of moderation somewhat in performing the marriage, is now galvanized into unwonted action. It is he who devises the sleeping potion and persuades Juliet to take it, he who entrusts the letter for Romeo to another friar without telling him of its importance, and he who, despite his insistence that "they stumble that run fast" (II,iii,94), literally stumbles in the graveyard as he rushes, too late, toward Juliet's tomb.

Even more striking, however, is the change in our view of the Nurse. Shakespeare emphasizes this by building into his play two very similar scenes, one of which takes place before the duel, the other after. In the first, we find that Juliet has sent her Nurse to Romeo, seeking news of the intended marriage. As always, the Nurse is late returning, and Juliet frets about the time; then when her Nurse at last appears, she presses her for news. But the Nurse is too preoccupied with her own physical ailments to give a report. With some remnant of good humor Juliet wonders aloud how she has breath to say that she is out of breath, and so the scene continues in a charmingly comic vein, until after many delays Juliet winkles from her informant the news that the wedding is planned for that very day. Altogether delightful on the stage, the scene is safely in the realm of comedy: The Nurse's fussy delay has caused no harm.

But notice how different the situation is the next time the Nurse arrives with a message. For now Mercutio has been slain by Juliet's cousin Tybalt, and Tybalt in turn slain by Romeo. Again Juliet waits impatiently, for it is her wedding night, and she is eager to be with her husband. As before, she spies the Nurse approaching and quizzes her at once. But the delayed and confused message the Nurse delivers on this occasion is a tragic one, and the more Juliet tries to learn the facts, the more obscure they seem, and the more desperate she becomes. Who is dead— is it Romeo? It seems to be Tybalt; but are they, then, both dead? No, it finally appears, only Tybalt is dead—but Romeo has killed him, and therefore Romeo is banished. The delay, so trivial before, is now profoundly distressing; the Nurse, so appealing in a comic context, takes on less pleasing qualities in the face of tragedy.

This device of twin scenes, one comic and one tragic, is used at least once more in the play, in an equally revealing way. In Act II, Scene iv, we see Mercutio engage Romeo in a battle of wits, rejoicing that his friend has become "sociable" once more. (The change in attitude, which Mercutio attributes to a return of common sense, has in fact resulted from Romeo's encounter with Juliet, and is yet another sign of her influence on his growth from self-absorption to self-knowledge.) As the puns and quips fly, Mercutio pretends to be overcome and finally calls upon a friend to part the combatants: "Come between us, good Benvolio! My wits faint" (66). The mood of the scene is comic, playful, and inconsequential—very like that of the first message scene between the Nurse and Juliet. But a few hours (and only three scenes) later, when the three friends encounter Tybalt, the same scenario results in tragedy. The weapons this time are swords rather than words, and it is Romeo who intervenes, while Mercutio is mortally wounded as a result of his intervention. Romeo's murmured explanation, "I thought all for the best" (III,i,102), tellingly reinforces the parallel between this duel and the previous one, for the name of Benvolio, the peacemaker in the duel of words, means literally "well-wisher"—one who "[thinks] all for the best."

We have mentioned a growth and change in Romeo, signified not only by his desire to heal the rift between the warring parties but also by a new vigor and originality in his language, profoundly different from the hackneyed phrases in which he expressed his passion for Rosaline. The most remarkable pattern of maturation in the play, however, is not Romeo's but Juliet's; indeed, it would not be excessive to say that she is the central figure in the play, despite the symmetrical balance of Montague with Capulet, or the even-handed justice of the title. And here again the playwright tips his hand—we must think, deliberately— by designing a series of steps by which the audience can clearly see a child become a woman. When we recall that the breakneck pace of *Romeo and Juliet* makes the entire drama occur within the course of four days, the transformation is even more astounding.

Juliet's growth to maturity is especially vivid for the audience because when first we see her she seems to have so far to go. In the opening scenes of the play she is wholly submissive, even passive, her sheltered life dominated by three authority figures: father, mother, and Nurse. Asked by her mother what she thinks of marriage, she replies "It is an honor that I dream not of" (I,ii,66). When she is told that Paris seeks to marry her, her answer is similarly dutiful: "I'll look to like, if looking liking move" (97)—but only, she hastens to add, if her mother gives consent. Given this initial glimpse of what is clearly a daughter rather than a mature woman, it is all the more startling for the audience to see what happens when first she sets eyes upon Romeo.

In the course of the Capulet ball, Juliet has spoken with Romeo and kissed him, but she does not yet know who he is. In order to find out, she devises a cleverly indirect ploy, first inquiring from the Nurse about the identities of two other young men in whom she actually has no interest. Only after she has learned their names, and thus diverted the Nurse's curiosity, does she ask about Romeo. Here for the first time we see Juliet act less than straightforwardly with one of her mentors, and in doing so begin to establish a separate adult identity. In a similar way, when her parents inform her of the marriage arranged with Paris, she replies with both overt defiance and covert cunning. "I will not marry yet," she tells her mother, "And when I do, I swear/It shall be Romeo, whom you know I hate,/Rather than Paris" (III,v,122–4).

From the time of this first meeting, but more particularly from the time of the tragic duel, Shakespeare shows us a Juliet whose self-knowledge is coupled with an increasing isolation, which separates her from friends and family, and leaves her, after Romeo's banishment, almost entirely on her own. As she develops from childhood to adulthood she undergoes a painful process of divestiture, stripping herself of former confidants one by one, as each appears to fail her. First she is forced to reject her parents, who insist blindly upon her marrying Paris; then, with even more pain, she must estrange herself from the Nurse, who, though an essential ally in happier days, now cheerfully urges her to commit bigamy. In effect Juliet, too, is "banished" by the Prince's edict. In dramatic terms, her isolation is symbolized by such events as the two soliloquies she speaks from the balcony (II,ii; III,ii), her refusal—on the Friar's order—to let the Nurse sleep in her chamber on the eve of the wedding, and her poignant observation as she reaches for the sleeping potion: "My dismal scene I needs must act alone" (IV,iii,19). Although she is for a moment tempted to call to her mother and Nurse for comfort, she realizes that the possibility of such comfort is lost. Finally, in the play's last scene, she will reject the Friar's inadequate though well-meant offer to "dispose" of her "among a sisterhood of holy nuns" (V,iii,156–7), and with it she rejects the Friar himself. This dismal scene, too, she must act alone.

But at the same time that she has lost her family and friends, she has gained a husband and lover—and in her scenes with Romeo, Juliet demonstrates a startling maturity of another kind by rejecting false modesty in favor of a frank declaration of love and an even franker declaration of sexual desire. The play invites us to contrast this behavior not only with her own previous naivete ("I'll look to like, if looking liking move") but also with the coy chastity of Romeo's first love, Rosaline, and with the coarse vulgarity of the Nurse. Thus, in the balcony scene Juliet is at first embarrassed to find that Romeo has overheard her private thoughts, but within half a dozen lines her "maiden blush" has given way to a direct and unashamed question: "Dost thou love me?" (II,ii,86; 90). Notice that it is she who asks the question, as it is she who has first spoken of love. Throughout the scene she remains the dominant figure, alternately advising, cautioning, and summoning Romeo, while he quite appropriately stands gazing at her from below. For a young woman of her age and her sheltered upbringing, this innocent forwardness is as remarkable as it is appealing.

A further advance toward maturity and self-knowledge is revealed in the soliloquy Juliet speaks on her wedding night, when she calls for the coming of night, and openly expresses her longing for the consummation of the marriage. "I have bought the mansion of a love,/But not possessed it," she tells us (III,ii,26–7); "So tedious is this day/As is the night before some festival/ To an impatient child that hath new robes/And may not wear them" (28–30). The impatient Juliet, no longer a child, not yet entirely a woman, once more puts aside modesty to speak forthrightly of love. When she speaks of learning "to lose a winning match/Played for a pair of stainless maidenhoods" (12–13) we may remember the many bawdy or "stained" references to maiden*heads* that have been made throughout the play. The difference between "maidenhood," which for Shakespeare means the condition of being a maiden, and "maidenhead," the purely physical evidence of virginity, is yet another clue to Juliet's full and healthy approach to life and love. It is entirely fitting that, in the final scene, she should reject the Friar's offer to place her in a convent. Having attained womanhood and sexuality at such cost, she will not, and cannot, return to the cloistered kind of life from which she began.

In our scrutiny of changes in Juliet's character, as well as our consideration of how the Nurse fails to change with changing circumstances, we have begun to see that there is much more to *Romeo and Juliet* than its plot. The way the play is put together, with certain scenes juxtaposed to one another, certain words and phrases repeated, certain characters designed to correspond to others or contrast with them, is as much a part of our experience as is the story of two young lovers and their tragic fate. By his arrangement of dramatic details into discoverable patterns Shakespeare teaches us how to understand and respond to his play. This is true not only on the level of character or action, but also on the level of language. In *Romeo and Juliet*, one of the most lyrical of all Shakespearean plays, patterns of verbal imagery complement or counterpoint events in the plot and lead an attentive audience to new insights.

From the first, the audience is made aware that there is something seriously wrong in the play's world. The Chorus delivers a Prologue in the form of a sonnet, a fourteen-line poem usually devoted in Shakespeare's time to a private declaration of love. But here we have a sonnet gone public, and a sonnet that speaks not of love but of civil war: "Where civil blood makes civil hands unclean" (4). Moreover, the Prologue is followed by the appearance of two servants of the house of Capulet who seem to have no object in life except to quarrel with their rivals, the servants of Montague. Lewdly jesting about the heads of maids and their maidenheads, the two servants continue the confusion between love and war, sexuality and violence, which was first suggested by the sonnet. Their squabble inevitably expands to envelop their masters, as Old Capulet, still wearing his nightgown, rushes into the street calling for his sword. There could be no more visible sign of the disorder endemic in Verona than the fact that servants draw masters into battle rather than the other way around.

As always in Shakespeare's plays, civil war is a symbol of conflict, not only within nations or cities, but also within individuals. As Verona is torn apart by the "ancient grudge" (Prologue, 3) between the Montagues and the Capulets, so will Prince Escalus be torn between strict justice and generous mercy, Juliet torn between loyalty to her family and love for her husband, Romeo torn between a desire to halt the feud and a need to avenge the death of his friend Mercutio. The very language of the play expresses this sense of conflict, opposition, and paradox:

"My only love, sprung, from my only hate!" cries Juliet (I,v,139), while the Chorus speaks of "Temp'ring extremities with extreme sweet" (II,14) and Friar Lawrence cautions that "These violent delights have violent ends" (II,vi, 9).

In fact, it may be useful for us to look at the feud between the Montagues and the Capulets not only as the central political fact of the plot but also as an underlying pattern that determines the nature of theme, image, and language throughout the play. The confusion of love and death we have already noted will occur again and again, for just as Friar Lawrence rhymes "womb" and "tomb," so, too, does the entire play. When Juliet first sees Romeo, she remarks in an aside to the audience that "If he be married/My grave is like to be my wedding bed" (I,v,134–5)— an innocent observation that, like so many others in *Romeo and Juliet*, ironically comes true. Similarly Lady Capulet, exasperated at her daughter's refusal to marry the County (i.e., Count) Paris, exclaims, "I would the fool were married to her grave!" (III,v,141). Several times we hear the curious image of Death as a bridegroom, and Romeo at the news of his lady's supposed death declares, "Well, Juliet, I will lie with thee tonight" (V,i,34). The double meaning here would have been reinforced for Shakespeare's audience by the fact that "dying" in Elizabethan England was a common synonym for sexual climax; if he cannot make love to her, he will lie with her, and die with her, in another sense. Even in terms of stage properties, the last moments of the two lovers combine sex and death. Romeo dies by drinking from a cup of poison, and a cup is a familiar Freudian symbol for the female. Juliet, finding the cup empty, stabs herself with Romeo's dagger— an equally familiar symbol for male sexuality, and one that has been the basis of jests by young men and servants on several occasions early in the play.

As it happens, one such jest will introduce another crucial "feud" or conflict within the dramatic texture of the play. Old Capulet, shouting for his "long sword" (I,i 73) as he rushes about in his nightgown, would have suggested to the audience a sense of his marital as well as his martial impotence, a sense that would have been underscored by his wife's tart comment: "A crutch, a crutch! Why call you for a sword?" (I,i,74). But the presence of Old Capulet and Old Montague in the thick of the battle also reminds us of the tension that develops in this play between youth and age. Prince Escalus, parting the sides, speaks of "ancient citizens" who "wield old partisans, in hands as old," forsaking the gravity proper to their years (I,i,90; 92). At the ball we hear from Old Capulet himself that he is long past his dancing days, and the conflict of generations is heightened by the evident age of both the Friar and the Nurse. Romeo argues that the Friar cannot understand love since he is no longer young, and the Nurse complains volubly about her aching bones and shortness of breath. "Old folks," says Juliet, are "unwieldly, slow, heavy, and pale as lead" (II,v,16–17). Ironically the old men and women in the play often behave like children—impetuous, willful, and dogmatic—while some of the children possess a wisdom and maturity foreign to their parents. Yet the older generation wields the power in Verona, though the younger men—to their cost— bear the swords.

The two oppositions we have noticed are in some ways analogous to one another; we might perhaps say that love is to death as youth is to age. A third antithesis, this time related to setting rather than to character or theme, fits the same pattern: It is the temporal "feud" between night and day. Again this split is prefigured in an early part of the play when Romeo, doting on the disdainful Rosaline, goes through all the motions of the lovesick suitor. After wandering through the woods till morning, he shuts himself in his room and, blocking out the daylight, "makes himself an artificial night" (I,i,138). This is an artificial night, for an artificial love. But once he meets Juliet they find reality and comfort only in darkness. All of the play's intimate scenes take place at night: the Capulet ball, the orchard or "balcony" scene, the night of marital consummation in Juliet's chamber, and the final night in the graveyard. Daylight brings public brawls, murderous duels, and the unwelcome threat of a bigamous marriage with Paris. Yet such is the tenuousness of their situation that light is continually breaking in on the lovers— either by the coming of day, or by the images in which they speak of one another.

The morning after their wedding night, in the lovely *aubade* or dawn-scene (III,v), Juliet tries to persuade her husband that it is the nightingale singing, and not the lark—that it is still night, and not yet time for him to go. But as Romeo is forced to point out, the day grows "More light and light—more dark and dark our woes" (36). As early as their first meeting the image of brilliant light in darkness has been used to describe their love. Romeo, glimpsing Juliet at the ball, says of her that "she doth teach the torches to burn bright!/It seems she hangs upon the cheek of night/As a rich jewel in an Ethiop's ear." (I,v,44–6). The surrounding darkness only makes her seem to shine the brighter. So, too, when he catches sight of her on the balcony, he will see her as the sun rising in the east—a sun who will "kill the envious moon" (II,ii,4), goddess of virginity and chastity. And yet, as in the *aubade*, the conjunction of light and darkness is all too often as ominous as it is fleeting. The Friar speaks of the "violent delights" of love as a kind of gunpowder—"like fire and powder/ Which, as they kiss, consume" (II,vi,10–11)—and the play contains several references to lightning, which is compared to love at first sight (II,ii,119–20), to the fateful duel (III,i,170), and to the curious merriment of prisoners awaiting death (V,iii,89–91). Perhaps the most threatening of all these images is spoken by Juliet on her wedding day, when she longs for the arrival of night, and for Romeo, "thou day in night." "When he shall die," she says, "Take him and cut him out in little stars,/And he will make the face of heaven so fine/That all the world will be in love with night/And pay no worship to the garish sun" (III,ii,17; 21–5). The innocent violence of this fantasy foreshadows the tragedy that will come, but at the same time it again suggests that tragic darkness will throw the brilliance of the lovers (and their love) into sharp relief. As if to confirm her prediction, "the garish sun" will not "show his head" (V,iii,306) in the closing moments of the play, as the survivors—and the audience—struggle to comprehend what has occurred.

The ultimate resolution of this conflict between light and darkness, as of all the others we have discussed, comes at Juliet's tomb, which Romeo will describe as a "lanthorn" rather than a "grave," and a "feasting presence full of light" illumined by her beauty (V,iii,84–6). It is interesting to note that in the public theaters of Shakespeare's time plays were performed in the afternoon, in full daylight, in a structure that was open to the sky. There was no stage lighting as we know it, only occasional props, like the torches in the ball scene—and the house, of course, was not darkened. Thus all the contrasts between night and day, darkness and light that seem so vivid in our reading of *Romeo and Juliet*—and so striking in modern productions—would have been achieved, originally, by the transforming power of language alone.

Romeo's word "lanthorn," incidentally, means not what we know today as a lantern, but rather a rooftop room with many windows. It is therefore the opposite of a "grave" in location as well as in brightness. And this juxtaposition of a very high place with a very low one brings us to yet another symbolic conflict in the play of *Romeo and Juliet*: that between rising and falling, or motion up and down. Once again, Shakespeare's own stage would have emphasized this, since like most Elizabethan theaters it had a balcony (the "upper stage") and a curtained space below (sometimes called the "inner stage"), which was used to represent enclosed spaces like caves, tombs, prisons, and monastic cells. Just as the lovers are safest in darkness, so they seem safer when they are either above or below the central stage. In part this is just another way of saying that they are safer in private places than in public places like the city square, but the up-down symbolism adds a new dimension of meaning: Like other Biblical (and Shakespearean) figures, these lovers will die to live, fall to rise again—as Juliet will do in the tomb.

In the balcony scene Juliet stands both literally and emblematically out of reach; Romeo can speak to her, but not touch her. Once they are married (below, in the Friar's cell) he climbs the rope ladder and the lovers are together aloft till dawn, when Juliet, watching him descend, sees him in her mind's eye "As one dead in the bottom of a tomb" (III,v,56). This central up-down pattern, from balcony to tomb, is supported by others of a secondary kind. At separate times Romeo and Juliet each literally fall down in despair—Romeo in Friar Lawrence's cell (III,iii), Juliet when she hears of his banishment. (This detail is supplied by the Nurse in conversation with Romeo at the time of *his* fall, so we may safely assume that it has taken place onstage in the previous scene, III,ii.) The Nurse's comic—and lengthy—account of Juliet as a child describes her as falling on her face and repeats her husband's bawdy suggestion that once grown up she will fall backward instead. "Standing," as we have already mentioned, is frequently used as a sexual pun. There is also much talk throughout the play of those who are up (i.e., out of bed) when they should be down (still asleep) connoting more disorder— talk that culminates in the Prince's double-edged words to Old Montague: "thou art early up/To see thy son and heir so early down" (V,iii,208–9).

As we have seen, these interwoven patterns of love and death, youth and age, night and day, dark and light, up and down mirror and symbolize the action of the plot. In a specialized sense, we might say that they *are* a plot, though a plot of a different sort from the sequence of scenes and development of dramatic action that more usually go by that name.

The importance of such patterns lies not only in the richness of texture and poetic beauty they supply—although their value in that regard is very great—but also in the fact that they help the audience to understand and interpret what is going on in the play. When, for example, we hear Juliet wishing for night, or imagining Romeo dead in the bottom of a tomb, we experience a sense of anticipated doom that is due not only to our perception as playgoers but to Shakespeare's excellence as a giver of clues. When old men admit they can no longer dance, we may legitimately question their wisdom in believing they can (or should) still fight, and when the Friar rhymes "womb" and "tomb" in the same speech in which he speaks of the powerful grace of his herbs, we are put on notice that his plan of the sleeping potion may possibly miscarry. A brief look at one final emblematic "feud," less prominent than those we have already mentioned, may suggest how such patterns may provide clues for interpretation of moments in the play that seem otherwise puzzling or ambiguous. The "feud" I have in mind here is that between silver and gold.

Silver is mentioned three times in the play. In the orchard or balcony scene Romeo speaks of the "blessed moon . . . That tips with silver all these fruit-tree tops" (II,ii,107–8). In the same scene he hears her call his name and thinks to himself "How silver-sweet sound lovers' tongues by night,/Like softest music" (II,ii,166–7), and later in the play, at the news of Juliet's "death," a group of musicians rather dispiritedly discuss why music is described as having a "silver sound" (IV,v). All these associations are pleasant, combining love, soul-stirring music, and the moon, protective goddess of unmarried girls.

By contrast the play's references to gold are frequently negative and debasing, connected with things that appear to be of questionable value. In the first scene gold is described as "saint-seducing" (I,i,212) with the displeasing implication that Romeo may have tried to bribe himself into Rosaline's favors. Lady Capulet's praise of Paris as a good book includes a mention of the "gold clasps" that lock in the "golden story" (I,iii,92)—a classic example of judging a book by its cover, for Paris, although certainly inoffensive, is much more victim than hero in the play as a whole. When Romeo is banished rather than put to death he protests to the Friar that the two sentences are the same—that "calling death 'banished'/Thou cut'st my head off with a golden axe" (III,iii,21-2), inflicting the same pain despite his effort to soften the blow. Finally, in the apothecary's shop Romeo is explicit in his condemnation: "There is thy gold—worse poison to men's souls," he says, "I sell thee poison [i.e., the gold]; thou hast sold me none" (V,i,80-83).

Having experienced—and remembered—all of this, what is the audience to make of the plan for atonement put forward by Old Capulet and Old Montague at the end of the play? Montague will "raise [Juliet's] statue in pure gold] (V,iii,299); Capulet, competitive to the last, will do the same for Romeo. But are the gold statues an adequate and appropriate memorial—or have those persons left on stage missed the point of the tragic happenings in Verona? Guided by the clues the playwright has given us, we may be justified in thinking that Shakespeare has provided us with an opportunity to be wiser than that other audience of these events, the surviving characters on the stage, and to realize that his play, rather than the golden statues, is the fit monument by which Romeo and Juliet will be remembered, and their tragedy understood.

Ralph Berry

Romeo and Juliet:
The Sonnet-World of Verona

Our general experience of *Romeo and Juliet* is not, I think, an
entirely settled matter yet—not settled to the extent that, say,
Macbeth or *Troilus and Cressida* or *Richard III* is. The play does
break sharply into two halves, following the death of Mercutio,
and the change of tone and (apparently) direction are marked.
We can cope with this, not necessarily crudely, by calling *Romeo
and Juliet* a comedy and a tragedy, but the critical problem of
unification is not altogether resolved.[1] The central transactions of
the play seem to invite a wide range of response. And the
language remains an underlying cause of unease, a faint yet
unmistakable stimulus and irritant to our responses. Every critic
notes that (in Clemen's words) 'the first scenes of *Romeo and
Juliet* strike us as more conventional in tone and diction than the
later ones.'[2] But what does 'conventional' imply, of approval or
disengagement, in this context? How is the partially 'liberated'
language of the later events to be taken? How, in brief, does the
language of the play guide our responses and imply a judgement?

I

The sonnet is the channel through which the play flows. Acts
I and II are preceded by a choric sonnet; Romeo and Juliet at their
first encounter compose a sonnet, chimingly, together. Several

Reprinted from pp. 37–47 of *The Shakespearean Metaphor* by Ralph Berry,
with permission of Macmillan, London and Basingstoke, and Rowman
and Littlefield, Totowa, N.J.

quatrains and sestets are scattered throughout the play, which closes with the Prince's sestet. Other passages hint broadly at parallels with the Sonnets: Montague's 'Many a morning hath he there been seen,/With tears augmenting the fresh morning's dew', for instance (I, 1, 129–30), and Romeo's 'O she is rich in beauty; only poor,/That, when she dies, with beauty dies her store' (I, 1, 213–14). The sonnet material helps to establish Verona as a country of the mind, a locale whose inhabitants place themselves through their mode of discourse. In the Veronese language, the most obvious adjunct to the sonnet is the rhymed couplet. It is an easier mode than the cross-rhymes of the sonnet, and the Veronese fall into it naturally. Capulet, for instance, has eleven consecutive rhymed couplets in I, 2, a record which Friar Laurence raises to fifteen in his first scene (II, 3). Romeo himself responds to the Friar in the same mode, and throughout the first half of the play slips easily into rhyme. Rhyme is the shared possession of this society. The Veronese think in rhyme, and communicate in rhyme: Friar Laurence's soliloquy (II, 3) changes not a whit in metre or tone after Romeo's arrival. But rhyme is psychologically more interesting than it looks. I discern two main varieties of the mode. With the elders, the heavy, jogging rhymes have the effect of a self-fulfilling prophecy. *Night* must follow *light* with the same inevitability that it does the day. The rhymes figure a closed system. The younger people, apt to confuse facility with penetration, seize on the other aspect of rhyme—that it can pick up the loose ends of a companion's speech. Thus, to the stimulus of Benvolio's 'I rather weep . . . At thy good heart's oppression', Romeo instantly reacts 'Why such is love's transgression' (I, 1, 181–3). It is a kind of game. The joint composition of the sonnet in I, 5 is, as I take it, a part-conscious event, a tranced process of courtly reciprocity. Juliet's 'You kiss by the book'[3] (I, 5, 110) combines an implied reproach for artificiality, with an acknowledgment of Romeo's dexterity at completing his own (and her) rhymes. Rhyme, in sum, is inward-turning, acquiescent, reflective of social forces. It tends to codify its own categories, and insulate them against erosion. It is Juliet who supplies the best internal comment on all this. Following her parting from Romeo, comes

> *Nurse.* What's this, what's this?
> *Juliet.* A rhyme I learned even now
> Of one I danced withal.   (i, 5, 142–3)

So 'rhyme' becomes a kind of crystallisation for the whole episode; a formula for the fluency, the intensity, and the superficiality of the means through which this society orders its experience, and its relationships.

II

The prime effect of the sonnet-material, coupled with this mass of rhyming, is to conduct us into a Petrarchan world. By this I mean a world conceived as a dramatisation of the Elizabethan sonnet collections. The grand cultural allusion that Shakespeare makes is to the explosion of amatory versifying in the early 1590s, a fashion inaugurated by the 'English Petrarke', Sidney. The main facts are well known, but the reader may care to be reminded of the sequence of dates leading up to *Romeo and Juliet. Astrophel and Stella* was published in 1591. In 1592 appeared *Delia*, by Samuel Daniel; and *Diana*, by Henry Constable (republished in 1594, with additions). 1593 saw *Parthenophil and Parthenope*, by Barnabe Barnes; *Licia*, by Giles Fletcher; and *Phillis*, by Thomas Lodge. Drayton's *Ideas Mirrour* came out in 1594. 1595 saw the publication of Spenser's *Amoretti*, besides Barnes' *A Divine Centurie of Spirituall Sonnets*. All these are sonnet-sequences, or collections including a large number of sonnets. It is not a complete list, merely an indication that between *Astrophel and Stella* and the composition of *Romeo and Juliet* (that is to say, 1594–6) no year passed without a significant public addition to the effusions of the sonnetteers. For our purposes here, certain characteristics of the sonnet-wave are salient. First, there is a definite acknowledgement of Petrarch himself as the inspiration of the school, and this is occasionally explicit in the verse. Daniel, for instance: 'Though thou a Laura hast no Petrarch found'; and Constable, 'Thy coming to the world hath taught us to descry/ What Petrarch's Laura meant . . .'[4] Second, the mode comprises certain personae, attitudes, situations—the cruel mistress, despairing lover, melancholy, insomnia, and so on. Third, the mode is inadequately described as 'conventional'. For several years it was *the* convention, a mental environment that nourished the greatest and smallest: Sidney, Spenser, Shakespeare drew from it the sustenance they needed, as did Fletcher, Barnes, Lodge. All defined themselves in relation to this central convention. Most of its individual exponents are unremarkable. 'Smoothness and standardization, abstractness and unreality, utter lack of criticism or analysis: these are the marks of the lyrical verse which, in the last years of the sixteenth century, was brought against something new.'[5] Shakespeare, however, is in *Romeo and Juliet* using the convention as a means of placing, and implicitly judging, his dramatis personae. J. W. Lever remarks of the minor sonnetteers of the period that 'Like Romeo and Juliet on their first encounter, these poets play delightedly with the conceits of "saints", "pilgrims", "palmers", and "prayers" . . .'[6] Precisely: and this is as true if the comparison is reversed. Romeo and Juliet are playing like minor poets within the current mode. As I take it, Shakespeare is combining an imaginative conception with a ready means of audience communication, for he would expect playgoers to pick up the fashionable expressions of Romeo and his social milieu. He thus combines immediacy of reference with interior, dramatic truth, for the characters assert their life to be exactly of their period. Lever is again à propos here: he reminds us of the extent to which 'life itself is patterned on literary modes: how men in one age tend to conduct their amours in all earnestness, like the heroes of Stendhal; in another, in all flippancy, like the heroes of Noel Coward.'[7] One of the most distinctive features of *Romeo and Juliet* is its almost journalistic flair in identifying the literary movement of the 1590s and the ways in which people modelled themselves upon the movement. Shakespeare's conception, then, synthesises the physical world of Renaissance Italy, the most famous literary expression of that world, and the Elizabethan reception to the expression.

The landscape of *Romeo and Juliet* has a precise inner consistency. It has the curious flatness of a trecento fresco. Not only are there young people and old people; they are young people's old people—and vice versa. The Montagues and Capulets, with their Prince, appear to us as they appear to the lovers—a formal, statuesque frieze of contention and judgement. Neither the Friar nor the Nurse needs a name; they are functionaries, purely. Nobody is middle-aged, nobody is even Hamlet's age. Mercutio aside, no one in the drama is capable of understanding it, and no one does. Nothing could be more indicative of the world the lovers inhabit than the sonnet they speak to each other—that, and the 'Aye me' (predicted by Mercutio) with which Juliet begins her soliloquy. There is no question here of inauthentic emotions (though Romeo, earlier, shows a certain awareness of role-playing). The young lovers feel intensely that which the mode incites them to feel. Confronted with the image of the ideal lover, each reverts to stereotype. What we have here is an existential drama of sonnet-life. The world of Romeo and Juliet, shared by Benvolio, the Montagues and Capulets, and the Prince, is a world of fixed relationships and closed assumptions. They appear as quotations, and they speak in quotations: the cliché, of which the sonnet is exemplar, is the dominant thought-form of Verona.

III

But the Petrarchan world comprehends anti-Petrarchan forces—the resistance movement, if you like. Of course an element of anti-Petrarchanism is implicit in the convention itself. An intelligent adherent to the mode is a prototype of the dandy, self-critically aware of the role he apparently acquiesces in. Such a one, perhaps, is the Romeo of the early scenes. But the resistance movement takes more overt forms than the polished oxymora that Romeo projects in I, 1. It can be observed in the Nurse, with her peasant's calculus of existence: 'I think it best you married with the County' (III, 5, 219). It is apparent in the servants' and musicians' dialogue of IV, 5, with its burlesque of grief: 'When griping grief the heart doth wound,/And doleful dumps the mind oppress . . .' (IV, 5, 123–4).[8] But the head and front of the resistance movement is Mercutio; and it is he, naming Petrarch to Romeo's face, who voices the dialectical challenge of this play:

> Now is he for the numbers that Petrarch flowed in.
> Laura to his lady was a kitchen-wench (marry, she had
> a better love to be-rhyme her), Dido a dowdy, Cleopatra
> a gypsy, Helen and Hero, hildings and harlots;
> Thisbe a grey eye or so, but not to the purpose—   (II, 4, 38–43)

Were Mercutio in love, he would write Sonnet 130 ('My mistress' eyes are nothing like the sun').[9] As he is not, he derides his friend in what is virtually a burlesque, rhymeless sonnet:

> Romeo! Humours! Madman! Passion! Lover!
> Appear thou in the likeness of a sigh;
> Speak but one rhyme and I am satisfied!
> Cry but 'Ay me!' pronounce but love and dove . . .   (II, 1, 7–21)

'Speak but one rhyme' implies a verdict, not only on Romeo, but on virtually everyone else in the play. Mercutio himself has a profound contempt for rhyme; he can scarcely bring himself to perpetrate a single one. His mode is a supple, virile prose, or a liberated blank verse; but preferably prose. The Queen Mab speech, as I take it, essentially validates and enlarges Mercutio. We cannot thereafter view him as a simple scoffer. His language is more *admirable* than Romeo's; it is a permanent judgement, coded into his aversion from rhyme and his mastery of the two major media. It is in prose that he presents, in a single speech, the issues, by which he demands to be judged:

> Why, is not this better now than groaning for love? Now art thou sociable, now are thou Romeo; now art thou what thou art, by art as well as nature, for this drivelling love is like a great natural that runs lolling up and down to hide his bauble in a hole.   (II, 4, 83–7)

The pun on 'art' directs us, via the art-nature opposition, to the issues of identity and role-playing that Mercutio detects in Romeo. The nature/natural gibe is a very serious critique of Romeo, and of what he terms love. But the point, and problem of the speech lies in the intensity of the anti-Petrarchan charge. 'Bawdy' is inadequate to describe the primitive force of this image, this sexual gargoyle. It is a grimace directed at the centre of the play; and even a strong-stomached modern critic may find it too much.[10] The gravest critical error concerning *Romeo and Juliet* is to assume that the play, more or less, identifies itself with the lovers; and the violence of Mercutio's commentary is on record to remind us of the counterforce whereby the ultimate poise is achieved.

In all this, Mercutio is an extended reflection of the play's cultural context—'topicality' is too limited and misleading a term. I am thinking of the wave of satirists who came in with the late 1590s—Hall, Marston, Donne. 'Dante and Petrarch go rudely through the door, with four centuries of European tradition. All that deifying of women amounts to nothing more than a self-deception, a projection of unsatisfied desire.'[11] Here A. J. Smith is writing of Donne, but the second sentence describes perfectly well the point that Mercutio is making to Romeo. I am not, of course, suggesting a crude reading of *Romeo and Juliet* that makes it a kind of debate between Spenser and Donne. I think rather that the dating of *Romeo and Juliet*, at the cross-roads of the 1590s, gave Shakespeare an opportunity to characterise the intellectual life of the period. It is an era of very rapid transition, and *Romeo and Juliet* assimilates and dramatises its conflicts. We can be certain that before the satirists of the fin-de-siècle had their public say, there must have been proto-Donnes and proto-Marstons of the capital's life concerned to make the—very sound—point that the bulk of sonnetteering was affected, unreal, and absurd. The thesis of Sidney and the antithesis of Donne are both, Hegelianly, present in the synthesis of 1595. And Shakespeare has described that synthesis.

Mercutio—to return to the play—is in fine the leader of the group which includes the Nurse and the comic servants. It exists to challenge the assumptions, the style, and even the diction of the Petrarchans in the centre of the stage. There is in this principle of organisation nothing original. Shakespeare had done it before, for this same city of Verona: the pretensions of the young gentlemen are savaged by everyone from Crab (parodically) upward. What is original is the means, of singular aesthetic appeal, whereby the suppression of the anti-Petrarchan voice initiates the coming of tragedy. The realist-critic of the Petrarchan world is the agent of a reality that destroys it. Mercutio's death does not refute him, it refutes the others. Without Mercutio, the position collapses. Lacking a strong, critical and intelligent impulse, the lovers with their helpers and elders are unable to cope with the demands of the new situation. The metamorphosis of Mercutio is decidedly the key to this curiously original drama.

IV

We might, I think, demonstrate the matter more elegantly by returning to the language of *Romeo and Juliet*. The central event of the play is the modulation of the realist into a governing reality. Well, but the antithesis of realism is nominalism; we might expect the first half of the play to be much engaged with the question of names. And this is in fact what we find. Of the play's thirty references to 'name', in all its forms, twenty-nine occur in the first three Acts. They are almost all associated with Romeo and Juliet, and with love. Mercutio initiates the motif parodically: 'Speak to my gossip Venus one fair word,/One nickname for her purblind son and heir,/Young Abraham Cupid . . .' (II, 1, 11–13) and continues with 'my invocation/Is fair and honest; in his mistress' name/I conjure only but to raise up him' (II, 1, 27–9). (This is the language, if not the tone, of Sonnet 151: 'flesh stays no farther reason,/But, rising at thy name, doth point out thee . . .') The balcony scene that follows is a sustained lyric on 'name'. The essential parts of Juliet's soliloquy are:

> O Romeo, Romeo, wherefore art thou Romeo?
> Deny thy father, and refuse thy name . . .
> 'Tis but thy name that is my enemy.
> Thou art thyself, though not a Montague.
> What's Montague? . . . O be some other name!
> What's in a name? That which we call a rose
> By any other name would smell as sweet. . .
> . . . Romeo doff thy name,
> And for thy name which is no part of thee,
> Take all myself.   (II, 2, 33–49)

Romeo's self-identification is

> By a name
> I know not how to tell thee who I am.
> My name, dear saint, is hateful to myself,
> Because it is an enemy to thee.   (II, 2, 53–6)

They are curiously obsessed by the relationship between names and vital essences. Juliet's 'Swear by thy gracious self, /Which is the god of my idolatry' (II, 2, 113–14) does seem to penetrate, via names, to essences; still, 'idolatry' is ominous, however consciously inflected. And Romeo, in a posture typical of the early Shakespeare's handling of young men in love, seems much more besotted with the appearance of things than his feminine counterpart. We cannot evade the ironic implications of his response to Friar Laurence's question, in the following scene:

> wast thou with Rosaline?
> *Romeo.* With Rosaline, my ghostly father? No.
> I have forgot that name, and that name's woe.   (II, 3, 44–6)

Romeo has a Caesar-like obsession with *name* as a third-person, objective entity. Note his paroxysm of grief at the news that Juliet cries on Romeo:

> As if that name,
> Shot from the deadly level of a gun,

Did murder her; as that name's cursed hand
Murdered her kinsman. O tell me, Friar, tell me,
In what vile part of this anatomy
Doth my name lodge? Tell me, that I may sack
The hateful mansion.   (III, 3, 102–8)

'Name', like 'rhyme', is a way of coding the apprehension of
values in this society. Appearance, and form, are the realities of
the Veronese. They are none the less genuine for that; but they
are vulnerable. No one has the grasp of meanings apparent in
'Make but my name thy love and love that still,/And then thou
lovest me, for my name is Will' (Sonnet 136).[12] This sonnet-society
lacks a major sonnetteer. Not one of the three perfect sonnets has
real quality, any more than the sonnet-fragments. The choric
sonnets (to which one can add the Prince's final sestet) do not
seek to grapple with the inwardness of the events and are, in a
profound sense, the play. The only man who could write sonnets
of the first order prefers to parody them; and he is dead at half-
way, or perhaps at the parting of octave and sestet. But even
Mercutio has the Veronese fascination with names—with Tybalt,
'Prince of Cats', the *bons* of the affected, 'villain', the fatal 'consort'
(the ministrel-word) that leads to the duel. Mercutio's final 'your
houses' is a reduction of the names that structure the first half of
the play. 'Houses' is a variant of 'Montague' and 'Capulet', the
terms that have sustained the nominalist duet of Romeo and
Juliet. The last words of the play's realist are a rejection of his
society's preoccupation.

V

This is a society as given to forms in grief, as in love and
war. I think the most daring scene in the play is IV, 5 wherein the
reactions of the Capulet household to Juliet's death are detailed.
Since her death is a deception, and since this scene must not
duplicate the final situation, Shakespeare can permit himself a
licence in characterising these people that is impossible later.
Capulet's reactions are interesting. First comes the unmatchably
simple and moving 'Death lies on her like an untimely frost /
Upon the sweetest flower of all the field' (IV, 5, 28–9). 'Death' is
perhaps as much an abstraction as a personification here: its
positioning at the beginning of the line conceals, as it were, the

capital. Now begins the movement to personification, to
formalisation:

> Death, that hath ta'en her hence to make me wail
> Ties up my tongue and will not let me speak.   (IV, 5, 31–2)

This is less moving. Now comes positively a conceit:

> O son, the night before thy wedding day
> Hath Death lain with thy wife. There she lies,
> Flower as she was, deflowered by him.
> Death is my son-in-law, Death is my heir . . .   (IV, 5, 35–8)

This is, of course, dramatically compressed time, but the
movement seems perfectly clear; it is from grief to mourning,
from the impulse to sorrow to the outward expression of that
sorrow. And the passages that follow border on the ludicrous, as
Lady Capulet, Nurse, Paris, and Capulet compete with each other
in an anthology of apostrophes. I do not know how these passages
should be staged; but I think Shakespeare is taking advantage of
a cultural fact, which is that patterns of mourning outside one's
own society tend to appear faintly absurd, a suggestion normally
overlaid by one's knowledge of the genuineness of the emotions.
But here we are freed from the obligation to react decently, and
we can admit that the Nurse's lamentation (especially) is a
burlesque:

> O woe! O woeful, woeful, woeful day!
> Most lamentable day, most woeful day
> That ever, ever I did yet behold!
> O day, O day, O day, O hateful day,
> Never was seen so black a day as this.
> O woeful day! O woeful day!   (IV, 5, 49–54)

The stupefying banality of this is no more than a lower-order
caricature—the device is standard Shakespearean—of the gentry.
And anyone in the audience who still feels that mourning, any
mourning, is a serious business can safely relax during the
musicians' interlude. It looks like being a good wake.

VI

The final stages of *Romeo and Juliet* are, however, the real thing, and it would be unseemly to permit the acidities of the pseudo-death scene to linger on one's tongue. The final events are essentially simple, and we should react simply to them. Nevertheless, our judgement has been carefully prepared throughout the entire play. The language of *Romeo and Juliet* is a notation that implies a judgement on its speakers, and Shakespeare exhibits, in his selection of styles, a profound detachment from the dramatis personae. Much of this detachment is, naturally, evident enough in the content of the play. I have no wish to reopen the question of the lovers' suicide—I am content with the evidence assembled by R. M. Frye that the Elizabethans would have found the suicides culpable.[13] Similarly, I accept F. M. Dickey's findings that the Elizabethans would have viewed the lovers in a much more comic light than we tend to.[14] And the play contains a clear refutation of Romeo's conduct, through Friar Laurence's rebuke in III, 3. But I want to extend this detachment to the entire dramatis personae, for it is, as I argue, at the root of the conception of tragedy here. W. H. Auden has listed ten occasions on which a character has made the wrong choice, with consequences that contribute to the ultimate fatality.[15] There is no need to weigh them here. Ten is sufficient. The point, surely, is that Verona is a wrong-choice society. It is a community fascinated with names, forms, rituals. Its citizens are passionate, impatient, intolerant, impulsive. It lacks a capacity for appraising its own values. Its Prince does not tell the community that the Montague-Capulet feud is an absurdity, he merely forbids brawling in the streets. The fatal chance of the thrust under Romeo's arm is bad luck: true. But someone would get killed in a duel, sometime; it was inevitable. Fate, then, is diffused back into the entire society. The seeds of tragedy are present even in the apparently comic world of the first two Acts—a world of young lovers and friends, comic servants and go-betweens, doddering seniors. To create a totally credible situation, which is habitually Shakespeare's objective, a much greater degree of social determinism is required than is generally understood. What we have in *Romeo and Juliet* is a complete social context for an action, a society that is unable to cope with consequences of its own deficiencies. Even at the end, Verona has learned little. The Prince, in his epitome of the non-committal, has only

> For never was a story of more woe,
> Than this of Juliet and her Romeo.

And Montague can only make his stylised public gesture, matched by Capulet:[16]

> For I will raise her statue in pure gold,
> That whiles Verona by that *name* is known,
> There shall no figure at such rate be set
> As that of true and faithful Juliet.   (v, 3, 299–302)

And all this is implicit from the beginning, in the characters' modes of discourse. Certainly their styles have improved—the second half of the play contains fewer rhymed couplets, more and less-stilted blank verse. But this is a relative improvement only. Their anagnorisis is as limited as the Prince's final sestet.

Closer than any other play in the canon, *Romeo and Juliet* stands near in spirit to *Love's Labour's Lost*. The Petrarchan world of Navarre, like that of Verona, is penetrated by an irrefutable and annihilating reality. And in each case the agent is a descendant of Mercury. 'Mercutio', we are told, 'is of course, mercurial; that is the humour concealed in the anagram of his name, and that is the way he behaves.'[17] Well, yes. Mercutio behaves mercurially; but so, in a different sense, does Mercade. Their relationship to the world of comedy is the same. The death of Mercutio is harsh, after the songs of Petrarch.

NOTES

1. Susan Snyder argues that 'the reversal is so radical as to constitute a change of genre.' '*Romeo and Juliet*: Comedy into Tragedy', *Essays in Criticism* XX (1970), 391. This leads to her final verdict that 'what Shakespeare wanted to convey was an ironic dissociation between character and the direction of events,' and that 'although the central characters have their weaknesses, their destruction does not really stem from these weaknesses' (p. 401). This analysis rests, I suggest, on a reaction to the play's mood, which unquestionably shifts from comedy to tragedy. My argument here is that the play, contrary to the impression one receives in the audience, does actually move in an (intellectually) straight line: that is, the catastrophe stems from certain communal and

individual weaknesses that are correctly diagnosed from the beginning.

2. Wolfgang Clemen, *The Development of Shakespeare's Imagery* (London, 1951), p. 64.

3. Harry Levin well emphasises the bookishness of Veronese society in 'Form and Formality in *Romeo and Juliet*', *Shakespeare Quarterly* XI (1960), 4–5.

4. *Delia*, Sonnet XL: and *Diana*, Sonnet VI in the manuscript edition. The quotations are from the joint volume in the *Elizabethan Sonnet Cycles* series, edited by Martha Foote Crow (London, 1896).

5. Patrick Cruttwell, *The Shakespearean Moment* (New York, 1960), p. 18. Cruttwell's main argument, concerning the decisive transitional conflicts of the 1590s, is both persuasive in itself and parallel to my own reading of *Romeo and Juliet*.

6. J. W. Lever, *The Elizabethan Love Sonnet*, second ed. (London, 1966), p. 146.

7. *Ibid.*, p. 57.

8. 'It develops and broadens—vulgarises, if you will—the irony of the bridal music brought to the deathbed.' Harley Granville-Barker, *Prefaces to Shakespeare*, 2 vols. (London, 1958) II, p. 319.

9. Cruttwell has a perceptive commentary on this sonnet and its relations with the convention. Cruttwell (New York, 1960), pp. 18–19.

10. See Brian Vickers, *The Artistry of Shakespeare's Prose* (London, 1968), p. 73.

11. A. J. Smith, 'The Poetry of John Donne', in *English Poetry and Prose 1540–1674*, ed. Christopher Ricks (London, 1970), p. 148.

12. The fourteen sonnets in which 'name' appears are 36, 39, 71, 72, 76, 80, 81, 89, 95, 108, 111, 127, 136, 151.

13. R. M. Frye, *Shakespeare and Christian Doctrine* (Princeton, 1963), pp. 24–7.

14. F. M. Dickey, *Not Wisely But Too Well* (San Marino, Calif., 1957).

15. In his Commentary to the Laurel edition of *Romeo and Juliet* (New York, 1958).

16. It is true that the reconciliation of Montague and Capulet can itself be a theatrical statement of knowledge. Once only have I seen this affectingly played: by the RSC (1976). After the Prince's penultimate speech, a long pause elapsed before Capulet hesitantly extended his hand, with 'O brother Montague, give me thy hand'.

17. Robert O. Evans, *The Osier Cage: Rhetorical Devices in Romeo and Juliet* (Lexington, Ky., 1966), p. 82.

Part II

Romeo and Juliet in Performance

James Black

The Visual Artistry of
Romeo and Juliet

The which if you with patient ears attend,
What here shall miss, our toil shall strive to mend.

The first-act prologue to *Romeo and Juliet* invites the audience to use its eyes as well as its patient ears. "Our toil"—the actors' efforts—will try to compensate visually for anything that may elude hearing. There is a more confident note here than can be found in Shakespeare's other first-act prologues: "think that you see" is the supplication common to the prologues of *Henry V* and *Henry VIII*, while the rather arrogant prologue-speaker in *Troilus and Cressida* comes armed "not in confidence/Of author's pen or actor's voice." Whether it is the sonnet form of *Romeo and Juliet's* prologue that curtails apology, or the assurance about his actors of a dramatist still comparatively new to his trade, it is appropriate that this prologue should emphasize looking as well as listening, for *Romeo and Juliet* is an especially "visual" play. Its story is told and its tragedy unfolded in a series of pictures as well as in dialogue; and indeed the play is a brilliant exercise in suiting the action to the word in such a way that both actions and words are given special intensity.

Shakespeare's pictorial sense is already active in his very earliest plays. When he turned the *Menaechmi* into *The Comedy of Errors* he added a second set of twins, and so obviously relished the possibilities for double exposures and double-takes. But the confusion is artfully controlled, and limited to the characters on the stage. As so much in *The Comedy of Errors* depends on what is

Reprinted from *Studies in English Literature 1500–1900* 15 (1975), 245–56,
by permission of Rice University.

seen, the audience is given the chance to "get its eye in" on the Dromios before being presented with two Antipholi. Antipholus of Ephesus does not appear until III.i; in this scene he orders a jewelled chain which in III.ii is—with much by-play for emphasis—hung around the neck of Antipholus of Syracuse, whom it thereafter identifies. Helped in this way to accept that the twins are visually the same yet different, the audience can go on to consider that philosophically they are different yet the same, for each brother seeking his counterpart finds himself.[1] Shakespeare's use of visual effects in other early plays has been noticed by W. Moelwyn Merchant, who says:

> In the immature *Henry the Sixth* plays, one of the principal pleasures at their 1953 revival in Birmingham was to realize Shakespeare's early mastery of stage grouping and symbolism as the plot moved on from tableau to tableau, gathered itself to a significant picture and then dissolved, each stage grouping contributing to a constantly mounting tension. Shakespeare and his contemporaries omitted no visual occasion or device which might add depth and complexity to the meaning and presentation of their plays.[2]

Each of the "stage-pictures" in *Romeo and Juliet* which I propose to discuss is shown twice or more than twice, and Shakespeare uses them to lead the careful onlooker through the experience of the play. The most obvious example of repeated pictures is given by the two "balcony scenes," II.ii and III.v. Each of these scenes perorates in a leavetaking just at dawn (II.ii.184–189, III.v.41–59); in each the "picture" is held for a considerable time of Juliet aloft in the balcony or window and Romeo below in the Capulet "orchard." The locale, the time of night or morning, the arrangement or disposition of the figures, the drawn-out leavetaking—all these features suggest that the second of these two scenes closes in a reduplication or reprise of the first.

But there is more than a simple repetition of setting and tableau here; more than a "visual rhyme." When Romeo and Juliet first stood thus at meeting and parting in the Capulet orchard it was dangerous for Romeo to be found there. Juliet's sober warnings were rapturously dismissed by him:

Juliet. If they do see thee, they will murther thee.
Romeo. Alack, there lies more peril in thine eye

Than twenty of their swords. Look thou but sweet,
And I am proof against their enmity. (II.ii.70–73)

Now, in III.v, all Verona is mortal to him: with the killing of
Tybalt death and banishment have shadowed their love. Under
this shadow it is Juliet who for a moment is desperately
impractical—"Wilt thou be gone?...Yond light is not daylight"—
and Romeo who protests "I must be gone and live, or stay and
die." When he gives in to Juliet's pleadings it is with a desperate
resignation far removed from his former rapture:

Let me be ta'en, let me be put to death;
I am content, so thou with have it so...
Come, death, and welcome! Juliet wills it so. (III.v.17f.)

Delight in new love and anticipation of future meetings made
their second-act parting "such sweet sorrow"; and goodnight was
said only "till it be morrow." But at their next—and final—
leavetaking Romeo's forced optimism cannot overcome Juliet's
fearful premonitions; he finally gives in to their mutual fears and
it is "dry sorrow" which informs this parting:

Juliet. O God, I have an ill-divining soul!
Methinks I see thee, now thou art so low,
As one dead in the bottom of a tomb.
Either my eyesight fails, or thou look'st pale.
Romeo. And trust me, love, in my eye so do you.
Dry sorrow drinks our blood. Adieu, adieu! (III.v.54–59)

The fact that in each of these scenes the setting is the same
and the stage picture reduplicated lends emphasis to the pathetic
alteration in the speakers' tones and circumstances. The parallels
emphasize the differences: things look the same but are painfully
altered. Thus the audience is looking at what it saw before, but is
being forced to see more intensely.

This process of intensification by parallel is carried forward
when in III.v Juliet is called from the window (as at her former
parting from Romeo), this time to receive a "new and deadly
blow"[3] from an element of the situation which also existed when
Romeo first came to the Capulet house. At that time Juliet was
officially betrothed to Paris; and still is though secretly married.
But in the scene just before her second parting from Romeo her
father has arranged for her to marry Paris in three days. In this
new dilemma Juliet decides to go to Friar Lawrence, and the

scene ends on her painful determination—in parallel and contrast
with its counterpart II.ii which closed with Romeo first setting
off rapturously from the orchard to tell Lawrence about his good
fortune:

> *Romeo.* Hence will I to my ghostly sire's close cell,
> His help to crave and my dear hap to tell.   (II.ii.188–189)
>
> *Juliet.* I'll to the friar to know his remedy.
> If all else fail, myself have power to die.   (III.v.241–242)

We are, of course, accustomed to thinking of *Romeo and Juliet*
in terms of patterns and re-echoings, but usually it is the patterns
of verse and image which commentators on the play have
emphasized. The "mighty opposites"[4] of the play's language—
love-hate, youth-age, light-darkness—can easily be thought of as
contributing nearly all the play's energy, with the tragedy
impelled more by its verbal kinetics than by its stagecraft. The
majority verdict on *Romeo and Juliet* is summarized by George Ian
Duthie in the New Cambridge Edition when he says that it is "in
certain important respects a dramatic failure, [but] a great poetic
success."[5] Thus it is especially easy to regard *Romeo and Juliet* as
lending itself most properly to "concert performance," in
confirmation of Samuel Johnson's view that we go to the theater
only "to hear a certain number of lines recited with just gesture
and elegant modulations,"[6] or Coleridge's opinion that
Elizabethan acting was more or less straightforward recitation.[7]
But to take this approach is to disregard the prologue's invitation,
which I have already mentioned, and to ignore what Hamlet
(who knew about plays) calls "the cunning of the scene."[8] Just as
patterned speech recurs in sonnets and fragments of sonnets
throughout the play so also do visual arrangements on stage.

As in the balcony scenes a stage picture or grouping comes
around for a second time complete in its details and with
intensified feeling, so when both of Juliet's prospective
bridegrooms encounter her at Lawrence's cell another picture is
reduplicated. Romeo and Juliet come together at the Friar's cell
to be married in II.vi; in IV.i Paris and Juliet also meet there. The
scenes are similar in arrangement: priest and bridgeroom enter
and talk about the marriage, and are joined by the lady,
whereupon the young couple talk exclusively to one another.
Other details strengthen the parallel. For example, in II.vi Romeo,

who has come to wed in a hurry, receives a sermon from
Lawrence on the advisability of moderate speed and passion,
while in IV.i Lawrence tries to suggest that Paris also should
moderate haste: "On Thursday, sir? The time is very short."
When Juliet enters it is Lawrence who in each scene breaks off
the conversation to announce her arrival; his words are conventional
but the echo is exact: "Here comes the lady." As with the balcony
scenes, the points of similarity serve to emphasize the tragic
alteration of mood between these two meetings of Juliet and her
betrothed, for the two cell scenes, like the balcony scenes, stand
on either side of the play's emotional watershed, which is
Mercutio's death. Juliet and Romeo met rapturously at Lawrence's
cell, swept along with a passion that Lawrence could only try to
direct, not suppress. And although Lawrence at that time
sermonized to Romeo in the ominous imagery of fire and
gunpowder which is characteristic of the play,[9] his counsel was
sententiously general. His words to Paris in IV.i are far more
immediately anxious, keyed to the urgency of a situation that
has developed gravely since last he met a bridegroom at this cell.
The images in his dialogue with Romeo in II.vi—"violent ends,"
"fire and powder," "light" and "flint"—are ominous, but also
triumphal, especially as they are reinforced by themes of joy and
wealth, published or "blazoned" in "rich music's tongue"; the
wedding scene has after all its epithalamium as well as its sermon.
In contrast to this scene's ardency, the predominant theme in its
counterpart is tears;[10] good-natured Paris puzzles and sympathizes
over Juliet's immoderate weeping for—as he thinks—Tybalt's
death. In place of the rich music in which Romeo and Juliet
celebrated their love and marriage day there is now wary fencing
in stichomythia as Juliet, keeping up a brave and Beatrice-like
front, fends off her suitor.

Each repetition of scene is used in *Romeo and Juliet* as a
dramatic milestone—a distance-marker, familiar and arresting
because seen before, which furthers as well as marks the
audience's guided progress across a tragic landscape. It may also
have become clear before now that the process of "visual
repetition with emotional intensification" which I have been
describing is none other than an adaptation for dramatic purposes
of the well-known poetic device of incremental repetition:
repetition with a variation that advances the narrative. *Romeo
and Juliet's* reduplicated groupings in orchard and cell serve the
function—though much refined—of a refrain in a ballad.

But this function is refined even further than the adding of an emotional charge to a picture seen the second time around. One stage grouping comes around for a third time, and at its second exposure cumulates, rather than fully releases, its charge, which is not to be spent until the optimum moment of the play's catastrophe. The picture in question here is that tableau in which Verona's Prince stands at each of his three appearances in "symmetrical assembly"[11] with his feuding subjects the Montagues and Capulets. At regularly-spaced intervals—Acts I, III, and V—Verona's rivalries break into open violence, and the Prince stands to arbitrate between the families in a stage-grouping as cumulatively ominous as Mercutio's thrice-repeated curse, "A plague o' both your houses!" For the increment added to each repetition of the picture is a growing freight of dead youth. Everyone is alive at the end of the first brawl, but when in Act III the Capulets and Montagues again stand to hear their Prince they face one another across Tybalt's dead body, with Mercutio newly dead off-stage. And when in Act V the participants in this same tableau reassemble they do so at the tomb where in plain sight lie Tybalt, Paris, Romeo, and Juliet. A reminder of Mercutio is added by the Prince:

> Capulet, Montague,
> See what a scourge is laid upon your hate,
> That heaven finds means to kill your joys with love!
> And I, for winking at your discords too,
> Have lost a brace of kinsmen. All are punished.   (V.iii.291–295)

Thus the same basic stage picture is made progressively tragic as it becomes more and more a pageant of death.

Perhaps the fact that only Tybalt's body appears in the second tableau of Prince and families, and not Mercutio's as well, may suggest that Shakespeare was thinking not only in terms of stage pictures but also of economy in the use of this one. As he is dead through an act of revenge for Mercutio's killing, and killed by Romeo, Tybalt's corpse sums up well enough in itself the intensifying situation. The single dead body is a very meaningful addition to the grouping already seen in Act I, but not so much of an addition as to compete with the spectacle of doom that will come at the third assembly in Act V. This is the "cumulative" aspect of the process: the situation as recapitulated in this third-act picture is now much more tragic, but still developing, and in arranging the picture economically with just a single dead body Shakespeare is storing (and building up) the full tragic energy for release in the catastrophe. This is not the only instance in *Romeo and Juliet* where Shakespeare conserves emotional energy: in IV.v. we see how the Capulet household's reaction to the supposed death of Juliet is carefully handled so as not to vitiate the real feeling which will be called forth when she actually dies.[12]

Closely linked to the repeated arrangement of Prince and families is the narrative which in each of these scenes recounts the events which have taken place. In I.i.106–115 Benvolio tells Romeo's father and mother how the first brawl started; in III.i.152–175 he recounts how Mercutio and Tybalt came to their deaths. At the play's end Lawrence has a forty-line speech recapitulating all that the audience has seen happen up to the lovers' deaths—a speech which "is often omitted in modern productions as being unnecessary."[13] In fact, of these three speeches, only one has any particular dramatic coloration, and that is Benvolio's second speech, in which he slightly distorts the events he is recounting so as to make Romeo appear less culpable.[14] Dramatic interest also is added here by the fierce rebuttals of Lady Capulet. But as Benvolio's first speech and Lawrence's last one are straightforward retellings of events the audience already has seen for itself, why then does Shakespeare include these two narratives, or indeed any of the three? T. J. B. Spencer gives an answer when he says that the Friar's recounting is necessary if there is to be a strong emphasis on the reconciliation of the two families. "We need this quiet narrative speech which helps us to put the sequence of events into true proportion, while we watch the heads of the two families realize what has happened and achieve their reconciliation," he says; and John Russell Brown suggests the stage effectiveness of the long silence of the Friar's auditors, a silence which bespeaks a growing "corporate acceptance of helplessness and ignorance in the face of catastrophe."[15] I feel it is important to emphasize that as audience we are looking on here as well as listening. What we are seeing as Lawrence explains is the same tableau presented in Act III, where a helpless participant in the tragic events stood by the human wreckage while he outlined the cause to Prince and parents. In each case there is plenty of time to take in the visual details (this time was given in Act I by the Prince's indictment). The additions and alterations to the second and third pictures are the more readily noticed because of this time given to study the tableaux, and because we not only have seen the picture before but also already know the events being recounted. In other words, all circumstances conspire to make the audience look, and look perhaps even a little harder than it may be listening.

The true focus of this stage picture is unquestionably the dead bodies in the tomb or inner stage. And should the audience at any time lift its eyes from the tomb, to look for example at a speaker or at the general picture before it, it would see as an alternative to the bodies of these dead youth nothing but their opposites—living, elderly men and women. For with the exception of that very minor character, Paris' Page, there are no young *dramatis personae* alive on the stage (Romeo's "man" Balthazar need not be young, and unlike Paris' servant is never addressed as "boy"). Where a young man, Benvolio, reported the details of the last two violent outbreaks, the reporter now is an old man, Lawrence. Hence this third exposure of the stage picture, with all the young protagonists dead and only the elderly left living, works as a great and visible antithesis, a visual complement to the opposites in the play's language, and a tragic summary of the central conflict between youth and age.

As the survivors of the two houses stand before their young dead and listen to Lawrence's story, the picture's emphasis is upon tragic waste. At this stage only the "ancient grudge" has survived, and the spectacle could be a reminder of that dissertation, early in the play, upon issueless death:

> *Romeo.* When [Rosaline] dies, with beauty dies her store.
> *Benvolio.* Then she hath sworn that she will still live chaste?
> *Romeo.* She hath, and in that sparing makes huge waste,
> For beauty, starved with her severity,
> Cuts beauty off from all posterity.   (I.i.215–219)

Most keenly of all, however, this spectacle of waste—the "plague" of Mercutio's curse—brings home Capulets early words about Juliet: "Earth hath swallowed all my hopes but she" (I.ii.14); and Montague's about Romeo:

> . . . the bud bit with an envious worm,
> Ere he can spread his sweet leaves to the air,
> Or dedicate his beauty to the sun.   (I.i.150–152)

The reconciliation which Granville-Barker and others call the play's true close[16] now is affirmed, and the former enemies delineate the richness of the double monument they will erect. Each is impulsively generous: but as they speak of Juliet and Romeo lying richly in effigy the actual bodies of the children are still there in sight. It is perhaps not fully appreciated that as Montague and Capulet detail the externals of a tomb we are looking on at the inside of one, at its contents.[17] Already the parents are, quite understandably, turning Romeo and Juliet into formal abstractions—figures which lie "like Patience on a monument,/Smiling at grief" (*Twelfth Night*, II.iv.117–118). It is the only way in which the elders can come to terms with their sorrow, "bury their strife" and quite literally cover up their guilt. In the disparity between the abstract gesture of a memorial and the seen reality of the bodies it will contain there is a bitter irony, which we might expect from the author of Sonnet 55, which points to the futility of "marble [and] the gilded monuments/Of princes," or from the coiner of the phrase "monumental mockery."[18] Perhaps Capulet senses the irony: he says antithetically: "As rich shall Romeo's by his lady's lie—/Poor sacrifices of our enmity!" The Prince is conscious of the bitterness of the moment: his expression "a glooming peace" hints at the true cost of this amity.

Thus in *Romeo and Juliet* first and last things are drawn together. Shakespeare uses for his purpose not only verse whose music and metaphors re-echo but also stage pictures which themselves look after and before—recapitulating what has happened, suggesting what is to come and finally, I believe, summarizing the whole tragic statement. In the assemblies which I have discussed we can see the major opposites of the play: private love in the orchard and cell scenes, public hate in the first two groupings with the Prince and the fusion of both in the final tableau. Perhaps, too, Shakespeare's use of the process which I have described helps answer the question of Benvolio's disappearance from the play. He vanishes just after his account of the second brawl—rather ironically, he fades out at that point of the action where his defense of Romeo has established him as a character in his own right, and not just a sounding-board for Romeo's sighs and Mercutio's wit. His departure has been noticed by editors, though usually only because of the problematical Q1 reading at V.iii.211, where Montague is made to say, "And young Benvolio is deceased too." "Who would notice the absence of Benvolio . . . at this moment [of tragic climax]?" asks T. J. B. Spencer, adding that the actor playing Benvolio was required for another role in this last scene.[19] But as the participants in Verona's mutinies have reassembled, to place themselves as they did before to "hear the sentence of [their] moved Prince," the reporter's role which before was filled by a young man has now been taken over by an old one. With nothing to say, Benvolio does not appear, yet in terms of what we see on stage his very absence is eloquent. If he appeared now he would mar the antithesis of young dead and old survivors.

Granville-Barker seems just to have missed *Romeo and Juliet*'s reduplication of scenes in his complaint that it is clumsy stagecraft to follow passionate Juliet in III.ii (where she has just learned of Tybalt's death and Romeo's banishment) with passionate Romeo in III.iii.[20] He is right so far as he goes: the paralleling of these scenes is more neat than progressive; and actors of Romeo know how fiendishly difficult it is to follow Juliet's scene.[21] But the scene of Romeo's passion at Lawrence's cell is more naturally answered by Juliet's quietly desperate interview with the Friar there in IV.i, when the impending wedding has made the situation even more threatening. John C. Adams asserts that Shakespeare "regarded the staging of *Romeo and Juliet* as inseparable from the total effect"[22]—although he, Richard Hosley, and others who have written (and debated) so usefully on this play have tended to concern themselves more emphatically with how the *stage* works than with how the play works. When *Romeo and Juliet* succeeds in performance the director may get the credit, as when Franco Zeffirelli is praised by John Russell Brown for his 1960 production in which "stage-business took its cue from the words spoken. . . . Phrases . . . were all directly and convincingly related to the action."[23] It is Shakespeare art—visual as well as verbal—which has prescribed the play's ideal performance in the first place.

The visual aspect of this art will be put to use again in his tragic maturity—in *King Lear*, for example. In the final scene of *Lear*, when Goneril and Regan are tidily dead off-stage, order is given to "Produce the bodies" (V.iii.230). Why should Shakespeare at this point, with Edmund dying on stage and with the calamitous entrance of dying Lear with dead Cordelia imminent, wish to burden his stage with two more bodies? Two answers come to mind: first, that Goneril and Regan have become such symbols of extra-human evil that they must be *seen* reassuringly dead; second, that Shakespeare wishes the tragic events to end as they began, bringing Lear together again with all his daughters— "The wheel is come full circle." And did Shakespeare, in an even later phase of his career when considering his stage, his *dramatis personae,* and the spirit and plot of the play he had in hand, perhaps glance back to the last scene of *Romeo and Juliet?* Towards the end of this very late play parents of great dignity and with an ancient grudge against one another meet before the inner stage in which their betrothed son and daughter are placed. The inner stage was Romeo's and Juliet's death-place, the persons now meeting before it could be in their assembling as in their old enmity reminiscent of the Montagues and Capulets, but

Here Prospero discovers Ferdinand and Miranda playing at chess.

After all, it has been said that in *The Tempest* "it is as if, at the end of his career, Shakespeare felt able at last to let Romeo and Juliet marry. But Montague must first shake hands with Capulet";[24] and the Romances with their promises of fulfilled and fruitful love (and with effigies which come to life) do counterpoise the tragic waste mourned in *Romeo and Juliet.* Whether or not Shakespeare deliberately glances at that tragedy in the last scene of *The Tempest,* it is certain that he knew the theater to be a visual as well as a verbal art. It is with this knowledge that he composes (in every sense of the word) his scenes, and in *Romeo and Juliet* as in his maturest work invites the audience to "look here, upon this picture, and on this."[25]

NOTES

1. Cf. *Comedy of Errors* I.ii.33–40 and V.i.417–418.
2. *Shakespeare and the Artist* (London, 1959), p. 17.
3. This is H. Granville-Barker's description of the new turn of events: *Prefaces to Shakespeare,* series II (London, 1930), p. 22.
4. *Hamlet* V.ii.62.
5. *Romeo and Juliet,* ed. John Dover Wilson and George Ian Duthie (Cambridge, 1955), p. xxxi. All quotations from *Romeo and Juliet* cite this edition.
6. "Preface to Shakespeare," in *Samuel Johnson: Selected Writings,* ed. R. T. Davies (London, 1965), p. 276.
7. S. T. Coleridge, *Select Poetry and Prose,* ed. S. Potter (London, 1933), p. 342.

8. *Hamlet*, II.ii.619.

9. Cf. T. J. B. Spencer's introduction to the New Penguin Shakespeare *Romeo and Juliet* (Harmondsworth, 1967), pp. 30–32.

10. Cf. IV.i. lines 6–12, 29–32.

11. T. J. B. Spencer's phrase, *Romeo and Juliet*, p. 276.

12. See Spencer's commentary on this scene, *Romeo and Juliet*, pp. 262–263.

13. Spencer, *Romeo and Juliet*, p. 277.

14. By suppressing the provocation that Mercutio gave Tybalt, Benvolio makes Tybalt seem the more guilty and Romeo a more justifiable revenger.

15. Spencer, *Romeo and Juliet*, p. 36; Brown, *Shakespeare's Dramatic Style* (London, 1970), pp. 67–68.

16. Granville-Barker, *Prefaces*, series II, p. 39; Spencer, *Romeo and Juliet*, pp. 36–37.

17. Waldo F. McNeir ("The Closing of the Capulet Tomb," *Studia Neophilologia* 28 [1956], 3–8) argues that the Prince's "Seal up the mouth of outrage for a while" is an order and cue for the tomb to be closed. "Shakespeare rightly felt, I think, that leaving the tomb and its contents open to view would interfere with a focus of interest on Friar Lawrence's story and perhaps blur the reconciliation of Capulet and Montague, the relieving note on which the tragedy ends" (7). Granville-Barker, on the other hand, writes of how at the end "plain to our sight within the tomb . . . Romeo and Juliet lie still," and points out that *Antony and Cleopatra* ends with a similar stage effect (*Prefaces*, series II, p. 30).

18. *Troilus and Cressida*, III.iii.153.

19. *Romeo and Juliet*, p. 276. Arthur Colby Sprague has found him doubled with Paris on at least one occasion (*The Doubling of Parts in Shakespeare's Plays* [London, 1966], p. 13).

20. *Prefaces*, series II, p. 20.

21. See, for example, John Gielgud, *Early Stages* (London, 1948), p. 214.

22. "Shakespeare's Use of the Stage in *Romeo and Juliet* III.v," *SQ* 7 (1956), 149. Cf. also Adams' "*Romeo and Juliet* as played on Shakespeare's Stage," *Theatre Arts* 20 (1936), 896–904 and his letters in *TLS* for Feb. 15, 1936 and May 23, 1936. Other views are expressed by Richard Hosley ("The Use of the Upper Stage in *Romeo and Juliet*," *SQ* 5 [1954], 371–384), Granville-Barker (*TLS* letters Feb. 22 and May 30, 1936), George Sampson (*TLS* letter Feb. 22, 1936), and W. J. Lawrence (*TLS* letters Feb. 29 and May 30, 1936).

23. *Shakespeare's Plays in Performance* (Harmondsworth, 1969), p. 183.
24. John Wain, *The Living World of Shakespeare* (London, 1964), p. 231.
25. *Hamlet*, III.iv.53.

Jack Jorgens

Franco Zeffirelli's *Romeo and Juliet*

Shakespeare's source for the story of Romeo and Juliet was Arthur Brooke's *The Tragicall Historye of Romeus and Juliet, written first in Italian by Bandell, and now in Englishe by Ar. Br.* (1562). In his "Address to the Reader," Brooke spoke of

> a couple of unfortunate lovers, thralling themselves to unhonest desire; neglecting the authority and advice of parents and friends; conferring their principal counsels with drunken gossips and superstitious friars (the naturally fit instruments of unchastity); attempting all adventures or peril for the attaining of their wicked lust; using auricular confession, the key of whoredom and treason, for the furtherance of their purpose; abusing the honourable name of lawful marriage to cloak the shame of stolen contracts; finally by all means of unhonest life hasting to most unhappy death.

In the story itself, however, he abandoned his heavy moralizing and showed great sympathy for both the young lovers and the Friar, and rather than tying the tragic ending to character and divine justice, rooted the cause in Fortune.

Certainly Shakespeare trusted the tale and not the teller. One of his most popular plays, written when he was about thirty and also at work on *A Midsummer Night's Dream, Romeo and Juliet* is an exuberant celebration of young love—its excitement, passion, and lyricism. Despite the ominous Prologue, which foretells the sacrifice of the young to "bury their parents' strife," critics often note that this love story has many of the characteristics of Shakespeare's romantic comedies: the fool Mercutio, the bawdy,

Reprinted from *Shakespeare on Film*. Bloomington: Indiana University Press, 1977, pp. 79–91, by permission.

funny Nurse, the stereotypical villain Tybalt, the blocking of the loves of the young by the values and laws of the old, ornamented verse, domestic detail, and even the motif of dreaming. Only with the death of Mercutio does the story become a tragedy of Fate and begin its breathless race toward the tomb.

What Romeo and Juliet lack in depth of character they make up in energy, beautiful innocence, and spontaneity. If the arc of their rise and fall seems unusually intense and brilliant, it is because it is set against a rich, dark background. Love clashes with hate, the ideal with the real. Romeo and Juliet's romance avoids sentimentality because it must pass through the fires of the Nurse's jokes and meandering, trivial, pragmatic mind, Mercutio's bawdy wit, the demands of duty and honor, the ugly rigidities of the old, and the feud, which though bound up with Fate seems to have a life of its own. Shakespeare's pattern seems true because it is never a simple one. If the parents want to live their lives over again through their children, they also have great affection and hope for them. Blended with the impulses of the young toward rebellion are hot tempers and the need to prove their maturity, which keep the feud alive when the old are ready to let it die. Analogous to the literal tragedy that the young and innocent are sometimes cruelly cut off in life is the figurative one that youth, innocence, spontaneity, passion die as we grow older—they are sacrificed to meaningless conflicts, adult responsibilities, and accommodating oneself to a fallen world.

Zeffirelli's *Romeo and Juliet*, based loosely on his energetic stage production for the London Old Vic in 1960, is the most popular and financially successful Shakespeare film yet made. It shares with his *Shrew* rich colors and textures, elegantly reconstructed Renaissance interiors and costumes bathed in idyllic golden light and resembling paintings by the old masters. It is spectacular, extravagant, full of nervous motion, energy, camera movement, rapid cutting. We find the same frenetically active extras and strenuous physicality in the clowning of the Maskers before Capulet's ball and the fights in the square that we find in Petruchio's pursuit of Kate and their destruction of Paduan proprieties. (The saturnalian pattern is at work here too, but the outcome is deadly, not festive.) The director fills his frame with motion, people, and things in an effort to give the film a realistic solidity, fullness, and spontaneity. At times it becomes almost operatic in its excess. As in *Shrew* there is so much music that one expects the actors suddenly to burst into song. Yet the acting, far from being operatic, is in a fresh, nontheatrical, nonelocutionary style. The director uses a pared down text, often interrupts the flow of the lines with entertaining gestures and sounds, and generally keeps the talk out of the way of the action according to the convention of film realism.

Critics have been harsh with Zeffirelli's rash, reckless style. John Simon complained of what he called "centrifugality."[1] In comparing *Romeo and Juliet* with Kozintsev's *Hamlet*, Ronald Hayman argued that

> wasting visual effects is quite as bad as wasting words, and where Kozintsev is tautly economic, Zeffirelli is loosely lavish. Each visual detail, each movement of the actors and each movement of the camera means something in Kozintsev, whereas Zeffirelli's camera wanders all over Verona, grabbing at anything that catches its eye, and putting in movements (or even dances like the gratuitous Moresca at the Capulets' ball) for the sake of their immediate photogenic appeal.[2]

Though we may question whether a "tautly economic" style would really suit this play, there is truth in Hayman's objections. Zeffirelli's films sometimes veer out of control, lapse into visual clichés, caricatures, and sentimentality, wander between muddled motivations and geography and a tendency to make everything simple and obvious. Still, he is no mere mindless popularizer of Shakespeare. Like *Shrew*, *Romeo and Juliet* is a critically underrated film which has some interesting dimensions. When he has things under control, Zeffirelli's images embody interpretative truths about the play very well.

The panoramic opening shot of *Romeo and Juliet* (a tribute to the opening of Olivier's *Henry V*—he even has Olivier reading the prologue) strikes many as a conventional establishing shot, an attempt to be "scenic." But Zeffirelli is doing here what the critics have not credited him with doing—using imagery in a significant way. To begin with, the shot provides a visual equivalent to the godlike, distant, formal tone and style of the prologue which contrasts so vividly with the passion and violence inside Verona's walls. As the camera pans over deathly still Verona, bathed in early morning light, the city is shrouded in fog. There is a formal rightness in this image, for the white shroud is one of the central motifs of the film. It recurs in Mercutio's white handkerchief, which at various times becomes his apron as he kneels in mock prayer and mimes the priest "dream-ing of an-o-ther ben-i-fice" (a glance at Friar Laurence?), his needle work (not long after, we see Juliet sewing), his contraceptive as he plays the gossip and the bawdy jokester with the Nurse, his deathlike mask ("blah, blah, blah") and washrag in the hot square, and finally his bandage which hides the bloody fatal wound and is rubbed in Tybalt's face by Romeo. The white shroud also appears in the Nurse's veil ("A sail! A sail!"), in the sheets and gauze curtains in Juliet's room, and in the winding sheets in Juliet's funeral and covering the corpses in the Capulet tomb. Opposing the fog-shrouded city of death in the opening shot is the burning circle of the sun. The camera zooms rapidly in on it (an overused device in this film) until it fills the screen with blinding orange light, making of it a symbol of the opposing passions of the play. It represents not only the love of Romeo and Juliet (the sun greets them in bed and shines at their funeral), of Romeo and Mercutio, and of the Nurse and Juliet, but also the general hatred unleased in the feud—the frustrated rage of Tybalt, Mercutio, Romeo, and Prince Escalus. The symbol captures the underlying unity of emotions which come together dialectically at the end of the play.

Zeffirelli's splashy style is evident in the two big scenes of the film, Capulet's ball and the fatal duels in the square. Each is shamelessly milked for emotion, the dance for the tenderness and lyricism and lyricism of young love, including the sticky sweet song "What is a Youth?" and the fights for the raw excitement of seeing mockery and tests of skill turn into a fight to the death as well as the shock and pain of seeing Mercutio die while his friends laugh, thinking it is another of his jokes. Each scene is filled with spectacle: the ball with swirling costumes, candles, torches, glasses of wine, heaps of fruit, diffused gold backgrounds, and the comic faces among the guests (including a tall, homely, moon-eyed girl who stares down at Juliet), and the duels with Mercutio's clowning and playing to his audience even in his bravura death, and the vicious, dirty, unromantic fight to the death between Romeo and Tybalt, shot in the midst of the dust with a hand-held camera and punctuated with nervous bursts of cuts, climaxing with Tybalt's running on Romeo's sword (a grim repetition of the accidental stabbing of Mercutio) and his sightless corpse falling on top of Romeo. Yet, in these scenes Zeffirelli does more than just immerse his audience in action and spectacle. Each scene presents a complicated pattern of characters, relationships, and themes central to Zeffirelli's interpretation of the play.

For Zeffirelli, language is primarily a key to character. He is more interested in "the poetry of human relationships" than in ideas, imagery, and the music of the words,[3] and he is not timid about fleshing out characters roughly sketched by Shakespeare. Lady Capulet, for example, is at the hub of the continuing feud. In her appearances before the ball, we learn that her marriage to the older Capulet is not a happy one. As the camera tastelessly zooms in on her sour face and a violin comically whines on the sound track, it is all too evident that Capulet has learned about girls being marred by early marriage and motherhood from personal experience. Capulet's remark to Paris that Juliet will be his only heir and, later, his joking lament for his lost youth at the ball suggest that he is impotent, that what is left of his marriage is the social arrangement. Lady Capulet, on the other hand, is still young, vain about her looks (we see her primping and being made up), uncomfortable with a nearly grown daughter, in need of the Nurse when she must broach the subject of marriage, in need of Capulet when Juliet is disobedient. At the ball we learn more about the conflict between Lady Capulet and her husband. He is a *nouveau riche*, lacking the polish and refinement of his guests, while she is a daughter of the old aristocracy, embarrassed by her *gauche*, gregarious spouse, positively withering in her irony as she reprimands Capulet and Tybalt for quarrelling at the ball (with a hostess's smile: "*well said* my hearts!").

In a sense, the Capulet marriage is a recapitulation of the larger conflict between the Capulets and the Montagues, who, Zeffirelli said, "are a noble, military family who have gone to seed. They are in decline. They produce only students—Romeo learns verses and Benvolio carries books. The Capulets are a rich merchant family, full of social climbers, men of wealth as well as men of action."[4] Louis Gianetti notes that the bright colors worn by middle aged, clean-shaven Capulet contrast with the dark robes of grey-bearded Montague.[5] Lady Capulet's refusal to help Juliet is thus more clearly motivated in the film. She is anxious to shore up the respectability of her family with an alliance with Paris; she is uneasy in the role of mother and annoyed that Juliet's stubbornness has subjected her to Capulet's anger. Underneath, too, one guesses that she welcomes the opportunity to subject Juliet (obviously Capulet's favorite) to the unhappiness she herself suffers by marrying her to a man she does not love. Lady Capulet is further implicated in the feud in that her refuge from her husband is handsome, virile, young Tybalt, her dancing partner at the ball, the "young princox" who submits to her when he will not to his uncle. The intensity of her grief when, with her hair down, she cries to Prince Escalus for justice (revenge) reflects the loss of much more than a favorite nephew.[6] This frustrating relationship also clarifies the keenness of Tybalt's anger, his anxiousness to prove his manhood, to uphold family honor, and to prevent Juliet from "consorting" with Romeo.

In the duels, Zeffirelli is once again interested in "the poetry of human relationships." There is deep friendship, even love, between Romeo and Mercutio. Mercutio's mercurial showmanship seems aimed at Romeo, and his anger, when Romeo is off sighing for love or making a milksop of himself before Tybalt, is tinged with jealousy. How could a friend abandon male comradery for "a smock"? These feelings, along with the oppressive heat, general boredom, and shallowness of Benvolio, make Mercutio push Tybalt too far and set the wheels of Fate in motion. The combatants are natural opposites. Tybalt fights with strength and skill, Mercutio with resiliency, wit, and a talent for doing the unexpected. Tybalt frightens and threatens his victim (he puts a sword to Mercutio's throat and lets him sweat, cuts off a lock of his hair), while Mercutio ridicules his (by bandying words while baptizing himself in the fountain, whistling nonchalantly when cornered, doing pratfalls and running in mock fear, arming Tybalt with a pitchfork, and forcing him to retreat by sharpening one sword on the other before his face). This ingrained antipathy between Mercutio and Tybalt—Tybalt's need to humiliate an opponent, Mercutio's need to flirt with danger (very near a death wish)—and Romeo's guilt, first at abandoning Mercutio and then at causing his death, come together to accelerate the tragic movement begun at the ball.

Zeffirelli's *Romeo and Juliet* does not have particularly distinguished readings of the verse, being in this respect at the opposite end of the spectrum from the articulate readings of Olivier's films or Peter Hall's *A Midsummer Night's Dream*. This was in part lack of skill and in part artistic choice. "What matters is modernity of feeling rhythm, modernity inside. The verse must always have an intimate rhythm, the rhythm of reality. It must never become music."[7] The ball and the fight heighten the contrast in the film between the young who *do* and the old who *talk*. "What

Zeffirelli suggests is that the means of communication between the young, or those who understand the young, is not essentially words, as it is for the older generation, but gesture and action."[8] Romeo and Juliet fall in love at the ball through looking and touching more than through words. Tybalt need only look at Juliet to know what has happened. In the duel, and earlier when he sports a death mask, raves in an empty square, and lifts up the Nurse's skirts, it is what Mercutio does as much as what he says that makes him so bawdy, irreverent, erratically alive. Like the lovers, the young bloods of the square "speak" with their bodies and their "weapons." The young distrust the rhetoric of the old: Juliet asks "what's in a name?" Mercutio responds to Benvolio's echoing of parental cautions with "blah, blah, blah," and Romeo is so impatient with Friar Laurence's tired saws while awaiting Juliet that he fills in the next word each time the holy man pauses. The impotent old, on the other hand, talk and talk, give worldly advice like the Nurse, send tardy letters and lend spiritual guidance like the Friar, or lecture and threaten like Capulet and the Prince. They seem overly deliberate, unspontaneous, slow compared with the young. That is why they are unable to help or even to understand.

Zeffirelli not only used the ball and the duel scenes to entertain, to further characterization, and to contrast young and old, he also displays something of Shakespeare's analogic habit of mind by underscoring the parallels between rituals of love and hate. Both scenes are ironic. Capulet intends the dance to provide a respite from the feud, to be a gesture of peace, a ritual of harmony in which his enemies are welcomed as his friends. Instead, it pours fuel on the glowing coals. Like Benvolio, Romeo tries to keep the peace in the fight scene, but he only manages to make "worm's meat" of Mercutio and Tybalt and get himself banished from Verona and his new wife. The good intentions of old and young go for naught. Hence, the ball and the fights are thematically linked by the motif of the circle,[9] which was first introduced in the opening shot of the sun, and is echoed later on the church floor at the marriage of Romeo and Juliet. The dance is choreographed as a symbolic feud, beginning with two separate circles of dancers and shifting to two concentric circles moving in opposite directions. In an analogue of the overall movement of the play, after the dance the crowd merges into one static circle as a singer of a melancholy song of love and death performs. The "dances" of the duellists also take place in a circle formed by spectators. Following Shakespeare, Zeffirelli shows that love and hate, and the rituals Verona has generated around these passions—the dance and the duel—are intimately related. In *Shrew* Zeffirelli found a play which celebrates the liberating and creative aspects of love. In *Romeo and Juliet* he found a play which focuses on *eros*, the destructive aspect of love (between Capulet and Lady Capulet, Romeo and Juliet, Romeo and Mercutio, the Nurse and Juliet, Lady Capulet and Tybalt, Friar Laurence and Romeo).

In many ways, this film is a "youth movie" of the 1960s which glorifies the young and caricatures the old, a Renaissance *Graduate*. While Romeo acquires a stubble of a beard and defies the stars, and Juliet learns that she must stand alone when her parents and the Nurse abandon her, we have little sense that they grow up. They are Adam and Eve in the Edenic greenery of Capulet's garden and never lose the golden aura of innocence which insulates them from reality. Romeo's way of opposing the feud is to wander the streets alone sniffing flowers and sighing with melancholy, avoiding his parents and friends, playing at love. Through cuts in the text, Romeo is not forced to take advantage of the ugly, dehumanizing poverty of the apothecary, nor is he guilty of a second murder, that of Paris.

Juliet begins the film as a laughing girl running playfully through the house, becomes a credible teenager in love at the ball and in the balcony scene, and at least starts to mature when, abandoned by her parents, she turns to the Nurse for comfort and finds none. Shakespeare expresses the moment verbally:

> Ancient damnation! O most wicked fiend!
> Is it more sin to wish me thus forsworn,
> Or to dispraise my lord with that same tongue
> Which she hath praised him with above compare
> So many thousand times? Go, counselor!
> Thou and my bosom henceforth shall be twain.

Zeffirelli says it with fewer words. Sadly advising Juliet to forget Romeo and marry Paris, forcing herself to praise the County, the Nurse makes up the bed in which Romeo and Juliet hours before consummated their marriage. To her a little straightening of the sheets can make everything as it was before. Juliet's response is simply "go!" The Nurse reaches out to touch and reassure her, but Juliet backs away. The Nurse goes to the door, looks back for the conciliatory look she had always found before, and, finding none, backs out of the room, crushed, bowing as she closes the door like one of the common servants. This, however, is the extent of Juliet's growth. Finally, there is no real sense of maturity or eroticism in their love. As Pauline Kael wickedly remarked, theirs is a "toy marriage."[10] It is damaging that Mercutio seems to feel and know more than Romeo and Juliet. He dies in irony and anger. They sob uncontrollably at losing each other. The limitations and the virtues of Zeffirelli's portrayal of Verona's youth are summed up in John Russell Brown's description of the original stage production.

> All the youth of Verona were at ease. Running and sauntering, they were immediately recognizable as unaffected teenagers; they ate apples and threw them, splashed each other with water, mocked, laughed, shouted; they became serious, sulked, were puzzled; they misunderstood confidently and expressed emotion freely. . . . [Zeffirelli] gave prominence to a sense of wonder, gentleness, strong affection, clear emotion and, sometimes, fine sentiment, as well as to high spirits and casual behavior.[11]

In comparison to the young, Brown noted, the old lacked conviction, and this carries over to the film. Their grief is not particularly moving. They often seem two-dimensional (in the zoom-in on Lady Capulet's face or Friar Laurence's leering at Juliet through his test tubes). The Prince has his moments of ferocity when breaking up the opening brawl on his magnificent, nervous horse with the sun burning behind him, and again at the conclusion. And the Nurse, a delightful mock nun who is eager to find in Juliet the daughter she lost, steals wine at the ball, refuses and then takes Romeo's money, rages at Mercutio, is human throughout—right to the moment when she stares stunned at the bodies of the two lovers at the end. But in general the older characters are less convincing, seem hastily sketched in, and this causes an imbalance. What keeps the film from being totally one-sided is the fatal, self-destructive urge in these youths. They are reckless, bored, cynical—children of the feud, just as a generation of Americans were children of Vietnam. They are *implicated* in keeping the feud going. It provides them an outlet for feelings of jealousy, insecurity, and rage not merely at the old and everything they are responsible for but at mortality in all its forms. Even Romeo is not always glamorized, turning into a bloodthirsty animal as he goes after Tybalt. In this sense, Zeffirelli does preserve Shakespeare's balance between old and young.

In shaping the text for the film, Zeffirelli and his fellow scriptwriters accelerated the already rapid sequence of events, reduced speeches to stress the inarticulateness of the young, and stripped away much of the self-conscious verbal artifice which clashes with realistic surfaces and colloquial readings. For example, Escalus's ornamented image is cut:

> What, ho! You men, you beasts,
> That quench the fire of your pernicious rage
> With purple fountains issuing from your veins!

Extended conceits are removed, such as Lady Capulet's urging Juliet to "read o'er the volume of young Paris' face" (the figure is elaborated in "beauty's pen," "margent of his eyes," "unbound lover," "gold clasps," and "golden story"). The film avoids the formal idiom of Juliet's grieving over the death of Tybalt or of the Capulets' mourning over the supposed death of Juliet. In the play Romeo uses oxymoron to embody the fundamental paradox of love and hate:

> Why then, O brawling love, O loving hate,
> O anything of nothing first create!
> O heavy lightness, serious vanity,
> Misshapen chaos of well-seeming forms,
> Feather of lead, bright smoke, cold fire, sick health,
> Still-waking sleep, that is not what it is!
> This love feel I, that feel no love in this.

Zeffirelli uses *visual* contrasts, shows the maimed survivors of the brawl and their mourning kin as they interrupt flower-sniffing Romeo's talk with Benvolio (Romeo throws the flower on the stones, walks away in disgust). Some of Zeffirelli's cuts (especially those in the cumbersome final scene) are usual on the stage and rescue what is in some ways an immature play from its own excesses. Some are compensated for by adequate gestures and visual imagery, such as the fierce, proud look on Tybalt's face as he turns to see Juliet sighing over Romeo at the ball, replacing "I will withdraw; but this intrusion shall/Now seeming sweet, convert to bitt'rest gall." Some substitutions are less successful, as when a dull shot of Italian countryside replaces

The grey-eyed morn smiles on the frowning night,
Check'ring the eastern clouds with streaks of light;
And flecked darkness like a drunkard reels
From forth day's path and Titan's burning wheels.

In keeping with the anti-intellectual tone of his films, Zeffirelli makes a philosophically thin play even thinner by cutting the Friar's thoughts that "The earth that's nature's mother is her tomb./What is her burying ground, that is her womb," and his wonder at a world where the vilest things do good and virtue can become vice. Also, occasionally cuts result in missed dramatic opportunities. For a director who underscores the structural and thematic relations between the Capulets' ball and the duels, as well as between the balcony scene and the deaths of the lovers, for example, it was a remarkable oversight to omit Shakespeare's striking transition from the Capulets' festive wedding preparations to mourning and funeral preparations when Juliet is found dead.

Many have complained that Zeffirelli's ornate brand of realism is inappropriate to tragedy. Certainly one would not like to see *King Lear* in his style. Yet in view of the strong elements of romantic comedy in the first half of *Romeo and Juliet*, the bright colors, constant movement, and rich detail seem true to the original. And often Zeffirelli foreshadows the darker, bleaker moments to come by cutting across this festive style: when Mercutio is bellowing in the empty square bathed in eerie blue light, when Juliet pauses in the shadows of Capulet's courtyard, and when Romeo is pursued along a dark, tunnellike street. The dust and stone of the hot town square contrasts with the warm, colorful interiors, and the imprisoning walls and mazelike streets symbolizing centuries of tradition and a social system hardened against change underscore the central theme of this and Castellani's film—"youth against a hostile society."[12]

Most important, the style of the film changes radically after the death of Mercutio; it is drained of its busy look and festive colors. Juliet's room dominated by whites, the somber tones of Friar Laurence's cell, the dark of Capulet's house, the subdued funeral for Juliet, Romeo's shadowy house in exile, the Capulets' tomb, and the desolate wind-blown square filled with mourners in black—all these serve to erase the festivity and effectively embody Shakespeare's shift in tone. And Zeffirelli not only shows his protagonists imprisoned in colorlessness and stone, he shows them imprisoned in a pattern of events. Visually, he emphasizes the symmetry of the escalating conflicts from the opening brawl to the deaths of Mercutio and Tybalt to the deaths of Romeo and Juliet. Three times the Montagues and Capulets come before the Prince, and three times he chastizes them, but only the last time, when the cost has been great enough, do the families see that they are destroying themselves by allowing the feud to continue. The love which blossomed in a garden withers in a tomb. The shrouded city becomes a tomb. As in *Throne of Blood*, the artistic patterning which provides the work with coherence and meaning becomes an embodiment of Fate which enmeshes the principal characters.

Some films of Shakespeare's tragedies end with a close-up of the face of the hero (Richardson's *Hamlet*, Brook's *King Lear*, Mankiewicz's *Julius Caesar*), placing emphasis upon the individual fall. Some conclude with a movement outward or upward, the society being involved in a final ritual (Welles's *Othello*, Olivier's *Hamlet*, Kozintsev's *Hamlet*). Some are circular (Kurosawa's *Throne of Blood*, Welles's *Macbeth*, Polanski's *Macbeth*), stressing the continuing power of the pattern. Zeffirelli's conclusion is a blend of the latter two. In the end the rituals of love and death merge. The bells which continually remind us of passing time, and celebrate the wedding, now become funeral bells. The Montagues and the Capulets, who streamed twice before into the square in parallel linear movements, now form a single procession as they bear Romeo and Juliet to be buried in their wedding garments. All the people we care about are dead, and with them have gone spontaneity, energy, and innocence. The silence in the sunlit square is broken only by the tolling bell, muffled footsteps on the stones, and the whistling wind. Compositions are rigidly symmetrical as the families gather on the steps of the church. The chaos of the brawls has been replaced by order, but it is a dead order. The camera picks out somber faces (especially the Nurse's), which reflect guilt, recognition, a sense of loss. Then emphasis shifts to the Prince and the Shakespearean theme of "responsibility learnt in adversity."[13] In the sole outburst of passion, the Prince's formal pronouncement, "all are punished," becomes a howl of rage and pain, "All are punished!"

As the two families file through the cathedral door toward the camera and the credits pass over the screen, there are gestures of consolement and reconciliation. The feud is over. But when they have all filed past, and the credits are through, the camera holds on the castellated wall towering over Verona's empty square, echoing the second shot of the film and providing a final symbol of division, war, imprisonment, continuity with the past. If *this* conflict has ended, conflict itself has not.

Zeffirelli's *Romeo and Juliet* is in most ways superior to the films by Cukor (1936) and Castellani (1954). It has energy, humor, and life where the others do not. No one would be tempted to say of it, as George Bernard Shaw said of Forbes-Robertson's production in 1895, that "the duel scene has none of the murderous excitement which is the whole dramatic point of it."[14] It avoids the static, ornate prettiness of the studio sets of the 1936 film, yet despite some excesses, never becomes a distractingly beautiful travelogue of Renaissance Italy the way the 1954 film often does. Leonard Whiting and Olivia Hussey are credible and likeable lovers as Leslie Howard and Norma Shearer or Laurence Harvey and Susan Shentall are not.

However, one may like the film for all its action, emotional power, and sense of theme and structure and still be aware that this *Romeo and Juliet*, transforming tragedy into a story of sentiment and pathos, is a less mature work than Shakespeare's. It is not merely that the hero and heroine do not ripen in understanding. It is that their deaths are conceived too simply. The sorrow, the sense of loss, the sexual overtones of "death" are present at the end, but the insight and defiant anger are missing. Neither Romeo nor Juliet senses the larger pattern. They never see what a corrupt and flawed world it is that they are leaving, never give any indication that they know how they contributed to their own downfall, and never understand that love of such intensity not only cannot last but is self-destructive. Sorrow at losing each other is not coming to terms with life or death. The clear-sighted calm and sense of inevitability with which Shakespeare's tragic hero and heroine greet their end have disappeared.

NOTES

1. John Simon, *Movies into Film* (New York, 1970), p. 107.

2. "Shakespeare on the Screen," *Times Literary Supplement* (London), Sept. 26, 1968, p. 1082.

3. Franco Zeffirelli in *Directors on Directing*, ed. Toby Cole and Helen Crich Chinoy (Indianapolis: Bobbs-Merrill, 1963), p. 440.

4. *Ibid.*, p. 439.

5. Louis Gianetti, *Understanding Movies* (Englewood Cliffs: Prentice-Hall, 1972), p. 154.

6. Albert R. Cirillo, "The Art of Franco Zeffirelli and Shakespeare's *Romeo and Juliet*," *TriQuarterly* 16 (Fall 1969), 81.

7. Zeffirelli, in *Directors on Directing*, p. 440.

8. Cirillo, "The Art . . .," p. 82.

9. *Ibid.*, p. 87.

10. Pauline Kael, *Going Steady* (New York: Bantam, 1971), p. 189.

11. John Russell Brown, *Shakespeare's Plays in Performance* (New York: St. Martin's, 1967), p. 168.

12. Paul Jorgensen, "Castellani's *Romeo and Juliet:* Intention and Response," *Film Quarterly* 10 (1955), 1.

13. Brown, *Shakespeare's Plays . . .*, p. 176.

14. *Shaw on Shakespeare*, ed. Edwin Wilson (New York: Dutton, 1961), p. 179.

Dame Peggy Ashcroft

From *Shakespeare in Perspective*

Every Shakespearean actor is frequently asked to name a favourite play or part.[1] There isn't really an answer, although I would unhesitatingly put both the title part and the play, *Romeo and Juliet*, in my top . . . four. There has been a recent fashion in the theatre to define a certain kind of play as a 'black comedy'. I would define *Romeo and Juliet* as a 'golden tragedy'. George Meredith wrote:

> . . . In tragic life, God wot,
> No villain need be! Passions spin the plot:
> We are betrayed by what is false within.

Tragic heroes such as Macbeth and Hamlet do have something 'false within'. It is after all the definition of a tragic character that his fate lies in himself and in his own weakness. Romeo and Juliet are thus not strictly speaking tragic characters, since they are betrayed by what is false without. They are the epitome of youth awakening to life, joy, love and fidelity. Theirs is the tragedy of circumstance, which perhaps makes it all the more poignant. Is it youth betrayed by age or love destroyed by hate? I think that both these are simplifications. It is true that they are the victims of a family feud, but as the play unfolds one sees everything that happens as a series of fatal accidents. We are never told the cause of the 'ancient grudge' between the Capulets and the Montagues, which the Chorus refers to at the very beginning of the play. It is accepted as a fact that the servants of the two houses, as well as the young bloods, should be ready to be at each others' throats. But we don't feel that this 'ancient

Reprinted with permission of the author from *Shakespeare in Perspective*, Vol. 1, edited by Roger Sales. London: Ariel Books, 1982, pp. 25–30.

grudge' is past remedy. After the opening brawl has been put down by Escalus, the Prince of Verona, Old Montague, who is Romeo's father, asks 'who set this ancient quarrel new abroach'. Lady Montague is concerned for Romeo's safety:

> O, where is Romeo? Saw you him to-day?
> Right glad I am he was not at this fray.   (1.1.114–5)

Capulet, who is Juliet's father, also appears to be concerned with keeping the peace. He refuses to let Tybalt attack the masked gate-crasher at the feast. But what we now call the collision course is already set in motion. The background of explosive anger and danger is an essential part of it, as is the heat of Verona and the high spirits of its youth, whether picking quarrels or falling in love.

And so the scene is set for the two lovers. Romeo is in love with love and so has no difficulty convincing himself that he loves fair Rosaline. Juliet is a child, not yet fourteen. When asked by her mother what she feels about marriage, she replies 'it is an honour that I dream not of'. Yet by the end of Act One she and Romeo have met at her father's feast and fallen in love at first sight. This is dramatised in the form of an exquisite sonnet:

> ROMEO: If I profane with my unworthiest hand
> This holy shrine, the gentle fine is this:
> My lips, two blushing pilgrims, ready stand
> To smooth that rough touch with a tender kiss.
> JULIET: Good pilgrim, you do wrong your hand too much,
> Which mannerly devotion shows in this;
> For saints have hands that pilgrims' hands do touch,
> And palm to palm is holy palmers' kiss.
> ROMEO: Have not saints lips, and holy palmers too?
> JULIET: Ay, pilgrim, lips that they must use in pray'r.
> ROMEO: O, then, dear saint, let lips do what hands do!
> Then pray; grant though, lest faith turn to despair.
> JULIET: Saints do not move, though grant for prayers' sake.
> ROMEO: Then move not while my prayer's effect I take.
>   (1.5-91–104)

It is only at the end of the feast that they discover that they have each fallen in love with their fated enemy.

I was fortunate enough to attempt Juliet three times in the theatre and a fourth on radio. The first time was when I was twenty-three in John Gielgud's first-ever production. This was for OUDS, the Oxford University Dramatic Society, with George Devine as Mercutio, Christopher Hassell as Romeo, William Devlin as Tybalt, Hugh Hunt as Friar Lawrence and Terence Rattigan as the First Musician. The First Musician only has a few lines, one of them after Juliet's apparent death: 'Faith, we may put up our pipes and be gone'. Terry told me many years later that he thought I looked extremely critical of his interpretation as I lay on my bed. In fact, I was steeling myself not to cry, knowing that Edith Evans as the Nurse was about to say:

> Honest good fellows, ah, put up, put up;
> For well you know this is a pitiful case. (4.5.97–9)

Philip Hope Wallace wrote, 'This is the Nurse as Shakespeare might have dreamt of seeing it played. Each syllable has a perfect identification with the character'. He was obviously thinking of Edith's interpretation of the Nurse's great speeches:

> Even or odd, of all the days in the year,
> Come Lammas Eve at night shall she be fourteen.
> Susan and she—God rest all Christian souls!—
> Were of an age. Well, Susan is with God;
> She was too good for me. But, as I said,
> On Lammas Eve at night shall she be fourteen;
> That shall she, marry; I remember it well.
> 'Tis since the earthquake now eleven years;
> And she was wean'd—I never shall forget it—
> Of all the days of the year, upon that day;
> For I had then laid wormwood to my dug,
> Sitting in the sun under the dove-house wall;
> My lord and you were then at Mantua.
> Nay, I do bear a brain. (1.3.17–30)

Perhaps for those who don't know this piece of ancient history I should explain that the OUDS always presented their winter production with a professional director and professional actresses. Whether that was a good idea or not is debatable. But I think it was a wonderful 'try-out' for John's original conception of the play. He saw it as above all a play about youth, to be acted by young men. It was a fast-moving, indeed a headlong and exhilarating production, on an open stage. There were no pauses between the scenes, which was unusual in those days. This kept the tension and the ironic twists of fate always before the audience.

Romeo and Juliet meet, they love and they marry. Tybalt kills Romeo's friend Mercutio. Romeo kills Tybalt and is banished. The lovers consummate their marriage. Juliet is then betrothed by her father to Paris. She goes to Friar Lawrence, who had married her to Romeo. He gives her a potion which will simulate death and she is taken to the family vault. Romeo, hearing of her death, returns and finds her on her bier. Juliet wakes to find that he has killed himself. She then kills herself with his dagger. In the finale the parents are reconciled over the bodies of their children after they have heard Friar Lawrence's account of the events. That is the play in synopsis, but because of its extraordinary vivid reality and the depth of all the characters in it, it is, as well as a lyrical tragedy, an intensely human domestic drama. The lovers are framed by marvellously rich characters: Capulet, Friar Lawrence, Peter, Paris, Tybalt and, above all, two of Shakespeare's greatest characters, the Nurse, a rival to Falstaff in her earthy humanity, and Mercutio, the wit and eternal joker who is always remembered for the Queen Mab speech and his death scene. This scene is a central climax in the play and it is from that moment on that all the disasters occur.

My first attempt at Juliet was inevitably agonising as I was plagued by the idea of it being 'a great tragic role'. I learnt after that production, in a subsequent one at the Old Vic a year later, that it is essential for Juliet to be a child of fourteen. If that is credible, then her awakening, her passion, her refusal to compromise and, finally, her tragedy take care of themselves. So I think my third venture, in John's second production of the play when Laurence Olivier and he shared the roles of Romeo and Mercutio, came near to fully achieving John's original conception of the youthful nature of the play. Olivier's Romeo, a rash boy of sixteen, was a definitive one and Edith was once again our cornerstone as the Nurse. I know that we were all very proud to hear that Harley Granville-Barker thought it was 'by far the best bit of Shakespeare' he had seen for years.

I know it has been said that Juliet is an impossible part to play because, by the time an actress is experienced enough to play her, she's too old to look the part. I really think that is nonsense. An actress up to twenty years older than Juliet, if she is really capable of playing the part, is not too old to be convincing. Of course a very young girl, especially on the screen, will be at a great advantage, but she has to encounter a number of technical difficulties. These difficulties are, I would say, two-fold. Firstly, she has to be able to sustain a very long and demanding part on the stage. Secondly, she has to deal at times with extremely complicated verbal fireworks. The part is all simplicity, whereas the language is often complex in the extreme. Shakespeare was still experimenting with language. He uses verse and prose alternatively, as in all the plays, but at the height of a dramatic scene in *Romeo and Juliet* he sometimes uses conceits and puns, which it is difficult to contain within the emotion. For instance, in the scene when the Nurse brings the news of the deaths of Tybalt and Mercutio, Juliet at first thinks that Romeo has been killed as well:

> What devil art thou that dost torment me thus?
> This torture should be roar'd in dismal hell.
> Hath Romeo slain himself? Say thou but 'I'
> And that bare vowel I shall poison more
> Than the death-darting eye of cockatrice.
> I am not I if there be such an 'I';
> Or those eyes shut that makes thee answer 'I'.
> If he be slain, say 'I'; or if not, 'No';
> Brief sounds determine of my weal or woe.   (3.2.43–51)

Compare the punning difficulties of such a speech with the directness of a later one, after the Nurse has tried to persuade her to marry Paris:

> Ancient damnation! O most wicked friend!
> Is it more sin to wish me thus forsworn,
> Or to dispraise my lord with that same tongue
> Which she hath prais'd him with above compare
> So many thousand times? Go, counsellor;
> Thou and my bosom henceforth shall be twain.
> I'll to the friar to know his remedy;
> If all else fail, myself have power to die.   (3.5.236–43)

Of the productions I have seen, by far the most memorable was Franco Zeffirelli's at the Old Vic. He achieved that heat, danger and Italianate inflammability that we had striven for. I only quarrelled with some of his 'cuts'. As I have already said, this background of explosive anger and danger is an essential part of the play, as is the heat of Verona and the high spirits of its youth in picking quarrels or falling in love.

NOTE

1. Dame Peggy Ashcroft, a director of the Royal Shakespeare
Company, played every leading lady in the canon except for Lady
Macbeth.

Julie Harris

From *The Guild Shakespeare*

I grew up in Michigan, and never saw a production of *Romeo and Juliet* on stage when I was young. I did see the movie starring Norma Shearer and Leslie Howard with John Barrymore as Mercutio. Those actors were not in their teens when they acted in the film, and I supposed that the roles should always be played by grown-ups. Later I attended a production of the play in England; it was in the early 1950s when I first went to visit London and traveled to Stratford-upon-Avon to see Shakespeare's home and the theatre where his plays are produced. Romeo was Laurence Harvey, and Zena Walker was Juliet. But for me it was still a play about older young people.

When Michael Langham asked me to play Juliet in 1960[1] at the Stratford Festival Theatre founded by Tyrone Guthrie in Stratford, Canada, I was terrified. Other than playing the Third Witch in the "Scottish" play (a production of *Macbeth* starring Michael Redgrave and Flora Robson), I had no experience acting in Shakespeare's plays.

Michael Langham came to New York City where I lived, and with great sensitivity and patience he guided me through the play scene by scene. He gave me a copy of the old Italian legend of Romeo and Juliet by Luigi da Porto. The legend found its way to England *and* to Shakespeare, for *Romeo and Juliet* was based on an English reworking of da Porto's story.

No matter how frightened I was of playing Juliet, I was challenged too: by the part, by the miraculous play itself, by the genius of the poetry, and by the uniqueness of the feelings

Reprinted from *The Guild Shakespeare*, Vol. 2. New York: GuildAmerica Books, 1989, pp. vii–x.

expressed by a girl not yet fourteen—and I was thirty-five years old!

With Michael leading me through the play, my understanding increased and my terrors fell away—well, a little way away. But I did wonder how I could ever play the scene in which Juliet's Nurse comes to Juliet and tells her that her kinsman Tybalt is dead. And killed by Romeo. *And* Romeo banished! Juliet must go from shock at the news of Tybalt's death, to relief that Romeo is alive, to despair at knowing that Romeo has been banished and she has lost him! All these feelings tumble out in a cascade of emotion.

After the period of rehearsals at Stratford I was prepared to play Juliet, and I longed to be able to fill every moment with truth. But I didn't really realize what strength it would take to carry those three hours. Fortunately I had so much help: Kate Reid as the Nurse, Christopher Plummer as Mercutio, Douglas Rain as Tybalt, Eric Christmas as Peter, Bruno Gerussi as my Romeo, Jack Creley as my father, and Leo Ciceri as Paris. We were all helped by a brilliant vocal coach and a beautiful human being, Iris Warren.

I will always remember that season in Canada: my mountain-climbing expedition, my ascent to Mount Everest. I hardly ever reached the summit, but when I did, Oh, Glory! And even to try was a rich experience.

I had a lovely English friend, Caroline D. Hewitt, born near Shakespeare's home in Warwickshire, who headed a girl's school in New York City and was a great Shakespearean scholar. When "Miss Hew" learned I was to play Juliet that season of 1960, she told me about the great Ellen Terry's performance of Juliet long ago. In the final scene, when Juliet wakes in the tomb to find Romeo dead, she holds Romeo for the last time, kisses him, and says "Thy lips are warm!" Miss Hew told me that when Ellen Terry spoke those words she whispered them; they went right to your heart as you realized that if Juliet had woken a few moments earlier she would have found her Romeo alive. In the old Italian legend, she *does* wake before Romeo dies—but he has already drunk the poison, and so there is between them the terror that Romeo knows that he must die and Juliet must witness her lover's death!

I wondered why Shakespeare didn't use that part of the story in his play. I spoke about it to Michael Langham when we were in rehearsal, and he decided that we would use a moment of that part of the old legend. As Romeo raised the vial of poison to his lips to drink, my fingers trembled and my arms moved ever so slightly. Bruno (Romeo) was looking away from me as he drank and didn't see that I had moved. It became an exciting moment.

Eventually, I did see two *young* actors, Leonard Whiting and Olivia Hussey, portray Romeo and Juliet in Franco Zeffirelli's film. I also saw the glorious work of the great choreographer John Cranko, when he produced *Romeo and Juliet* for the Stuttgart Ballet with Marcia Haydée and Richard Cragun—heartbreakingly beautiful that work is.

So my dream has come true. I have seen the play done perfectly and had the great good fortune myself to work with an inspired director who gave me the opportunity to play one of the greatest parts ever written in a play of Divine inspiration.

> . . . when he [Romeo] shall die,
> Take him and cut him out in little Stars,
> And he will make the Face of Heav'n so fine
> That all the World will be in love with Night
> And pay no Worship to the garish Sun.

Has language ever been used more beautifully?

NOTE

1. Julie Harris has performed such diverse roles as Emily Dickinson in *The Belle of Amherst*, Blanche du Bois in *A Streetcar Named Desire*, and Mary Lincoln in *The Last of Mrs. Lincoln*, for which she won the Tony Award in 1972. Her Shakespearean roles include Juliet in *Romeo and Juliet*, Blanche in *King John*, Ophelia in *Hamlet*, and the Third Witch in *Macbeth*.

Brenda Bruce

Nurse in *Romeo and Juliet*

Nurse is one of those *famous* roles in Shakespeare.[1] The theatrical history books are full of references to the brilliance of revered actresses, each seemingly 'definitive'. Some of them Dames! If Nurse was a part played by Dame Edith Evans and Ellen Terry and Mrs Stirling and Beatrix Lehmann and Celia Johnson, to name but a few, who was I to waver at the chance? I had always felt that if I played Nurse whilst I was still young enough I would take as starting-point her lines from her first speech, referring to her own baby Susan. 'Susan and she [Juliet] were of an age. Well, Susan is with God, she was too good for me.' If Nurse's baby died eleven years ago and she became Juliet's wet nurse, she could not be older than forty. Later in the same speech, describing her weaning of Juliet, she says to Lady Capulet, 'My Lord and you were then at Mantua.' This suggests that Nurse has been responsible for Juliet's upbringing. She is in fact the Mother, the person in whom Juliet lays her trust and confides her secret love. She sees Paris as the perfect answer to all her hopes for her 'baby', Juliet—love, marriage, children—simply the woman's lot, which can be pleasurable. Lady Capulet is mainly interested in the social position that will be gained for the Capulets through such a marriage.

In my opinion, Nurse is no country bumpkin. She holds a very important position with an important family in Verona. She is the Italian equivalent of a bright Cockney with all the same energetic vulgarity and warmth, and the only interest in her life is Juliet and Juliet's happiness. A fairly simple premise. However

From *Players of Shakespeare*, ed. Philip Brockbank. Cambridge: Cambridge University Press 1985, pp. 91–102. Reprinted with the permission of Cambridge University Press.

the complications within the part are tremendous. As so often with Shakespeare's major supporting parts, the subtext is very difficult to play. The jokes are obscure:

> NURSE. Doth not rosemary and Romeo begin both with a letter?
> ROMEO. Ay, Nurse, what of that? Both with an 'R'.
> NURSE. Ah, mocker, that's the dog's name. 'R' is for the—
>
> (2.4.206–10)

But Nurse stops herself saying whatever rude word she has in mind. The reference books state, 'Nurse cannot read'! I decided to face that problem with an audience! Along with Maria in *Twelfth Night* and Gertrude in *Hamlet*, Nurse is a reporter. In almost every scene she reports happenings to the other characters, most often repeating what has already been seen by the audience. She nudges Juliet sexually as Mercutio nudges Romeo in the same manner.

I realized that work at home was out of the question. The reaction of Tybalt, Mercutio, Romeo, Juliet and the Capulets and a director who allowed *room* for Nurse's subtext and did not treat her as a garrulous joke was the only way to find a true character. We did not read through the play at the first rehearsal. Nor did we see any designs. The set was a piece of cardboard two feet by one foot with two angled walls that were to move about, plus a bench the size of a matchbox and a bed two inches square. I saw that 'we' were on our own! None of us had ever worked together before. We eyed each other with respect, but gingerly, and plunged in scene by scene. I made some instant coffee for myself and shared it with a glamorous lady who turned out to be the dress designer, Nadine Bayliss. She explained that the boys were in leather, the girls in 1980 up-market hand-knitted silk dresses. 'And Nurse?', I said. 'Oh yes, you too, with an outrageous purple and silver cloak and long glass earrings for the street scene.' Tentatively I suggested red bubble curls for my hair. She would check with Ron Daniels (director). He approved this, so at least I knew how I would appear. If I had found myself weighed down with layers of heavy woollen skirts, my face and head half hidden in a wimple, the feeling of lightness and delight I was hoping to achieve in the first scene would have been a much more difficult task. The first time I played Gertrude in *Hamlet* I was encased in white sheepskin. I felt and looked like a bedside rug. Ron also liked my idea of a young Nurse and so work began.

My first rehearsal work was on Act 3, Scene 2—Nurse returning with the news of Tybalt's death. Realizing that Juliet had fallen in love with him, she had arranged their marriage; the Capulets, Paris, protocol, meant nothing to her; only Juliet's happiness mattered. If the fight between the households had not taken place, Nurse, I am sure, could have pleaded Romeo and Juliet's case. The first scene of Act 3 was all too familiar in 1981. The children, carrying their elders' bitterness and aggression and bigotry into the streets, fight and kill each other. The audience watch the scene but Nurse must repeat it to Juliet. Although she is not in the scene, she reports Tybalt's death in detail. She cries, 'Tybalt, Tybalt the best friend I had'. Why? She never speaks to Tybalt. We decided that Nurse should arrive at the party in Act 1 with Tybalt, that he and Nurse should lead the dancing and that Nurse should be very aware of the ensuing arguments between Tybalt and Romeo and Tybalt and Capulet. So during the weeks we tried to cope with all our various problems. We began sonnet classes with Terry Hands and Cicely Berry. She is in charge of voice, speech, and the presentation of the text. These sessions were nerve-racking but gradually broke down the barriers between the actors. Generalization was not allowed; we had to be specific; we had to learn to look each other in the eye and *tell* the sonnets to each other. Cicely Berry took speeches at random; we sat in a circle and, starting with the first word, spoke one each, in correct sequence, slowly, halting at first; but gradually one forgot oneself, picked up the word and passed it on to the next actor. We learned to *listen* to the actor on the left and *give* to the actor on the right. With practice it became like a near-perfect relay race; accepting and passing, we became one voice. We began to listen to each other, share with each other, keep Shakespeare's rhythm without falling into meaningless rhetoric, choose words specific to the speech without chopping up the rhythm—difficult at first, but when carried into rehearsal most helpful.

I like to start with a simple outline of character and fill in details as I work with fellow actors, quite often elaborating, then discarding; always trying to keep in mind that the audience will have a great influence on one's performance.

But I determined to tell the story from Nurse's point of view; with every report *tell* the story; no striving for laughs, no stressing of the verbal juggling.

The street scene with Mercutio, Benvolio and Romeo was a 'pig'. There was nothing in the script to suggest what the boys

do to Nurse to cause her extreme indignation: 'Now, afore God, I
am so vexed that every part about me quivers.' We struggled on,
trying to invent outrageous business. We did not solve the scene
satisfactorily before the first preview. After weeks before
audiences who were patently not very amused, Jonathan Hyde
(Mercutio) came into my dressing-room for our nightly two-
handed note session, with the answer. I had fallen between two
stools. I had not quite thrown off the old Nurse image. I was
playing old Nurse taking umbrage. Wrong. The boys were leather-
clad, greasy-haired, *menacing*. Wrong. The audience was not
prepared to laugh at the ill-treatment of Nurse. I was distasteful.
Since by now we knew each other rather well and trusted each
other as actors, we agreed to improvise the next night. The boys
were light and frivolous and I *enjoyed* their fun. Instead of using
my fan to make a ladylike image, I hit them about their heads. It
was a Japanese paper fan and made a sharp noise. The audience
laughed. After three slaps they laughed and clapped. After a few
performances the fan broke and the prop boys substituted another
fan. It was short and the ribs were made of plastic, instead of
cane. When I hit the boys the smart crack was missing. The
wonderful tingle of comedy-timing disappeared. On my free days
I drove to all the Japanese emporiums from Oxford to East
Finchley in search of the correct fan, without much luck. Comedy
is almost impossible to explain. A sharp noise evoked by a quick
light slap is very amusing. Hard hitting is *not* so funny. We four
went on working with our audiences and the scene grew in sheer
fun.

In time we started to rehearse Act 2, Scene 5, Nurse's return
from the street scene. My Nurse could not truthfully (and I had
to believe in my chosen interpretation) be so utterly exhausted
after a trip into town. It had to be Mother saying, 'Let me get in
and sit down before you badger me—I'll tell you everything you
want so much to know, after a sit down. Wait, calm down, my
back aches, my head throbs and I think Romeo is a poor choice.'
After some teasing, Nurse with one of her inevitably bawdy
comments sends Juliet off to Friar Laurence to be married:

I am the drudge and toil in your delight
But you shall bear the burden soon at night.   (2.5.75–6)

At the Royal Shakespeare Company we always have *solus*
calls. It gives one the chance to work on personal problems

without pressure. The time had come to look at Nurse in the scenes up to the marriage of Romeo and Juliet. Nurse's long speech in 1.3 was giving me great trouble. I was very afraid it was boring. Ron pointed out that I was rushing it, not enjoying the language. He told me to *talk* to him. Look him in the eye and *tell* him the story of the weaning of Juliet. We spent an hour on that one speech. It was weeks before I got anywhere near what Ron wanted but in that first hour I began to enjoy the picture of the hot afternoon before the earthquake.

> Sitting in the sun under the dovehouse wall . . .
> And then my husband—God be with his soul!
> 'A was a merry man—took up the child. (1.3.27, 39–40)

Quite apart from giving an audience information about Nurse, the speech paints a wonderful picture of the domestic life of the Capulets. Technically, the energy must keep right through to the lines:

> Peace, I have done, God mark thee to his Grace,
> Thou was the prettiest babe that e'er I nursed.
> An I might live to see thee married once
> I have my wish. (1.3.59–62)

Nurse would be completely fulfilled if Juliet might be 'A happy Mother made.' Juliet *is* Nurse's life. In fact after Juliet's apparent death, Nurse fades out of the play. When Juliet is dead, there is no Nurse.

The work on the first half of the play had reached a point when I must decide on Nurse's basic qualities, her philosophy, character, morality and position with regard to the Capulet family. I made a list of notes for myself. These were to cover the first half of the play; the question of Nurse's morality after the death of Tybalt was yet to come. The philosophy: it is a man's world, it is a young world. Very young girls must prepare for love, especially the physical aspect of love and the inevitable outcome, 'women grow by men'. But she believes in romantic love and happiness and babies; yet she is a religious woman who calls upon God a great deal. Her position in the Capulet family is that of a servant, who once her position as wet nurse is over and Juliet is weaned, is kept in their employ. She teaches Juliet to 'run and waddle about'. She runs the household, she is a 'retainer' and she is Juliet's confidante. She is not, so far, a deep-thinking woman; she has only learned to live with the inevitable happenings of a life such as hers. Her infant dead, her husband dead, she dedicates her life to Juliet. If Juliet really loves Romeo, then Nurse will do everything in her power to see them married. There is nothing to indicate that she has any qualms with regard to the Capulet/ Montague feud.

Nurse's bawdiness is part of her character. She cannot resist sexual innuendo. It is a running joke; often after a bawdy remark she says 'May God forgive me.' Her sexual jokes are never intended to be leering or lascivious. I was brought up in a working-class family. The general good-natured innuendo shocked my young romantic feelings. In retrospect I saw it for what it was: a running joke against a woman's lot; a built-in sense of timing; what a music-hall comic would call 'a throw away'. But like the female members of my family, Nurse has a very moral attitude; for instance in 2.4, in one of her speeches to Romeo: 'the gentlewoman is young and therefore, if you should deal double with her, truly it were an ill thing to be offered to any gentlewoman, and very weak dealing' (2.4.167–70). Nurse is as severe in her interviewing of Romeo as a possible suitor as Capulet is in his interviewing of Paris. Of one thing I was certain, I must not shy away from Nurse's bawdiness, neither must I demand audience reaction (some of the references and puns are anyway too obscure). Shakespeare had written a Cockney wit into a Veronese nurse. Until the death of Tybalt Nurse must enjoy every second. As I have said before, but for the death of Tybalt, Romeo and Juliet might have lived happily ever after. Nurse would have pleaded their case and might have won the Capulets over. That is not the story of Romeo and Juliet. Those were my notes to myself for the first half of the play!

We started work on 3.2. Ron, cleverly I think, set the scene in exactly the same way as for Nurse's return from the street scene (2.4, 5), when she was quite knowingly teasing Juliet. 3.1 had been a very different street scene. The jokes are over. We are facing tragedy. Nurse once again talks at cross purposes—not, as I see it, because she is hysterical, but because she is in a state of shock. Mercutio killed, her best friend Tybalt murdered by Romeo, Romeo banished, out of her despair she turns on 'men' with quiet deep bitterness, as though she is discovering the darker side of human relationships for the first time:

> There's no trust,
> No faith, no honesty in men; all perjured,
> All forsworn, all naught, all dissemblers.
> Ah, where's my man? Give me some aqua vitae. (3.2.85–8)

Here in the speech I took a liberty! I cut 'give me some aqua vitae', using 'Ah, where's my man?' as a cry for my dead husband, someone of my own to help my anguish:

> These griefs, these woes, these sorrows make me old.
> Shame come to Romeo. (3.2.89–90)

Life is not only love, marriage, babies. There is bitterness and loss and waste. Yet once again she cannot resist Juliet. As she takes the desperate child in her arms, she promises to find Romeo and help them consummate their marriage.

Morally how does Nurse stand? Does one protect, in fact encourage one's child to harbour, a convicted murderer? The answer must be yes, if, like Nurse, one believes that happiness with one's chosen man, however fleeting, is the very essence of life. There have been murderers and deserters since the beginning of history who have gained respite because of the loyalty of their women.

In 3.5, Nurse stands silent, horrified as Capulet rages against his daughter. Nurse alone knows that Romeo and Juliet are married. She alone knows the real cause of Juliet's hysterical agony. She speaks once, briefly turning on Capulet:

> God in heaven bless her!
> You are to blame, my lord, to rate her so. (3.5.168–9)

Nurse has until this moment been treated by the Capulet's rather as they would treat a poor relation; used, teased and shown a certain aloof kind of affection, but Capulet's reply

> Peace you mumbling fool!
> Utter your gravity o'er gossip's bowl,
> For here we need it not (3.5.173–5)

reminds us that Nurse is after all 'only a servant'.

I think the most terrible moment for Nurse is Lady Capulet's withdrawal of all motherly comfort:

> Talk not to me, for I'll not speak a word,
> Do as thou wilt, for I have done with thee. (3.5.202–3)

Why doesn't Nurse tell the truth and confess her part in the marriage? Out of loyalty to Juliet? Out of some mistaken idea that all may yet be well? Out of the fear of dismissal? Shakespeare gives no indication. When the parents have left the room, Juliet begs Nurse for help:

> What sayest thou? Hast thou not a word of joy?
> Some comfort, Nurse.   (3.5.211–12)

Now came the 'crunch', Nurse's advice to Juliet; I think it best to write the speech in sections and explain my specific decisions. Capulet's anger with Juliet (especially 3.5.176–95) serves as my subtext:

> Graze where you will, you shall not house with me . . .
> An you be mine, I'll give you to my friend,
> An you be not, hang, beg, starve, die in the streets.
>   (3.5.188, 191–2)

Nurse could advise Juliet to run away with her to Friar Laurence, seek refuge in a nunnery, follow Romeo into Mantua, call her mother and father, confess to them, pray for their understanding and forgiveness, and with their help plead with the Prince to forgive Romeo. If any of these solutions had been in Shakespeare's *Romeo and Juliet* the play would be a drama, not a tragedy. As it is, Juliet is unschooled in life—a fourteen-year-old girl—and her closest companion is Nurse, with whom she shares her waking and sleeping hours (in 4.3.10 Juliet refers to Nurse not sharing her room as usual, but sitting up with Lady Capulet). Nurse is incapable of sending Juliet out into the world; Juliet's parents are moreover full of grudge against the Montagues, a 'continuing rage'. Nurse has only one answer and it is immoral and against the law. It is damnation in the eyes of the church, but better than starving on the streets. Her solution is *bigamy*. How to begin to give this advice? I wrote earlier of a director who gives space for subtext. Ron Daniels gave it to me. I've written beside the speech to Juliet, 'Take all the time in the world.' 'Faith, here it is.'

> Romeo is banished; and all the world to nothing
> That he dares ne'er come back to challenge you.   (3.5.213–14)

There must be no hint of emotion in the voice, no attempt at physical comfort. Those two lines are a simple statement of fact.

> Then, since the case so stands as now it doth,
> I think it best you married with the County.   (3.5.216–17)

Anything is better than family rejection, starvation. There would be nothing for a girl, alone in the world—only begging on the streets. Parental control and approval and marriage were the only possibilities for a woman. Independence for the Juliets of that time was out of the question. As though to soften the shock for Juliet of 'I think it best you married with the County', Nurse says,

> Oh he's a lovely gentleman!
> Romeo's a dishclout to him.   (3.5.218–19)

If Nurse sounds as though she believed this, she will get a laugh from the audience. What I wanted was a reaction of shock. When I play well I often get this reaction. I would like the audience to feel let down by someone whose motives they have trusted. Nurse carries on to the end of the speech with her advice, not believing a word of it in her heart.' Then Juliet asks, 'Speakest thou from thy heart? And Nurse answers, 'And from my soul too. Else beshrew them both.' In an attempt to make the advice acceptable, Nurse fusses about, making the bed, trying to make everything 'sensible and acceptable'. But Juliet answers, 'Amen'—in other words, 'Devil take you!'

From then on Nurse is watchful; Juliet returns from Friar Laurence's cell, happy, it seems, after her meeting with Paris. Nurse is not certain; she watches her child's reactions. 'See', she says, 'where she comes from shrift with merry look.' Juliet seems merry. She leaves Nurse to choose her wedding gown—again subtext ('Ay, those attires are best,' 4.3.1)—and then:

> I pray thee leave me to myself tonight.
> For I have need of many orisons
> To move the heavens to smile upon my state,
> Which, well thou knowest, is cross and full of sin.   (4.3.2–5)

Nurse knows; it was Nurse's advice; she knows Juliet is married, and advised her to commit bigamy. At this moment Shakespeare does not give Nurse any lines. Lady Capulet kisses her child and goes happily to bed. Nurse can only search Juliet's face for a second and scurry off to prepare the wedding-breakfast.

In 4.5 Nurse comes to awaken Juliet. All fears allayed, a conscience stifled; teasing, bawdy Nurse once again. Juliet is dead. Here Shakespeare abandons Nurse. She joins in a formal lament and disappears from the story. In 5.3, the Friar confesses his part in the tragedy and says, 'and to the marriage/Her nurse is privy'. Nurse is not in the scene to put *her* case. Why? Might it be that she is the epitome of the woman who lives on the fringe of other people's lives, helping to shape their destiny, but no more than that?

NOTE

1. Brenda Bruce, an Associate Artist of the Royal Shakespeare Company, has been with the Company since 1964. Her acting experience has been in every sense extensive. She has appeared in theatres all over the world (including South America and China), in films, and on television, where her performance in *The Winter's Tale* won her the Best Actress Evening Standard Award. At Stratford, she has played at both The Other Place and the Royal Shakespeare Theatre, where her range has covered Mistress Page, Paulina, Maria in *Twelfth Night*, Gertrude, Lady Capulet and Mistress Quickly in *Henry V*. She first played the Nurse in the *Romeo and Juliet* production of 1980, repeating her performance in the 1981 seasons at Newcastle and the Aldwych. With her were Anton Lesser as Romeo and Judy Buxton as Juliet, and the production, designed by Ralph Koltai, was directed by Ron Daniels.

Stanley Wells

Juliet's Nurse: The Uses of Inconsequentiality

Lady Capulet. Thou knowest my daughter's of a pretty age.
Nurse. Faith, I can tell her age unto an hour.
Lady Capulet. She's not fourteen.
Nurse.   I'll lay fourteen of my teeth—
And yet, to my teen be it spoken, I have but four—
She's not fourteen. How long is it now
To Lammas-tide?
Lady Capulet.   A fortnight and odd days.
Nurse. Even or odd, of all days in the year,
Come Lammas Eve at night shall she be fourteen.
Susan and she—God rest all Christian souls!—
Were of an age. Well, Susan is with God;
She was too good for me. But, as I said,
On Lammas Eve at night shall she be fourteen;
That shall she, marry; I remember it well.
'Tis since the earthquake now eleven years;
And she was weaned—I never shall forget it—
Of all the days of the year, upon that day;
For I had then laid wormwood to my dug,
Sitting in the sun under the dove-house wall.
My lord and you were then at Mantua.
Nay, I do bear a brain. But, as I said,
When it did taste the wormwood on the nipple
Of my dug, and felt it bitter, pretty fool,
To see it tetchy, and fall out with the dug!
Shake, quoth the dovehouse. 'Twas no need, I trow,

Excerpt from *Shakespeare's Styles*, ed. Philip Edwards et al. Cambridge:
Cambridge University Press, 1980, pp. 51–66. Reprinted with
permission of Cambridge University Press.

To bid me trudge.
And since that time it is eleven years;
For then she could stand high-lone; nay, by th'rood,
She could have run and waddled all about;
For even the day before, she broke her brow;
And then my husband—God be with his soul!
'A was a merry man—took up the child.
'Yea,' quoth he, 'dost thou fall upon thy face?
Thou wilt fall backward when thou hast more wit,
Wilt thou not, Jule?' And, by my holidam,
The pretty wretch left crying, and said 'Ay'.
To see, now, how a jest shall come about!
I warrant, an I should live a thousand years,
I never should forget it: 'Wilt thou not, Jule?' quoth he;
And, pretty fool, it stinted, and said 'Ay'.
Lady Capulet. Enough of this; I pray thee hold thy peace.
Nurse. Yes, madam. Yet I cannot choose but laugh
To think it should leave crying and say 'Ay'.
And yet, I warrant, it had upon it brow
A bump as big as a young cock'rel's stone—
A perilous knock; and it cried bitterly.
'Yea,' quoth my husband, 'fall'st upon thy face?
Thou wilt fall backward when thou comest to age;
Wilt thou not, Jule?' It stinted, and said 'Ay'.
Juliet. And stint thou too, I pray thee, nurse, say I.

                              (*Romeo and Juliet*, I,iii,11–59)

The style of the Nurse's speeches in Act I, scene iii of *Romeo and
Juliet* makes a vivid impact on both readers and spectators. It is
described by Nicholas Brooke as 'something altogether new, both
in this play and, in fact, in Shakespeare's output'. He finds its
'nearest antecedent', not in verse, but in 'the prose of I,i'. While
'it goes far beyond that', nevertheless 'its characteristic is that it
is close to prose, or rather to prosaic speech, developing its own
rhythmic momentum'.[1] By the time that Shakespeare wrote *Romeo
and Juliet* he had written much dialogue that approximates to
prosaic speech rather than to literary prose; and I should like to
begin this essay by examining some of the characteristics of the
Nurse's utterance which may account for the claim that it
represents 'something altogether new'.

It is easy to point to aspects of the style which create the
illusion of spontaneity. There are colloquial expressions such as
'Come Lammas Eve at night', 'Shake, quoth the dovehouse' (so
personal as to be obscure in meaning), 'stand high-lone', and

'broke her brow'. The diction is familiar, even vulgar: 'dug', 'tetchy', 'trudge', 'waddled'. There are emphatic or asseverative expressions, including 'Well,' 'as I said', 'marry', 'Nay', 'I trow', 'by th'rood', 'by my holidam', 'I warrant'. Some of these words and phrases, and others, are repeated or slightly varied in a manner that would be avoided by a literary artist but which helps to bind the speech together and to give the impression that they are idiosyncratic to the speaker: 'God rest all Christian souls!' . . . 'God be with his soul!': is this sententiousness or piety?—the performer may decide; 'I remember it well . . . I never shall forget it . . . I never should forget it'; 'pretty fool . . . pretty wretch . . . pretty fool'; and 'To see it . . . To see, now. . .'.

These devices might equally well be discerned in the racy prose dialogue of Act I, scene i, or in individually longer prose speeches, such as Launce's principal soliloquies in *The Two Gentlemen of Verona* (II,iii; IV,iv). More individual to the Nurse is the structure and argument of the speech (or, in effect, its denial of structure and argument): the sequence of ideas and images, and the aim to which they are applied. Coleridge referred to them in an 'Essay on Method in Thought'[2] as an example of Shakespeare's exhibitions of 'the difference between the products of a well disciplined and those of an uncultivated understanding'. He remarks that 'the absence of Method, what characterises the uneducated, is occasioned by a habitual submission of the understanding to mere events and images as such, and independent of any power in the mind to classify or appropriate them'. One very obvious symptom of the 'absence of Method' in the Nurse's disquisition is the frequency with which she interrupts herself. Sometimes this is because she follows an associative train of thought irrespective of its relevance to her listeners:

> I'll lay fourteen of my teeth—
> And yet, to my teen be it spoken, I have but four—
> She's not fourteen.

Is her self-interruption here a conscious playing with 'four' and 'teen', or rather the subconscious struggle to clear her mind of verbal entanglements? Again, the performer may choose.

Part of the comedy of the Nurse's utterance lies in the fact that what she interrupts has in itself no logical sequence. The information that she has to convey in her main speech is entirely contained in its second line:

Come Lammas Eve at night shall she be fourteen.

This fact might well be pointed by stage business, Lady Capulet endeavouring to resume the conversation after this statement. But the Nurse's well of recollection has been tapped, and the flow cannot be quenched. Coleridge parallels this speech of the Nurse with one of Mistress Quickly. In answer to Falstaff's question 'What is the gross sum that I owe thee?', she replies

> Marry, if thou wert an honest man, thyself and the money too. Thou didst swear to me upon a parcel-gilt goblet, sitting in my Dolphin chamber, at the round table, by a sea-coal fire, upon Wednesday in Wheeson week, when the Prince broke thy head for liking his father to a singing-man of Windsor—thou didst swear to me then, as I was washing thy wound, to marry me and make me my lady thy wife. Canst thou deny it? Did not goodwife Keech, the butcher's wife, come in then and call me gossip Quickly? Coming in to borrow a mess of vinegar, telling us she had a good dish of prawns, whereby thou didst desire to eat some, whereby I told thee they were ill for a green wound?
>
> (2 *Henry IV*, II,i,81–94)

Here, Coleridge remarks that 'the connexions and sequence which the habit of Method can alone give have in this instance a substitute in the fusion of passion'. The Nurse lacks Mistress Quickly's vituperative passion of self-righteous indignation, but her recollections, too, are grounded in emotion, provoked by the memory that she had had a daughter of the same age as Juliet. The very fact that Susan's relationship with the Nurse is not explicitly stated is itself an aspect of Shakespeare's dramatic style here. It tells us obliquely of the Nurse's intimacy with the family in which she lives, an intimacy which the performers can use by suggesting a sympathetic, if bored, acceptance that once the Nurse has embarked on this tack, she must be indulged. And it engages the audience by requiring them to make the inference. The death of an infant has an inevitable poignancy, and one which must link the Nurse to the Capulets since Juliet has thriven on the milk which should have reared Susan. And we may recall that the shadow of infant mortality has already darkened the play, in Capulet's 'Earth hath swallowed all my hopes but she' (I,ii,14).

The Nurse's recollection that Juliet and Susan 'Were of an age' is interrupted by the pious commonplace 'God rest all Christian souls!', leading us to infer that Susan is dead, and is followed by two more clichés: 'Susan is with God;/She was too good for me.' The ordinariness of these expressions is surely part of their point; they come naturally from the mouth of a simple-minded woman. To say, as G. I. Duthie does in the New Cambridge edition,[3] 'She knows she has faults. When she declares that little Susan was too good for her, she is speaking partly jocularly but partly, for a second, seriously, with self-knowledge', is surely to ignore the stereotyped quality of the assertion.

After her digression, the Nurse's pulling herself up with 'But, as I said', and coming full circle with

On Lammas Eve at night shall she be fourteen,

marks another point at which she might have concluded. But her recollections have a self-generating momentum, and as she goes on, she becomes increasingly self-absorbed. Coleridge's 'Method' implies consideration for the listener (or reader), an ordering of statements requiring the application of fundamental brainwork such as is associated with literary artistry or conscious rhetoric, and is thus outward-looking; the 'absence of Method', on the other hand, implies a delving into the subconscious which produces the kind of monologue that achieves communication rather by accident than by design. The Nurse makes no pretence that her ramblings are relevant to the situation. They are a form of self-indulgence which is also a form of both self-investigation and (when conducted in public) self-revelation, so the response of listeners is a measure of their response to the speaker's character. The Nurse's listeners allow her to continue; whether they do so with complete indulgence or with some degree of indifference, and with attempts to interrupt, is open to interpretation. The Nurse's repetitions of 'But, as I said' may be regarded as a method of staving off interruption, or they may be less outward-looking, her own method of attempting to exert some control over her discourse.

After concluding the first paragraph of her speech, she marks time for a moment with 'That shall she, marry; I remember it well' before embarking on another paragraph whose beginning also is to reappear as its ending. And from the recollection of one landmark—Lammas Eve as the time of the infant's birth—she passes to another—the day of 'the earthquake' as that on which Juliet was weaned. That Shakespeare was here considerately making a topical allusion in order to help scholars of the future to know when he wrote his play is improbable. An 'earthquake' is chosen as the kind of event which would be significant in the lives of all who experienced it, an episode certain to engrave itself upon the collective memory. It serves again to link the masters with their servants. The coincidence of Juliet's being weaned on the day of the earthquake is stressed in the phrase 'Of all the days of the year', and seems to confer importance upon the event; but always, as these facts emerge, they are linked and given significance by being shown as part of the life-experience of the woman who recollects them. It is her memory in which they dwell—'I remember it well', 'I never shall forget it'; and it is her body with which they are associated.

So far we have had only statements; now, as she becomes more immersed in her topic, she becomes anecdotal. The absence of intellectual logic in what she says is apparent in the false connective 'For'—'For I had then laid wormwood to my dug'— but the sudden sequence of nouns in this and the succeeding line—'wormwood . . . dug . . . sun . . . dovehouse' and 'wall'— helps to create a vivid picture of peaceful normality which gains in credibility by its association with a violently abnormal event. Yet another association obtrudes—'My lord and you were then at Mantua'—and the pressure of recollection becomes so great that the Nurse returns to the present in wonderment at her own mental powers—'Nay, I do bear a brain.'[4]

She resumes her anecdote, losing herself again in memories which allow no acknowledgement that the baby of whom she speaks is the girl who stands beside her. Her style is not expository but exclamatory, deepening the suggestion that she is re-living the experience:

> pretty fool,
> To see it tetchy, and fall out with the dug!

This exclamation is followed by another, elliptical and slightly obscure,[5] which recalls the earthquake's shocking disruption of normality—'Shake, quoth the dovehouse.' Again she is jolted back to the present as she recalls her hasty flight and rounds off the second paragraph with a return to the statement with which it began: 'And since that time it is eleven years.'

The final part of the speech again begins with a false connective, and has no logical link with what precedes it, nor even any obvious associative one, unless it is that the Nurse's memory of her need to 'trudge'[6] leads from her own legs to Juliet's, and thus to the recollection that Juliet was able to *stand* by herself. The second anecdote features another newly introduced character, the Nurse's husband; the touch of sadness that he is dead is offset by her memory of him as 'a merry man'. For the first time now she quotes direct speech, in her husband's somewhat bawdy, familiar remark to the child 'Jule'. The Nurse's own, self-absorbed delight in her recollections is evident in her repetition of the anecdote. Whether she has carried her stage audience along with her is again a matter for interpretation. Lady Capulet's interruption,

Enough of this. I pray thee, hold thy peace

appears to demonstrate impatience, yet it can be played against its sense, in full enjoyment of the comedy of the tale. Coleridge referred to the Nurse's 'childlike fondness of repetition in her childish age—and that happy, humble ducking under, yet resurgence against the check—

Yes, madam! *Yet* I cannot choose but laugh.'[7]

And she adds the circumstantial and bawdy detail of the 'bump as big as a young cock'rel's stone' before winding herself to a standstill with her fourth telling of the tale.

I have written of the speech so far as if it were composed in prose, not verse. I have referred to the 'prose' characteristics of its diction and structure, and to the fact that it quotes a passage of (supposedly) prose speech. Although in modern editions we read the speech as verse, it is a curious fact that it was printed as prose in all the early editions: the bad quarto (1597), the good quarto (1599), and the First Folio (1623). It is less surprising that verse should appear as prose in the memorially reconstructed bad quarto than that most of the Nurse's speeches in this scene are set in italic type in both quartos. There is evidence that in Q2 the first thirty-four lines of the scene are reprinted directly from Q1,[8] and it is likely that this fact influenced the Q2 compositor to go on setting these speeches as prose even though they were presumably written out as verse in the holograph from which he is believed to have set the remainder of the scene. Not until Capell's edition (1768) were the Nurse's speeches arranged as verse. In the meantime Thomas Otway had adapted and amplified them, while retaining their substance, in unmistakable prose in his *Caius Marius* (1679). Garrick, naturally, set them as prose in his adaptation of 1748, followed, in spite of Capell, in John Bell's acting edition (1774). At least two nineteenth-century editors— Staunton (1857) and Keightley (1865)—did the same, and so does Frank A. Marshall in the *Henry Irving Shakespeare* (8 vols., 1888– 90), with a note condemning 'the modern editors who have tried to make verse of what was surely never intended for it', and asking: 'Why should Shakespeare be made to violate every rule of rhythm and metre, for the sake of trying to strain this conventional prose into blank verse?' (vol. 1, p. 240). Irving's acting edition of 1882, however, prints the expurgated remnants as verse.[9] G. B. Harrison reverted to prose in his Penguin edition (1937), and even Dover Wilson wrote that 'editors have never been able to make anything but very rough verse out of these speeches and it is quite possible that Shakespeare intended them to be rhythmical (i.e. easily memorized) prose'.[10] But this statement is impressionistic rather than accurate. G. Walton Williams (p. 107) analyses the scene carefully and shows that the earlier section of the Nurse's long speech 'is marked by irregular verse': the nineteen lines include one four-syllable line (35), three hypermetrical lines with unaccented final syllables (18, 22, 31); and five hypermetrical lines with accented final syllables (23, 25, 26, 28, and 32); these are not violent irregularities, and several of them may be explained as contractions in pronunciation; the remainder of the scene, Williams finds, is 'in smooth verse' with minor exceptions. Minor rhythmic irregularities may be expected in verse which is so clearly intended as this is to represent 'prosaic speech'; as Kenneth Muir says, 'Shakespeare obtains some subtle effects by the verse rhythm underlying the apparently colloquial speech.'[11] Little more than a glance is needed to show that in both the inauthentically and the authentically derived sections, the ends of lines are almost invariably also the ends of sense-units: the only enjambment in the main speech is at lines 31–2 ('the nipple/Of my dug . . .'). There can be no question that Shakespeare was fully conscious that he was writing verse, nor, to my mind, that he was going further than ever before in the experiment of combining the diction, rhythms, and even the mental processes normally associated with prose utterance within the over-all rhythms of blank verse. The speeches would be remarkable enough as an exhibition of the 'quick forge and working-house of thought' if they had indeed been in prose; it is the fact that in them prose rhythms are counterpointed against a verse structure that makes them 'something altogether new, both in this play and . . . in Shakespeare's output'.

I should like now to draw back from a close focus on the speech itself to a broader consideration of its function in the play as an aspect of Shakespeare's dramatic style. *Romeo and Juliet* is often dated 1594–5, a fact that it has in common with *Love's Labour's Lost, The Two Gentlemen of Verona, The Comedy of Errors, The Taming of the Shrew, A Midsummer Night's Dream, The Merchant of Venice, Richard II, King John*, and *Titus Andronicus*. Obviously the composition of these plays must have been spread over a period of several years, but it is fair to regard *Romeo and Juliet* as one of a group of early plays in which Shakespeare shows an experimental interest in verbal style. *King John* and *Richard II*, along with the earlier *1* and *3 Henry VI*, but like no other plays in the canon, are written entirely in verse. In them Shakespeare seems to be deliberately limiting his stylistic range, seeking intensity rather than diversity. In other plays he seems rather to be seeking a wide range of stylistic variation. Part of the effectiveness of the Nurse's speech derives from the fact that, though it occurs no later than the opening of the third scene, it has been preceded by passages written in very different styles, including the sonnet form of the Prologue; the colloquial prose of the opening dialogue of the servants; Prince Escalus's dignified blank verse; the more lyrical blank verse of Benvolio's description of the lovesick Romeo; Romeo's own rhapsodic verse, which includes rhyming couplets and has some of the qualities associated with metaphysical poetry; the comic prose of Capulet's servant; and sonnet-type sestets from both Benvolio and Romeo.

This rich stylistic diversity has helped to establish verbal style as a guide to character, and has encouraged us to respond to verbal effects. We know that this is to be a play in which plot is not all-important, and this is essential, since in terms of plot the whole of Act I, scene iii could exist without the Nurse. Her big speech is a set-speech in more senses than one. It is an extended show-piece for the performer, and also for the Nurse herself. This is, we may well suspect, an oft-told tale. Do we not feel, as soon as she says 'I can tell her age unto an hour', that she is about to give us every detail? And may we not feel, too, that her on-stage audience has heard it all many times before? This seems to me to be suggested by the line, completing a verse couplet, with which Juliet almost succeeds in bringing the Nurse's recollections to an end. 'And stint thou too, I pray thee, nurse, say I.' What is the tone? Is Juliet embarrassed or bored? indulgent or irritable? imploratory or imperative? Again, there is room for variety of interpretation.

If the Nurse's speech is irrelevant to the plot, we may ask how Shakespeare came to write it, and why he was disposed to lavish so much of his artistry on it. Is it merely an exuberant exercise of virtuosity, a set-piece for the author as well as for the actor and the character? Is it an inartistic irrelevance, a fanciful embroidery of the situation unnecessarily pursuing a hint suggested by the source? There is, indeed, some basis for it in Arthur Brooke's *Tragicall Historye of Romeus and Juliet*,[12] which may provide pointers to the style in which the scene should be played as well as help to explain the style in which it is written. One vexed question relates to the Nurse's age. Brooke clearly thought of her as old: he calls her 'an auncient dame' (1. 344), an 'olde dame' (1. 345), an 'auncient nurse' (1. 689). Yet 'in her youth' she 'had nurst' Juliet 'with her mylke' (1. 345). Brooke's Juliet is sixteen, more than two years older than Shakespeare's; but this still leaves some awkwardness about the Nurse's having been able to suckle the infant Juliet, and have a child of the same age herself, and yet now being 'auncient'. In a narrative poem, the point may pass unnoticed; on the stage it is more obtrusive. Thus St John Ervine, reviewing Edith Evans's legendary performance in 1935, remarked that though the character was 'superbly played' she was 'made to totter as if her legs had been racked with rheumatism for half a century'.[13] Terence Spencer attempts to reconcile the discrepancy, suggesting that she is not 'to be imagined as an aged crone but as, perhaps, in her early fifties'.[14] But perhaps the performer is best advised to ignore logic and to play for effect.

One function of the Nurse's repetitiveness is to lay great stress on Juliet's age, which has created a different problem. Shakespeare makes her younger than either Brooke or Painter (who says that she is eighteen). Geoffrey Bullough suggests that this is intended 'to emphasise the charm of her girlish directness, the pathos of her passion and resolution'. Charles Armitage Brown (quoted in the New Variorum edition) had a more practical suggestion: 'Juliet's extreme youth was, at the time, an apology to the audience for the boy who played so arduous a part.' Whatever the truth of this, actresses playing the role have frequently chosen not to include among its ardours the effort to look fourteen. Theophilus Cibber (1744) offers what might have

been classed as an emendation if it had not occurred in a mere
acting edition: Lady Capulet says: 'She's but fifteen', and the
Nurse replies 'She's not fourteen' (but Cibber spoils the impression
of thoughtfulness by then having her say 'come Lammas-Eve at
night shall she be fifteen'). In Garrick's acting text (followed by
Bell) Juliet is 'not yet eighteen' (with appropriate alterations to
the number of the Nurse's remaining teeth and to other figures);
Benson, like Garrick, relieved his leading lady from the strain of
attempting to look no more than a fortnight under eighteen.

These are considerations that relate to the style of acting the
Nurse's role. Shakespeare also derived hints from Brooke for the
style in which he wrote it. Brooke's 'prating noorse', too, is
repetitive and anecdotal; she makes a 'tedious long discoorse'.
The crucial lines are worth quoting:

> And how she gave her sucke in youth she leaveth not to tell.
> A prety babe (quod she), it was when it was yong,
> Lord how it could full pretely have prated with it tong,
> A thousand times and more I laid her on my lappe,
> And clapt her on the buttocke soft and kist where I did clappe.
> And gladder then was I of such a kisse forsooth,
> Then I had been to have a kisse of some olde lechers mouth.
> And thus of Juliets youth began this prating noorse,
> And of her present state to make a tedious long discoorse.
>
> (II.652–60)

Here, as in Shakespeare, we have prosaic speech cast into the
form of verse. Shakespeare's diction is related to Brooke's ('prety
babe', 'quod she','it' for 'she', 'thousand'). So also are the mode
and tone of the Nurse's discourse. The comic earthiness of 'clapt
her on the buttocke soft and kist where I did clappe' is reflected
in the Nurse's unabashed acknowledgement of the physical details
of breast-feeding and in the bawdy implications of the anecdote
about her husband. Needless to say, this was not to the taste of
the Victorians. Bowdler (1818) omitted the whole of the anecdote
about falling backwards; he retained the breast-feeding while
altering 'dug' to 'teat'. Lacy's acting edition of about 1855 outdoes
Bowdler in purification, omitting even the breast-feeding,
reducing the major speech to only eleven lines (compared with
Bowdler's twenty-two), and entirely omitting the following
speech. Henry Irving's acting edition of 1882 is even more brutal,
and results in nonsense. Mary Anderson, at the Lyceum four
years later, allowed Mrs Stirling her anecdote, but Forbes-

Robertson, in 1895, omitted the bawdy, while curiously retaining
the lead-in to it, as if to encourage the audience to recall (or
imagine) it if they will:

> 'Yea,' quoth he, 'dost thou fall upon thy face?
> Thou wilt —'
> *Lady Capulet.* Enough of this.

To show that Shakespeare found some suggestions in his
source for both the content and manner of the episode is not, of
course, to provide artistic justification for it. But if it is irrelevant
to the plot, it is far from irrelevant to the greater entity which is
the play. Terence Spencer has remarked that the 'momentous
and breathtaking four days' to which the play's action is confined
'are given a context in the passage of time much larger and longer,'
and that 'Old Capulet and the Nurse, in particular, carry the
mind outside the framework of the play to events and emotions
which nevertheless put Juliet and her Romeo in perspective'.[15]
The Nurse's ramblings do indeed give us a sense of the past; and
they do so in a particularly poignant context. The stage situation
shows us a girl poised on the brink of womanhood. We have not
met her before, and one function of the Nurse's speeches is to
engage our sympathetic interest in the play's heroine. As the
Nurse talks, her memories not only throw our minds back to the
infancy of this girl, they also recall a prediction made at that time
of how Juliet would react when she had 'more wit' and came 'to
age'. The child who is talked about as an innocent infant is now
before us, the subject of marriage plans. She retains the vulnerable
innocence of the baby that 'stinted and said "Ay"', as we see in
her reaction to the question 'How stands your dispositions to be
married?' 'It is an honour that I dream not of', says Juliet. This is
in naïve contrast to the sexuality of 'Thou wilt fall backward
when thou hast more wit', and it partakes of the infantile naïveté
of Juliet's earlier response: 'Ay.' Thus the Nurse's delving into
the past recalls an anecdote which looked forward to beyond,
but only just beyond, the present in which she speaks. The
temporal complexities of the situation are subtle and ironical.

One function of the episode is, of course, to establish the
Nurse's personality, and in this it has succeeded so notably as to
have become a classic instance of Shakespeare's genius for
character portrayal. Nicholas Brooke finds that her utterance here
'offers a very telling contrast to the hollow courtliness of I.ii:

earthy, sentimental, warm-blooded, bawdy, repetitious. At all levels delightful, and most refreshing in its unselfconsciousness' (p. 93). And G. I. Duthie goes further in sketching a personality on the basis of what she says here: 'despite all her crudities, we can never forget the essential good-heartedness of this old woman who, vulgar and earthy as she is, looks back on past days and compresses precious memories into words which, while brief, suggest a loving and happy married life, with sorrow philosophically endured' (p. xxxvi). These comments testify to her credibility; but this is not enough. Coleridge, replying to suggestions 'that her character is the mere fruit of observation', spoke of it rather as a 'character of admirable generalisation'.[16] He betrays an implicit concern that the dramatic character should relate, at least, to recognisable characteristics of certain types of human beings. 'Let any man conjure up in his mind all the qualities and peculiarities that can possibly belong to a nurse, and he will find them in Shakespeare's picture of the old woman: nothing is omitted.' Some of these qualities are admirable, some not; so he finds in her 'all the garrulity of old age, and all its fondness . . . the arrogance of ignorance' and 'the pride of meanness at being connected with a great family,' and 'the grossness, too, which that situation never removes' (p. 145). These observations are, of course, elicited by the Nurse's behaviour in all the scenes in which she appears, but it is significant that most of her qualities can be discerned in her initial speeches. The appeal that she exerts is as a 'character' in the sense that we speak of someone as 'a great character': one, that is, who is so self-consistent, so roundedly and immutably himself, so much of a fixed point in a landscape, that we can delight in his idiosyncrasies without needing to declare judgement on him. So Shakespeare, we feel, gives us the Nurse in her totality on her first appearance; she is herself a landmark, a constant against which the changes and developments in other characters can be measured. And here we come to those aspects of Shakespeare's portrayal of the Nurse which make her not just credible as an individual and recognisably representative of a class, but of essential importance to the play in which she is found. The 'fondness' for Juliet which she clearly conveys draws us to Juliet as well as to the Nurse. And her limitations, suggested here, will later be tragically relevant to Juliet. Nicholas Brooke follows his expression of pleasure in the Nurse's character by saying that: 'It is also, humanly speaking, shallow enough in its own way, and this will

be sharply exposed later; but here, the judgement is withheld.'
Judgement comes, of course, when (only a few days later in the
play's time-scheme) Juliet, a bride, is shown to have passed far
beyond any understanding that the Nurse can offer. Then she
becomes in Juliet's eyes 'Ancient damnation! O most wicked
fiend!' (III,v,236). To this extent she is seen as a foil for Juliet, a
rounded, developed but static character that serves as a measure
of the speed and extent of Juliet's spiritual and emotional
development. These opening speeches lay the groundwork of
this relationship.

I have written of the Nurse's speeches in relation to their
verbal style, and also to what we may call Shakespeare's theatrical
and dramatic styles. Many aspects of the speeches can be admired;
the one that seems most original, and most important for
Shakespeare's later development, is their exploitation of
inconsequentiality. By a carefully controlled representation of
utterance which is characterised by an absence of linguistic
control, Shakespeare creates interstices which can be filled with
nuance. This is a splendidly theatrical mode, because it leaves
something to the performer, who, by means of gesture, movement,
facial play and subtlety of intonation, may create an appropriate
physical realisation of all that the speech implies.

And such realisations may be very different from one another.
As long ago as 1902, a theatre critic remarked that 'By tradition
of the stage this is a comic character, the confidential retainer,
rustling with silks and rattling with keys, interfering in everything,
prone to take offence at imaginary slights, tyrannising over those
she nominally serves, and all the time English to the finger-tips.
Mrs Stirling [who played with Ellen Terry in Henry Irving's
production, and with Mary Anderson] was a perfect embodiment
of that type. Miss [Tita] Brand [who played in the Ben Greet
production under review] gives us a very different person. Here
is an Italian crone, just such a figure as may be met by the dozen
in the streets of Rome or Naples; a southern face, with parchment
skin and hairy growth, and the four teeth to which the owner
confesses much in evidence. . . .'[17] Such openness to interpretation
is surely a mark of the truly theatrical conception.

As well as leaving something to the actor, the role no less
importantly leaves something to the audience. Allusions, oblique
references, incomplete logical connections, implications, half-
concealed trains of thought require the audience's intelligent
collaboration to be wholly meaningful. The audience is, as it

were, drawn into the speaker's mind, engaged with a lively intensity which can be much greater than response to a harangue composed with complete 'Method'.

Whether Shakespeare derived the style of the Nurse's speech from sources in literature and life we cannot say.[18] Arthur Brooke contributed suggestions for their effect, but no model for their method. I suspect it is relevant that, at about the time the play was composed, Thomas Nashe was demonstrating his capacity in what he calls the 'extemporal vein'. What is clear is that, having, as it were, learnt the trick, Shakespeare, as we should expect, went on to develop and vary it. The Nurse's inconsequentiality arises from the fact that her mental processes are too feeble to create an adequate syntactical structure; or—to look at it from her creator's point of view—in the Nurse Shakespeare employs broken syntax and inconsequentiality to suggest a mind that is naturally lacking in intellectual control. He does something similar, though in prose, with Mistress Quickly, as we have already seen. The Nurse's speech patterns are related to those of Justice Shallow, in whom they suggest the effects of senility. All these characters give the impression of complete spontaneity. Lacking the power to order their thoughts and control their expression, they display no disjunction between the impulse to speak and the terms in which their thoughts are formulated. This gives them a kind of innocence. Pompey, in *Measure for Measure*, may seem rather to be using these tricks of language to pull the wool over his interlocutors' eyes than to be incapable of greater coherence:

> As I say, this Mistress Elbow, being, as I say, with child, and being great-bellied, and longing, as I said, for prunes; and having but two in the dish, as I said, Master Froth here, this very man, having eaten the rest, as I said, and, as I say, paying for them very honestly; for, as you know, Master Froth, I could not give you three pence again.   (II,i,94–100)

These are speakers of prose. In verse, Shakespeare learnt that inconsequentiality could be a powerful means of portraying mental anguish, the overthrowing of a noble mind. Hamlet's soliloquies—like the Nurse's speech—encompass familiar diction, exclamations, repetitions, self-interruptions, and broken syntax within a verse structure:

    Why, she would hang on him
As if increase of appetite had grown
By what it fed on; and yet, within a month—
Let me not think on't. Frailty, thy name is woman!—
A little month, or ere those shoes were old
With which she followed my poor father's body,
Like Niobe, all tears—why she, even she—
O God! a beast that wants discourse of reason
Would have mourned longer—married with my uncle,
My father's brother; but no more like my father
Than I to Hercules   (I,ii,143–53)

In *King Lear*, too, the breakdown of linguistic control is used
to high emotional effect:

    No, you unnatural hags,
I will have such revenges on you both
That all the world shall—I will do such things—
What they are yet I know not; but they shall be
The terrors of the earth.   (II,iv,277–81)

And the same play exhibits at its most powerful Shakespeare's
technique of counterpointing speech rhythms with a verse
structure:

And my poor fool is hanged! No, no, no life!
Why should a dog, a horse, a rat have life,
And thou no breath at all? Thou'lt come no more,
Never, never, never, never, never.
Pray you undo this button. Thank you, sir.
Do you see this? Look on her. Look, her lips.
Look there, look there!   (V,iii,305–11)

It seems to me that the Nurse's speeches in Act I, scene iii of
Romeo and Juliet show Shakespeare to be suddenly the master of
a technique that enabled him greatly to extend the expressive
resources of dramatic language.

NOTES

1. *Shakespeare's Early Tragedies* (London, 1968), p. 92.
2. In *The Friend*, 1818; *Coleridge on Shakespeare*, ed. Terence Hawkes,
    Penguin Shakespeare Library (Harmondsworth, 1969), pp. 87–8.

3. 1955, p. xxxvi.

4. There is ample evidence that this phrase, recorded as a proverb (M. P. Tilley, *A Dictionary of the Proverbs in England in the Sixteenth and Seventeenth Centuries* [Ann Arbor, 1950], B 596) is self-gratulatory, meaning, as Isaac Reed glossed it, 'I have a perfect remembrance or recollection'; though the opposite meaning may easily suggest itself to a modern reader, resulting in George Skillan's note, in French's Acting Edition (London, 1947), 'then suddenly realising that she is getting somewhat away from her subject and admitting it'. T. J. B. Spencer seems to concede some doubt in his New Penguin (Harmondsworth, 1967) gloss: '(perhaps) I have a good memory still'.

5. Barbara Everett, in her subtle essay 'Romeo and Juliet: The Nurse's Story' (*Critical Quarterly* [Summer 1972], 129–39), writes that '"Shake, quoth the dovehouse!" has not been quite helpfully enough glossed, presumably because few Shakespeare editors are sufficiently acquainted with what might be said to a very small child about an earthquake. It does not simply mean, as has been suggested, "the dovehouse shook"; it allows the unfluttered dovecote to satirise the earthquake, as in a comical baby mock-heroic—to be aloof and detached from what is happening to it' (p. 135).

6. I take it that the Nurse is saying that she was so shaken by the earthquake that she 'trudged' without having to be told to do so. Barbara Everett's comments on the passage (p. 136) seem rather to imply that the Nurse is saying that Juliet, in her tetchiness, had no call to send the Nurse packing, that the dovehouse was unimpressed equally by the fury of the earthquake and by the infant's crossness, and (possibly) that the Nurse was no more impressed by either. This seems to me to be an equally acceptable interpretation.

7. *Coleridge on Shakespeare*, p. 135.

8. See *William Shakespeare: The Most Excellent and Lamentable Tragedie of Romeo and Juliet, A Critical Edition*, by G. Walton Williams (Durham, N.C., 1964), p. xii.

9. It is of only incidental interest that the published screen script of Metro-Goldwyn-Mayer's film starring Norma Shearer and Leslie Howard prints *all* the verse as prose, with the explanation that this helped the actors 'to speak their lines as Hamlet wished his players to speak theirs, "trippingly on the tongue"' (*A Motion Picture Version of Shakespeare's 'Romeo and Juliet'* [New York, 1936], p. 249).

10. 'The New Way with Shakespeare's Text', *Shakespeare Survey* 8 (Cambridge, 1955), p. 98.

11. *Shakespeare's Tragic Sequence* (London, 1972), p. 40.

12. References are to the reprint in Geoffrey Bullough's *Narrative and Dramatic Sources of Shakespeare*, 8 vols. (London, 1957–75), vol. I (1957), pp. 284–363.

13. *The Observer*, 3 November 1935.

14. New Penguin edition (1967), p. 184.

15. *Ibid.*, pp. 33–4.

16. *Coleridge on Shakespeare*, p. 145.

17. W. Hughes Hallett, reviewing Ben Greet's production at Ealing, in *The Pilot*, 17 May 1902, p. 528.

18. Jonas Barish cites the Nurse as the earliest specific illustration of his claim that Shakespeare 'virtually invented linguistic satire on the English stage' (*Ben Jonson and the Language of Prose Comedy* [Cambridge, Mass., 1967], p. 284).

Philip C. McGuire

On the Dancing in
Romeo and Juliet

Romeo and Juliet first exchange words, hands, and lips against the backdrop of the dancing which occurs during Act I, Scene v. The significance of that dancing—the full range of its possible functions—comes most clearly into view if the "old" strategy of examining the cultural context within (and against) which Shakespeare worked is combined with a "new" approach that calls upon us to think about Shakespeare's plays not just as literature but also, perhaps even primarily, as theatre. The chapters on dancing in Sir Thomas Elyot's *The Boke Named the Governour* (1531) demonstrate the insights into *Romeo and Juliet* which such a combination of "old" and "new" approaches can generate. Elyot explains that dancing is an "exercise of the body" which is

> . . . of an excellent utilitie, comprehendinge in it wonderful figures, or, as the grekes do calle them, *Ideae*, of vertues and noble qualities, and specially of the commodiouse vertue called prudence. . . .[1]

Elyot's shaping premise that ordered movement of the human body can convey complex abstractions to those who are, in his words, "diligent beholders and markers" (241) is also a central assumption of advocates of a performance-centred approach responsive to the extra-verbal dimensions of Shakespearean drama. Conversely, Elyot's explication of the precise, extensive correspondences that he sees between dancing and "the commodious vertue called prudence" can contribute considerably

Reprinted with permission of author and *Renaissance and Reformation/ Renaissance et Réforme* from n.s. 5, No. 2 (1981), 87–97.

to making us "diligent beholders and markers" of *Romeo and Juliet* both on the page and in the theatre.

In explaining "howe in the fourme of daunsinge, nowe late used in this realme amonge gentilmen, the hole description of this vertue prudence may be founden out and well perceyued" (240–41), Elyot links each of the "meuyngs" or "motions" common to all dances with one of the seven branches of prudence.[2] Especially pertinent to *Romeo and Juliet* is Elyot's analysis of the correspondence between the second "motion" of dancing and the second branch of prudence:

> By the seconde motion, whiche is two in nombre, may be signified celeritie and slownesse, whiche two, all be it they seme to discorde in their effectes and naturall properties . . . yet of them two springeth an excellent vertue where unto we lacke a name in englisshe. Wherfore I am constrained to usurpe a latine worde, calling it *Maturitie.* . . .
>
> Maturitie is a meane betwene two extremities, wherin nothing lacketh or excedeth. . . . The grekes in a prouerbe do expresse it proprely in two wordes, whiche I can none other wyse inteprete in englisshe, but speede the slowly. . . .
>
> *Maturum* in latine maye be enterpreted ripe or redy, as frute when it is ripe, it is at the very poynte to be gathered and eaten. . . . Therfore that worde maturitie is translated to the actis of man, that when they be done with suche moderation, that nothing in the doinge may be sene superfluous or indigent, we may saye, that they be maturely done. . . .
>
> In the excellent and most noble emperour Octauius Augustus . . . nothinge is more commended than that he had frequently in his mouthe this word *Matura*, do maturely. As he shulde have saide, do neither to moche ne to litle, to sonne ne to late, to swiftly nor slowely, but in due tyme and measure.
>
> (243–45)

The passage suggests several ways in which the dancing during Act I, Scene v, does more than provide an interlude of communal harmony that contrasts with and thereby accentuates the violence stalking the streets and squares of Verona. Elyot's remarks help us to see how that violence arises from the absence— in the civic and familial structures of Veronese society as well as in specific characters—of virtues, particularly prudence and maturity, which the dancing during Act I, Scene v, might very well have signified to Renaissance audiences. As Elyot explains them, prudence and maturity are not necessarily incompatible with youth nor are they inevitably acquired with age. Capulet in his rage at Juliet's refusal to marry Paris, the Prince in his feeble efforts to preserve civil peace, perhaps even the Friar in his futile attempt to establish harmony in Verona by using his ecclesiastical offices to assist the young lovers—each acts in ways which are, by Elyot's criteria, as immature and imprudent as any actions undertaken by Romeo and Juliet, Tybalt and Mercutio and Paris.[3] For "diligent beholders and markers," then, the measures[4] through which the dancers move can function to define a norm of prudence and maturity applying to individuals and to the city and families of which they are members. That norm is, on the one hand, less harshly condemnatory of the lovers than the judgement found in Shakespeare's source,[5] but, on the other, it undercuts a modern audience's impulse uncritically to glorify Romeo and Juliet as flawless lovers.

Elyot's interpretation of *Maturum* also clarifies possible links between the dancing and the imagery of ripening articulated during the play. Capulet associates that imagery with Juliet when he rejects Paris's first proposal of marriage to her with the comment: "Let two more summers wither in their pride,/Ere we may think her ripe to be a bride" (I.ii.10–11). Juliet extends the imagery of ripening to include the love which she and Romeo share: "This bud of love, by summer's ripening breath,/May prove a beauteous flower when next we meet" (II.ii.121–22). The dancing can be seen as a "figure," a choreographic representation, of the processes of ripening which are aborted during the play, principally through the unknowing actions of the only two characters who declare that they will not dance—Romeo and Capulet.[6] Capulet's abrupt decision to have Juliet marry Paris forces Friar Lawrence, a character well-versed in the properties of herbs and flowers, to improvise a plan which calls upon Juliet to imitate the withering and subsequent ripening of plants by seeming to die and then, "in due tyme and measure" (245), re-appearing as Romeo's spouse. That plan, which is tantamount to having Juliet enact the Proserpine myth signifying the cycle of the seasons,[7] miscarries when the Friar's message to Romeo fails to reach him and Romeo returns too soon from exile, in effect cutting short the process of "ripening" which the Friar has set in motion.

Elyot's reference to "celeritie and slownesse" also directs attention to dancing as an activity which reconciles the extremes of speed and slowness which are repeatedly presented during

Romeo and Juliet. The sight of people "kepynge iuste measure and tyme" as they "daunse truely" (241) during Act I, Scene v, alerts us to other pairings during the play which juxtapose, rather than harmonize, speed and slowness in moving. One such pairing comes into focus at the conclusion of Act II, Scene iii, as we watch Romeo rushing to leave ("O let us hence; I stand on sudden haste"—l. 93) while the Friar, moving less quickly after him, warns: "Wisely and slow; they stumble that run fast" (l. 94).[8] A similar pairing emerges when the Nurse enters in Act II, Scene v, and Juliet, eager for word of Romeo, rushes toward the slow-moving figure whose lack of speed afoot she has just been lamenting:

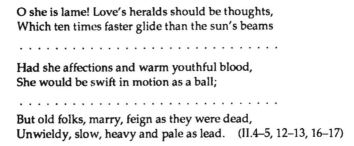

> O she is lame! Love's heralds should be thoughts,
> Which ten times faster glide than the sun's beams
>
> . . . .
>
> Had she affections and warm youthful blood,
> She would be swift in motion as a ball;
>
> . . . .
>
> But old folks, marry, feign as they were dead,
> Unwieldy, slow, heavy and pale as lead.   (II.4–5, 12–13, 16–17)

The "slouhte and celeritie" (245), to use Elyot's terms, of the characters' physical movements are analogous to the leaden tenacity with which most characters cling to old hatreds and, at the other extreme, the suddenness, "Too like the lightning" (II.ii.119), with which Romeo and Juliet are caught up in their new affections. Those affections give rise, in turn, to desires that move with extreme speed or slowness. Waiting for Romeo to come and their marriage to be consummated, Juliet yearns for the sun to speed across the heavens:

> Gallop apace, you fiery-footed steeds,
> Towards Phoebus' lodging; such a waggoner
> As Phaethon would whip you to the west,
> And bring in cloudy night immediately.   (III.ii.1–4)

Later, their night together spent, she refuses to acknowledge that the sun's movement has proceeded apace: "Yond light is not daylight, I know it, I;/It is some meteor that the sun exhales" (III.v.12–13). Romeo is willing to agree:

I am content, so thou wilt have it so.
I'll say yon grey is not the Morning's eye,
'Tis but the pale reflex of Cynthia's brow;
... Let's talk; it is not day.   (III.v.18–20, 25)

In filming *Romeo and Juliet*, Franco Zeffirelli[9] gave the motif of quick and slow movement prominence of a kind it probably cannot have on stage. Our first sight of Juliet during the film is as she dashes through the house in response to the Nurse's calls, a sequence which is later inverted when we see Juliet's parents running frantically in response to the Nurse's cries upon finding Juliet's "corpse." After first showing us Romeo, love-sick for Rosaline, walking lethargically through the streets of Verona, Zeffirelli gives us a prolonged shot of him running ecstatically through shrubs and trees after leaving Juliet on the balcony. In addition, the fight between Romeo and Tybalt is choreographed so that they repeatedly race after one another or after weapons that have been knocked away from them.

Zeffirelli's film departs from Shakespeare's script in ways which further emphasize speed and slowness afoot. While Shakespeare calls for Tybalt to return after Mercutio dies, Zeffirelli has Romeo dash through the streets in pursuit of Tybalt, and in Zeffirelli's film Friar Laurence's message to the exiled Romeo arrives too late not because the Friar carrying it has been held in quarantine but because Balthasar, whom we see astride a galloping horse, outpaces the Friar, whom we glimpse sometimes riding upon, sometimes walking beside a slow-footed donkey.

A moment—in both the play and Zeffirelli's film—which allows special emphasis to fall upon the motif of movement which is unduly quick or slow comes with Juliet's hurried entrance immediately after Friar Laurence has counseled Romeo: "Therefore love moderately; long love doth so;/Too swift arrives as tardy as too slow" (II.vi.14–15). The lovers can move to embrace with an eager swiftness that visually undercuts the Friar's words, in which "diligent beholders and markers" might detect an echo of Elyot's paraphrase of Octavius Augustus' injunction, *Matura:* " ... do neither to moche ne to litle, to soone ne to late, to swiftly nor slowely, but in due tyme and measure." The dancing during Act I, Scene v, can be seen, then, as the articulation through orderly bodily movements of a norm of properly-timed, mature action which is also expressed verbally through the Friar.

The connections between the dancing and the Friar's advice which Elyot's paraphrase of "*Matura*" helps to bring into focus are particularly relevant to the play's final scene, during which young Romeo, moving swiftly, arrives too early at the tomb of the Capulets and the Friar, his "old feet" (V.iii.122) stumbling over the graves, arrives too late. Their entrances, both equally "tardy," complete a pattern of mis-timed arrivals initiated in the opening scene when Tybalt enters just as Benvolio has drawn his sword in an effort to stop the fray (I.i.72). The same pattern also manifests itself not only in Tybalt's untimely return after Mercutio has died but also at a point the full significance of which Elyot's remarks help us to appreciate—the exchange between Romeo and Benvolio before they move on to the dancing at the house of the Capulets:

> *Ben.* Supper is done, and we shall come too late.
> *Rom.* I fear too early. . . .   (I.iv.105–06)

Friar Laurence's comments when Romeo comes to his cell after leaving Juliet turn on the question of whether Romeo has risen too early or, not having slept at all, has been awake too late.

> What early tongue so sweet saluteth me?
> Young son, it argues a distempered head
> So soon to bid good morrow to thy bed. . . .
> Therefore thy earliness doth me assure
> Thou art up-rous'd with some distemp'rature;
> Or if not so, then here I hit it right,
> Our Romeo hath not been in bed to-night.   (II.iii.32–42)

Thus, the dancing is preceded, and the balcony scene followed, by dialogue explicitly concerned with the issue of whether actions are timely—undertaken neither "to soone ne to late. . . . "

If the dancing embodies a norm of appropriately-paced, timely action, the relationship between the dancing and the lovers which each production of the play establishes is of potentially crucial significance. The possibilities are numerous. In the Royal Shakespeare Company's 1976 production of *Romeo and Juliet* (directed by Trevor Nunn with Barry Kyle), Romeo virtually snatched Juliet from amidst the dancers, who then drifted off-stage—a playing which isolated the lovers, in the force of their awakening affections, from the order implicit in the dancing. Zeffirelli in his film, on the other hand, had Romeo look on as

Juliet participated in a slowpaced, formal dance, then join—heedless of his earlier resolution not to dance—in a second dance, the Moresca, which pairs him occasionally with Juliet and concludes with the dancers whirling more and more quickly and wildly in two circles, one within the other, moving in opposite directions. Zeffirelli thus links the emerging love between Romeo and Juliet with energies that burst the confines of order, be it the civil order of Verona or the formal order of the dance. Another possibility is to have the dancing continue as Romeo and Juliet speak, join hands, and kiss, thus juxtaposing the lovers who are held almost motionless by the force of their new passions against the background movement of those who are keeping "due tyme and measure" as they dance.

While discussing "celeritie and slownesse," Elyot observes that those qualities "may be well resembled to the braule in daunsing (for in our englisshe tonge we say men do braule, when betwene them is altercation in wordes) . . ." (242). The different meanings of "braule" which Elyot notes point us towards affinities between kinds of actions in *Romeo and Juliet* which at first glance seem antithetical: the dancing during Act I, Scene v, and the battles, always preceded by an "altercation in wordes," which flare up during the play.[10] When Romeo, after his first entrance, becomes aware of the signs of fighting scattered about, he exclaims "O brawling love" (I.i.182), a phrase equally appropriate for the dancing in which he later refuses to join. Mercutio's characterization of Tybalt as "More than prince of cats" (II.iv.19) suggests that in his swordsmanship Tybalt displays a talent for "kepynge just measure and tyme" that is also apt in those who "daunse truely." Tybalt handles his sword, Mercutio warns Benvolio,

> . . . as you sing prick-song; keeps time, distance, and proportion;
> he rests his minim rests, one, two, and the third in your
> bosom. . . .   (II.iv.20–23)

In addition, Mercutio draws his sword against Tybalt with words that explicitly link dancing and duelling: "Here's my fiddlestick; here's that shall make you dance" (III.i.50–51).

In performance the affinities between dancing and duelling established by Shakespeare's script can be amplified by extra-verbal means. The Royal Shakespeare Company's 1976 production of *Romeo and Juliet*, for example, allowed the audience to watch actors who were shortly to do battle in the opening scene as Montagues and Capulets going through warm-up exercises and, ballet-like, practising thrusts and parries, advances and retreats. In Zeffirelli's film the second of the dances—the Moresca in which Romeo joins, momentarily linking hands with Juliet—ends with the movie audience looking on through the lens of a camera held waist-high in the centre of two circles of dancers whirling faster and faster.[11] That visual composition is repeated during the fight between Tybalt and Romeo, as a low-placed camera pans several times around the circle of Montagues and Capulets which forms, breaks, and re-forms around the two young men locked in battle. The choreography of gesture and movements during a production can also be patterned so as to direct attention to the parallels between the dancers who are "holding eche other by the hande or the arme" (235) and the swordsmen who find themselves paired in combat, sometimes at swords' or arms' length, sometimes hilt-to-hilt or hand-to-hand. The gestures common to such disparate activities can help to bring into focus the play's presentation of a major gestural pattern, one in which characters repeatedly join hands—in fighting, in dancing, in friendship, in love, and, when Montague and Capulet join hands (V.iii.296) over the corpses of their children, in mutual grief.

Common to both kinds of "braule" is the process of people pairing off with and moving in response to one another, and that process is a major structural element in *Romeo and Juliet*. In dancing, as Elyot points out, the pairings are between men and women:

> In every daunse, of a moste auncient custome, there daunseth
> to gether a man and a woman, holding eche other by the hande
> or the arme, whiche betokeneth concorde.   (235–36)

Romeo and Juliet presents us with pairings of men with other men—as friends and as antagonists—which clash with and disrupt the concord implicit in "the association of a man and a woman in daunsing" by which, Elyot adds, "may be signified matrimonie" (233). The interplay between the pairing of men with women and the pairing of men with other men in friendship or in enmity is most prominent in Act III, Scene i.[12] Mercutio dies from a hit taken when the newly married Romeo, acting out of love for Juliet, steps between his friend and his new kinsman Tybalt, the antagonist with whom Mercutio paired himself with the words, "Here's my fiddlestick; here's that shall make you dance" (ll. 50–51). Zeffirelli's film underscores the force of the friendship between Romeo and Mercutio by having the dying Mercutio cup Romeo's face in his hands as he asks, "Why the devil came you between us?" (l. 107). Earlier, on their way to the dance at the Capulets' house, Romeo had cupped Mercutio's face in his hands, seeking to quiet the terrors stirred in Mercutio by his musings upon Queen Mab: "Peace, peace, Mercutio, peace" (I.iv.95). The dying Mercutio's repetition of that gesture visually asserts the bond of friendship which Romeo, with this second effort to entreat Mercutio to a peace, has violated in ways which Romeo himself makes explicit:

> This gentleman, the Prince's near ally,
> My very friend, hath got this mortal hurt
> In my behalf. . . .
>   O sweet Juliet,
> Thy beauty hath made me effeminate
> And in my temper soft'ned valour's steel!   (ll. 114–16, 118–20)

The pairing of a man and woman in sexual love has, in Romeo's eyes, emasculated manly courage and friendship, both of which manifest themselves in the pairing of men with men.[13]

By stepping between Mercutio and Tybalt as they brawl, Romeo is caught up in a process which sees him subsequently paired in diverse ways with a succession of people. With Mercutio's dying, Romeo is paired with him in a bond of friendship which, momentarily overriding his pairing in matrimony with Juliet, moves him to pair himself in mortal combat with Tybalt. Romeo is afterwards paired sexually with Juliet in a union which consummates their marriage, and still later he is paired in combat with Paris before the tomb of the Capulets. That pairing of husband and would-be-husband—of antogonists in love—directly precedes the final pairing, in death, of lovers who first saw and kissed one another during a dance.

The interplay among the various modes of pairing—in dance, in sexual love, in marriage, in friendship, in mortal combat— helps to make manifest one of the fundamental structural configurations in the play. As characters move from pairing to pairing, they are in effect changing one "partner" for another and participating in a "dance" radically unlike the dancing in Act I, Scene v. That dancing, which paired men with women, signified the generative potential of sexual union and matrimony, but the "dance" in which all the characters are moving is the one by which Death leads all human beings to the grave. A detail of George Murcell's 1976 production of *Romeo and Juliet* at the St. Georges Theatre in London directed the audience's attention to the link between the dancing and the process by which characters move towards death. Romeo and Juliet exchanged their first words standing downstage while other couples continued dancing, one by one exiting upstage centre. As the last pair of dancers exited, the male (Benvolio, I believe) paused, turned, and stared for a moment or two towards the audience, covering his face as he did so with a death's head mask. The effect was to have the audience see the lovers joining hands and lips in the foreground while a figure of death looked on from the background. *Romeo and Juliet* is, we should note, the only Shakespearean play which concludes with its characters—living and dead—assembled in a graveyard, and the dancing during Act I, Scene v, can make visible to "the diligent beholder and marker" an order implicit in and giving shape to the events which bring them there. All in Verona "dance" towards the graveyard.

Elyot's commentary on dancing also suggests how the measures through which the dancers move during Act I, Scene v, can function as a means of assessing, of "measuring" the dance-like process by which the characters move towards death and the graveyard. To be most illuminating for today's actors, directors, and audiences, that "measure" of the play's actions need not—and probably should not—be rooted in the specific virtues of prudence and maturity but in Elyot's perception that dancing signifies the coming into being of a mean through the uniting of extremes. Elyot defines maturity as "a meane betwene two extremities, wherin nothing lacketh or excedeth" (244) and, using terms more specific to dancing, as "the meane or mediocrities betwene slouthe and celeritie, communely called spedinesse" (245). Elyot also discusses how "all qualities incident to a man, and also all qualities to a woman lyke wyse appertaynynge" (236) are "knitte to gether and signified in the personages of man and woman daunsinge" (238). "Wherefore," he explains,

> when we beholde a man and a woman daunsinge to gether, let us suppose there to be a concorde of all the saide qualities, being ioyned to gether. . . . And in this wise *fiersenesse* ioyned with *mildenesse* maketh *Seueritie; Audacitie* with *timerositie* maketh

> *Magnanimitie;* wilfull opinion and *Tractabilitie* (which is to be
> shortly persuaded and meued) makethe *Constance* a vertue;
> *Cousitise of Glorie,* adourned with *benignitie* causeth honour; *desire*
> *of knowlege* with *sure remembrance* procureth *Sapience; Shamfastnes*
> ioyned to *Appetite of generation* maketh *Continence,* which is a
> meane betwene *Chastitie* and *inordinate luste.*   (237–38)

The specific qualities which Elyot sees as "knitte to gether" in
dancing are less important in clarifying the dancing in *Romeo and*
Juliet than is the underlying principle of a mean being generated
by the reconciliation of extremes.[14]

The dancing during Act I, Scene v, of *Romeo and Juliet*
functions most deeply as a non-verbal but intelligible paradigm
of that principle—the "tempr'ring" of "extremeties" (II.Prol.14)—
which is shown breaking down in individuals, in families, and in
Verona itself during the course of the play. The dancing which is
the occasion of the lovers' meeting accentuates the fact that the
other pairings which emerge during the play do not moderate
extremes but intensify them. The all-male pairings arise from
and sharpen the untempered extremes of loving friendship and
mortal enmity, and those extremes, which clash most bloodily in
the pairings of Act III, Scene i, undercut the principle of the
mean "signified in the personages of man and woman daunsinge."
The relationship between Romeo and Juliet on which the male
pairings impinge most directly involves the opposite of the
process of reconciling masculine and feminine qualities which
Elyot sees as implicit in the act of dancing. Their affections do
not balance one another in generative concord. Instead, enflamed
by the very process of being shared and reciprocated, their
affections prove to be as consuming and deadly as the hatred
between their families.[15]

In the Verona of *Romeo and Juliet* the very act of people coming
together, of meeting—which is a fundamental condition of urban
society—marks not a moment of potential reconciliation (as in
the dancing) but a flashpoint. Extremes are not tempered by being,
in Friar Laurence's words, "incorporate/two in one" (II.vi.37).
Instead, they collide, destroying one another in the very act of
meeting and touching—"like fire and powder,/Which as they
kiss consume" (II.vi.10–11). Romeo and Juliet die, we recall, "with
a kiss" (V.iii.120), and the meeting of the Prince and the Friar
amidst the devastation which has emerged from the dance of
events stresses the failure of forces—civil and ecclesiastical, secular

and religious—to sustain that mean which is the basis for human order. Meeting in that same graveyard, Montague and Capulet—as fathers the agents of another mode of order, the familial, which has also collapsed—are moved for the first time to exchange words and hands in what the Prince characterizes as "A glooming peace" (V.iii.305). They do so over the paired and motionless bodies of their children, who first spoke, touched, and kissed amidst the dancing of Act I, Scene v.

NOTES

1. Sir Thomas Elyot, *The Boke Named the Governour*, ed. Henry Herbert Stephen Croft, I (London: 1883; rpt. New York: Burt Franklin, 1967), p. 239. Another work which illustrates the significance which certain Renaissance thinkers saw in dancing is Sir John Davies' *Orchestra or A Poem of Dancing* (1596). Davies argues that dance is the order which Love imposed on the formless void when creating the universe and then extended to human society by teaching mankind to dance:

   > Since when all ceremonious mysteries,
   > All sacred orgies and religious rites,
   > All pomps and triumphs and solemnities,
   > All funerals nuptials and like public sights,
   > All parliaments of peace and warlike fights,
   > All learned arts and every great affair,
   > A lively shape of dancing seems to bear.   (stanza 77)

   Davies stresses what might be called the civil and societal implications of dance, Elyot the personal and moral.

2. The seven branches of prudence are honor to God, maturity, providence, industry, circumspection, election, experience, and modesty (discretion).

3. As Elyot defines them, two of the other branches of prudence signified by dancing, providence and industry, also apply with particular force to the Prince and Friar Laurence.

   > Providence is wherby a man nat only forseeth commoditie
   > and incommoditie, prosperitie and aduersitie, but also
   > consulteth, and therewith endeuoureth as well to repelle
   > anoyaunce, as to attaine and gette profite and
   > aduauntage. . . . Semblably it is the part of a wyse man to

forsee and prouide, that either in suche things as he hath
acquired by his studie or diligence, or in suche affaires as
he hath in hande, he be nat indomaged or empeched by
his aduersaries.

In lyke maner a gouernour of a publike weale ought to
prouide as well by menaces, as by sharpe and terrible
punisshementes, that persones iuell and improfitable do
nat corrupte and deuoure his good subiectes . . . .

Industrie . . . is a qualitie procedyng of witte and
experience, by the whiche a man perceyueth quickly,
inuenteth freshly, and counsayleth spedily. Wherfore they
that be called Industrious, do moste craftily and depely
understande in all affiars what is expedient, and by what
meanes and wayes them maye sonest exploite them. And
those thinges in whome other men trauayle, a person
industrious lightly and with facilitie spedeth, and fyndeth
newe wayes and meanes to bring to effecte that he
desireth. (246–49)

4. Note how both the choreographic and the normative meanings of
"measure" converge in Benvolio's lines: "But let them measure
us by what they will,/We'll measure them a measure and be
gone" (I.iv.9–10). All quotations from *Romeo and Juliet* follow *The
Complete Plays and Poems of William Shakespeare,* ed. William Allan
Neilson and Charles Jarvis Hill, New Cambridge edition
(Cambridge, Mass.: Houghton Mifflin, 1942).

5. Arthur Brooke's *The Tragicall Historye of Romeus and Juliet* (1562).
The following excerpt from Brooke's Address to the Reader
accurately conveys the work's moral stance:

To this ende (good reader) is this tragicall matter written,
to describe unto thee a couple of unfortunate lovers,
thralling themselves to unhonest desire, neglecting the
authorite and advise of parents and frendes, conferring
their principall councells with dronken gossyppes, and
superstituous friers (the naturally fitte instrumentes of
unchastitie) attemptyng all adventures of peryll, for the
attaynyng of their wished lust . . . abusyng the honourable
name of lawefull mariage, to cloke the shame of stolne
contracts, finallye by all meanes of unhonest lyfe, hastening
to most unhappye deathe.

6. See I.iv.11, 14–16, 35–38 and I.v.32–35.

7. Perdita—like Juliet, a daughter whose parents think her dead—
explicitly refers to this myth in IV.iv.116–27 of *The Winter's Tale.*

8. Brents Stirling traces the theme of hastiness in his chapter on *Romeo and Juliet* in *Unity in Shakespearean Tragedy* (New York: Gordian Press, 1956), pp. 10–25.

9. Jack J. Jorgens provides a fine discussion of the film in *Shakespeare on Film* (Bloomington and London: Indiana University Press, 1977), pp. 79–91.

10. David A. Samuelson first called my attention to correspondences between the dancing and the fighting.

11. The whirling circles of dancers are then juxtaposed against the circle of those who listen motionlessly to the boy singing of mortality and the transience of love while Romeo and Juliet talk, touch, and kiss beyond that circle.

12. The efforts of Lady Montague and Lady Capulet to keep their husbands from joining in the opening brawl (I.ii.83, 87) could be taken as an earlier example of this conflict.

13. The tension between sexual love and male friendship is present in other Shakespearean plays, most prominently in *Two Gentlemen of Verona* and *The Merchant of Venice*.

14. Elyot's emphasis on finding a mean between extremes is also a central motif in Castiglione's *The Courtier*, which includes, in Book III, a discussion of how "from the union of male and female there results a composite which preserves the human species, and without which its parts would perish" (III.14).

15. The dance sequence provides the finest moments of Alvin Rakoff's television production of *Romeo and Juliet* for "The Shakespeare Plays," and the failure to link that sequence effectively with other moments in the play is an important facet of that production's over-all weakness. The production does little more than establish a simple contrast between the peace, order, and beauty of the dance and the violence, disorder, and death which ensue.

Robert Hapgood

West Side Story
and the Modern Appeal of
Romeo and Juliet

There is a sense in which a modern adaptation can be regarded
as a form of critical interpretation of the original, its emphases
and omissions, successes and failures serving to sharpen our
awareness of the original and its modern appeal. For a student of
Shakespeare, that is the primary interest of *West Side Story* today.[1]
Not that the creators of *West Side Story* ever intended to set
themselves up as Shakespearian commentators. Jerome Robbins,
its chief progenitor, director, and choreographer, was inclined to
play down the connection with Shakespeare, to whom no official
credits were given. As he told an interviewer when the musical
was in rehearsal, "*Romeo and Juliet* is merely a spring-board . . .
Basically, this is to be a tough contemporary story and a jazz
piece."[2] Yet no one has a keener sense of what is currently most
alive in the theater than do our leading theater artists. And when
artists of the international appeal of Robbins and his
collaborators—Leonard Bernstein (music), Stephen Sondheim
(lyrics), and Arthur Laurents (book)—transfer Shakespeare's
feuding Verona to the gang-ridden West Side of New York, their
choices are bound to be revealing.

By studying these choices and weighing their success, a
theater scholar should be able to reflect some light on the original
work, especially those parts of it that have spoken to the adapters
and their audiences.

Reprinted from *The Shakespeare Jahrbuch* 8 (1972), 99–112, with the
permission of the Shakespeare Gesellschaft.

In a cogent discussion of the aesthetics of operatic adaptations, Winton Dean sensibly maintains that an adaptation deserves to be considered not only in relation to its original but also on its own merits.[3] Certainly, *West Side Story* still has its moments as an independent work of art. While preparing this article, I have had two opportunities to see the film. I found some of the dancing as exciting as ever, most of all at the beginning—where the finger-snapping swagger of the rival gangs rises with a lift of the arms or a stylized skip to the condition of modern dance, relaxes, and rises again to a ballet-like kind of basketball before descending to a brawl. The sophisticated hoodlumism of "Gee, Officer Krupke" is still amusing, as in the mock lament:

> *My father is a bastard,*
> *My ma's an S.O.B.*
> *My grandpa's always plastered,*
> *My grandma pushes tea.*
> *My sister wears a mustache,*
> *My brother wears a dress.*
> *Goodness gracious, that's why I'm a mess!*

This skit anticipated, and perhaps suggested, the sequence in *Hair* satirizing Margaret Mead and others who make profession of "understanding" delinquent youth.

Over the years *West Side Story* has also taken on a nostalgic appeal, comparable to that of an earlier (1944) Robbins-Bernstein musical about New York, *On the Town*, revived this season on Broadway. One of the film showings I attended was part of a fund-raising gathering for a municipal homecoming, complete with mixed-up slides of the previous year's celebration narrated by the imperturbably talkative president of the local Lion's club. In its boosterism, the film was remarkably apt for the occasion.

Unabashedly, it glorifies America's largest city, not only its glamorous skyscrapers (as in the visual accompaniment to Bernstein's overture, a variously-colored abstract design that finally dissolves into the New York skyline) but what is picturesque about its slums. For all its focus on inter-racial conflict, the musical is bouyed by a hopefulness about American life that now seems gone forever.

West Side Story is thus already well on its way to becoming a period piece. Its intrinsic interest today seems to me mainly historical. When first produced in New York City in 1957, it was a great hit and was generally felt to be, as Robbins hoped, "as modern as tomorrow's headlines." The original cast then made a triumphal tour of the nation, before returning to renewed success in New York. A no less successful world tour followed. In 1961 the United Artists film version won ten academy awards.

West Side Story pioneered some important developments in the American musical. In her able study of *Das amerikanische Musical* (Munich, 1969), Ursula Gatzke devotes a chapter to it as the representative musical for the Fifties. At the time Agnes de Mille, the choreographer, saw the work as "a point of departure. After this we shall move into a more fluid, mobile theatre."[4] Bernstein lists the "theatrical risks" the innovators ran by daring to include "death and racial issues and young performers and 'serious' music and complicated balletics."[5] This was not of course the first American musical to adapt Shakespeare, nor has it proved to be the latest. It was preceded by Rodgers and Hart's *Boys from Syracuse* (1938, based on *Comedy of Errors*), *Swingin' the Dream* (1939, an ill-fated translating of *A Midsummer Night's Dream* to a Louisiana plantation, featuring Louis Armstrong as Bottom), and Cole Porter's *Kiss Me Kate* (1948, based on *Taming of the Shrew*), and followed by *Your Own Thing* (1968, based on *Twelfth Night*) and the current musical version of *Two Gentlemen of Verona*. It remains, however, the only such adaptation that does not have a happy ending.

As late as 1964 a revival of *West Side Story* in New York was still being received with enthusiasm. By its 1968 revival, however, the work was beginning to seem dated. Clive Barnes was remarking that he had never much cared for it and judging its jazz-dance old-fashioned and a dead end.[6] The musical has led an after-life in occasional reshowings of the film, in summer stock productions, and as a high school text. But it no longer has the impact it once did. A topical adaptation of *Romeo and Juliet* for the Seventies would inevitably focus not on gang warfare between Puerto Ricans and first-generation Americans but on the relationships of blacks and whites, as is borne out by the "related reading" of a recent high school study-guide to *West Side Story,* all of which has to do with blacks in America.[7]

Although *West Side Story* has in some respects lost its timeliness, it still can throw light on the contemporary appeal of *Romeo and Juliet*. For one thing, it confirms yet again that Shakespeare has become our Homer, his works having assumed the quality of myth. For Bernstein, one of the excitements of creating the musical was in finding "a contemporary setting echoing a classic myth."[8] Shakespeare himself seems to have been doing something similar. In her analysis of the "liebestod myth" in *Romeo and Juliet*, M. M. Mahood finds that Shakespeare treated the adventures of his Veronese lovers "with the detached judgment we accord history as well as with the implicated excitement we feel for myth . . . The resultant friction between history and myth, between the story and the fable, kindles the play into great drama."[9] Something of the same might be said of the *Romeo and Juliet* myth in *West Side Story*. For the adapters have used the parallel in knowing ways. As Laurents reports, they decided that the musical should not follow the play "closely and almost paraphrase the original" but rather "use the original as a reference point and let the story wind its own way, led by the character of today and today's youth."[10] There are obviously many resemblances, large and small. Similarities of character and plot have been thoroughly surveyed by Norris Houghton. Shakespeare seems also to have suggested subtler effects. The irony of Juliet's dream of her wedding night with Romeo, "Gallop apace, you fiery-footed steeds" (III, ii), unsuspecting that he has just been banished, is approximated in the stage-version by Maria's "I Feel Pretty" song. (In the film this bold irony is lost because the song precedes the settlement house dance.) Did Shakespeare's recurring imagery of sudden light against darkness suggest the following passage?: "Tonight, tonight, The world is full of light,/With suns and moon all over the place./Tonight, tonight,/The world is wild and bright, Going mad, shooting sparks into space." The differences between the play and the musical are equally clear, particularly toward the end; Laurents stresses that "the entire second half of the Shakespearian play rests on Juliet swallowing a magic potion," a device that he feels would not be acceptable in a modern play.

The resulting effect is of a modern story that moves in and out of myth. We are not, I believe, continually being invited to draw parallels—to see Friar Laurence in Doc the concerned druggist, Paris in the approved suitor, Chino, and so on. Such identifications take place only in retrospect. Only at high points does the *Romeo and Juliet* story come to mind: as the lovers first meet at the neighborhood dance, make their balcony-scene declarations of love on Maria's fire-escape, and are torn apart by the "rumble" between the two "houses," climaxing in the deadliness not of the sword but the switchblade.

This mythic heightening of key moments also contributes to the special genre of *West Side Story*. Very deliberately, the adapters were seeking a middle area, above a conventional musical yet not pretending to the status of opera or ballet, as a direct treatment of *Romeo and Juliet* would have invited. They drew inspiration from first-hand observation of West Side street life but were careful to avoid "slice of life" realism; Laurents points out, "the dialogue is my translation of adolescent street talk into theatre: it may sound real but it isn't." At the same time they were alert to the "opera trap," as Bernstein put it. This was not to be another *Porgy and Bess.* The chief problem, he felt, was "to tread the fine line between opera and Broadway, between realism and poetry, ballet and 'just dancing,' abstract and representational . . . The line is there, but it's very fine, and sometimes takes a lot of peering around to discern it."[11]

Their success in doing so in the stage version may be appreciated by contrast with the film and with the novelized treatment. Robbins recognized that a transfer from stage to screen raises new questions of style: "The main problem is welding together a realistic scene with dancing which is not realistic. In the stage version, we have quite stylized settings—very unreal. In a full-length picture, such settings would seem silly. And so I've had to adapt the choreography to the more realistic setting in the film."[12] Unfortunately, a unified style was never found; Robbins himself withdrew from the film in mid production.[13] To Oliver Smith, whose "basically abstract" designs for the staged *West Side Story* remain his favorite work, the film seemed to have "no consistency."[14] The most effective real settings are those that most resemble stage sets, for there is something incongruous about teen age gangs singing and dancing down an ordinary street.

Such incongruity is still more striking in the naturalistic "novelization." In the musical, the only theft is that of a vegetable during the opening give and take between the Jets and the Sharks, but the novel begins: "Riff Lorton looked at the wrist-watch he had rolled off a drunk the week before" and goes on to muse over the various muggings that he and his gang might undertake. When Tony mounts the fire-escape for the novel's balcony scene, his mind is full of calculations for flight if caught; and the scene is set thus: "Across the yard a toilet flushed with a throaty gargle and rumbling of old pipes . . ." In the staged musical, the *Romeo and Juliet* parallels work together with the semi-classical style of the music, dance, and design to raise the tone of the work above such squalor.

Another salient feature of *Romeo and Juliet* that *West Side Story* capitalizes upon is its youthfulness, not only in its subject of young love but in its manner of presentation. It was "the intensity of adolescent feeling" in the play that first prompted Robbins to think of making an adaptation. Shakespeare intensified his pace by compressing the time of his source from months to less than a week. Laurents went still further, confining the action to two successive evenings, five o'clock to midnight. Shakespeare's "hot days" became the "last days of summer"; Robbins remarked about the real West Side: "Those kids live like pressure cookers. . . . There's a constant tension, a feeling of the kids having steam that they don't know how to let off."[15] Stephen Sondheim was later to regret the insouciance of some of his lyrics: "I was so anxious to show off—to demonstrate I could rhyme anything that I still wince over some of the lyrics. Maria would just not say 'I feel pretty/I feel charming/it's alarming/how charming I feel.'"[16] Certainly, the word-play in the last line of this song ("I'm in love with a pretty wonderful guy") seems forced. But at their best his lyrics have an appropriately brash exuberance.

In the original production the dancing had a headlong energy that made it physically hazardous. Newspaper accounts mention that Carol Lawrence (Maria) was "sidelined for four weeks by a broken foot" and that Larry Kert (Tony) "has used almost as much bandage-and-liniment as greasepaint, suffering at various times a fractured rib cage, a serious cut over one eye, a temporarily dislocated spine, and various minor cuts and bruises." The music, especially for the scenes of conflict, has the same kind of drive. Even the love songs had a fresh force when sung by the original cast that was softened in the film. Later Bernstein would reconcile himself to the decision to cast primarily for dancing rather than singing ability: "I guess that we were right not to cast 'singers'; anything that sounded more professional would inevitably sound more experienced, and then the 'kid' quality would be gone."

Beyond anything else it is the feud and the tragic attempt of the young lovers to bridge the conflict that is at the heart of what the creators of *West Side Story* saw in *Romeo and Juliet*. As the credits always indicate, the adaptation is "based on a conception of Jerome Robbins." The conception has a fascinating history. The idea for such an adaptation may first have occurred to George Balanchine. Recalling the film, *Goldwyn Follies* (1938), Leo Lerman explains that "in Balanchine's opus, *Romeo and Juliet* was danced and mimed in period, and then it all transformed to a Manhattan East Side tenement area replete with local toughs and festoons of drying wash."[17] Clive Barnes points out that for Robbins *West Side Story* "was not the first time he had introduced a modern variant of *Romeo and Juliet* to the New York stage, for in 1949 he staged his ballet *The Guests* for the New York City Ballet, and this also had a theme (in this case made virtually abstract) of ill-matched lovers crossing caste lines of either race or social class.[18] Robbins himself dates the conception from being asked by an actor friend to read the part of Romeo: "I began to think of how to transpose this violence of emotion to the world today. I began to explore possibilities of making it come alive. I looked for analogous situations today."[19] In 1949, too, Bernstein reports:

> Jerry R. called today with a noble idea: a modern version of *Romeo and Juliet* set in slums at the coincidence of Easter-Passover celebrations. Feelings running high between Jews and Catholics. Former: Capulets; latter: Montagues. Juliet is Jewish. Friar Lawrence is a neighborhood druggist. Street brawls, double death—it all fits.

At this stage, Laurents adds, the working title was *East Side Story*, depicting "the lower East Side of New York: specifically Allen Street for Juliet and the Capulets, Mulberry Street for Romeo and the Montagues." Despite the enthusiasm of the collaborators (all of whom are Jewish) for this conception, it was delayed by other career preoccupations until it began to seem "not very fresh." "*Abie's Irish Rose* to music," was a mocking friend's term for it. Then in 1955, when Bernstein and Laurents were in Hollywood, "discussion of the racial problems of Los Angeles led quickly and directly to shifting the locale of our work from the lower East Side of New York to the upper West Side; and the conflict to that between a Puerto Rican gang and a polymorphous self-styled 'American' gang." Several weeks later, Bernstein records that Robbins "loves our gang idea." The work became known as *Gang Way*, not becoming *West Side Story* until shortly before its opening.

Although the adapters were responsive to the changing topicality of the conflicting groups, their engagement with the pattern of divided groups trying to come together was basic and longstanding.[20] This pattern is deeply rooted in the nature of American theater, which often functions as one of the "melting pots" of a diverse society. It is there that Jewish, black, and homosexual writers and performers have been able to address a general American audience and celebrate their common humanity. Robbins has been explicit about his personal desire for community. While insisting that *West Side Story* is not "preachy," he told an interviewer: "The story has a hopeful as well as a tragic side . . . It says that the price of prejudice is too high to pay . . . Love and peace cannot exist in a world in which there are such hostile forces as now exist."[21] The same desire prompted his work on *Fiddler on the Roof*, which he directed and choreographed:

> For research, Robbins had everyone reading Zborowski and Herzog's sociological study of "shtetl" (the Yiddish word for a village community) life in Russia, *Life is with People*. As for the company, he says, "I wanted to make a *shtetl* out of *them*. To make them understand what the community in *Fiddler* was like. I told them to think of the Jews in Anatavka as though they were a theatrical company trying out a new show out of town. Each person was trying to build something in common with his neighbors."[22]

The adapters of *West Side of Story* seem to have discovered such a feeling. After its opening night, Bernstein exulted that "we all really *collaborated*; we were all writing the *same* show. Even the producers were after the same goals we had in mind." The company also shared this spirit. As Agnes de Mille commented, the strength of the production "lies not in individuals but in its group anger, group clashes, group emotions."

This longing for community is everywhere in *West Side Story* itself. What holds the Jets together is a sense of belonging: "You're never alone,/You're never disconnected!/You're home with your own." In showstopping "America," Rosalia dreams of Puerto Rico, but she is overwhelmed by Anita and the other girls who rejoice in their new home: "Immigrant goes to America,/Many hellos in America." At their make-believe wedding, Tony and Maria sing of their union: "Make of our hands one hand,/Make of our hearts one heart,/Make of our vows one last vow:/Only death will part us now." The theme is clearest in their dream of a world "Somewhere," a world without hostility, in which they can find "a new way of living . . . a way of forgiving." The stage direction reads:

The lovers hold out their hands to each other; the others follow suit: Jets to Sharks; Sharks to Jets. And they form what is almost a procession winding its triumphant way through this would-be world, as they sing the words of the song . . .

By common consent, this was the least effective number in the stage-version (the dance part was omitted altogether from the film). Such direct wish-fulfillment seemed sentimental in an otherwise "tough" production.

Plainly, the moment in *Romeo and Juliet* that was most seminal for *West Side Story* was that in III, i, in which Romeo tries in vain to make peace with Tybalt. Such an effort is unknowingly parodied by Glad Hand , the "overly cheerful" recreation director, who attempts ineffectually to organize "a few get-together dances." It is cynically parodied by the self-serving peace-keeping of the police officers. At Maria's urging and at the cost of being called "chicken," Tony like Romeo seeks to minimize and finally to stop the "rumble," only to compound and become complicit in its violence.

The pattern is most convincingly realized in what is still for me the most moving part of *West Side Story*, the duet toward the end between Maria and Anita. At first Anita upbraids Maria:

A boy like that who'd kill your brother,
Forget that boy and find another!
One of your own kind—
Stick to your own kind!

Maria then counters, using Anita's melody but her own words:

I hear your words—
And in my head
I know they're smart . . .
But my heart
Knows they're wrong.

Then both sing at once, Maria's love soaring over Anita's hate. At last Anita is won over as Maria sings her tender lyric.

I have a love, and it's all that I have.
Right, or wrong, what else can I do?
I love him; I'm his,
And everything he is
I am, too.

Elsewhere the musical motifs of love and hate are separate, or at most juxtaposed (as in the pre-Rumble rendition of "Tonight," in which the gangs, the lovers, and Anita are all "waiting expectantly for the coming of night, but for very different reasons"). Here, they directly conflict, in the music as well as in the words. The lyrics are for once simple and direct, free from over-cleverness. As a result, the play's central concern with the melting of hatred through love is powerfully dramatized.

Maria's success with Anita is immediately undone by the cruelty of the Jets, and she tells them the lie that clinches the tragedy: "Bernardo was right . . . If one of you was bleeding in the street, I'd walk by and spit on you. Tell the murderer Maria's *never* going to meet him! Tell him Chino found out and—and shot her!" Only Tony's death and Maria's grief and gestures of forgiveness toward "both their houses" bring any softening in the rival gangs. It is thus as a social drama that *West Side Story* finds its resolution. There is a suggestion of a love-death when Tony cries out: "Come and get me, too, Chino." But primarily the tragedy is of young love thwarted not by fate but by social determinism, the workings of a condition in which everybody is involved in the violence (as Maria says of Tony at the end, "We all killed him") and yet in which nobody means for it to happen.

If the emphases and strengths of *West Side Story* reveal something of the original, so do its limitations and difficulties. Robbins aspired to create a work that would make Shakespeare's poetry "come alive in 20th century terms, through the cadence of Arthur Laurents' lines and Leonard Bernstein's music."[23] Regrettably, this does not happen. Although the dialogue succeeds in rendering "articulate inarticulate adolescence," it never achieves eloquence. The vitality of Bernstein's music is in the scenes of violence. There it genuinely finds a semi-classical level, drawing on the harmonies and rhythms of classical as well as jazz and Latin traditions.[24] But the love songs are scarcely more than Tin Pan Alley "hits." It takes a Prokofieff to match the lyricism of Shakespeare's words.

A related difficulty was in finding a modern Romeo. Tony was the great casting problem for the stage musical. It required a long, nationwide search to find Larry Kert, and he remained in the part through a series of Juliets. Apparently, there are not many actors who are to the right degree at once romantic and virile. The movie Tony was neither. Combining comedy with tragedy is of course thoroughly Shakespearian; but it is a tricky mixture and *West Side Story* overdid it. Even Shakespeare may have erred in the attempted humor of incidents after the death of Mercutio: the exchange between Peter and the musicians (IV, v) seems to me a failure. Certainly, the stage-version of the musical went wrong in this respect. Originally, the "Officer Krupke" number was drastically misplaced; coming after the rumble, its manic, Mercutio-like cleverness clashed with the sobered mood that the fatalities brought. It is much more effective when, as in the film, it comes early in the story.

To some extent even the more durable part of what *West Side Story* has to tell us about *Romeo and Juliet* may well have had its day. Many of its lessons have already been applied to the play in Franco Zeffirelli's stage and screen versions. He too cast unknowns in the leading roles and in general capitalized on the youthfulness of the work. He too (although with no more success) sought to substitute music for the lyricism of the lines. Interestingly, he seems to have recognized but played against the conventional view of the *Romeo and Juliet* myth, refreshing it by stressing the physical rather than the ethereal side of their love. Alan Downer was not far wrong in summing up Zeffirelli's approach as "*West Side Story* without Leonard Bernstein."[25]

Yet it can be the final interpretive contribution of an adaptation to make contemporary tendencies so extreme that it helps to predict the next swing of the theatrical pendulum. What can *West Side Story* disclose about the *Romeo and Juliet* of the Seventies? One such tendency is the movement away from Shakespeare's dialogue. Zeffirelli cut more than half of his text; *West Side Story* did not use Shakespeare's words at all. Now that Peter Brook in *A Midsummer Night's Dream* and the film of *King Lear* has found a new way of delivering Shakespeare's lines— very much as poetry, freely stylized, often spoken by actors directly facing the audience—it seems likely that the dialogue of *Romeo and Juliet* will soon be honored in the same way. Along with this should come a renewed emphasis on the private tragedy of the lovers (the astonishing success of Segal's *Love Story* indicates the popular hunger for such an emphasis). And with these developments should come a keener awareness of their individuality. The emphasis might, indeed, shift from the "intensity of adolescent feeling" of Romeo to the relative maturity of Juliet, which grows until it leads, very disturbingly, to suicide.

But a theater scholar must not presume on his opportunities for prophecy. The next step in the theatrical interpretation of

Romeo and Juliet is of course ultimately unpredictable. For it depends not only on the times and the reverses of tradition but on the gifts of its interpreters: on what they can find in their own lives that will—as did *West Side Story*—bring Shakespeare's play to renewed life, however brief.

NOTES

1. The script of *West Side Story* is most readily available in *Romeo and Juliet and West Side Story*, introd. by Norris Houghton (New York, 1965); it also appeared in *Theater Arts* (Oct. 1959). The vocal score has been published by G. Schirmer, New York, 1957. Recordings include the original New York cast (Col. OL-5230: OS 2001; Phi [E] BBL 7272: SBBL 504 [s]) and the film soundtrack (Col. OC-5670: OS-2070 [2]; CBS [E] BPG 62058; SBPG 62058 [s]). A "novelization of the Broadway musical" by Irving Shulman was published in New York (1961). Thanks are due to Miss Martha Whitten, who undertook as an undergraduate independent-study project to recreate the 1957 production.

2. David Boroff, "West Side Story," *Dance Magazine*, August 1957, p. 19.

3. *Shakespeare in Music*, ed. P. Hartnoll (London, 1967), pp. 89–96.

4. Quoted by Peter Brinson, *London Times*, Dec. 7, 1958.

5. Leonard Bernstein, "Excerpts from a West Side Log." *Playbill*, 1957.

6. Clive Barnes, "A New Look at *West Side Story*," *New York Times*, Sep. 1, 1968.

7. Daniel Fader and Elton McNeil, *Hooked on Books* (New York, 1968), pp. 121–122.

8. David Ewen, *Leonard Bernstein* (Philadelphia, 1967), p. 124.

9. *Shakespeare's Wordplay* (London, 1957), p. 59.

10. Arthur Laurents, "Musical Origins," *Playbill*, 1957. All subsequent quotations from Mr. Laurents are taken from this source.

11. Bernstein, "Excerpts." All subsequent quotations from Mr. Bernstein are taken from this source.

12. Quoted by D. Lyle, *New York Herald Tribune*, August 21, 1960.

13. Stanley Kaufmann, "West Side Glory," *Dance Magazine*, Oct. 1961.

14. "The Designer Talks," *Plays and Players*, Nov. 1970, p. 20.

15. Boroff, p. 15.
16. Patricia Bosworth, "A Conversation with Steve Sondheim," *Playbill*, 1971.
17. "At the Theatre: *West Side Story*," *Dance Magazine*, Nov. 1957, p. 12.
18. Barnes, "A New Look."
19. Boroff, p. 15.
20. Cf. Peter Ustinov's *Romanoff and Juliet* (1957), a Shavian comedy depicting an American girl and her Russian lover.
21. Boroff, p. 18.
22. Robert Kotlowitz, "Corsets, Corned Beef and Choreography," *Show*, Dec. 1964, p. 91.
23. Boroff, p. 18.
24. Wilfred Mellers, *Music in a New Found Land* (New York, 1965), pp. 428–432; Robert Evett, "Bernstein's Romeo and Juliet," *New Republic*, Sep. 9, 1957.
25. "For Jesus' Sake Forbear: Shakespeare *vs.* the Modern Theater," *Shakespeare Quarterly*, Spring 1962, p. 220.

Barbara Hodgdon

Absent Bodies, Present Voices: Performance Work and the Close of Romeo and Juliet 's Golden Story

To begin with endings, consider two brief texts. Although neither comes from the Elizabethan age or its drama, both, I want to argue, have much to do with *Romeo and Juliet's* close in performance. The first is a late nineteenth-century poem by A. E. Housman:

> With rue my heart is laden
> For golden friends I had,
> For many a rose-lipt maiden
> And many a lightfoot lad.
>
> *
>
> By brooks too broad for leaping
> The lightfoot boys are laid;
> The rose-lipt girls are sleeping
> In fields where roses fade.[1]

The second text, a news account, carries a dateline of 11 March 1987, Bergenfield, New Jersey:

> Four teenagers—two sisters and two young men—killed themselves together today in a suicide pact. The victims were found at about 6:30 a.m., seated in a car with its engine running in a garage at a sprawling garden apartment complex. At the community's high school yesterday, sorrowful students said abuse of alcohol and other drugs was common among local teen-agers, and they said school officials had been slow to respond to the problem. Only when the principal announced

Reprinted from *Theatre Journal*, 41:3(October 1989), 341–59.

244 Romeo and Juliet

that a "terrible tragedy" had taken place did most of the school's 1,200 students learn of the suicides. "The whole place was quiet for a while, except for people crying," said Fernando Marrero, a junior. . . . On the front seat of the car was "a lengthy suicide note" written in pen on a brown paper bag, said the Bergen County Prosecutor, Larry J. McClure, who added that the deaths occurred "by way of an obvious agreement." "The note had been signed by all four of them," Mr. McClure said. In the note, he said, they asked to be "waked together" and "buried together."[2]

Seven days later, two other teen-agers, Lisa L. Klaeger and Christopher Herdt, attempted suicide in the same garage but were rescued by a police rookie who was checking the site as part of his routine patrol. *The New York Times* concluded its story of this second incident with the following description—reporter as set designer, constructing images of waste for a final tableau without actors:

> Today that cinder block enclosure was empty except for a battered hubcap, an empty bottle of Hawaiian Punch, the cardboard carton from a six-pack of beer and the slats of the garage door, which the police had torn from its hinges. Under the splintered boards was the cover of a music cassette by the heavy-metal rock group AC/DC. Its title: "If You Want Blood, You've Got It."[3]

Housman's lyric writes a double epitaph memorializing the speaker's anguish as well as the value and beauty of youth, celebrating both in a romantic, even sentimental, freeze-frame, which joins the speaker, across time, to his own loss in condensed, perfected images suspended in and simultaneously escaping time's natural decay. Although not as seemingly transhistorical as Housman's verses, *The Times*'s account documents one incident among many. A year earlier, that same newspaper reported 5,000 adolescent suicides per year, noting that many more are categorized as accidents or other deaths in order to spare families and that, for each completed, there are some one hundred attempts.[4] According to Gay Luce, author of *Why Adolescents Kill Themselves*,

> Adolescent suicide is horrifying, unthinkable and a little unreal to most adults, for we tend to be complacent about the troubles of the young. To the modern adult, *Romeo and Juliet* may seem

only a story. Yet many adolescents cling to one another in similar
love, with the desperation of a last hope in a lonely world. . . .
Literary descriptions of childhood suicides seem bizarre, yet
they resemble modern case histories.[5]

Housman's verses and *The Times*'s report of a tragedy that shocked
not just a particular middle-class community but the entire nation
articulate two opposed and often, though not necessarily,
contradictory paradigms for the history of *Romeo and Juliet*'s close
in performance. On the one hand there is a powerfully
conservative impulse, rooted in nineteenth-century theatrical
tradition as well as in its cultural milieu, to enclose its *Liebstod*-
like myth of timeless tryst in the tomb, to preserve its "golden
story"—including all the lyrical beauty of its verse—inviolate as
a precious icon of young love, glorified tragedy, and immortal
"Shakespeare." Such a *Romeo and Juliet* permits audiences to
mourn—not only for "Juliet and her Romeo" but also for their
own youthful (or not so youthful) desires—while simultaneously
protecting them by offering a familiar, comfortable relationship
to Shakespeare's tragedy, a relationship that may be, and often
is, further distanced by period costumes and Renaissance decor,
which isolate its historical moment, engaging spectators with a
celebrated Elizabethan past and with one particular, and
particularly famous, artifact of its privileged genre. This
performance model assumes a vision of the play not unlike that
of Housman's "lightfoot boys" and "rose-lipt girls"—intact,
timelessly universal, transcendent. On the other hand, a second
model for *Romeo and Juliet* in the theatre begins from an equally
powerful, and potentially radical, impulse to appropriate
Shakespeare's playtext in order to address contemporary cultural
circumstances. Such versions have at least two theatrical
antecedents—the 1956 Laurents-Bernstein-Sondheim-Robbins
West Side Story and Bertolt Brecht's alienation aesthetic, analogues
which, either singly or together, generate what might be called
naked or unfamiliar Shakespeare—potentially unsafe, not "the
real thing." In responding to this second performance model,
reviewers' and critics' mourning focuses not so much on the
star-crossed lovers' tragedy but on the loss of Shakespeare's poetic
lyricism and of traditional staging conventions. These judgments,
however, may mask a further potential source of discomfort—
that such *Romeo and Juliet*s may confront spectators with their
own complicity, not only in the playtext's events but also with

those which, as in *The Times*'s 1987 account, make front-page headlines: "We all killed him," says Maria at *West Side Story*'s end; the final stage direction reads, *"The Adults—Doc, Shrank, Krupke, Glad Hand—are left bowed, alone, useless."*[6]

*   *   *

However articulated, such a consistent sense that *Romeo and Juliet* in performance bespeaks loss invites further inquiry. What seems especially intriguing here is that Shakespeare's playtext, which takes loss as one of its central subjects, not only engenders a similar experience in its spectators but also reproduces that experience in the circumstances of its theatrical performance. For, in the theatre, the history of the playtext itself is a history of loss. Because this history is most especially and acutely visible at the close, I want, first, to trace that process through several contemporary stagings and, then, in confronting the issues posed by this performance variorum,[7] to argue for repositioning the study of Shakespearean performance within a cultural framework.

From Juliet's death forward, *Romeo and Juliet* describes a series of seemingly anti-climactic events analogous to those in the final scene of a detective fiction: alarmed discoveries by the Watch, the Prince, and the lovers' parents; accusations; hurried questions; appeals to authority and patience; the Friar's lengthy explanation; the evidence of imperfect near-witnesses, Balthasar and Paris's Page; Romeo's letter to his father, appropriated by the Prince just before he accuses the feuding families; the fathers' reconciliation, including their somewhat discomforting commercial rivalry over the golden statues; the Prince's conclusive pronouncement. Even though Shakespeare's playtext crowds multiple entrances and explanations together, repeating a pattern initiated by the other two crowd scenes (I. i and III. i), it seems almost perverse, especially in a play that calls attention to its characters' impatience and the speed of its events, for the action to slow down (once it's too late), to have and take all the time in the world to resolve its "two hours' traffic." Particularly at issue are the Friar's forty-one lines, retelling the story for the assembled community, asking for pardon.[8] Following Samuel Johnson, who thought it "much to be lamented that the poet did not conclude the dialogue with the action, and avoid a narrative of events which the audience already knew,"[9] eighteenth- and nineteenth-century theatrical practice concentrated upon the lovers' deaths and then provided a symbolic tableau of reconciliation, constructing closure as a condensed image of the privileged lovers, one which not only has affinities with narrative painting (and, later, with the still photograph) but which has persisted throughout theatrical history as an almost obligatory finale.[10] Although he admitted that *Romeo and Juliet's* ending lacks the "resourceful breadth of effect" characteristic of *Cymbeline*, Harley Granville-Barker argued for restoring not just the Friar's speech but Shakespeare's full scene.[11] Contemporary theatrical practice, however, pays only selective attention to his suggestion. Details of several recent stagings can provide a kind of composite map of this history of loss, restoration, and further loss.

Peter Hall's 1961 Royal Shakespeare Company *Romeo and Juliet*, for example, offered fairly representative cuts.[12] Hall compressed the Watchmen's dialogue and cut fourteen lines of the Friar's speech—including its somewhat contradictory opening, "I will be brief, for my short date of breath/Is not so long as is a tedious tale" (V. iii. 229–230)[13]—as well as the explanations of Balthasar and Paris's Page, moving directly from the Prince's "We still have known thee for a holy man" (270) to "Where be these enemies?" (291) and so on through to the conclusion of Shakespeare's text. Following the Prince's last lines, a mass exit generated the familiar stage picture of Romeo and Juliet's entwined bodies, positioned slightly off-center, their presences overwhelmed by the massive walls of the tomb. Slow drumbeats from offstage marked the growing distance between mourners and dead; finally, the single lantern, carelessly left behind, which had illuminated their faces, went out.

In 1976, Chris Dyer, Trevor Nunn's designer, transformed the Royal Shakespeare Theatre into a Globe-like auditorium, with an open stage, the proscenium arch disguised, and two balcony rows of seats running across the back of the stage.[14] Nunn's Romeo, Ian McKellen, carried Francesca Annis's Juliet from a midstage trap, let her stand, and then held her close, her arms encircling his neck as he sat, his feet in the tomb-trap on "Here will I remain." As he drank the potion, one of Juliet's hands fluttered with life, and Romeo fell, Juliet in his arms, just as her hand moved to touch his cheek. From this point forward, Nunn's staging played a nearly complete text, which concluded by recognizing the double function of the final speech as both narrative close and epilogue. Whereas the Prince spoke the first two lines, Chorus addressed the rest to the audience, splitting this last partial sonnet between two speakers as though to echo the sonnet Romeo and Juliet shared when they met at the Capulets' ball. And then, on this simulated Elizabethan stage, the play immediately dissolved as Chorus waved on the rest of the company for the usual bows.

Another variant, Ron Daniels's 1980 Royal Shakespeare Company staging, consistently emphasized the repetition—and transformation—of actions: bed and bier were similarly positioned; in the three public scenes, people stood in precisely the same relationship to the Prince.[15] At the close, Capulet extended his hand to Montague, and they embraced before the Prince spoke his last words. As the music played earlier for Juliet's funeral returns—a setting for Thomas Nashe's "Adieu, farewell, earth's blisse"—a general exit isolated the dead in a spotlight, framed by the shadowed presences of the play's three father figures, together with Lady Capulet. But Daniels's vision of *Romeo and Juliet* as *A Midsummer Night's Dream* become nightmare suggested a different original strategy: "If I were really bold," he mused during a late rehearsal period, "I would have you all going round to reconcile in an echo of the final dance at the Capulet ball."[16]

Precisely such a "dance"—expressed through an exchange of speaking looks—closed and enclosed Franco Zeffirelli's 1968 film of *Romeo and Juliet*. Omitting the discovery scene entirely, Zeffirelli's filmtext cut from the lovers to a high-angle long shot of Verona's public square, seen through veils of early-morning mist. The Montagues and Capulets, who twice before exploded into this space in parallel intercut movements, now joined in single, solemn procession, bearing Romeo and Juliet's bodies, dressed in their wedding garments, to be buried. To the sounds of tolling funeral bells and torches sputtering in the wind, the mourners' footsteps echoed on the stones as the families gathered on the church steps. The camera isolated individual faces (especially the Nurse's), which reflected guilt, sorrow, and loss. Then, in a low-angle close-up, the Prince's "All are punished!" admonished both on-screen and off-screen watchers, equally complicit in the play's tragedy.[17]

As the two families filed through the cathedral door toward the camera, a brief pan, from full shot to mid-close-up, isolated the dead lovers, side by side on the bier. Then the credits began to roll up: next, the film image was further enclosed with a lattice-like golden frame. Again, the camera singled out particular faces and groups. Intriguingly, the women remained separate, aloof and hesitant; it was the men who touched or embraced. Like Shakespeare's, Zeffirelli's Verona threw the weight of privilege to masculine power. The film's last shot held on Verona's massive walls, seen from the empty square, while Laurence Olivier's sonorously authoritative tones, in voice-over, spoke the story's epilogue. As in the film's opening shot, the sun was just rising, and if it seemed that Romeo and Juliet's story was over, with the Montague-Capulet feud resolved on a conciliatory note and the picture firmly set within an enclosural frame, it could also have seemed that this story is possibly, perhaps infinitely, repeating itself—just as the film, as cultural product, is infinitely repeatable, always the same.

Among these performance variants, Hall's finale typified not only the prevailing stress on the Prince's patriarchal authority but also the option of a kind of viewer's choice, which replaces one final stage picture—the familial reconciliation—with another—the spotlit image of the two lovers, abandoned by their parents—thereby offering spectators a last, painfully perfect, voyeuristic glimpse of timeless union. Like Hall's, Nunn's staging also "belongs" to Romeo and Juliet. Although splitting the Prince's speech with the Chorus blurs the distinctions between play and "after-play," between onstage and offstage communities, and thus joins stage and world, implicating both in the tragedy, the earlier moment when Juliet wakes almost in time to catch her Romeo generates a poignant emblem of haste and loss, captured in memory (as well as on the poster sold in the theatre lobby), which seems to override these last emphases and to crystallize both the play's events and the spectator's experience. And both Daniels's and Zeffirelli's finales—the first with its reduced community of stilled figures, facing their own guilt; the second with its satisfying circular return to beginnings—contain and enclose Shakespeare's tragedy within a fictional frame, distancing spectators from loss.

Whereas each of these *Romeo and Juliets* certainly invited spectators to recognize that loss, each also (though perhaps in varying degrees for particular spectators) memorialized the lovers' story in a Housman-like, restorative project, one which not only featured/privileged the assuring (especially to academic interpretative communities) familiarities of a full or nearly full text but which also permitted individual spectators either to negotiate their own contemplative relationship to that story or, in the case of Zeffirelli's film, to assuage and subsume their responses within the final, amplified, and overly sentimental sequence of atonement. Two other *Romeo and Juliets*, forty years apart, effected a more unsettling negotiation between Shakespeare's playtext and its audiences. For very different reasons, each constructed a sense of ending from textual absence; both constitute examples of my second, confrontational, model of *Romeo and Juliet*'s performance history.

The time is 4 April 1947; the place, once again, Stratford-upon-Avon. In the week preceding the opening of Peter Brook's *Romeo and Juliet*, the First Festival offering at The Memorial Theatre, press announcements touted the twenty-two-year-old director's revolutionary (at the time) decision to cast young unknowns, eighteen-year-old Daphne Slater and twenty-six-year-old Laurence Payne, in the title roles. Assured of violence and passion—Brook's tag-line for the production was "for now, these hot days, is the mad blood stirring"—and promised no sweetness or sentimentality but rather "a genuine Elizabethan spirit," the first-night audience gathered outside the theatre in the early April evening.[18] *The Irish Times* records the scene:

> Here there were all the signs of peace—sleek limousines outside the door, stiff shirts and long dresses, cigars passed recklessly in the foyer from film producer to ambassador and back again. Around the distinguished guests the theatre was packed with the undistinguished pilgrims—the young men in their windbreakers, the small Chinese, the elderly ladies, the burly girls. There was most decidedly the atmosphere of an occasion.[19]

"To muted French horns the production began hauntingly with John Harrison's voice, grave and gentle, speaking the sonnet for Chorus," reported J. C. Trewin. In silhouette, the actor made a slow exit through the dark, his voice faded, and light blazed suddenly upon a stage bare of scenery except for a single stand of crenellated wall, backed by an indigo cyclorama,[20] what Brook later called "the great tent of Mediterranean blue which hangs over every moment of [the play], from the first brawl in the dusty market to the calm and peaceful cadence in the grave."[21] Although Brook and his designer, Rolf Gérard, started with elaborate (and expensive) scenery, they began throwing it out at dress rehearsal, gradually reducing the stage to an empty hot-orange arena and a few sticks. Much later, Brook justified this decision by claiming that "[*Romeo and Juliet*] is a play of wide spaces, in which all scenery and decoration easily become an irrelevance, in which one tree on a bare stage can suggest the loneliness of a place of exile, one wall an entire house."[22] But if for Brook, coming to Shakespeare addicted to ballet's open, uncluttered stages and spatial poetry, *Romeo and Juliet* offered a vehicle for exploring a stagecraft "which could give freedom and space to the sweep of the poem,"[23] his critics—those Mercutio's phrase aptly labels "these strange flies, these fashion-mongers, these pardon-mes" (II. iv. 32–33)—condemned its reckless spectacle, "which sacrifices poetry, acting, and even the story itself, to pictorial splendor."[24] "BALLET V. THE BARD, AND THE BARD LOST," proclaimed the *Daily Mail*'s review headline; the *Birmingham Post* complained that "Mr. Brook's fondness for stage pictures more than once carries him outside the framework of the play . . . and he allows Gérard's settings to create a scene of architectural isolation which suggests anachronistic air raids."[25]

Brook's critics did not confine their objections to what one called "flashes of almost Technicolour vehemence" and another "too much production and too little play."[26] Stratford's reared-on-Shakespeare audiences began to murmur when they failed to hear Benvolio's long speech about the Mercutio-Tybalt-Romeo fight (III. i. 150–173) and the Friar's explanation of the potion's effects to Juliet (IV. i)—omissions that seemed especially odd since Brook had made room for figures often cut in performance: Simon Rebeck, James Soundpost, and Hugh Catling, the musicians who argue while Juliet lies dead, offering a counterpoint to the Capulet mourning (II. v. 96–141). And finally, as *The Times*'s reviewer noted, "Mr. Brook is so little interested in the characters that he omits altogether the reconciliation of the houses over the grave of the 'poor sacrifices of their enmity!'"[27] These as well as other comments about the production's localized features finally crystallized into a generalized critique of failure. Brook's *Romeo and Juliet* lacked "the urgency of Shakespeare's rhetoric," "the high emotional requirements of the infinite tragedy," sacrificing "sentimentality and starshine" to the unfamiliar.[28] "If to be lean and harsh, with glowing purple patches here and there," said the *Guardian*'s critic, "is also to be unmoving in the deeper sense, what happens to the famous claim of tragedy on our pity and terror?"[29] In the wake of World War II, a tragedy for Britain's own youth, not only was Gérard's setting a harsh reminder of that recent past but Brook's cavalier treatment of Shakespeare's classic—and his apparent disregard for what a group of trained spectators considered its poetic value—generated a *Romeo and*

Juliet "as pitiless as the April weather."[30] It presaged change to
an audience who desired to pretend that nothing had changed,
to be reassured that the past was not only infinitely familiar but
infinitely repeatable. For this particular interpretative community,
hot, inventive, experimental Shakespeare was not just lacking
what one critic called "the true strain"[31]: in voicing a profound
threat to time-honored stage traditions, it flaunted its own—as
well as its spectators'—engagement with the potential loss of an
inherited cultural ethos.

As though mimicking the several Quarto and Folio versions
of Shakespeare's playtext, Brook's prompt copy exists in two
states.[32] The first reveals that the play as rehearsed included a
heavily cut version of the final sequence, omitting the Watchmen's
discovery, eight of the Friar's lines, and the reports of Balthasar
and the Page and replacing the Montague-Capulet speeches of
reconciliation with a handshake. The second, which cuts directly
from Juliet's death to the final speech, constitutes the playing
version. As John Harrison, who played Benvolio as well as
Chorus, recalled, Brook decided on the cut at dress rehearsal,
when he also awarded the Prince of Verona's final speech to
Chorus. Indeed, Chorus had from the beginning been
improvisatory: Brook had originally intended a recorded
disembodied voice—he even tried recording it himself.
Responding to criticism, Brook justified his choice by faulting
Shakespeare as well as his company: the scene, he said, is
"elongated [and] contains extremely clumsy writing . . . we could
not bring it to life."[33] Curiously attuned to the playtext's own
emphases on fate and chance, Brook's ending seems more like a
hasty accident resulting from his own youthful frustration than a
deliberately crafted, distinctive directorial innovation.

Nearly half a century following Brook's impulsive decision
to drop Shakespeare's last scene on the rehearsal-room floor, the
close of Michael Bogdanov's 1986–87 *Romeo and Juliet*—one of
the Royal Shakespeare Company's entries in the category of what
some might call contemporary decorated Shakespeare—revealed
a more purposefully radical erasure at work: 140 lines of
Shakespeare's playtext absent; in their place eight lines from the
Chorus's opening sonnet, the tenses changed from present to
past. Although only two of Brook's reviewers noted the absence
of *Romeo and Juliet's* final scene, nearly every report of Bogdanov's
version described, and sought to interpret, its use, or misuse, of

Shakespeare's playtext. Briefly, let me reconstruct its dominant features.

As Juliet stabbed herself with Romeo's knife—"there rust, and let me die" (V. iii. 170)—a blackout, accompanied by music (a signal that the play was not yet over), covered what was to be revealed as a spectacular transformation: when the lights came up, Romeo and Juliet stood on the tomb, their faces masked and bodies caped in shimmering golden fabric. Family members, friends, and bystanders—including several photographers—gathered around the statues as the Prince presided over their unveiling; he read a cut version of the first Chorus from two note cards. As he finished, more *papparazzi*, flashbulbs popping, rushed down the aisles to orchestrate posed pictures of the Mafioso Prince, the two fathers shaking hands, the two sets of parents, Friar Lawrence, the Nurse (who seemed reluctant to pose or to speak with reporters, even though she had brought along the rope ladder as evidence), and the drug dealer-apothecary, who had supplied Romeo with a foil-wrapped packet of, presumably, heroin for "cordial" injection. Once the moment was recorded, milked of its potential publicity value, the Prince swept off with his entourage, refusing further comment; the others left as well—some pursued by reporters, some ignored. Lady *Montague* (still living) placed a rose at the foot of Romeo's statue. Benvolio remained, seated down left at a café table. He rose, crossed toward the statues for a last look, and slowly walked away as the lights went down on the two figures, the final sign of what, much earlier—and speaking of Paris, not Romeo—Lady Capulet called "the golden story."

Whereas Shakespeare's close concerns discovering the true story behind the final melodramatic tableau of bodies, Bogdanov's finale constructed an ironic, near-parodic substitution for melodrama—by rewriting those bodies as the spectacle Shakespeare's playtext places in an imagined future and by fixing *Romeo and Juliet*'s story as different from that which spectators have seen and (presumably) been complicit with. Irving Wardle of *The Times* found this particular representation a harsh transformation of Shakespeare's "pious thought that the lovers' deaths have patched up the family feud [into] an irreconcilable clash between affection and property"; Benedict Nightingale of the *New Statesman* called it "a grotesque distortion of Shakespeare, who wanted to suggest that out of love, pain, death, good might come."[34] For the critical community, Bogdanov's brashly unique collaborative endeavor, which used Shakespeare's playtext as a trampoline, broke through its textual envelope, and bounced into postmodern flight, simply was not *Romeo and Juliet* "as they liked it." Rather, appropriating Shakespeare's playtext to represent—and confront—contemporary cultural phenomena risked connections which critics described, at best, as unnecessary relevance, at worst, as anachronistic, transgressive violations of *Romeo and Juliet's* presumably transhistorical meanings.

* * *

Bogdanov's finale illustrates several of the perceived threats contemporary performances represent: the reappropriation of textual elements; the potential enslavement of text by spectacle; the disappearance, destruction (as opposed to deconstruction), and ultimate consumption of the text.[35] In order to unpack and demystify these threats, I would like to propose several ways in which performance criticism can more firmly inscribe itself in relation to other critical discourses, theorize itself into something close to privileged status, and reposition its centrality. I say reposition because in Elizabethan times, as Louis Montrose, among others, has argued, the theatre existed both as a marginal institution and also, contradictorily—through the metaphor joining stage and world—as the precise and powerful center of the social sphere.[36] Yet even after twenty years or so of variously-informed justifications, the study of performance remains a somewhat marginal project—largely, it would seem, because the status of performance in relationship to other textual categories remains highly indeterminate.

Increasingly, however, contemporary textual scholarship suggests that the playtext itself is mutable, subject to change from its very inception. Several of Shakespeare's playtexts—*Hamlet* and *A Midsummer Night's Dream*—not only enact this mutability but even specifically authorize Elizabethan versions of what critics and scholars have called directorial interference and actors' corruptions, terms which assume an ownership over the written text not unlike that of overly protective fathers preserving, from all the world, their daughters' chastity as a sign of their own patriarchal power. When the players come to Elsinore, Hamlet takes the First Player aside: "Can you play 'The Murder of Gonzago'? . . . You could for a need study a speech of some dozen or sixteen lines which I would set down and insert in't, could you not?" (II. ii. 523; 525–527). Hamlet tailors an extant text in order to make it "speak . . . with most miraculous organ" to a particular audience at a particular time, to represent his personal and political designs. And, like Hieronimo's play in *The Spanish Tragedy*, Hamlet's newly-adapted play depends on a typically Tudor premise, that the action of a play could decisively alter the course of real events.[37] Similarly, the alterations Peter Quince and his fellows make during rehearsals of "The Most Lamentable Comedy and Tragic Death of Pyramus and Thisbe" are designed to suit the play to its performance space, its occasion, and its audience, and they occur because of casting limitations as well as (probably) economic constraints. Quince's original script names two characters—Thisbe's mother and Pyramus' father—who are transformed, during the course of rehearsals, into a moon—a technical effect that glances at all of *Dream*'s actual and implied virgin queens—and a wall—a stage property that literalizes Egeus' function as a blocking parent. These radical changes require that new material be written for both Moon and Wall; additional worry over frightening the ladies prompts another prologue proclaiming that Lion is Snug the Joiner. In both instances, the resulting performances depend upon a view of the playtext as a flexible, unfixed entity, open to a process of adaptation and cocreation in the theatre as well as in the mind.[38]

Fortunately for dramatic history (and for both plays), someone called (apparently) William Shakespeare documented not only Prince Hamlet's production concept and its intent but also pertinent features of the rehearsal process and performances of Quince's play. Both exist as texts. But Bogdanov's final scene for *Romeo and Juliet*, with its minimal textual authority—eight reappropriated lines—belongs to another category—playing— which in Shakespeare's own time had primacy over "the play" as a printed object. Indeed, he wrote within and against a system of performed representations, which was at least as privileged, if not more so, than the published (literary) text of the play. Today, however, scholars tend to measure performances against a peculiarly obsessive brand of Shakespearean quality control— the extent to which the performance successfully (or unsuccessfully) competes with the printed text or, more significantly, with each reader's private, ideal construction of that text, for authority. To some extent, such an attitude assumes that a Shakespearean playtext will not only speak for itself but will also (miraculously) ventriloquize and make accessible its past historical moment. Theatre history, however, suggests a more specific historicity for the representation of Elizabethan playtexts. Peter Brook, a director who claims no interest in history, only one in the aesthetic relations between performances and their audiences, posits, in a statement seemingly designed to protect his own work from history, the particularly ephemeral life of theatrical representations: "A production is only correct at the moment of its correctness, and only good at the moment of its success. In its beginning is its beginning, and in its end is its end."[39] Reflecting on such representations as well as on Shakespeare's own practice invites considering Bogdanov's body play, as well as the other versions of *Romeo and Juliet*—for which I have admittedly provided less than complete descriptive maps— as *performance texts.*[40]

Quite obviously, such a label seeks textual authority for theatrical representation. Here, what is first of all essential is to encounter the conceptual illusion behind the term "text." The very word appears inviolate, enclosed—an "x" or "nexus" fenced in by two powerful t's. Appropriating the term and coupling it with "performance" intentionally threatens both the notion of an established, authoritative written text of a Shakespearean play and the notion that those written words represent the only form in which a play can possess or participate in textuality. An apparent oxymoron, "performance text" freely acknowledges the perceived incompatibility between the (infinitely) flexible substate(s) of a Shakespearean play and the (relative) fixity of the term "text." Certainly the contemporary critical climate recognizes and gives value to the multiple, imperfect states of many Renaissance texts, challenges the notion of an inviolate canon, and generates renewed attention for the collaborative atmosphere which gave rise to theatrical representations. Why, then, not give equally privileged attention to radically imperfect and radically variable performance texts? Although some forms of discourse acknowledge such variability—particularly the so-called stage-centered reading, which attempts to create the equivalent of a performance text in rehearsal by generating multiple options for representation—the result is often just as empty and static as the original "ideal" architecture, uninhabited by live bodies. If, however, we permit specific theatrical representations to participate in and own the privileges accruing to textuality, to read what we see and hear on the stage as a text, such a project would generate a more precise, more historically- and culturally-engaged model of performance criticism. Writing this sort of cultural history is essential if the profession's newly-dominant discourse, new historicism, is to separate itself from "essentialist old historicism." For the new historicism, which by and large equates plays with their texts, and thus focuses on that which gives the illusion that it "abides," reproduces the assumption that only reading can yield insights about those texts.[41] Yet the principles of the "new discipline" invite, if not compel, a focus that moves beyond texts to examine how present-day theatrical representations perform cultural work.

To return, then, to Bogdanov's performance text and to interrogate its choices. In the strictest sense, his rewritten ending neither violated nor distorted "Shakespeare's text" (whatever that may be) at all. Rather, by leaping over those 140 lines, Bogdanov began after the playtext ended, in the white space following the written words, a space which invites inhabitation and representation. In choosing to reappropriate and truncate the opening Chorus at the close, Bogdanov was listening to, and reproducing, the broken sonnet that ends Shakespeare's own playtext. The use (or killing) of that sonnet not only enforced a confrontational connection between the beginning and ending of the original by rewriting ending as beginning but also invited rereading the story as a tabloid, late-night news-fiction, a commodity of scandal providing the occasion for a photo opportunity. The Prince's central position and his indifferently casual reading from cue cards revealed how authority exploits such spectacle to reconstitute its power. That spectacle connected with others in the performance text, most notably the apothecary scene, where Romeo wandered through a Mantuan street observing a carnival procession where, in the manner of *Spitting Image* video puppets, giant heads representing Thatcher, Reagan, and Kohl mocked contemporary authority figures. Not only did Bogdanov literalize the play's various reporters—the Friar, the Nurse, and Benvolio—in the newsmen, but he also foregrounded Benvolio's isolation from the others' apparent publicity hunger. By privileging his last goodbye to his friend, this performance text introduced a last reminder of Verona's male community, which substituted a young for an old final witness, inverting the final overriding presence of age rather than youth, and it reproduced a closural feature of many other Shakespearean playtexts, a single male figure. Excluding himself from Verona's preoccupations with commercial power, this Benvolio seemed to function as a potential anchor of audience attitude toward the authority figures who have exploited a tragedy for their own purposes. Rather than attempting to appropriate a missing past or recapture a lost reality, Bogdanov's close situated itself as an integral part of contemporary cultural production driven by images or simulacra.[42] Here, the ideological purpose of spectacle was turned against itself, its parodic construction simultaneously enslaving those on stage and (potentially) empowering those in the audience.

In the late 1980s, the intertextual connections between Bogdanov's performance text and our own social space have a weekly, if not daily, familiarity. The program for the production invited, even enforced, those connections. Rather than quoting a range of critical opinions on the play or providing background material on Elizabethan culture, that program reproduced excerpts from current cultural studies of love and marriage and suicide. This document, together with the poster, reviews, "thick descriptions" of the entire performance text;[43] Bogdanov's prompt copy, a series of photographs taken at dress rehearsal (many of which were designed as star shots), and a videotape shot with a single camera equipped with a zoom lens, point the way toward an even larger notion of textuality. Following reception theory models such as Jane Feuer's work on *Dynasty*,[44] such an archive of texts would also include an existing interview with Sean Bean and Niamh Cusack, who played Romeo and Juliet;[45] gossip about the actors' fears that their performances were overwhelmed by Chris Dyer's set; hiring policies at Stratford, including an exchange of letters in the press about black actors cast in the season; and Niamh Cusack's remarks to Jay Halio's 1988 NEH Seminar that, although she understood Bogdanov's reading of the close, she thought they could have achieved similar ironies by using the language.[46] To extend further the open or dispersed textuality of Bogdanov's performance text as a cultural event, it would be necessary to gather additional interview and biographical material from actors, director, and designers; descriptions of the rehearsal process; information on the economic circumstances of production; whatever critical perspectives figured in the shaping of the performance text; and the decodings of the production generated by particular interpretative communities—including hostile spectators.[47]

This *bricolage* of discourses, this potential archive, constitutes not just the exclusive province of theatre historians but the foundation for a more global project of criticism, one which I call

performance work. By this I mean the interrelated phenomena
Montrose has described in noting the theatre's ability to do
cultural work—to trace, intersect with, and intervene in the
dimensions of the social sphere.⁴⁸ Such an enterprise requires
that we rethink the compartmental, mutually exclusive
formulations we apply to that floating entity we call "the play."
It requires that we give up the conventional opposition between
a so-called authoritative text and performance, find ways to
negotiate contradictory worlds—Renaissance and postmodern—
and permit those contradictions to energize rather than limit our
discourse. It requires that we view theatrical representations not
as fraudulent rites enacted by rival priests, rites where we mourn
the loss of desired familiarity or signs of a glorious past, but as
activities that participate in historical processes and in the
ideological work of shaping present-day reality. Such performance
work invites a redirected critical praxis—one which embraces
Shakespeare's playtexts, their variant critical re-formations, and
performance texts in order to dance a new historical rag, a kind
of present historicism (another oxymoron), which addresses
current cultural practice—so that what we now attempt to
recuperate for Shakespeare's time we also do for our own. In
evoking the absent bodies of a number of *Romeo and Juliet*
performance texts, giving them a present voice, my own
performance work writes a brief history of its close—a history
which re-inscribes the playtext's own remembering, interpretation,
and confrontation within a cultural framework and which
attempts to re-imagine the theatre's ability to participate in the
ideological work of giving varied shapes to our loss, endowing it
with a "local habitation," offering us pardon—and, on occasion,
naming us as the chief, though not the only, begetters of that
loss.

NOTES

1. A. E. Houseman ["With Rue My Heart is Laden"], August 1893,
   1896, from *Chief Modern Poets of England and America*, ed. Gerald
   DeWitt Sanders, John Herbert Nelson, and M. L. Rosenthal, 4th
   ed. (New York: The Macmillan Company, 1969), I, 13.
2. *The New York Times*, 11 March 1987, pp. A1, B6.

3. *The New York Times*, 18 March 1987, pp. A1, B2.

4. *The New York Times*, 2 March 1987, p. 8:5. See also *The New York Times*, 13 March 1987, p. 3:1 and 27 May 1987, p. 3:5.

5. Quoted in program notes for Michael Bogdanov's 1986–87 *Romeo and Juliet*. See also *The New York Times*, 11 September 1987, p. 13:1, which summarizes a study by David P. Phillips and Lundie L. Carstensen of the University of California at San Diego and Madelyn S. Gould and David Shaffee of Columbia University, published in the *New England Journal of Medicine*, indicating that television news coverage of suicides and television dramas about the topic appear to cause a temporary increase in the number of teenage suicides.

6. Arthur Laurents, *West Side Story*, in *Romeo and Juliet/West Side Story*, ed. Norris Houghton (New York: Dell Publishing Co., Inc., 1965), p. 224.

7. For the notion of a performance variorum, see Cary Mazer, "Shakespeare, the Reviewer, and the Theatre Historian," *Shakespeare Quarterly* 36:5 (Special Issue), 650–51.

8. Natalie Zemon Davis includes an intriguing discussion of the historical context of, and the issues surrounding, the Friar's pardon tale (as well as the possibility that Romeo would be able to seek, and gain, pardon), in *Fiction in the Archives: Pardon Tales and Their Tellers in Sixteenth-Century France* (Stanford: Stanford University Press, 1987), pp. 70–76.

9. *Johnson on Shakespeare*, ed. Arthur Sherbo (New Haven: Yale University Press, 1968), VII, 956.

10. For an overview of eighteenth- and nineteenth-century practices, see Jill L. Levenson, *Shakespeare in Performance: Romeo and Juliet* (Manchester: Manchester University Press, 1987).

11. Harley Granville-Baker, *Prefaces to Shakespeare* (Princeton: Princeton University Press, 1946), IV, 58–61, 67.

12. Prompt copy at The Shakespeare Centre Library, Stratford-upon-Avon.

13. All line citations are from *The Pelican Shakespeare*, ed. Alfred Harbage (New York: Viking Press, 1969).

14. Prompt copy at The Shakespeare Centre Library, Stratford-upon-Avon.

15. Prompt copy at The Shakespeare Centre Library, Stratford-upon-Avon.

16. Miriam Gilbert, rehearsal log for Daniels's production, personal communication. I am grateful to Professor Gilbert for sharing these materials with me.

17. For more complete readings of Zeffirelli's film, see Jack Jorgens, *Shakespeare on Film* (Bloomington: Indiana University Press, 1977), pp. 79–91 and Albert R. Cirillo, "The Art of Franco Zeffirelli and Shakespeare's *Romeo and Juliet*," *TriQuarterly* 16 (Fall 1969), 68-93.

18. *Stage*, 3 April 1947; Peter Brook, "Shakespeare Isn't a Bore," reprinted in *The Shifting Point, 1946–1987* (New York: Harper & Row, Publishers, 1987), pp. 71–72.

19. *The Irish Times*, 7 April 1947.

20. J. C. Trewin, *Peter Brook: A Biography* (London: MacDonald, 1971), p. 33.

21. Peter Brook, "Style in Shakespearean Production," in *The Modern Theatre: Readings and Documents*, ed. Daniel Seltzer (Boston: Little, Brown and Company, 1967), p. 255.

22. Brook, "Style," p. 255. Brook's single tree anticipates the minimalist set for Samuel Beckett's *Waiting for Godot* (1948–49), produced in Paris in 1953; given Brook's admiration for Beckett's work, it seems possible to conjecture, in spite of the dating, that his set choices react to it.

23. Brook, "Style," p. 255.

24. *The Irish Times*, 7 April 1947.

25. *Daily Mail*, 7 April 1947; *Birmingham Post*, 7 April 1947.

26. *Manchester Guardian*, 7 April 1947; *The Irish Times*, 7 April 1947.

27. *The Irish Times*, 7 April 1947.

28. In order, the phrases are from the *Coventry Evening Telegraph*, 7 April 1947; *Wolverhampton Express and Star*, 7 April 1947; *Daily Sketch*, 7 April 1947.

29. *Manchester Guardian*, 7 April 1947.

30. *Manchester Guardian*, 7 April 1947.

31. *Birmingham Post*, 7 April 1947.

32. Prompt copies from the Shakespeare Centre Library, Stratford-upon-Avon.

33. Trewin, *Peter Brook*, p. 35.

34. Irving Wardle, "Irreconcilable Clash between Affection and Property," *The Times*, 10 April 1986; Benedict Nightingale, "Sight-Seeing," *New Statesman*, 18 April 1986. At least one version of *Romeo and Juliet* fulfilled, even overfulfilled, Nightingale's wish.

The first part of the Royal Shakespeare Company's 1980 *Nicholas Nickleby* closed with a performance of *Romeo and Juliet* staged by the Crummles's theatre company. Juliet woke, seized Paris's dagger, and was about to kill herself when Romeo revived. Paris came to life as well (he was just stunned), and then all the characters, plus a few who seemed to come from some other play—a Fool, for example—came onstage. In the midst of explanations, Mercutio dashed in (also not dead), and Benvolio turned out to be a girl, Benvolia, disguised for the love of Paris. The Prince, played by the company's drunken actor, leaned against the canvas arches, causing a perilous swaying. Even the Apothecary, played by Smike, wrapped in a dark cloak, was present. This happy ending led to a tableau, an exit, and a return of the entire company for a curtain call, accompanied by Mrs. Crummles's appearance as Britannia with a Union Jack draped over her massive bosom. All sang England's praises—"a land victorious in war shall be victorious in peace." Then, as the lads from Dotheboys Hall as well as all the other cast members joined the Crummles's company, the play-within-the-play curtain call turned into the real curtain call, which ended with a triumphant burst of sound and laughter.

35. In Bertolt Brecht's view, such consumption was characteristic of Elizabethan theatrical practice, "where theatre was so potent that it could swallow immortal works of art greedily and bare-facedly as so many 'texts'" (*Brecht on Theatre*, ed. John Willett [New York: Hill and Wang, 1966], p. 166).

36. Louis Adrian Montrose, "The Purpose of Playing: Reflections on a Shakespearean Anthropology," *Helios*, n.s. 7 (1980), 51–74. See also the work of Stephen Greenblatt, especially the essays in *Shakespearean Negotiations: The Circulation of Social Energy in Renaissance England* (Berkeley: University of California Press, 1988).

37. For a full discussion, see Joel B. Altman, *The Tudor Play of Mind* (Berkeley: University of California Press, 1978).

38. On these issues, see Philip C. McGuire, *Speechless Dialect: Shakespeare's Open Silences* (Berkeley: University of California Press, 1985), especially pp. xiii–xxv. In *Puzzling Shakespeare: Local Reading and Its Discontents* (Berkeley: University of California Press, 1988), Leah Marcus mobilized some of these features of *Hamlet* and *Dream* in an argument parallel to my own (see especially pp. 46–50).

39. Brook, "Style," p. 256; see also p. 251.

40. My term derives from Richard Schechner, who refers to performance texts as theatrical events that grow primarily from

rehearsal and laboratory work and, at times, are supported only by a minimal printed text. I appropriate the term, then, to refer to the end result of a process that begins with a (usually) cut version of any existing text. See Schechner's discussion in "Collective Reflexivity: Restoration of Behavior," in *A Crack in the Mirror: Reflexive Perspectives in Anthropology*, ed. Jay Ruby (Philadelphia: University of Pennsylvania Press, 1982), pp. 39–81. See also Richard Schechner, *Performance Theory* (1977); rpt. (New York and London: Routledge, 1988), and Victor Turner, *The Human Seriousness of Play* (New York: Performing Arts Journal Publications, 1982). For pertinent work on semiotic rather than anthropological approaches to performance, see Keir Elam, *The Semiotics of Drama and Theatre* (London: Methuen, 1980) and *Shakespeare's Universe of Discourse: Language-games in the Comedies* (New York: Cambridge University Press, 1984), and Patrice Pavis, *Languages of the Stage: Essays in Semiology of the Theatre* (New York: Performing Arts Journal Publications, 1982). To some extent, I have synthesized the two approaches—though as I have attempted to trace cultural patterns by mobilizing "signs" within particular performance texts, I have not absorbed those signs into the rather rigorous systems Elam and Pavis used. For yet another related approach, see David M. Bevington, *Action is Eloquence: Shakespeare's Language of Gesture* (Cambridge: Harvard University Press, 1984).

41. My thanks to Philip C. McGuire for a conversation which helped to formulate these ideas.

42. The notion constitutes one of the focal points in the debate on defining postmodernism. See, for example, Andreas Huyssen, "Mapping the Postmodern," *New German Critique* 33 (1984), 5–52; Frederic Jameson, "Postmodernism: The Cultural Logic of Late Capitalism," *New Left Review* 146 (1984), 53–92.

43. The phrase comes from Clifford Geertz's chapter title, "Thick Description: Toward an Interpretive Theory of Culture," *The Interpretation of Cultures* (New York: Basic Books, 1973).

44. Jane Feuer, "Reading *Dynasty*: Television and Reception," *South Atlantic Quarterly* 88:2 (Spring 1989), 443–60.

45. Lesley Thornton, "Stratford's New Romantics," *Observer*, April 1986.

46. Miriam Gilbert (personal communication) reports Cusack's view of the ending. Henry Woronicz's 1988 *Romeo and Juliet* for the Oregon Shakespeare Festival season offered just such an alternative interpretation. Although neither Woronicz nor his designer, William Bloodgood, had seen Bogdanov's performance text, their set and costume choices—which combined various styles

of architecture to reflect the various levels of history and culture, classical to contemporary, existing side by side in a European cityscape and eclectic costuming that found equivalents between sweeping greatcoats and Renaissance capes—were remarkably similar. For the close, Woronicz played a nearly full text; the performance text ended with superimposed tableaux, one dissolving into the other. The first revealed the entire community of mourners; the second, as lighting redefined the survivors as the background of a final composition, privileged the lovers' bodies in a pale glow before the final blackout. Indeed, the close constituted an emblem *combinatoire* of the entire performance text. Although Woronicz retained the traditional tableau, his staging positioned the lovers apart from one another rather than joined in death, a choice which prevented sentimentality and invited spectators to read their deaths as hasty and disarranged—the stuff of unplanned, raw experience. By avoiding an icon of transcendence, Woronicz's final emphasis captured the juxtaposition of private and public sorrow directly preceding Bogdanov's finale—before Romeo and Juliet's story became a media event. Certainly two performance texts with some similarities in macrodetail occurring within two years of one another indicate that both Bogdanov and Woronicz share an ideological framework, one which attempts to make connections between what was, for the Elizabethans, a popular story and what is, for the late 1980s, an equally popular preoccupation with examining familial, as well as other forms of, social conflict.

47. The reception history of Zeffirelli's filmtext offers an especially intriguing example. Whereas critics complained of Zeffirelli's cuts (over half of Shakespeare's lines missing), popular opinion seemed undisturbed at the substitution of romantic, full-of-the-joy-of-life-and-the-agony-of-love sequences borrowed from "B" movies for Shakespeare's tensely counterpointed sonnets, sestets, and rhymes. In the context of late 1960s ahistoricism, with its emphatic notion of new beginnings, what Pauline Kael called "the music of the great lines" had less relevance than Nino Rota's insistently luscious sound track, pumping sentiment into (among other spaces) the Capulet tomb. In 1967, the year before *Romeo and Juliet's* release, fifty to seventy-five thousand young pilgrims flocked into the Haight-Ashbury district for the Summer of Love: music, drugs, and sex became the center of a national fantasy life celebrated in Scott McKenzie's plastic-hip "San Francisco"—"If you're going to San Francisco/Be sure to wear a flower in your hair." And two weeks after *Romeo and Juliet's* release, *Sergeant Pepper's Lonely Hearts Club Band—the* album that condensed the late sixties' phenomena—returned, bringing the Beatles, re-represented as

cartoon figures in *Yellow Submarine*, to rescue Pepperland from the Blue Meanies with music and love. In a cultural milieu that freed teenage bodies from parental and *in loco parentis* control, Zeffirelli's film became one among many cult objects for the "age of Aquarius." And, although the film's initial interpretative communities divided along generational lines, as though reproducing the playtext's own feud between youth and age, in the late 1980s Zeffirelli's *Romeo and Juliet* performs a different kind of cultural work. Curiously and somewhat contradictorily, the voices of age and experience who once viewed the film as a threat to Shakespeare now urge it upon the young. Largely through its institutionalization within the secondary-school curriculum, Shakespeare according to Zeffirelli has become a cultural product that reconciles the (academic) desires of the old with the (perhaps) refractory claims of the young—surely one of the oddest reversals in *Romeo and Juliet*'s strange and eventful performance history. For one of the film's most acid reviews, see Pauline Kael, "She Came At Me in Sections," reprinted in *Going Steady* (New York: Bantam Books, Inc., 1971), p. 186; for a sense of the sixties' culture, see Todd Gitlin, *The Sixties: Years of Hope, Days of Rage* (Bantam Books, Inc., 1987), pp. 214-21.

48. Montrose, "The Purpose of Playing." See also "'Shaping Fantasies': Figurations of Gender and Power in Elizabethan Culture," *Representations* 1:2 (1983), 61-94.

Part III

Romeo and Juliet as a Product of Elizabethan Culture

Franklin M. Dickey

"To love extreamely,
procureth eyther death or danger"

The play is uniquely constructed in that the same passions which make us tearful or indignant before the action ends, do amuse us with little interruption for almost half the acting time. Even the events leading up to Mercutio's death promise comedy rather than tragedy, and it must have startled the first audience to see laughter so quickly turn to mourning. Yet the play is an exceptionally powerful tragedy, even if it sometimes embarrasses critics. Where the first half delights us with love comedy, the last three short acts explore the tragic potentialities of young love. Fortune and hatred threaten to turn the lovers' bliss to ashes, but the immediate cause of their unhappy deaths is Romeo's headlong fury and blind despair. Thus in both the beginning of the play and at the end Shakespeare's view of love remains sound philosophically and dramatically.

Only if we recognize love as potentially dangerous will the structure of the play stand examination. The source from which Shakespeare created his tragedy fails in this respect, for its plentiful moral discourses do not really show anything except the author's orthodox bias in favor of reasonable action over passion. Where [Arthur] Brooke's jigging *Romeus and Juliet* (1562–63) leaves the relationship between the three great themes of the story unresolved, Shakespeare has constructed a drama with signposts to guide his audience through the argument.

In fairness to Brooke, however, it should be said that the central meanings of the action are also central in Shakespeare's

Excerpt from Chapter VIII, pp. 102–117, of *Not Wisely But Too Well*.
Reprinted with permission of the Henry E. Huntington Library.

tragedy. Sometimes Shakespeare paraphrases Brooke's Friar with the same astonishing virtuosity with which he transforms chronicles into living history. The essential philosophical patterns of Brooke reappear in Shakespeare, and we may say of this source, as of so many others, that more than its plot inspired Shakespeare. The potential meanings of the action stimulated one side of his mind as surely as the external events excited his sense of theater.

Let me hasten to add that Brooke's professed conception of the meaning of the action and Shakespeare's dramatic presentation of it are often poles apart. In a Preface which is insistently Protestant, Brooke tells us that the "well disposed mynde" will profit from "The glorious triumphe of the continent man upon the lustes of wanton fleshe." Brooke solemnly advises the "good Reader" that this tragic matter was written

> to describe unto thee a coople of unfortunate lovers, thralling themselves to unhonest desire, neglecting the authoritie and advise of parents and frendes, conferring their principall counsels with dronken gossyppes, and superstitious friers (the naturally fitte instrumentes of unchastitie) attemptyng all adventures of peryll, for thattaynyng of their wished lust, usyng auriculer confession (the kay of whoredome, and treason) for furtheraunce of theyr purpose, abusyng the honorable name of lawefull mariage, to cloke the shame of stolne contractes, finallye, by all meanes of unhonest lyfe, hastyng to most unhappye deathe.

After this preliminary sermon it is odd to find that in the poem itself the "superstitious frier" is a pattern of kindly wisdom and that the love of the two young people is "perfect," "sound," and "approved." It is equally odd to find that Brooke attributes to fortune the fatal course of the action, while at the same time giving to the Nurse, to Romeus, and to the Friar long disquisitions on the power of reason to triumph over fortune.

For *Romeo and Juliet* Shakespeare has taken from Brooke what he needed to make an effective tragedy and has discarded the rest. We saw that he altered Brooke's conception of the story by making the Nurse, Capulet and Montague, and Mercutio comic characters, and that he altered Brooke still further by handling the early love scenes in the manner of comedy. He has also intensified the tragedy by making his characters more consistent, so that the moral philosophy of the Friar, which Shakespeare adapted from Brooke, has a real function in the action. He has likewise changed Juliet's character to contrast with Romeo's and has given Romeo more responsibility for the rash and passionate ending of love. He has rearranged Brooke's statements on the consequences of passionate action so that, instead of appearing as interpolated moral preachments, they serve to explain the tragedy. And he has added to Brooke a dramatic irony which further underlines the meaning of the plot.

One way in which Shakespeare has tightened the loose structure of his source is by giving Juliet more maturity. Brooke's Juliet, although two years older than Shakespeare's heroine, is much more a child. On hearing of Tybalt's death she swoons. The Nurse brings her to consciousness only with great difficulty, and once conscious, Juliet indulges in a long, self-pitying complaint, the gist of which is "Goe hence, and let me dye." Nor can she be comforted until the Nurse has preached reason to her for fifty lines.

We await her suicide with pity, but since she has threatened to die so often before the end, her final act has none of the real terror of Juliet's death in the play. Since Shakespeare's Juliet has constantly displayed more courage and good sense than Romeo, when her spirit breaks at the sight of her lover's corpse, the audience may experience a real catharsis.

The great change which Shakespeare has made in the relationship of the lovers appears most clearly when we watch Brooke's Romeus bid Juliet goodbye before going to Mantua. Juliet threatens to throw herself out the window if she may not follow him disguised as a boy. Romeus, who in Shakespeare becomes a creature all fire and ice, preaches the necessity of patience:

> if (my loving wife)
> Thou banish from thy mynde/two foes that counsell hath,
> (That wont to hinder sound advise)/rashe hastines and wrath;
> If thou be bent tobay/the lore of reasons skill,
> And wisely by her princely powre/suppresse rebelling will,
> If thou our safetie seeke,/more then thine owne delight . . .
> So shall I safely live abrode . . .   (ll. 1654–62)

These are fit words in the mouth of a young man who allows the counsels of reason to cool his early love for the unknown fair whom Shakespeare calls Rosaline. They are not in keeping with the nature of Shakespeare's passionate hero. Where Shakespeare has Romeo disdain Benvolio's repeated advice to look on other

beauties, Brooke's Romeus tamely acquiesces to the reasonable
platitudes of an older friend:

> The yong mans lystning eare/receivde the holesome sounde,
> And reasons truth yplanted so,/within his head had grounde:
> That now with healthy coole/ytempred is the heate:
> And piecemeale weares away the greefe/that erst his heart
> dyd freate.
>
> (ll. 141–144)

Where Shakespeare's hero never really heeds the Friar's
consolations of philosophy, Brooke's Romeus allows himself to
be talked out of despair, so that "affections veale" is

> removed from his eyes,
> He seeth the path that he must walke,/and reson makes
> him wise.
>
> (ll. 1487–88)

It is hard to believe that so dutiful a young man could bring
about his own destruction, and Brooke therefore leans heavily
on "false fortune" to justify the tragedy. Thus where Shakespeare's
tragedy brings love, fate, and hatred into an understandable
relationship, the three themes remain at odds in Brooke, and his
poem is both philosophically and aesthetically chaotic.

Shakespeare has recast Brooke's Romeus so that his character
maintains philosophic and dramatic unity. Throughout *Romeo
and Juliet* Romeo is precipitate in love. Juliet, who loves as
faithfully, is much less subject to the gusts of passion which
blind Romeo. Romeo never examines the consequence of his
actions, but Juliet fears that their love may be "too rash, too
unadvis'd, too sudden." Romeo never shares Juliet's insight. After
they have pledged love at Juliet's window, his only concern is
that the love he feels seems too delightful to be true. It is Juliet
not Romeo who thinks practically of arranging for marriage and
who remembers to ask what time she is to send her messenger in
the morning.

On Romeo's inability to control either his passionate love or
his passionate grief, his death and Juliet's depend. The boundless
love which Romeo felt at the sight of Juliet turns as suddenly to
despair, just as any well-versed Renaissance philosopher might
have predicted, for the man in the grip of one passion was easily

swayed by another. Once a man had suffered burning love, he bore the "prints and skarres" of love all his life.

Romeo's character then is one key to the tragedy. The key to the significance of Romeo's attitudes toward love and fortune is Friar Laurence, whom Shakespeare has made a much more effective critic of the action than has Brooke. Although Brooke's Friar is a wise old man to whom the Prince himself as well as both "Montagews" and "Capilets" go for advice, he dabbled in magic when young and still has a secret bedroom where he was wont in youth "his fayre frendes to bestowe." Furthermore Brooke gives much of the Friar's moral commentary which illumines the action of the play to other characters whose judgment we cannot trust. When Romeus and the Nurse preach reason it is hard to take them seriously; but in Shakespeare Friar Laurence's sermons predict the course of Romeo's love.

Much of this material is adapted from Brooke, as of course are the lovers' despair and suicide. Shakespeare has also taken over, sometimes practically word for word, the Friar's warnings to Romeus. But Shakespeare has sharpened the point of Brooke's homilies and raised them out of the realm of platitude. Where Brooke's discourses on reason, passion, and all the customary proper conduct read like set pieces of moral uplift, Shakespeare's Friar wastes no time with generalities but tells Romeo in terse homilies what happens to those who dote.

Shakespeare's Friar unlike Brooke's is a true chorus whose words give the necessary moral base from which to judge the tragedy. Our introduction to the Friar's philosophy is the homily on herbs in which he compares the world of nature and the soul of man. The metaphor he uses gives the gist of Elizabethan ethics:

Within the infant rind of this weak flower
Poison hath residence and medicine power;
For this, being smelt, with that part cheers each part;
Being tasted, slays all senses with the heart.
Two such opposed kings encamp them still
In man as well as herbs, grace and rude will;
And where the worser is predominant,
Full soon the canker death eats up that plant.   (II, iii, 23–30)

Romeo interrupts the Friar's soliloquy to tell him about Juliet, and the Friar replies in one of the most amusing speeches of the play, a passage of friendly mockery which is not only in keeping with the comic tone of Act II but serves like Mercutio's lustier jests to underline Romeo's early folly.

Romeo takes refuge from the Friar's well-meant ridicule by trying to turn his own earlier counsel back on him. "Thou chid'st me oft for loving Rosaline," he reproaches his friend, who answers dryly,

> For doting, not for loving, pupil mine.   (II, iii, 82)

After a few bantering lines the Friar promises to marry the lovers in order to end the hatred of their houses. The scene ends without more ado as Romeo characteristically implores,

> O, let us hence; I stand on sudden haste.   (II, iii, 93)

a sentiment to which the Friar gives the equally characteristic answer,

> Wisely and slow; they stumble that run fast.   (II, iii, 94)

At this point in the action love still promises to triumph and give us a happy ending. But even here Shakespeare has managed to give us a clue to the meaning of the play without boring us with the dull sort of moral lecture of which Brooke is fond. The whole scene is in lively couplets and is shot through with humor as well as wisdom. Only by making this scene as brilliant and as witty as it is could Shakespeare make the Friar's observations on Romeo's dotage convincing after the comedy we have just seen. To present bald moralizing here would have put the Friar in the class of scolding parents whose counsel young lovers traditionally ignore.[1]

When we next see the Friar he is standing with Romeo waiting for Juliet to come to her wedding. "So smile the heavens upon this holy act," the old man prays, "That after-hours with sorrow chide us not!" Romeo eagerly cries "Amen, amen," but blurts out his own passionate philosophy, that love means more to him than life:

> come what sorrow can,
> It cannot countervail th' exchange of joy
> That one short minute gives me in her sight.
> Do thou but close our hands with holy words,
> Then love-devouring Death do what he dare;
> It is enough I may but call her mine.(II, vi, 3–8)

Alarmed, the Friar drops the gentle mockery with which he has instructed Romeo and prophesies that

> These violent delights have violent ends,
> And in their triumph die, like fire and powder,
> Which as they kiss consume . . .
>   love moderately; long love doth so;
> Too swift arrives as tardy as too slow.   (II, vi, 9–15)

Here for the first time the Friar tells Romeo what happens to those who allow themselves to be carried away by love, yet the truth of this Cassandra-like warning will not appear until the play is almost over.

The Friar's warning is the first of a series which build up tension through the play. Set side by side passion and reason in the person of Romeo and the Friar oppose each other to the end.[2] In Romeo's defiance of fate Shakespeare has supplied the audience with one more indication that Romeo's impetuous nature will result in catastrophe. Second he has provided an answer to Romeo's transport which the audience would have recognized as a universal truth, that "to love extreamely, procureth eyther death or danger."[3] He has given this answer to the Friar, whom all the characters in the play treat with the utmost respect. Most important he has put into the Friar's mouth two images which epitomize the whole plot, the image of fire and powder which we shall hear him use again shortly, and the statement, "Too swift arrives as tardy as too slow," that predicts what lies ahead when Romeo rushes back from Mantua to die.

Having killed Tybalt, Romeo is ready to kill himself despite the old man's reminder that banishment is a light enough sentence for a crime which the law punishes with death. In the frantic rhetoric of love, almost comic in its extravagance, Romeo denies the mercy of the Prince's judgment and rails against fate:

> 'Tis torture, and not mercy. Heaven is here,
> Where Juliet lives; and every cat and dog
> And little mouse, every unworthy thing,
> Live here in heaven and may look on her;
> But Romeo may not. More validity,
> More honourable state, more courtship lives
> In carrion-flies than Romeo; they may seize
> On the white wonder of dear Juliet's hand
> And steal immortal blessing from her lips . . .
> This may flies do, when I from this must fly . . .   (III, iii, 29–41)

Again the Friar gives us the moral background against which we see Romeo's agony. The Friar calls him "fond" and "mad" because he will not help himself, and Romeo cries in distraction, "Hang up philosophy!" If you were, he charges his friend, "Doting like me and like me banished," then you might act like me. In a frenzy he throws himself upon the ground, refusing to get up to hide when someone knocks, despite the fact that disclosure would be fatal. Fortunately it is only the Nurse, who begins to chatter about Juliet's sorrow.

Romeo now threatens suicide and Friar Laurence, thoroughly aroused, delivers one of his longest and most eloquent speeches, some fifty lines which again foreshadow the course of the action. "Hold thy desperate hand!" he rebukes Romeo,

> Art thou a man? Thy form cries out thou art;
> Thy tears are womanish; thy wild acts denote
> The unreasonable fury of a beast.
> Unseemly woman in a seeming man,
> And ill-beseeming beast in seeming both . . . [4]

Repeating the image of fire and powder, he warns that if misery follows, it will be Romeo's fault, for if Romeo commits suicide in an access of despair, Juliet too will die:

> Thy wit, that ornament to shape and love,
> Mis-shapen in the conduct of them both,
> Like powder in a skilless soldier's flask,
> Is set a-fire by thine own ignorance,
> And thou dismemb'red with thine own defence.
>
>   (III, iii, 130–134)

Tragedy must follow if self-hatred conquers love and if Romeo rejects the blessings of fortune. Fortune will not destroy the lovers but frantic despair will:

> Take heed, take heed, for such die miserable.   (III, iii, 145)

Shakespeare does not let us forget that disregard of the Friar's reasonable counsel rather than the turning of fortune's wheel dooms Romeo's love.

At the beginning of Act V Romeo relates a dream he has had in which he lay dead but was revived by Juliet's kisses. Delighted with the memory of it, he exclaims cheerfully,

My dreams presage some joyful news at hand.   (i, 2)

Immediately his servant Balthasar enters with the premature news that Juliet is dead. Agonized, Romeo abandons hope, crying,

Is it even so? Then I defy you, stars!   (V, i, 24)

Echoing the Prologue's "misadventur'd piteous overthrows," Balthasar begs his master to have patience. "Your looks are pale and wild," he pleads, "and do import/Some misadventure." Patience, however, is the philosopher's virtue, not Romeo's. Fully aware that he is desperate and that what he does is irrational, Romeo muses,

> O mischief, thou art swift
> To enter in the thoughts of desperate men!   (V, i, 35-36)

He goes to an apothecary and, in persuading him to sell poison, echoes the same metaphor with which the Friar has earlier tried to dissuade him from dismembering himself in his own defense. "Let me have/A dram of poison," he demands, so potent

> that the trunk may be discharg'd of breath
> As violently as hasty powder fir'd
> Doth hurry from the fatal cannon's womb.   (V, i, 59-65)

The complicated irony of Romeo's dream and his immediate despair accentuate the meaning of the tragedy. The audience, knowing that Juliet is not dead, understand what poor Romeo does not, that never has he been closer to the realization of permanent happiness but that at the same time it will be forever out of his reach. The full truth of the Friar's warning strikes us now. When Balthasar echoes the Prologue we are prepared to see Romeo, whose nature bears the seeds of its own destruction, bring about the piteous misadventures for which he wrongly blames the stars.

Meanwhile Friar Laurence is still working to save Romeo from himself. Having discovered that a quarantine has kept his letters from reaching Mantua, he lays plans to take Juliet from her tomb that night and to send another message to Romeo. Romeo's haste prevents his foresight.

From here on the tragedy moves rapidly to its inevitable conclusion. The setting of Scene iii is the churchyard and tomb of the Capulets. Paris enters with his page to strew flowers on Juliet's grave. He sends the boy away to warn him should anyone approach; when the boy whistles, Paris hides. Savagely, Romeo threatens Balthasar with violent death if he does not withdraw at once. Paris, justifiably outraged at the sight of the Capulets' worst enemy breaking into the tomb of the girl he himself has loved, steps out to arrest him.

Romeo, mad with desperation, is resolved even to murder, if necessary, rather than be hindered from killing himself on the body of his beloved. Using strange terms for a man whom so many critics consider absolutely guiltless, Romeo cries,

> Good gentle youth, tempt not a desperate man.
> ... I beseech thee, youth,
> Put not another sin upon my head,
> By urging me to fury: O, be gone!
> ... live, and hereafter say
> A madman's mercy bid thee run away.   (V, iii, 59–67)

It is most interesting that Paris uses proper legal terminology in accosting Romeo; he does not challenge him to fight but demands that he come with him to judgment. Indeed he sounds almost like a constable when he tells Romeo:

> I do defy thy conjurations
> And apprehend thee for a felon here.   (V, iii, 68–69)

Paris of course although perhaps a stuffy fellow is quite right legally, and Romeo is wrong. The whole scene is Shakespeare's invention, and one wonders why he chose to arrange the events leading up to Paris's death as he did. It would have been equally plausible dramatically to have had Paris dash in challenging Romeo to draw and defend himself. If the object of the scene is merely to provide a contrast in character which will make us approve Romeo's valor, it is odd to find Romeo eulogizing the man he has just killed, "Mercutio's kinsman, noble County Paris!"

It seems more logical to interpret the scene as another of the signposts which Shakespeare has given us to help make the tragedy a real tragedy in which the catastrophe depends not upon fate but upon the passionate will of Romeo. Only after he *has* put another sin upon his head does Romeo understand whom he has killed and remember that Balthasar has told him of Paris's love for Juliet. Dazed by despair, however, he heard all as if in a dream:

What said my man, when my betossed soul
Did not attend him as we rode? I think
He told me Paris should have married Juliet.
Said he not so? Or did I dream it so?
Or am I mad, hearing him talk of Juliet,
To think it was so?   (V, iii, 76–81)

Greeting Paris as another like himself, slain by love, he drags the body into the monument:

O, give me thy hand,
One writ with me in sour misfortune's book!
I'll bury thee in a triumphant grave.   (V, iii, 81–83)

He gazes at Juliet tenderly, on whose blushing cheek "death's pale flag is not advanced." Although she looks so lifelike that Romeo almost guesses the secret, his own mortal frenzy drives him on. His last desperate act will free him from the blows of fate:

O, here
Will I set up my everlasting rest,
And shake the yoke of inauspicious stars . . .   (V, iii, 109–111)

Early in the play Romeo has felt strange forebodings before going to the Capulets' feast where he meets Juliet; "my mind misgives," he confides to his friends,

Some consequence yet hanging in the stars
Shall bitterly begin his fearful date
With this night's revels, and expire the term
Of a despised life clos'd in my breast
By some vile forfeit of untimely death.   (I, iv, 106–111)

We recall that he concludes this same speech by placing his fate in God's hands:

But He that hath the steerage of my course
Direct my sail!   (I, iv, 112–113)

Now, however, he is himself the steersman and rejects the heavenly guidance he has trusted earlier. In his last breath he assumes the responsibility for the wreck of his hopes. "Come, bitter conduct," he cries,

Thou desperate pilot, now at once run on
The dashing rocks thy sea-sick weary bark!   (V, iii, 117–118)

Just as the Friar has promised, Romeo condemns himself. Love turned too hastily to despair is "unreasonable fury." Truly, too fast arrives as tardy as too slow. Juliet wakes and, seeing her lover dead, kills herself with his dagger.

Romeo therefore is a tragic hero like Othello in that he is responsible for his own chain of passionate actions. When we first see him he is already stricken with love. This first love is comic, but nevertheless it is a real attack of the sickness of love, as his father makes clear when he complains that Romeo's humor will turn "Black and portentous" unless checked.

Since the man stricken with passion could not readily defend himself against new onslaughts of passion, Romeo's sudden passionate about-face when he sees Juliet would have seemed realistic to an Elizabethan audience. Romeo's transports for Juliet differ from his first melancholy because she returns his affection. For a time he is cured and conducts himself so reasonably that even Mercutio comments on the change in his temper.

But with Mercutio's death Romeo casts aside all reason and begins a chain of passionate action which leads to death. Rejecting the reasonable conduct with which he had first answered his enemy, he attacks and kills Tybalt. It would certainly have spoiled the play for Romeo to have waited for the law to punish Tybalt, but the fact remains that this reasonable action would have turned tragedy into comedy. In this choice between reasonable and passionate action lies one great difference between the genres. Forgiveness produces the happy ending of comedy; revenge produces the catastrophe of tragedy.

Romeo's next passionate mistake is to fall into frantic despair after the Prince sentences him to banishment. When Romeo cries out against his lot, Friar Laurence, the consistent voice of moderation and wisdom, warns him that he is truly unfortunate only in giving way to uncontrolled grief.

The next step in Romeo's march to destruction is his sudden and complete despair when he learns that Juliet is dead. The direct result of Romeo's frenzied desire to kill himself is his killing of Paris, an incident which Shakespeare adds, like the death of Lady Montague and the death of Mercutio, to his source. Thus Brooke's Romeus dies with less on his conscience than does Shakespeare's hero. In Brooke Romeus kills Tybalt only to save

his own life, not to revenge a friend, and at the end of the play
dies guiltless of any additional blood save his own. In our play,
however, Shakespeare is careful to make Romeo guilty of sinful
action under the influence of passion, while at the same time
making us sympathize with Romeo's agonies of despair. In his
encounter with Paris Romeo announces both his own mad
desperation and the fact that in bringing the chain of passionate
folly to its close, he puts one more sin upon his head.

Romeo's last passion-blinded act is to kill himself just before
Juliet awakes, and her suicide may be thought of as the direct
result of his. Although Shakespeare does not preach, the
Elizabethan audience would have realized that in his fury Romeo
has committed the ultimate sin. It must be remembered that,
despite Hamlet's passionate wish, God had "fix'd/His canon
'gainst self-slaughter."

Romeo's death is not the cold-blooded action of a mortal
sinner though, and it should inspire us with both pity and terror.
It is true that in Renaissance ethics suicide is a mortal sin, but
under certain circumstances, God was inclined to be merciful to
passionate sinners. Those who suffer the madness of love have
hope of grace, for persons who are temporarily beside themselves
or are "found to have been long melancholy, and that in
extremity," in Burton's words,

> know not what they do, deprived of reason, judgement, all, as
> a ship that is void of a pilot must needs impinge upon the next
> rock or sands, and suffer shipwrack.   (p. 373)

Yet the tragedy of Romeo and Juliet is a true tragedy,
preserving the ambiguous feelings of pity and terror which
produce catharsis. Romeo remains a free agent even though he
scarce knows what he does. Those who allowed passion to carry
reason headlong were guilty of the very fault that Elizabethan
ethics were designed to prevent. It is exactly because love could
unseat the reason that few men who loved excessively could
look forward to a virtuous life and a happy death.

The word of one contemporary playgoer, at least, has survived
to assure us that the theme of the play is not *amor vincit omnia*
but that "Death is the common Catastrophe" of those who love
unwisely. From love, writes Burton,

comes Repentance, Dotage, they lose themselves, their wits, and make shipwreck of their fortunes altogether: madness, to make away themselves and others, violent death.

Doting love does not, to use Dowden's phrase, "exalt and quicken the inner life." On the contrary

if this passion continue . . . it makes the blood hot, thick, and black; and if the inflammation get into the brain, with continual meditation and waking, it so dries it up, that madness follows, or else they make away themselves.

To prove his point Burton quotes, alongside lines of Ovid and Virgil, the concluding couplet:

Who ever heard a story of more woe,
Than that of Juliet and her Romeo?   (pp. 763–764)

Does this mean that Burton and the spectators in his day, or that Shakespeare himself, looked upon the play as an edifying lesson in how not to conduct oneself in love? I hardly think so. The pattern of the action, given shape by Friar Laurence's warnings, Mercutio's satiric ebullience, and the Prince's scattered judgments, revolves around two of the most attractive young lovers in all literature. But the patterns of moral responsibility are necessary to give the action its perspective, and it is these patterns of the destructive as well as the creative force of love and the dependence of fate upon the passionate will which most contemporary criticism neglects or denies. We, who have moved so far from Shakespeare's world, need to be reminded of these things. They would have touched his audience far more deeply than they touch us today.

NOTES

1. Brooke's handling of the incident is entirely different. He conventionally tells us that the Friar argued with Romeus about the dangers of marriage in vain (ll. 597–610), and the Friar informs us at the end that the lovers forced his hand by threatening "in sinnefull state to live" if he did not do as they wished (ll. 2923ff.)

2. Because Brooke has not maintained the contrast, his poem lacks tension. He chose to give Juliet the lines Shakespeare gives Romeo:

> let Fortune do/and death their woorst to me.
> Full recompensd am I/for all my passed harmes,
> In that the Gods have graunted me/to claspe thee in
> myne armes.
>
> (ll. 860–862)

Her words are touching (Romeus bursts into tears) but they do not further the action in any real way; they are pathetic but serve no other purpose that to wring our hearts. Shakespeare has used these sentiments to better purpose.

3. *Politeuphuia*, f. 130.

4. III, iii, 109-113. Shakespeare apparently found Brooke's words and sentiments appropriate in this instance, for he has taken them over without much change:

> Art thou quoth he a man?/thy shape saith, so thou art:
> Thy crying and thy weping eyes,/denote a womans hart.
> For many reason is/quite from of thy mynd outchased,
> And in her stead affections lewd,/and fansies highly
> placed.
> So that I stoode in doute/this howre (at the least)
> If thou a man, or woman wert,/or els a brutish beast.
>
> (ll. 1353–58)

J. W. Draper

Shakespeare's "Star-Crossed Lovers"

Romeo and Juliet is a tissue of improbable coincidence: Capulet's illiterate servant happens by mere chance to ask Romeo to read the list of those invited to his master's entertainment; Romeo, by a most unusual chance, decides to attend his arch-enemies' festivities, and so chances to fall in love with Juliet; at just this time the Prince chances to make a stringent edict against brawling, and Romeo chances to kill Tybalt and so is banished; and, also at just this time, Old Capulet chances to betroth Juliet to the Count Paris. Any one of these chances might singly be accepted; but why should they all occur within two days and just in the right order to set the plot in motion? Even more a matter of fortuity is the catastrophe: by chance, the Friar's letter to Romeo miscarries; by chance, Romeo meets and kills Paris at the tomb; by chance, the Friar is too late to intercept Romeo; and, by chance, Juliet awakens just too late to save her lover's life and just too soon for her father to save her from suicide. Indeed, never was love-affair more perfectly ill-timed; and yet, as if to emphasize this very fault, the master-dramatist, more than in any other play, marks, scene by scene, the days of the week and sometimes the very hours of the day. Truly, as Rümelin declares, "mere accident"[1] seems to guide the order of events; and, if this be so, the play has no integration of plot, does not illustrate the inevitable working of any general truth, and so can have no theme; without a theme, it has no ethos or significance; and, for all the gorgeous trappings of Shakespeare's lyric style, it is not tragedy but mere melodrama.

Indeed, the critics have had difficulty in assigning to *Romeo and Juliet* any universal meaning. Ulrici, Rötscher, Vehse,[2] and

Originally printed in *Review of English Studies* 15 (1959), 16–34.
Reprinted by permission of Oxford University Press.

more recently Erskine[3] seem to feel that it expresses the evils of
civil feuds; but, in sharp contrast to Shakespeare's later, political
tragedies,[4] neither the action nor the dialogue emphasizes the
general injury to the state that feuds were supposed to effect;
and, furthermore, the Prince himself declares that his objection
to brawling chiefly arises not from such dangers but from the
killing of his kinsman Mercutio.[5] Tieck and Maginn seem to
consider that the tragic outcome derives from Romeo's
impetuosity and too great haste; but is it Romeo's haste that
brings him to the Capulet feast or that so crucially keeps the
Friar's letter from arriving? Dowden says that "the moral theme
of the play is the deliverance of a man from dream into reality"[6];
but surely such a change would improve the hero's chances for
meeting the problems of life, and so result rather in comedy.
Horn, more vaguely, suggests that the play expresses "the grand
irony of life"; and Bodenstedt and Erskine feel that "tragic fate"
directs it; but the ironies are as nothing compared with those of
Hamlet, Othello, or *Lear*; and there is no fatal antecedent action, as
in the *Oedipus,* that decrees an inescapable tragic consequence.
Thus most critics, despite the obvious predominance of
coincidence, seem to feel that the play has some sort of system or
governing purpose; and they accordingly assign it various vague
and rather divergent themes, none of which closely fits the plot
or explains its sudden leaps without causality from one episode
to another. Shakespeare generally gave the stories that he used a
timely realism and *vraisemblance*; and his utter failure to link the
events of *Romeo and Juliet* in any certain, or even probable,
connection is a strange departure from his usual artistry.

In the main trend of the story, Shakespeare follows rather
closely Brooke's poem, which is generally recognized as the chief
source for the play. Brooke tells the tale as a "wofull chance,"
with little effort to explain the chances that occur; and he and
Paynter, Shakespeare's other possible source, agree in repeatedly
ascribing the course of events to "Fortune" or "false Fortune."[7]
Shakespeare, however, makes little reference to Fortune as
governing the action; and these references appear too late to
explain the motivation of the plot.[8] A few passages somewhat
casually ascribe the direction of events to "God" or "heaven";[9]
but the play has no clear-cut Christian moral, unless it be the
evils of brawling, as indeed Paynter suggests, or the wickedness
of a secret marriage, as Brooke implies; and the catastrophe is
not the inevitable consequence of either of these things.

Nevertheless, over the play hangs a certain tragic fate. Juliet cryptically answers Paris, "What must shall be";[10] and reiterated premonitions suggest an evil end: the Prologue refers to the "death-mark'd love" of the two protagonists; Lady Capulet,[11] the Nurse,[12] and Friar Lawrence[13] give voice to ominous predictions; Romeo twice dreams—the second time that his lady found him dead; both lovers are "pale" and melancholy at parting; Romeo,[14] even while arranging his marriage, casts his defiance at "love-devouring death"[15]; he says that the killing of Mercutio "but begins the woe"[16]; and he declares that he and Paris are "writ in sour misfortune's book."[17] Juliet compares her love to the dangerous speed of lightning[18]; her "all-divining soul" sees Romeo "As one dead in the bottom of a tomb"[19]; she describes her case as "past hope, past cure, past help"[20]; and, as she takes the poison, "a faint cold fear" as to the outcome "thrills" her veins.[21] Is all this the mere convention of dramatic prolepsis—a mere pious pretence of inevitable catastrophe where no inevitability exists? Is Shakespeare no more than a theatrical charlatan, or did he really see in this issue of circumstance a *rationelle* and motivation that is not clear to us?

Not only is the play replete with ominous predictions, but many of these predictions are associated with the hours and days and with the heavenly bodies that mark time. The Prologue refers to Romeo and Juliet as "star-cross'd lovers." At the very beginning of the action, when Romeo starts for the Capulet feast, he says:

> . . . my mind misgives
> Some consequence, yet hanging in the stars,
> Shall bitterly begin his [its] fearful date
> With his night's revels, and expire the term
> Of a despised life closed in my breast,
> By some vile forfeit of untimely death. . . .[22]

In Act II, Friar Lawrence invokes the good will of "the heavens,"[23] but he fears that "after-hours will chide" all those concerned in the marriage.[24] When Capulet forces Juliet to the unwelcome match with Paris, she cries out: "Is there no pity sitting in the clouds . . ."[25] and later, "Alack, alack, that heaven should practise stratagems" against her.[26] At Juliet's seeming death, Lady Capulet and the Nurse blame the day and hour as "Accurst" and "black" and "lamentable," as if the very calendar were responsible; and the Friar, even more clearly, imputes the misfortunes of Capulet to astral influence:

The heavens do lour upon you for some ill;
Move them no more by crossing their high will.[27]

In Act V, when Romeo learns of Juliet's supposed death, he cries aloud, "then I defy you, stars!"[28] And when he is resolved to kill himself, he says that death will "shake the yoke of inauspicious stars From this world-wearied flesh."[29] Friar Lawrence imputes the killing of Paris to "an unkind hour,"[30] as if the blame lay on the heavenly bodies that mark the passing time. Thus, if Shakespeare meant what his characters seem to say, astral influence actually governs the lives of these "star–cross'd lovers"; and, like so many of Chaucer's figures,[31] they are the puppets of the stars and planets and of the days and times of day.[32]

Although the stricter theologians looked askance and a few astronomers such as Copernicus must have had doubts, nevertheless the sixteenth century generally accepted astrology as a science[33]; Queen Elizabeth regularly employed the learned Dr. Dee to compute for her the lucky days and hours for undertaking her affairs; and, though only specialists mastered the more esoteric mysteries of casting a horoscope, yet all classes devoured books of popular astrology, edition on edition, [34] so that Ben Jonson could make it the basis of his masque, *Mercury Vindicated*. Everyone knew that the moon governed the rise and fall of tides; and what was man that he should escape such power?[35] Indeed, the farmer had to know the changes of the moon for the planting of his crops; and almanacs, which supplied this astrological information, were so plentifully produced that the Lambeth Palace Library, for the year 1595 alone, has no less than six by as many different publishers. Shakespeare himself makes constant reference to astrology; and Schmidt's *Lexicon* lists thirty–six examples of his use of *star* as "influencing human fortune," and four uses of *astronomer* as "astrologer."

To the Elizabethans, astrology had come down with some accretions from its Babylonian origins. They knew Greek astrology, partly from pseudo-Aristotle, Galen, and Ptolemy, and partly through Arabic and mediæval authors; and a bevy of translators such as Warde,[36] Wither,[37] and Newton,[38] and popularizers such as Moulton,[39] Harvey,[40] and above all that assiduous compiler Thomas Hill,[41] supplied them with the traditional lore of astrology and its associated pseudo-sciences. Indeed, the Greeks, by a curious schematism, had linked astrology with their other learning; and the result, as transmitted by the

Middle Ages, was an integrated and complex theory that embraced and co-related physical and biological knowledge. Human beings were divided into four types, depending on which "humour," or bodily fluid, dominated their physique; and each of these humours was associated with a certain day, with certain planets and constellations, with a chemical "element," a season of the year, a period of a man's life, a colour, a metal, and a bodily condition of heat or dryness. This astro-biological lore, being largely a matter of tradition, shows less variety and disagreement than one might expect in different Elizabethan authors; and, without attempting to plumb the mysteries of "judicial" astrology, *i.e.* the casting of horoscopes, one can, at least approximately, set forth the more obvious phases of the subject. Perfect health of mind and body arose from a perfect balance of the four "humours"; but, in most men, one humour or another predominated, either by nature from birth or by the circumstances of the occasion. Blood, supposed to be generated in the stomach, gave to those whom it controlled a sanguine temper; it was considered hot and moist and was associated with youth and spring-time. Sanguine persons were thought to be under the influence of the constellations Gemini, Libra, and Aquarius and of the planet Jupiter, and so were of a jovial disposition. This disposition especially prevailed from midnight to six in the morning, and its day was Thursday. Its colour was white, its metal electrum, and its chemical element the air. The sanguine man was handsome and lucky, and Jupiter was called "the greater fortune." A superfluity of phlegm, supposed to be generated in the liver or perhaps the stomach, made a man easy-going, slow-witted and "phlegmatic"; this humour was cold and moist and generally fortunate, and was associated with the element water, with middle age, and with autumn; such persons were under the influence of the constellations Cancer, Scorpio, and Pisces, and under either the planet Venus, which was grouped with Friday, copper, and yellow, or the moon, which was grouped with Monday and silver. The phlegmatic humour achieved its greatest power from six in the evening until midnight, and especially on Mondays. A superfluity of bile, called "choler," generated in the heart and found chiefly in the gall-bladder, made a man wrathful or "choleric"; this humour was hot and dry, and was associated with fire, youth, and summer; such persons were presumed to be under the influence of Aries, Sagittarius, and especially Leo, and of the ill-omened planet Mars, whose day was Tuesday, or, more luckily, of the sun, whose day was Sunday; their hours were from six in the morning until noon; their metal was gold, and their colour red. A superfluity of black bile, generated chiefly in the brain and found chiefly in the spleen, made a man melancholy; this humour was cold and dry, and was associated with winter and old age; such persons were under the influence of Taurus, Virgo, and Capricorn, and of that most ill-omened planet Saturn, and were therefore of saturnine disposition; their hours comprised the afternoon and their day was Saturday; their metal was lead, their colour grey, and their chemical element the earth. The present study proposes to examine the chief characters of the play to ascertain how well they fit into these four types, and how well their actions and the outcome of these actions accord with their days and times of day.

Gervinus[42] and Law[43] note the sharp contrast between Tybalt, Benvolio, and Mercutio; and this contrast, upon close examination, seems to spring from the fact that each represents a distinct type in the medical and astro-biological theory of the day. Tybalt is clearly of the choleric or wrathful type: he is always ready to fight, a quality that brings about the tragic catastrophe; he is "fiery" and "furious" and admits his "wilful choler"[44]; and Benvolio refers to "the unruly spleen of Tybalt deaf to peace."[45] Although the spleen was often associated with melancholy, yet it was also considered the seat of anger[46]; and, as the choleric man, of disposition hot and dry,[47] was supposed to be much given to anger in its entire gamut from mere "chyding" to "fighting, murther, robbery, sedition,"[48] Benvolio's reference to Tybalt's "unruly spleen" is quite appropriate to the latter's choleric nature. Choler, moreover, might properly predominate in early maturity[49]—about the right age for Old Capulet's nephew—and in the hot, dry months of summer when the play takes place. Of Tybalt's personal appearance, Shakespeare gives no direct clue[50]; but certainly the timing and the outcome of the events in which he participates agree with the dominant hours of the choleric man: Capulet manages to quiet him at the festivities when Romeo appears; for it is between 6 p.m. and midnight in the phlegmatic period of the day; and Tybalt's fight and death on Monday afternoon are quite correctly timed: the day itself was phlegmatic and the time of day melancholy, and consequently his martial powers would have ebbed at noon, when the choleric part of the day was over. A complete accord of each character and his every act with the appropriate times would hardly be dramatically possible; and yet the part of Tybalt, minor and fragmentary though it is, agrees with scheme of the Elizabethan pseudo-sciences, as to his bodily humour and his psychological bent, as to his age and the season of the year, as to the timing of events by the day and time of day. Nothing of this appears in Shakespeare's sources: the season is winter, with the days and hours only vaguely marked. Could Shakespeare, by mere accident, have introduced so many consistent details; and would an Elizabethan audience, steeped in such lore, have failed to realize their significance?

Also choleric, perhaps by nature, perhaps because of the season of the year, is Old Capulet. His wife, quite properly, thinks this humour inappropriate to his age; and, when in the first street-brawl he demands his sword, she suggests that a crutch would be more fitting. He is "too hot," *i.e.* too angry, toward Juliet[51]; and his impetuous, headstrong nature, like that of Tybalt, directly contributes toward the tragic catastrophe. His blood is still young; and, even at night, he complains of heat rather than of chill[52]; and, though he is "old,"[53] he seems to long for his "dancing days" and the masquerades of thirty years before.[54] Such another testy old gentleman is Montague, who itches to fight the "villain Capulet."[55] Among the Elizabethans decrepitude set in at about the age of forty; for they lived hard and were primitive in their hygiene and sanitation.[56] Thus Capulet, whose reference to his "dancing days" would place his years about fifty or beyond, is certainly enjoying a very green old age.[57]

In sharp contrast to these choleric types is the phlegmatic Benvolio; and Shakespeare points and repoints this contrast.[58] As Benvolio's name suggests, he is easy-going and friendly. "Fleame" was thought to be cold and moist and "wearyish"; and Benvolio is "weary."[59] Such men were supposed to be affable, slow, dull, forgetful, soft of flesh, of small appetite, fat, short, possessed of little hair, of pale complexion, and given to dreams of rain and swimming.[60] Mercutio, to be sure, compliments Benvolio by calling him "as hot a Jack . . . as any in Italy"[61]; but the latter's obvious preference for peace gives the lie to such a description: at the very beginning of the play he tries to avoid a brawl; and he opens the crucial third act with a speech of similar import to Mercutio:

> I pray thee, good Mercutio, let's retire:
> The day is hot, the Capulets abroad,
> And, if we meet, we shall not 'scape a brawl;
> For now these hot days is the mad blood stirring.

He urges the swashbucklers to drop their swords and "reason coldly"[62]; and, after the fray is over, he refers to "The unlucky manage of this fatal brawl."[63] In the first act, moreover, he pursues his phlegmatic humour by not pursuing Romeo.[64] Heat was supposed to make persons of this temperament more sanguine[65]; and perhaps this influence makes Benvolio hopeful of avoiding brawls and, at the beginning of the play, of curing Romeo's lovesickness; but the heavens prevent his purposes; and, as the momentum of the tragedy develops, he drops out of sight as if his phlegmatic temper and sanguine hopes and lucky influence were inappropriate to the catastrophe.

The name Mercutio, which Shakespeare derived from his source, doubtless suggested that the character be depicted as of the mercurial cast; and, indeed, this may have supplied the hint from which Shakespeare conceived his whole tragedy of humours. The mercurial temper is most difficult to define; for persons under that planet's influence might by attraction partake of any one of the four humours, and so were chameleon-like in their variety:

> *Mercurie* in all things is common and mutable, he is good with
> the good, and euill with the euill, with the Masculine, masculine,
> with the Feminines, feminine, hote with the hote and moyst
> with the moyst, infortunate with the infortunes, and fortunate
> with the fortunes, especially when he is ioyned or corporally
> applying vnto them, or beholdeth them with some good aspect.[66]

Just so, Mercutio changes to the wrathful type at the entrance of the angry Tybalt; and this same quick adaptability he urges vainly upon Romeo.[67] The mercurial type was supposed to be a "nimble person" and a go-between in love-affairs[68]; and Mercutio by nature has "dancing shoes with nimble soles"[69]; and he joins with Benvolio in trying to distract Romeo and cure him of the unhappy love for Rosaline. This type, moreover, was supposed to be "volatile, sprightly, and ready-witted."[70] Both Brooke and Paynter agree in calling Mercutio "pleasant and courteous" and popular with ladies; and they add that he had a fiery mind but cold hands—a suggestion of the inconsistent mercurial temperament. Shakespeare's Mercutio is certainly garrulous: he "talks of nothing"[71]; he "loves to hear himself talk"[72]; and he "will speak more in a minute than he will stand to in a month"[73]; and, on occasion, he takes the stage for forty-two lines on the "inconstant" topic of dreams.[74] He calls himself "the very pink of courtesy,"[75] and readily adapts his talk to the occasion, witty, consolatory, or obscene[76]; and he is so susceptible to environment that he seems to feel the chill of night more even than Old Capulet.[77] He is quite fitly killed on Monday afternoon—a phlegmatic day and a melancholy time of day that would depress the mercurial temperament and subject him the more easily to Tybalt's onslaught.

Juliet's old Nurse should also, perhaps, be accounted of the mercurial type. Juliet, to be sure, impatiently accused her of having the phlegmatic and melancholy symptoms of old age, "unwieldy, slow, heavy and pale as lead"[78]; but, at the time, she is doubtless under the phlegmatic influence of Monday, and certainly her interminable garrulity and her willingness to shift from Paris to Romeo and back suggest that by nature she shares Mercutio's cast of mind. These minor characters, especially Tybalt and Mercutio, conform rather closely to their astrological prototypes; and an examination from this point of view of the two principals in the play would seem to be worth while.

Juliet is clearly of a hot, passionate temperament. She falls in love with Romeo at first sight, and she even dares to gainsay her father's orders to his face. The Nurse calls her "hot"[79] and tells an anecdote of her babyhood that the credulous might interpret as a sign of passion.[80] At the beginning of the play, she is not quite yet fourteen,[81] and so has hardly had an opportunity to show her nature; but the stars had given her this nature even from her birth, and Shakespeare carefully impresses on the audience the horoscope of her nativity; and twice we are told that she was born on "Lammas-eve at night,"[82] that is when the sun was in the house of the constellation Leo.[83] Those born under Leo were supposed to be choleric and passionate if not incontinent, inclined to be stout and often barren; and the type was associated with youth and summer.[84] If then Juliet is of this hot complexion, her planet should be Mars or the sun; and with the latter the text constantly associates her: she shines so brightly that she shames the torches[85]; she is called the "sun"[86]; Romeo refers to her "light"[87]; Friar Lawrence compares her to "the sun" clearing away Romeo's sighs[88]; Juliet herself compares her love-thoughts to "the sun's beams"[89]; she is a "lantern" and "her beauty makes This vault a feasting presence full of light"[90]; and, at her death, the Prince declares that "The sun for sorrow will not show his head."[91] The Nurse cannot find Romeo for her until the sun is in the ascendant at high noon[92]; and the poison, counteracting her natural impulse, makes her "cold and drowsy."[93] Some of these references may be mere metaphor, but they are too numerous and too apt to Juliet's choleric nature to be entirely accident; and, moreover, metaphor was so commonly a part of the method of scientific thought that a metaphoric use does not preclude a strictly technical one. Juliet, therefore, like Tybalt and Old Capulet, is hot and dry, but only moderately so, for she is under the influence of the sun rather than of Mars.[94] Choler was supposed to be most active in summer[95]; and the characteristics of this type were amply chronicled in contemporary pseudo-science: such an one was slender, of moderate stature, "lyuely, daper, quycke,"[96] and "prouoketh to ye works of Venus"[97]; and "neyther can they so well rule theyr own affections because in their reasonings and discourses they be so very earnest and hastye."[98] Thus the heat of summer clearly brings out in the maturing Juliet the traits of character fixed by her birth when her planet[99] the sun was in the sign of the zodiac Leo.

The most complex of all these figures is Romeo. He first appears as an example of the melancholy type, and so suffers under the influence of Saturn,[100] which was styled "the greatest infortune." Even before he enters, his father describes his tears and sighs, and declares that his "humour" is "Black and portentous."[101] He has been avoiding the sun, and "locks fair daylight out"[102]; and, when he enters, he declares that the love for Rosaline that afflicts him is a "choking gall."[103] Clearly, Romeo, whatever his natural humour, is suffering from love-melancholy. Heaviness and the metal lead were particularly associated with this bodily condition;[104] and Romeo is "heavy"[105]; he "cannot bound a pitch above dull woe"[106]; he has "a soul of lead"[107]; and he compares his love to a "heavy lightness" and a "Feather of lead."[108] Melancholy often brought on madness[109]; and Mercutio fears for his sanity[110]; and Benvolio proposes the proper cures of diversion and counter-attraction.[111] Romeo's condition is like that of Orsino at the beginning of *Twelfth Night*; but his case is more violent, perhaps because, as the learned Friar says, his disposition is not well "temper'd."[112] At all events, he is obviously given to "extremities."[113]

On falling in love with Juliet, however, Romeo rebounds to his natural self. Melancholy is cold and dry, unhappy, and saturnine; but Romeo, in the bloom of youth and lofty station, could partake of such a humour only because of some immediate, overpowering impulse, for "trouble and affection" can change one's disposition.[114] Romeo, by nature sanguine,[115] quickly returns to his innate merry self.[116] Indeed, at the very moment that he climbs Juliet's garden wall, he would seem to renounce his former bitter mood: earth, as a chemical element, was associated with melancholy[117]; and Romeo cries out: "Turn back, dull earth, and find thy centre out."[118] This tendency to variable extremes was in itself a sign of a hot disposition; for such a humour was described as "variable and changeable."[119]

In the last four acts, Romeo clearly shows the effects of his sanguine humour. His whole love-affair betrays a cast of mind that is hopeful against obstacles, and impatient of cold reason; and this very quality helps to induce the tragic ending. Even as he leaves Juliet, condemned to exile from Verona, he is still hopeful, and protests against "Dry sorrow" because it "drinks our blood"[120]; and he prosecutes his wooing and insists upon the marriage, with an untimely haste. His association with the moon,[121] to be sure, rather suggests the phlegmatic; but this may be mere contrast to Juliet as the sun; and folklore, moreover, takes the moon as the source of moisture that causes decay and growth[122]; and so perhaps Romeo, of a hot and moist complexion, might be associated with it. Romeo's sanguine humour, moreover, fits with his good looks: the Nurse catalogues his physical attractions *seriatim* in the best sonnet style[123]; and the sanguine man was supposed to be "mery, pleasant [witty], fayre, and of a ruddy colour,"[124] to have "comely" stature and a handsome appearance "consonăte to manly dignity."[125] Indeed, blood was the "best of all the humours" and was associated with youth and spring.[126] Romeo is by nature "mery" and "pleasant" and can overcome even the volatile Mercutio at persiflage[127]: truly, he seems to show all the good qualities of the sanguine man. He has also the weakness of the humour: blood could produce "riot and wilfulness"[128]; and those who had a superfluity, when "too much chafed," are prone to act "like mad-men"[129]; quite of this sort is Romeo's rage against Tybalt, and his rage against himself when he has killed Tybalt, "The unreasoning fury of a beast."[130] In short, Romeo, in his rapid changes from saturnine love-melancholy to his natural joyous disposition, and thence on occasion to unreasoning rage, is a rather clear portrayal of the sanguine man: he woos Juliet in one night and marries her next day in defiance of all obstacles; he has the sanguine man's good looks and wit and dignity of bearing, and also his wilful fury under provocation. The choleric Tybalt, Capulet and Montague, all under the influence of Mars, the choleric Juliet under the influence of Venus, the phlegmatic Benvolio, the mercurial Mercutio and the Nurse, and the sanguine Romeo, now under the power of love-melancholy and now of fury: all of these surely make of *Romeo and Juliet* an astrological tragedy of humours.

The Elizabethan pseudo-sciences, however, were associated not only with human character but also with the calendar; and, as the month and the days of the week are rather clearly marked throughout the play, a review of the action day by day should indicate how far the periods of predominance of certain humours govern the outcome of the episodes. The reference to "Lammastide,"[131] *i.e.* August 1, as "A fortnight and odd days" to come, clearly places the action in the "hot days" of the middle of July, when "the mad blood [is] stirring"[132]; and summer was associated with the hot, dry, choleric temperament. In the very first scene, moreover, the word-play on "choler" strikes at once the keynote of the season as well as of the action. This setting in the heat of summer is Shakespeare's own deliberate change from his two reputed sources, in both of which the story begins in winter and drags on into spring. Shakespeare, in fact, even has Juliet declare that "summer's ripening breath" has matured their "bud of love"[133]; and thus one may impute both the love and the hate that motivated the tragedy to the season of the year and the sign of the zodiac.

The old mediæval system of "elections" according to which each hour after dawn brought one luck or misfortune under a changing astral influence, varying according to the time of dawn and according to the day of the week—all this system was far too complex for an audience to follow, and would have required too much rapid calculation on their part to be effective: Shakespeare, therefore, was obliged to use some simpler method wherever he proposed to govern his plot by the luck or ill-luck of days and hours. In his sources, the action of the play consumes several months; he begins it on Sunday and ends it early Thursday morning.[134] The first act and the first two scenes of the second occupy Sunday, that is Juliet's day. The opening street-brawl apparently takes place in the morning, a part of the day when the choleric humour was predominant; and the second scene, in which Romeo reads the list of guests to be invited to Capulet's supper, seems to occur that afternoon; and, at about the same time, the third scene in which Lady Capulet and the Nurse discuss Juliet's age. Scene four is in the evening; and the maskers are hurrying to the Capulet residence. Benvolio declares: "Supper is done, and we shall come too late"; and Romeo answers him:

I fear, too early: for my mind misgives
Some consequence yet hanging in the stars,
Shall bitterly begin his [its] date
With this night's revels . . .[135]

This speech, spoken by the hero and coming at the final climax of the scene, seems particularly significant: Romeo quite properly fears bad influence at that time of the day; for the evening would not usually be favourable either to his natural sanguine disposition or to the melancholy humour that for the time afflicts him. Indeed, how else can one explain his fear of being "too early" coupled with his misgivings of bad astral consequences? In the fifth scene, the maskers arrive as the hall is cleared for dancing; and, at first sight, Romeo and Juliet fall in love, converse in a perfect sonnet, and then kiss and part. The time of day is phlegmatic, and Tybalt's anger is restrained by Capulet; but, even so, it is no lucky hour for the two lovers. In the first scene of Act II, Romeo gives the slip to his merry companions; and, in the second, he is under Juliet's window. This famous dialogue in which the two plight their troth clearly takes place in the sanguine period after midnight; for, near the end, Juliet remarks that it is "almost morning."[136]

While "grey-eyed morn smiles on the frowning night" Friar Lawrence is out gathering herbs; he meets Romeo and advises prudence. The next scene is in the late morning. The Nurse, having searched since nine o'clock, at last comes upon Romeo in the company of his merry friends. Her slowness in finding him is stressed both here and in a later scene; but the situation and the dialogue that explain it seem alike without dramatic reason; and perhaps one should suppose that the Nurse, though perhaps by nature mercurial, has, with advancing age, grown phlegmatic or even melancholy.[137] If melancholy, her lucky hours did not begin till noon; and, just after Mercutio says that it is noon,[138] the Nurse finds Romeo, and so can make the appointment for him to marry

Juliet that afternoon. Thus the marriage takes place in the time of day dominated by the unlucky melancholy humour, for melancholy was associated with Saturn and his malefic influence. That same fatal afternoon, Mercutio and Tybalt are both killed and Romeo, "fortune's fool,"[139] is banished by the Duke. These are the critical hours of the play; and Juliet may well wish the sun's "fiery-footed steeds"[140] to hurry by, for evening will bring less dangerous auspices. So Juliet is wed; and that night the marriage is consummated[141]; but the unfriendly streaks of morning bring in Tuesday, the choleric day of Mars and of dead Tybalt's vengeance, for on that day Romeo's exile starts.[142]

Old Capulet, meanwhile, intent on marrying Juliet to Paris, sets Thursday for the happy event,[143] and then moves it forward to Wednesday,[144] and on this same unlucky Tuesday forces the already wedded Juliet to consent. This Tuesday, which comprises most of the fourth act, is a welter of ill-omened preparations; Romeo hastens to depart; the Capulet household is preparing for the wedding; and Juliet is preparing, by the use of the Friar's drug, to frustrate their preparations. She takes the potion with deep misgivings, as well she may. The working of this drug has caused great trouble to commentators. The Friar declares that it is supposed to last "two and forty hours"[145]; and his calculations must be true, for he reaches the tomb about the time that Juliet actually awakes.[146] Forty-two hours, however, from Tuesday night when she takes the potion would bring her waking to the following Thursday afternoon or early evening; and, in fact, she wakes very late at night and apparently on Wednesday. The present writer hazards the suggestion that "two and forty" is a textual slip for "four and twenty," which would agree with both the metre and the circumstances.[147] On this same Tuesday occurs one of the most fatal chances of the tragedy: the Friar's letter fails to reach Romeo, and so Romeo fails to do his part in the plan that was to unite him with his bride.

Wednesday, the day of changeable Mercury, begins with the discovery of Juliet's seeming death; and, indeed, Wednesday is full of change and violent reversal; the wedding is quickly turned into a funeral; Juliet seems to die, then lives, then dies; the hopes of the good Friar change to bitter failure; and Romeo, fresh from happy dreams,[148] hears of his wife's death and believes the news, returns, kills Paris, and takes poison. When Juliet is first discovered in seeming death, the Nurse and Lady Capulet lament the "Accursed, unhappy, wretched, hateful day"[149] no less than fourteen times: surely they thought that the day had something to do with their misfortunes. Mercury was supposed to be good or evil depending on its relation to other influences[150]: Juliet's cold body is found in the morning; the funeral apparently takes place in the afternoon, when melancholy was the predominant humour; and the death of the lovers, before midnight. The final reconciliation of the rival houses seems to occur in the early hours of Thursday,[151] a sanguine day and time of day: perhaps by this Shakespeare meant that the reconciliation was well-founded and permanent.

Contemporary scientific theory, in short, does much to explain the plot of *Romeo and Juliet*, and reduces considerably the amount of apparent coincidence. Shakespeare changes the time of the tragedy to mid-July, when "summer's ripening breath" matures both the love of the protagonists and the hate of the rival houses. The sub-major figures, in their characters and actions and sometimes even in their physiques, fit into the scheme of humours. The passionate character of Juliet, necessary to her part in the tragedy, agrees with her association with the sun and her birth under the sign of Leo; and the impetuous fervour of Romeo, careless of results, is consonant with his sanguine disposition. Some of the actual coincidences, moreover, can be traced to the day or time of day: the choleric morning hours would seem to give rise to the initial brawl; and this brawl in turn causes the Prince's edict, which in turn causes Romeo's fatal banishment. Romeo's going to the Capulet festivities "too early" makes possible his meeting with Juliet and his falling in love with her; the phlegmatic hours of evening explain Capulet's success in restraining Tybalt at the moment; and the thoughtless abandon of the balcony scene is quite proper to the sanguine hours after midnight. The crucial deaths of Tybalt and of Mercutio, furthermore, take place in the afternoon, when ill-omened melancholy was supposed to rage; and Romeo's banishment and Juliet's wedding fall on Tuesday, the unlucky day of Mars. Indeed, again and again, not only the forebodings of the characters but also the auspices of the humours and the calendar point to a tragic catastrophe: the "death-mark'd love" of "star-cross'd lovers" cannot end happily. Thus the theme of the play is not the evils of civil faction, as in Paynter, or the wickedness of "stolne contractes," as in Brooke, but rather, as in Greek tragedy, the hopelessness of defying the heavens' will. Both the Elizabethan theory of tragedy that derived from Seneca and Horace[152] and the general taste of the age[153] demanded an obvious moral theme; and Shakespeare, snatching a grace beyond the reach of Chapman or Kyd or Marlowe, seems to have turned popular science to his purpose to give the plot of his drama something of the inevitable sequence of Hellenic tragedy.

NOTES

1. *Romeo and Juliet*, ed. Furness Var., p. 466.

2. *Ibid.*, pp. 451 *et seq.*

3. J. Erskine, "Romeo and Juliet," in *Shakespearean Studies*, by members of the department of English in Columbia University (New York, 1916), p. 219.

4. *See* the present author, "Political Themes in Shakespeare's Later Plays,"*J.E.G.P.*, xxxv. 61 *et seq.*

5. *Romeo and Juliet*, III. i. 138 and 181, *et seq.*

6. Dowden, *Shakespeare, a Critical Study* (London, 1876), pp. 106–7.

7. On the history of "fortune," see H. P. Patch, *The Goddess Fortune in Mediæval Literature* (Cambridge, Mass., 1927).

8. *Romeo and Juliet*, III. v. 61; v. ii. 17; and v. iii. 82.

9. *Ibid.*, IV. i. 56; v. iii. 260; and v. iii. 292.

10. *Ibid.*, IV. i. 21.

11. *Ibid.*, III. iv. 4.

12. *Ibid.*, III. iii. 92.

13. *Ibid.*, III. iii. 1–3 and 145; v. iii. 135–136 and 153–154.

14. *Ibid.*, III. v. 55.

15. *Ibid.*, II. vi. 7.

16. *Ibid.*, III. i. 112–113.

17. *Ibid.*, v. iii. 82.

18. *Ibid.*, II. ii. 119.

19. *Ibid.*, III. v. 55.

20. *Ibid.*, IV. i. 45.

21. *Ibid.*, IV. iii. 15.

22. *Ibid.*, I, iv. 106 *et seq.*

23. *Ibid.*, II. iv. 1–2.

24. *Ibid.*, II. vi. 1–2.

25. *Ibid.*, III. v. 196.

26. *Ibid.*, III. v. 209.

27. *Ibid.*, IV. v. 94–95.

28. *Ibid.*, v i. 24.

29. *Ibid.*, v. iii. 111–112.

30. *Ibid.*, v. iii. 145–146.

31. See W. C. Curry, *Chaucer and the Mediæval Sciences* (New York, 1926).

32. Writers on Shakespeare and astrology barely refer to *Romeo and Juliet*: W. Wilson, *Shakespeare and Astrology* (Boston, 1903); *Shakespeare's England* (Oxford, 1917), I. 444 *et seq.*; and C. Camden, "Astrology in Shakespeare's Day," *Isis*, XIX. I *et seq.*

33. The debate on the validity of astrology started with Pico della Mirandola just before 1500 (L. Thorndike, *History of Magic* [New York, 1934], Chap. lxi) and developed later in England (Camden, *op. cit.*).

34. L. B. Wright, *Middle-Class Culture in Elizabethan England* (Chapel Hill [N.C.], 1935), p. 593 *et seq.*

35. L. Lemnius, *Touchstone* (London, 1581), leaf 79ʳ. Almanacs are said to have been of "readier money than Ale and cakes." *See* T. Nashe, "Have with You" (*Works*, ed. McKerrow), III. 72.

36. W. Warde, tr., *The Most Excellent Booke of Arcandam* (London, 1592). Most of these rare volumes are to be found in the Folger Shakespeare Library.

37. F. Wither, tr., C. Dariot, *Astrologicall Iudgement of the Starres*, (London, 1598).

38. T. Newton, tr., L. Lemnius, *Touchstone of Complexions* (London, 1581).

39. T. Moulton, *Myrrour or Glass of Health, ed. princ.* (London, 1539).

40. R. Harvey, *Astrological Discourse* (London, 1582; supplement 1583).

41. T. Hill, *Schoole of Skill* (London, 1599), etc. On Hill and his writings see Wright, *op. cit.*, p. 565.

42. *Romeo and Juliet*, ed. Furness Var., p. 456.

43. *Ibid.*, ed. Arden, p. xvi.

44. *Ibid.*, ed. Furness Var., I. i. 102; III. i. 114; I. v. 87.

45. *Ibid.*, III. i. 150–151. Tybalt is "a gentleman of the very first house" (II. iv. 22–23); and this may refer to Aries, which governed the choleric type. His name signifies a cat; and perhaps this also is significant. *See* Lemnius, *op. cit.*, leaf 96^v *et seq.*

46. Lemnius, *op. cit.*, leaf 138^r and 138^v. Cf. *N.E.D.*, *s. spleen*.

47. Ptolemy, *Tetrabiblos*, tr. Ashmand (London, 1827), pp. 149, 198; Hill, *op. cit.*, leaf 8^v; and Lemnius, *op. cit.*, leaf 86^v.

48. Arcandam, *op. cit.*, sig. M2^r; and Lemnius, *op. cit.*, leaf 23^r.

49. L. Campbell, *Shakespeare's Tragic Heroes* (Cambridge, 1930), p. 60.

50. Hill (*op. cit.*, leaf 8^v) imputes to this type thick, black, bushy hair; but Ptolemy (*op. cit.*, 149) thinks red hair of moderate growth; and Arcandam (*op. cit.*, sig. M1^r) seems to agree.

51. *Romeo and Juliet*, III. v. 174.

52. *Ibid.*, I. v. 25–26.

53. *Ibid.*, I. ii. 2–3.

54. *Ibid.*, I. v. 29 *et seq.*

55. *Ibid.*, I. i. 72.

56. *Cyuile and Vncyuile Life* (*ed. princ.*, 1579) in *Inedited Tracts*, ed. Hazlitt, Rox. Lib. (London, 1868), p. 75; E. Tilney, *Flower of Friendship* (London, 1568); sig. Biiij^r; [? I.M.], *General Practise of Medicine* (London, 1634), sig. B2^v, L. Lemnius, *op. cit.*, leaf 29^v *et passim*; and Arcandam, *op. cit.*, sig. M2^v.

57. *Cf.* Falstaff. *See* Ruth Sims, *The Green Old Age of Falstaff*, about to appear.

58. *Romeo and Juliet*, III. i. 16 *et seq.*

59. *Ibid.*, I. i. 121. He is also fortunate in that he escapes the catastrophe.

60. *Batman upon Bartholome*, London, 1582, leaves 31^v and 32^r; Arcandam, *op. cit.*, sig Mi^r and Mi^v; Lemnius, *op. cit.*, leaves 23^v, 86^v, 111^v; 122^r; 146^r; Hill, *op. cit.*, 16 and 26; and Dariot, *op. cit.*, sig. D4^r.

61. *Romeo and Juliet*, III. i. 11–12.

62. *Ibid.*, III. i. 47.

63. *Ibid.*, III. i. 136 *et passim*.

64. *Ibid.*, I. i. 122–123.

65. Campbell, *op. cit.*, p. 59.

66. Dariot, *op. cit.*, sig. Di^r.

67. *Romeo and Juliet*, I. iv. 27–28.

68. *N.E.D.*, *s. mercury*.

69. *Romeo and Juliet*, I. iv. 14–15.

70. N.E.D., s. *mercurial*. Mercury's influence, moreover, was supposed to make men ingenious. See Hill, *Schoole, ed. cit.*, leaf 50ᵛ.

71. *Romeo and Juliet*, I. iv. 96.

72. *Ibid.*, II. iv. 132.

73. *Ibid.*, II. iv. 133–134.

74. *Ibid.*, I. iv. 53–95.

75. *Ibid.*, II. iv. 52.

76. *Ibid.*, II. iv. 100–101. He talks bawdry to the Nurse, perhaps appropriately.

77. *Ibid.*, II. i. 40.

78. *Ibid.*, II. v. 17.

79. *Ibid.*, II. v. 61.

80. *Ibid.*, I. iii. 42 *et seq.*

81. *Ibid.*, I. ii. 9; I. iii. 12 *et seq.*

82. *Ibid.*, I. iii. 17 and 21.

83. Lammas-eve would be July 31, O.S., *i.e.* August 10 N.S. The sun is in the sign of Leo from July 21 to August 21.

84. Dariot, *op. cit.*, sig. Biiiʳ and Biiiᵛ. Venus and Leo were thought to incite lust. See Burton, *Anatomy of Melancholy*, III. 3, 2, 2, 1.

85. *Ibid.*, II. v. 42.

86. *Ibid.*, II. ii. 3.

87. *Ibid.*, II. ii. 155.

88. *Ibid.*, II. iii. 74.

89. *Ibid.*, II. v. 5.

90. *Ibid.*, v. iii. 84 *et seq.*

91. *Ibid.*, v. iii. 305.

92. *Ibid.*, II. v. 9.

93. *Ibid.*, IV. i. 96.

94. Dariot, *op. cit.*, sig. Diʳ.

95. Campbell, *op. cit.*, p. 59.

96. Lemnius, *op. cit.*, leaf 129ʳ and 129ᵛ. Many of these details could hardly apply to a young woman, and so are omitted.

97. *Batman, op. cit.*, leaf 32ᵛ.

98. Campbell, *op. cit.*, p. 59; and Dariot, *op. cit.*, sig. D3ᵛ.

99. Of course the sun was a planet according to the generally accepted Ptolemaic system.

100. Dariot, *op. cit.*, sig. Civ*.

101. *Romeo and Juliet*, I. i. 133.

102. *Ibid.*, I. i. 124 *et passim*.

103. *Romeo and Juliet*, I. i. 187. *See* John Cole, "Romeo and Rosaline," about to appear.

104. Hill, *Schoole, ed. cit.*, 25.

105. *Romeo and Juliet*, I. i. 130; I. iv. 12, 15 and 35–36.

106. *Ibid.*, I. iv. 21.

107. *Ibid.*, I. iv. 14.

108. *Ibid.*, I. i. 171 *et passim*.

109. See the present author, "Hamlet's Melancholy," *Ann. Med. Hist.*, IX n.s., p. 142.

110. *Romeo and Juliet*, II. iv. 5.

111. *Ibid.*, I. ii. 46 *et seq.* Lemnius prescribes "Moderate myrth and banqueting," leaf 154*.

112. *Ibid.*, III. iii 115. *See* the present author, "The Melancholy Duke Orsino," the *Bulletin* of the Johns Hopkins Institute of the History of Medicine, about to appear.

113. *Romeo and Juliet*, I. v. 156.

114. Lemnius, *op. cit.*, leaf 92ʳ and 92ᵛ.

115. *Romeo and Juliet*, II. iv. 78 *et seq.* The sanguine type was supposed to be particularly susceptible to love. *See* Burton, *op. cit.*, III. 2, 2, 1; J. Ferrand, 'Ερωτομανια (Oxford, 1640), p. 64; and N. Coeffeteau, *Table of Humane Passions* (London, 1621), p. 551.

116. *Ibid.*, II. iv. 79 *et seq.*

117. Lemnius, *op. cit.*, leaf 86ᵛ.

118. *Romeo and Juliet*, II. i. 1–2.

119. Lemnius, *op. cit.*, leaf 45ᵛ.

120. *Romeo and Juliet*, III. v. 58.

121. *Ibid.*, II. ii. 107; and III. ii.1 *et seq.*

122. Sir J. G. Frazer, *Golden Bough* (London, 1919), VI. 132 and 137.

123. *Romeo and Juliet*, II. v. 39 *et seq.*

124. Arcandam, *op. cit.*, sig. M2ʳ.

125. Lemnius, *op. cit.*, leaves 48ᵛ and 49ʳ

126. *Ibid.*, leaf 86ᵛ; *Batman, op. cit.*, leaf 30ʳ; Campbell, *op. cit.*, 58; and Dariot, *op. cit.*, sig. D2ᵛ.

127. *Romeo and Juliet*, II. iv. 63–64.

128. Lemnius, *op. cit.*, leaf 101ᵛ.

129. Arcandam, *op. cit.*, Miʳ.

130. *Romeo and Juliet*, III. iii. 111.

131. *Ibid.*, II. iii. 14 *et seq.*

132. *Ibid.*, III. i. 2–5.

133. *Ibid.*, II. ii. 121.

134. Daniel ends the play Friday (*Trans. New Shak. Soc.* [1877–79], 194); for a discussion of his mistake, see old Rolfe ed., 202–19. See also Ferrand, *op. cit.*, Chap. xxi, who seems to feel that the stars had only a very limited influence over the human body; and P. Boaystuau, *Theatrum Mundi*, tr. Alday (London, 1574), pp. 202–3, who also seems to think the humours more important.

135. *Romeo and Juliet*, I. iv. 106 *et seq.*

136. *Ibid.*, II. ii. 176.

137. *Ibid.*, II. v. 17.

138. *Ibid.*, II. iv. 100–101.

139. *Ibid.*, III. i. 129. In Paynter, the marriage takes place on Saturday, and much time elapses before the catastrophe.

140. *Ibid.*, III. ii. 1.

141. *Ibid.*, III. iii. 164 and 172.

142. *Ibid.*, III. iii. 167 *et seq.*

143. *Ibid.*, III. v. 111 and 152.

144. *Ibid.*, IV. ii. 24 *et seq.*

145. *Ibid.*, IV. i. 105.

146. *Ibid.*, V. iii. 252.

147. Juliet took the potion an hour or more after it was "near night" (IV. ii. 39).

148. *Romeo and Juliet*, V. i. 1 *et seq.*

149. *Ibid.*, IV. v. 17 *et seq.*

150. Dariot, *op. cit.*, sig. D1ᵛ.

151. At the end of the scene, the Prince refers to "this morning" as if the sun were about to rise.

152. See A. H. Gilbert, "Seneca and the Criticism of Elizabethan Tragedy," *P.Q.*, XIII. 370 *et seq.*; and Campbell, *op. cit.*, pp. 5 *et seq.*

153. Wright, *op. cit.*, pp. 403 *et seq.* See also W. Farnham, *The Medieval Heritage of Elizabethan Tragedy* (Berkeley, Calif., 1936).

Douglas L. Peterson

Romeo and Juliet and
the Art of Moral Navigation

The major interpretive problem presented by *Romeo and Juliet* is
that of determining who or what is finally responsible for the
calamity that overtakes the young lovers. The evidence seems
contradictory. The allusion in the Prologue to the lovers as "star-
crossed," the extent to which chance seems to conspire against
them (especially after Romeo has slain Tybalt), and the
premonitions of disaster experienced by both lovers seem to
indicate that the play is fatalistic, perhaps even, as one
commentator has argued, a tragedy of "astrological
determinism."[1] On the other hand, there is a good deal of evidence
throughout the play which points to defects of character as the
determining cause of the catastrophe: the lovers' rashness in love
and their desperation in the face of adversity (each threatens
suicide when learning of Romeo's exile) are forcibly identified as
sinful by Friar Laurence.[2]

This apparently conflicting evidence has led some
commentators to conclude that the play is defective—the work
of an immature dramatist who has "failed to convey a certain
tragic conception which points toward his maturity."[3] "What we
actually have," according to the New Cambridge editor, "is a
drama of fate involving the destruction of two innocent victims
who have defects of character which are not properly worked
into the pattern."[4]

But the inadequacy has been ours, not Shakespeare's.
Whatever else in the play may suggest immaturity—the mannered

Originally printed in *Pacific Coast Studies in Shakespeare*. Eugene:
University of Oregon Books, 1966, pp. 33–46. Reprinted with permission
of the University of Oregon and the author.

courtly dialogue, the lack of depth in characterization, and a degree of inflexibility in the pentameter line—it discloses a tragic conception that is fully worked out and which looks forward to the mature tragedies, to *Hamlet*, especially. The contradictions attributed to Shakespeare are very much in evidence in Arthur Brooke's narrative, and it is certain from the ways in which Shakespeare replotted his source that he was quite aware of them. In place of Brooke's Fortune and her wheel, Shakespeare introduces Providence and the Renaissance idea of order; in place of Brooke's victims of Fortune, whose love at first sight was a "mischief" brewed by the whimsical goddess, Shakespeare introduces the only children of the feuding families, whose destiny is to end the feud and thus to restore civic order in Verona.[5]

"The time is out of joint" in Verona just as surely as it is in Hamlet's Denmark, and the lovers, like Hamlet, are "born to set it right." They are "star-crossed" in a quite literal sense: Providence, having decreed that they will settle the feud, has selected the stars as the agency through which its determination will be effected.[6] Once they meet, they will be powerfully attracted to each other. But it does not follow that since their love at first sight is providentially ordained, they are deprived of freedom of choice, or that their deaths are inevitable as the only means of restoring civic order. How they manage their affections, once they have met—hence how they will fulfill their destiny—will be up to them.

That the stars could influence though not directly determine choice is common Renaissance doctrine. Jack Cade, in *The Mirror for Magistrates*, observes:

It may be well that planets do incline,
And our complexions move our minds to ill;
But such is reason that they bring to fine
No work unaided by our lust and will.[7]

It is the physical nature of man, and hence the passions, that are subject to astrological influence. His reason is free. The doctrine is stated more fully by George Wither:

Hee, *over all the* Starres doth raigne,
That unto Wisdome can attaine.

. . . We know (and often feele) that from above
The *Planets* have, on us, an *Influence*;

And, that our Bodies varie, as they move.
  Moreover, *Holy Writ* inferres, that these
Have some such pow'r; ev'n in those Places, where
It names *Orion,* and the *Pleiades;*
Which, *Starres* of much inferiour *Nature* are.
  Yet, hence conclude not, therefore, that the *Minde*
Is by the *Starres* constrained to obey
Their *influence;* or, so by them inclin'd
That, by no meanes resist the same we may.
For, though they forme the *Bodies* temp'rature,
(And though the *Minde* inclineth after that)
By *Grace,* another *Temper* we procure,
Which guides the *Motions* of *Supposed Fate.*
The *Soule* of *Man* is nobler than the *Sphæres;*
And, if it gaine the Place which may be had,
Not here alone on Earth, the Rule it beares,
But, is the *Lord,* of all that *God* hath made.
    Be *wise in him;* and, if just cause there bee,
    The *Sunne* and *Moone,* shall stand and wayt on thee.

                                                                (lines 10–30)[8]

The stars may influence the mind and therefore choice, but
only indirectly and only to the extent that man allows his mind
to "incline after" the body, whose "temp'rature" is affected by
their influence. What Wither summarizes Aquinas has elaborated
in detail:

> . . . the heavenly bodies make no direct impression except on
> bodies . . . Consequently, if they are the cause of our choosing,
> this will be by an impression made either on our bodies or on
> external bodies. Yet in neither way can they be a sufficient
> cause of our choosing. For the objective presentation of some
> corporeal thing cannot be the sufficient cause of our choice,
> since it is clear that when a man meets with something that
> pleases him, be it meat or woman, the temperate man is not
> moved to choose these things, whereas the intemperate is . . .
> No possible change wrought in our bodies by an impression of
> the heavenly bodies can suffice to cause us to make a choice.
> For all that results therefrom are certain passions, more or less
> violent, and passions, however violent, are not a sufficient cause
> for choosing them, since the same passions lead the incontinent
> to follow them by choice, and fail to induce the continent man.
> Therefore, it cannot be said that the heavenly bodies cause our
> choice.[9]

Viewed in the light of Aquinas' remarks, the position of the lovers is clear. Once they meet they may surrender to passion, following its dictates, as Aquinas' intemperate man does, by choice; or they may temper it as, in fact, Friar Laurence recommends in II.iii.94. Whichever they choose, their love, decreed by Providence and initiated by the stars, will be the means of reconciling the feuding families and restoring order in Verona. What Providence has decreed is irrevocable; but how the decree is fulfilled—whether order will be restored through the normal operation of the laws of nature or through violence, retribution, and purgation—will be up to them.

The choice of means confronting Romeo and Juliet is not confined to a single occasion. Rather, they are given a series of opportunities for choice. Each time they choose wrongly they make their situation more difficult, but—and the dramatic tension in the play is lost unlesss the audience realizes this—even as late as Romeo's return from exile it is possible for the play to end happily with the peaceful reconciliation of the feuding families. Up to the moment of Romeo's suicide Providence is sympathetic with the young lovers; on each occasion that they have the responsibility of choice, Providence offers them counsel, either directly through premonition or through Friar Laurence. If they will listen, if they will be properly guided, they will emerge safely from even the worst of their troubles.

The first occasion for choice occurs in the fourth scene of the first act. Mercutio, Benvolio, and Romeo are about to proceed to the Capulet ball when Romeo announces his reluctance. "'Tis no wit to go," he says; and when Mercutio asks him why, he discloses that he has had a dream warning him of the grave dangers to be risked by going. Mercutio meets his concern with a scoff and attributes dreams in general to the imagination. But Romeo is unmoved. He is convinced that dreamers "do dream things true."

> ... my mind misgives
> Some consequence, yet hanging in the stars,
> Shall bitterly begin his fearful date
> With this night's revels, and expire the term
> Of a despised life closed in my breast
> By some vile forfeit of untimely death.   (lines 106–111)[10]

But his decision is to ignore the premonition and proceed to the ball:

But He that hath the steerage of my course
Direct my sail! On, lusty gentlemen.   (lines 112–113)

The premonition whose authenticity is borne out by the fact that Romeo's decision to ignore it initiates a series of events ending in his death, like those omens preceding Caesar's death, is unmistakably a warning from Providence.[11] The time is not appropriate for the stars to exert their influence. To ignore the premonition is, in short, to invite the consequences specified in it.

It is obvious, then, that "He" in line 112 is not, as most editors have assumed, a reference to God, since Romeo's decision ignores a warning that can only have God as its source. In the terms of the nautical metaphor, "He that hath the steerage of my course / Direct my sail!," Romeo is rejecting the course charted by God as pilot. Romeo's decision is therefore in no sense an expression of faith in a special "divinity that shapes our ends, / rough-hew them how we will." It is an expression of a reckless indifference. He is a victim of unrequited love. Rosaline will have nothing to do with him. Melancholy has made him indifferent, careless of who will assume the charting of his course.

The identity of the "pilot" to whom Romeo entrusts his future is no mystery. It is Cupid. Romeo had agreed originally to Benvolio's suggestion to attend the ball only because it would allow him the opportunity to "rejoice" in Rosaline's incomparable beauty (I.ii.105–106). It is Cupid who guides him to the Capulet entertainment, and it will be Cupid who continues to chart his course after he meets Juliet. In fact, Romeo himself identifies his helmsman as Cupid in II.ii. Juliet, discovering Romeo beneath her balcony, asks him, "By whose direction foundst thou out this place?" Romeo answers:

By love, that first did prompt me to inquire.
He lent me counsel, and I lent him eyes.
I am no pilot, yet wert thou as far
As that vast shore washed with the farthest sea,
I would adventure for such merchandise.   (lines 80–84)

Shakespeare's purpose here in picking up the metaphor again is perfectly clear. Romeo has given over the steerage of his course through the troubled waters of the family feud to the blind god, who earlier in the play (II.i.9–14) has been identified as the personification of passion unenlightened and uninformed by reason. Having initially rejected Providence as a guide, he now entrusts himself to the guidance of a blind pilot.

But Romeo's commitment need not be in any sense final, although the longer he allows Cupid to control his course the greater the difficulty he will meet in attempting to avoid the catastrophe his first premonition had warned him of. How, finally, the lovers will fulfill their destiny will depend on whether Romeo continues to follow Cupid or whether he will entrust his course to Friar Laurence.

The next occasion for choice occurs in II.iii, when Romeo must decide between satisfying the urgency of his passion through a secret marriage or proceeding "wisely and slow," as his spiritual adviser counsels. Laurence's remarks about the "opposed kings," "grace and rude will," which reside "in man as well as herbs" remind the audience of the ethical principle in terms of which Romeo's ardor is to be judged. His passion, tempered, is a good; but left uncontrolled it is poisonous and self-destructive. Laurence is reluctant to believe that Romeo's love for Juliet is any more authentic than his infatuation for Rosaline has been, but he sees, and correctly, that it can be a means of ending the feud:

> But come, young waverer, come, go with me,
> In one respect I'll thy assistant be;
> For this alliance may so happy prove,
> To turn your households' rancor to pure love.   (lines 89–92)

Romeo's passion is neither good nor evil; rationally ordered it will be a good and, furthermore, may have the virtue of turning family rancor to love. But it is evident from Romeo's insistence upon an immediate secret marriage, despite the Friar's warning, that Cupid is still steering Romeo's course.

The alternatives available to Romeo and Juliet that have been identified in II.iii, reasonable caution and reckless haste, are re-introduced in II.vi, the scene in which Laurence reluctantly agrees to their secret marriage. The Friar's opening lines indicate his fear of what the consequences may be:

> So smile the Heavens upon this holy act
> That afterhours with sorrow chide us not!   (lines 1–2)

He knows that "violent delights have violent ends," but a secret and hasty marriage is better than fornication:

> . . . we will make short work,
> For, by your leaves, you shall not stay alone
> Till Holy Church incorporate two in one. (lines 35–37)

This scene, ending with the lovers and the Friar setting out to church and followed by a time lapse during which the marriage takes place and is consummated, concludes what Shakespeare has plotted as a distinct and complete action. It began when Romeo ignored a providential warning and recklessly gave the "steerage" of his course over to Cupid. As a consequence he has met Juliet and thus come prematurely under the influence of the stars. Faced now with the alternatives of allowing Cupid to continue to direct his course or of accepting Laurence as a new helmsman, he settles for Cupid. He will marry Juliet immediately to satisfy his desire.

Up to now Providence has seemingly favored the lovers. They are about to be married, and they will consummate the marriage that night. But Romeo has ignored a divine warning, and Juliet has ignored her own sound judgment:

> I have no joy of this contract tonight,
> It is too rash, too unadvised, too sudden. (II.ii.117–118)

Both have ignored the advice of Friar Laurence. Having committed themselves to passion, they will have to endure the consequences; and order in Verona will have to be restored by other than rational means.

The two ways recognized in the Renaissance by which Providence gains its ends are identified by Thomas Browne as the "ordinary and open" and the "obscure" ways. The operation of the laws of nature, he says, constitutes the "ordinary way"; the other way men call fortune:

> This [i.e., the operation of natural law] is the ordinary and open way of His Providence which Art and Industry have in a good part discovered; whose effects we may foretel without an Oracle: to foreshew these, is not Prophesie, but Prognostication. There is another way, full of Meanders and Labyrinths . . . and that is a more particular and obscure method of His Providence, directing the operations and single Essences: this we call *Fortune*, that serpentine and crooked line, whereby He draws those actions His Wisdom intends, in a more unknown and secret way. This cryptick and involved method of His Providence have I ever admired . . . Surely there are in every man's life

certain rubbings, doublings and wrenches which pass a while
under the effects of chance, but at the last, well examined,
prove the meer hand of God.[12]

By rejecting reason the lovers have rejected "the ordinary and
open way" of fulfilling their destiny and chosen, in effect, the
"obscure" way. They will discover in it that they are beset by
chance and accident.[13]

But if the new action begun in III.i, following the marriage, is
dominated by what seems to be chance, the lovers' responsibility
is not diminished. They still have the opportunity for decisions
which will directly affect the manner in which they accomplish
what Providence has ordained.

The first opportunity for decision in the new action is
presented to Romeo just after Tybalt has killed Mercutio. It is an
ironical accident that Romeo should have inadvertently given
Tybalt the opportunity to kill Mercutio when in the role of
peacemaker he stepped between the two swordsmen. Now it is
up to him to decide whether to honor Escalus' directive to the
feuding families,

> If ever you disturb our streets again,
> Your lives shall pay the forfeit of the peace,   (I.i.103–104)

or to satisfy the code of revenge. Again he allows passion to
direct his decision:

> Away to Heaven, respective lenity,
> And fire-eyed fury be my conduct now!   (III.i.128–129)

He is, or course, not responsible for Mercutio's death, but by
defying Escalus' edict and slaying Tybalt he becomes responsible
for the consequences resulting from Tybalt's death. Furthermore,
in accusing Fortune for what has happened ("O, I am fortune's
fool!" [line 141]) he is guilty of impatience, and impatience is
blasphemy. Joseph Hall writes:

> Am I a foole, or a Rebell? A foole, if I be ignorant whence my
> crosses come: a Rebell, if I know it, and be impatient. My
> sufferings are from a God, from my God; he hath destin'd me
> every dramme of sorrow that I feele: thus much thou shalt
> abide, and here shall thy miseries be stinted ... I must therefore
> either blaspheme God in my heart, detracting from his infinite
> justice, wisdome, power, mercy ... or else confesse that I ought
> to be patient.[14]

Guillaume Du Vair levels the same change against those who blame Fortune for the apparently chance occurrences which are really the workings of Providence:

> Men attribute unto Fortune the accidents whose causes they comprehend not. And from thence it is come, that some being grown so brutish, as they observed no causes of the effects which they saw, they deemed all did happen by chance. So out of their ignorance and brutalitie, they have made themselves a Goddesse, which they call Fortune, and paint her out blindfold, turning with a wheele worldly affairs, casting at randome, and throwing her presents, and favours by chance.[15]

Providence makes Romeo an unwitting agent in Mercutio's death, but Romeo decides to slay Tybalt.

From the time that Romeo kills Tybalt to the end of the play, the lovers are faced with mounting adversity in which chance is notoriously conspicuous. How they endure adversity will now determine how they fulfill their destiny as agents of Providence. If their faith is strong enough, if they can be "constant in adversity"—and this is repeatedly stressed throughout the final three acts—they may escape calamity, unite the families, and live happily as man and wife.

Again it is the Friar who, in counseling Romeo, discloses the doctrine that is essential to the correct interpretation of the action. His instructions to Romeo on how to accept exile might have come from any of a number of texts on Christian patience. His opening lines,

> Romeo, come forth, come forth, thou fearful man.
> Affliction is enamored of thy parts,
> And thou art wedded to calamity, (III.iii.1–3)

are not merely indulgence in an idle conceit. The amorous figure is based upon a commonplace of Renaissance consolatory literature: *affliction is proof of God's love*. According to Bacon, whereas "Prosperity is the blessing of the Old Testament, adversity is the blessing of the New."[16] Du Vair advises those who have suffered affliction to "give thanks to God for it, as for a great favour. Yea, I say, that that which we call miseries and calamities are gifts of God most precious and profitable."[17] He, too, uses the navigation figure: "The Sailor groweth to be a Pilote amongst Tempests and stormes: and man becomes not a man indeed, that is, constant and courageous, but in adversity."[18] But Romeo is unwilling to take the helm of his ship from the pilot to whom he had originally surrendered it. When Laurence offers him "Adversity's sweet milk, philosophy," he throws himself on the ground, tears his hair, and finally, learning of how Juliet has received the news of Tybalt's death, draws his sword to commit suicide. It is only after the Friar, confronted by the threat of the unpardonable sin, has given Romeo *secular* or *worldly* cause for hope that he pulls himself together. His sin, so identified by the Friar, is despair—an insufficient faith in the ways of God to man.

Romeo's reaction to the news of his exile is paralleled by Juliet's reaction to the same news in III.ii.97ff., as the Nurse points out in her comparison of their despair in III.iii.83–89.[19] It is also paralleled by Juliet's tearful reaction to her father's decision that she will marry Paris. Again, in Capulet's response to her tears, the nautical metaphor appears:

> . . . What, still in tears?
> Evermore showering? In one little body
> Thou counterfeit'st a bark, a sea, a wind.
> For still thy eyes, which I may call the sea,
> Do ebb and flow with tears; the bark thy body is,
> Sailing in this salt flood; the winds, thy sighs,
> Who raging with thy tears, and they with them,
> Without a sudden calm will overset
> Thy tempest-tossed body.   (III.v.130–138)

The Friar, again faced with a potential suicide, is forced to the extreme plan of deception involving the trance-inducing herb. In this instance the end justifies the means: the prevention of suicide justifies deception. The strategy misfires because of what again appears to be a sheer accident. An important letter does not get delivered.

But again it is Romeo, not Fortune or Providence, who is responsible for the ensuing consequences. Once more he fails to meet adversity as he should. He despairs, again ignoring a reassuring premonition and Balthazar's advice to control himself. The final act opens with Romeo's disclosure that he has had another dream:

> If I may trust the flattering truth of sleep,
> My dreams presage some joyful news at hand . . .
> I dreamed my lady and found me dead—

Strange dream, that gives a dead man leave to think!—
And breathed such life with kisses in my lips
That I revived and was an emperor.   (V.i.1–9)

The news which Romeo then receives of Juliet's death seemingly contradicts the assurance of the dream that all will work out well. The dream seems in fact to be a cruel joke until we realize that it is a veiled assurance by Providence that the news he is about to receive is misleading, that death may be only apparent. The situation in the dream is of course reversed—"I dreamed my lady came and found me dead"—but the essential fact is there, and Romeo ponders it momentarily: "Strange dream, that gives a dead man leave to think!" If he had taken the premonition to heart, either of two things might have happened. He might not have taken the news of Juliet's death as final and therefore not have rushed out to buy the poison; or, after returning to Verona and finding her apparently dead, he might have remembered the dream and the feelings of reassurance it had given him and perhaps have awakened her, as she in the dream had awakened him, with a kiss.

In any event, his reaction to the letter is indefensible. Balthazar advises him to be patient:

I do beseech you, sir, have patience.
Your looks are pale and wild, and do import
Some misadventure.   (V.i.27–29)

But he remains desperate, buys the poison, and rushes back to Verona. Even a few minutes' delay and he might have returned to find Juliet awakening. But he is impatient; he sees suicide as the only release from his "world-wearied flesh." His last words are to invoke again the pilot to whom he has entrusted his course:

Come, bitter conduct, come unsavory guide!
Thou desperate pilot, now at once run on
The dashing rocks thy seasick weary bark.   (V.iii.116–118)

Again, when Romeo has most need of a seasoned and resolute pilot, he allows a love grown desperate to end his voyage on the rocks of despair.

It is impossible, therefore, to maintain the romantic view of Romeo's suicide, and of Juliet's which immediately follows, as a beautiful sacrifice on the altar of innocent, ideal love. The families for their disruption of civic order, Tybalt and Mercutio for their impetuosity, Escalus for his "winking . . . at discord," and Friar Laurence for his assuming that a happy reconciliation of the feuding families might be accomplished through untempered passion—all must share in the blame for the lovers' "misadventured piteous overthrows." But the lovers themselves must bear the final blame. Destined to end the "ancient grudge," they are nevertheless free to choose the means by which they fulfill what Providence has ordained. Repeatedly, they reject divine and rational guidance, following passion as their blind pilot instead, until, finally, they take their own lives, fulfilling what Providence has ordained—but only in a final act of irrational and unpardonable defiance.

NOTES

1. J. W. Draper, "Shakespeare's 'Star-Crossed Lovers,'" *RES* XV (1939), 16–34.

2. Although most commentators have assumed that the play is a tragedy of fate rather than of character, this deterministic view has always had its opponents. Early in the nineteenth century Tieck insisted that "the tragic fate lies in the character of Juliet, and especially of Romeo. Had he been calmer, more cautious, less familiar with the idea of suicide, he would not have been Romeo; he ought to have investigated the matter [of Juliet's reported death], taken pains to inform himself, visited the Friar, and there would have been no tragedy. He must, Juliet must, perish; the necessity lay in their very natures" (Furness *Variorum* ed. of *Romeo and Juliet*, p. 449). Ulrici, another nineteenth-century critic, attributed the catastrophe to the perversion of love into lust: "Both [lovers] are high-born, richly gifted, and noble of nature; both have earth and heaven within their bosoms; but they pervert their loveliest and noblest gifts into sin, corruption, and evil; they mar their rare excellence by making idols of each other, and fanatically sacrificing all things to their idolatry" (Furness *Variorum* ed., pp. 451–452). The most recent challenger of the deterministic view of the play is Franklin M. Dickey, who sees in Romeo "a tragic hero like Othello in that he is responsible for his own chain of passionate actions," *Not Wisely But Too Well* (San Marino, 1957), p. 114.

3. John Lawlor, "Romeo and Juliet," *Early Shakespeare*, Stratford-Upon-Avon Studies, 3 (New York, 1961), p. 123.

4. G. I. Duthie, ed., New Cambridge *Romeo and Juliet* (Cambridge, 1961), p. xxx.

5. Both Franklin Dickey and Irving Ribner recognize that Romeo and Juliet are the agents through which Providence restores order. According to Dickey, they are free agents and hence responsible for the catastrophe which befalls them, but nevertheless destined by Providence to end the feud (*Not Wisely But Too Well*, pp. 95–115 *passim*). Ribner, on the other hand, insisting on their innocence, argues that their deaths are unavoidable—the means decreed by Providence for ending the feud, punishing the parents, and restoring civic harmony: "Out of the evil of the family feud—a corruption of God's harmonious order—must come a rebirth of love, and the lives of Romeo and Juliet are directed and controlled so that by their deaths the social order will be cleansed and restored to harmony." *Patterns in Shakespearean Tragedy* (London, 1960), pp. 26–27. See also Irving Ribner, "Then I denie you starres': A Reading of *Romeo and Juliet*," in *Studies in the English Renaissance Drama*, ed. Bennett, Cargill, and Hall (New York, 1959), pp. 269–286.

6. See Aquinas, *Summa Contra Gentiles*, "That the Inferior Bodies are Ruled by God by Means of the Heavenly Bodies," *Basic Writings of Thomas Aquinas*, ed. Anton C. Pegis (New York, 1945), XI, 153–155.

7. Lilly B. Campbell, ed. (Cambridge, 1938), p. 171.

8. Emblem No. 31 in *A Collection of Emblemes* (London, 1635) Huntington Library Copy, No. 79918.

9. *Summa Contra Gentiles*, "That the Heavenly Bodies are not the Cause of our Willing and Choosing"; Pegis ed., pp. 160–161.

   D. C. Allen in his extensive survey, the *Star-Crossed Renaissance* (Durham, N.C., 1941), does not notice the influence of Aquinas on Renaissance astrological thought. He does point out, however, that the English were generally agreed that although the stars affected the lives of men they did not determine them: "None of the English opponents of astrology was willing to say that the stars were without influence; at most, they denied that the planets had the governing of the human will and that the influence of the stars could either be measured or predicted. On the other hand, the formal defenders of the art were reasonably moderate. The English proponents distinguish carefully between the base and the upright astrologer; they cling to the doctrine of free will and try to effect a compromise between it and the tenets of astrology" (pp. 143–144).

10. All quotations from the play are from *Shakespeare: The Complete Works*, ed. G.B. Harrison (New York: Burlingame, 1952).

11. See my "'Wisdom Consumed in Confidence': An Examination of Shakespeare's *Julius Caesar*," *SQ* XVI (1965), 19–28.

12. *Religio Medici* (Everyman ed.), pp. 19–20.

13. The notion that he who fails to attain wisdom or fails properly to order his passions places himself in the power of Fortuna is a commonplace in Renaissance thought. See, e.g., the anonymous engraving, Wisdom and Fortune, from Bovillus, *De sapiente*, 1511; reproduced in Eugene F. Rice, *The Renaissance Idea of Wisdom* (Cambridge, Mass., 1958), pp. 128ff.

14. *Heaven upon Earth and Characters of Virtues and Vices*, ed. Rudolph Kirk (New Brunswick, N.J., 1948), p. 107.

15. *A Buckler Against Aduersitie* (London, 1622), p. 75. Huntington Library Copy No. 60013.

16. "Of Adversity," in *Essays of Francis Bacon* (Garden City, N.Y., n.d.), p. 25.

17. *A Buckler Against Auduersitie*, p. 91.

18. *Ibid.*, p. 94.

19. Having discovered Romeo "on the ground with his own tears made drunk," she remarks the similarity of their reactions: "Oh, he is even in my mistress' case,/Just in her case!" And again, after the Friar's "Oh woeful sympathy!/Piteous predicament!" She notes: "Even so lies she,/Blubbering and weeping, weeping and blubbering."

James C. Bryant

The Problematic Friar
in *Romeo and Juliet*

Friar Laurence has been traditionally called by critics the voice of wisdom and moderation in Shakespeare's drama of impetuous young lovers. For instance, George Ian Duthie[1] sees him as 'a very worthy man', 'prudent', 'worldly-wise;' and G. B. Harrison[2] sees him as 'sympathetically treated', 'grave, wise, patient.' Such a view of Friar Laurence is little altered after more than a century of critical studies.[3] Perhaps it is the very security of this venerable interpretation that prompted the following statement by Mutschmann and Wentersdorf:

> Shakespeare reveals no trace whatever of the wide-spread prejudices of non-Catholics in connection with this aspect of the life of the Roman Church. On the contrary; he does everything in his dramatic power to show his friars and nuns, their lives and customs, in an unequivocally favorable light.[4]

Yet Shakespeare's Friar Laurence deserves further examination in spite of the conventional statements handed down from one generation to another about his good intentions. This is not to disparage his worldly wisdom or his fundamental beneficence, but it may suggest that he is more problematic than most critics have recognized in the past. For in view of his questionable conduct in the drama, one senses the need to judge Friar Laurence as an ecclesiastic, perhaps as the stereotype of comical friars derived from medieval fabliaux and *commedia erudita*, rather than as an ordinary man of worthy motives.

Reprinted from *English Studies* 55 (1974), 340–50 by permission of Swets & Zeitlinger.

Without attempting to enter the controversy over Shakespeare's use of ecclesiastical figures in the drama, one nevertheless would do well to recall the historical climate as well as Shakespeare's use of Arthur Brooke's poem. It should be recalled that Shakespeare's England was particularly hostile to friars and other representatives of Roman Catholicism, especially following Philip's abortive invasion of 1588. Consequently, an original audience in 1594 was conditioned by years of political propaganda from pulpit, stage, and published works to recognize in Roman Catholic sentiment a political threat to England and to the Reformation. What may have appeared innocuous enough on the stage was in real life often synonymous with political subversion. In Muriel St. Clare Byrne's words, 'Refusal to conform to the doctrines of the established Church became thereafter no longer heresy, but a refusal of loyalty to the State, the body politic'.[5] In short, since Shakespeare wrote for a popular audience, it is therefore unlikely that he would compromise his popularity as a dramatist by making himself vulnerable to the ever watchful eyes of the Establishment. But rather than compile evidence in support of this side issue, one should consider instead the common sense advice of Kenneth Myrick to inquire first what were 'the instinctive religious beliefs' of the people for whom Shakespeare wrote his plays.[6]

An audience in 1594 would also have been aware of the literary convention which often used friars and other ecclesiastics as the butt of ribald humor. In certain ways, as shall be pointed out later, Shakespeare seems to depict Friar Laurence in that long standing tradition of the comical friar dating backward in time to the songs of the Goliards, the medieval fabliaux, and the Italian *novellatori* which frequently made the religious, particularly the friars, subjects of their broad humor.[7] This is not to say, however, that Shakespeare expected the same kind of emotional response for his friar that would have been possible in England at an earlier date, as for example in some of the entertaining pieces about clerics by John Heywood. For by Shakespeare's time the polemical element was too considerable to serve the cause of good-spirited humor merely. Moreover, Shakespeare in 1594 apparently saw no compulsion to follow the obvious derogation of some of his contemporaries: witness, for example, from Peele's *Old Wives Tale* (ca. 1591), 'a friar indefinite . . . a knave infinite'; from Marlowe's *Faustus* (ca. 1592) to Mephistophilis, 'Go, and return an old Franciscan friar; That holy shape becomes a devil best'; and from *The Jew of Malta* (ca. 1591), 'have not The nuns fine sport with the friars now and then?'. Shakespeare is more subtle. But by mildly discrediting the friar as an ecclesiastic, the result may have been as effective to an anti-papal audience as was Peele's commonplace derogation or Marlowe's bitter invective.

Part of the difficulty modern readers have in assessing Friar Laurence objectively lies perhaps in an insistence upon seeing him with myopic focus as a sympathetic man with good intentions. At this point, however, an inherited romantic sympathy for the man should be distinguished from any completely objective consideration of the friar as an ecclesiastic. For to sympathize with him as a man must at the same time be to suspend his role as a religious, sequestered from ordinary secular engagement and devoted rather to a life of piety. His function in the drama, then, would be as a well-meaning friend to Romeo more than as a representative of 'true felicity' and transcendental values. One expression of this problem becomes apparent in Joseph Kennard's comment:

> Our short-sighted human wisdom speaks soberly and acts foolishly. And because Friar Laurence is not a saint, but just a man like our nextdoor neighbor, with all the weakness and warm feelings of real life, do we love him dearly. . . . Friar Laurence has quite forgotten that he is a friar, and we, too, are quite ready to forget it, and to see only the man fighting, not wisely, but with all his might against cruel misfortune.[8]

While one may easily appreciate the sentimentality of such an evaluation, there yet remains the problem of judgment by a standard which the man necessarily renounces whenever he assumes the vows of an ecclesiastic. To judge the friar merely as a 'nextdoor neighbor' who has 'quite forgotten' his holy calling is to restore to him a status of carnality and secularism which he—and presumably the Church—would have found abhorrent. Indeed it is this disparity between *ought* and *is* that lay at the root of the comic tradition of friars in the fabliaux and in the bawdy tales of Boccaccio and Chaucer as well as in the contemporary drama. One must assume, then, that Shakespeare's audience would have seen Friar Laurence as one who *ought* to be 'ghostly sire' under the *regula* rather than as a 'nextdoor neighbor'. It is when he deviates from his spiritual function that he becomes problematic theologically.

Franklin M. Dickey's excellent examination of love in Shakespeare's plays reminds the modern student that passionate and doting love was the usual matter of comedy during the Renaissance, rarely of tragedy.[9] By application of the Renaissance dicta of romantic love—dicta to which Shakespeare was undoubtedly committed—Dickey points out that Shakespeare treats love in the first half of the action as 'more comic than has been realized'.[10] 'No other tragedy', he writes, 'preserves the comic spirit for so long a time'.[11] And although Dickey sees Friar Laurence in the traditional manner as a 'sweet old man'—the voice of Renaissance moderation to hasty and passionate young love—his conclusions about the comical aspects of *Romeo and Juliet* do not prohibit a view of the friar as an essential part of that comic spirit. Indeed, if Dickey's thesis is valid—and it is—Friar Laurence can be seen in relation to this concept of 'Love and the follies of lovers' as the substance of Elizabethan comedy.[12] Moreover, it is significant that Shakespeare's first borrowings from Arthur Brooke's tragic poem appear in a comedy, *Two Gentlemen of Verona*.[13]

If Shakespeare modeled the love comedy in *Romeo and Juliet* upon the *commedia dell' arte*, an alternative which Dickey suggests,[14] then the dramatist would have been aware of a long Italian tradition of depraved friars as stock characters. For even in the early sacred drama (*rappresentazioni sacre*) some ecclesiastics tended to become caricatures, such as 'the friar sly and tricky'.[15] And the Latin humanistic comedy of the early fifteenth century sometimes followed the tradition of derogating clerics for comic amusement. One example of this type is *Janus sacerdos*, which centers around a trick played upon a priest named Janus, 'a kindly old man but a pederast'.[16] Perhaps the most notable stage friar in the comic tradition appears in Machiavelli's *commedia erudita* entitled *Mandragola* (1513–1520). His Fra Timoteo, sensual and lusty, is villainous, 'but always a comic figure and trusted by others to conduct the business of a Churchman'.[17] But while Shakespeare's friar seems quite out of company with those cited in the Italian tradition, as far as moral depravity is concerned, nevertheless the tradition itself was too popular to be ignored by modern readers, far removed as they are from contemporary associations of friars with moral depravity. It is quite possible that Shakespeare retains something of the comical friar tradition by implying a disparity between the cleric's holy commitment and his actual behavior in the drama rather than following a form thoroughly familiar and often over-worked by the time of his own writing. And if Friar Laurence lacks an obvious association with Fra Timoteo, he at least bears kinship with him in a thoroughgoing 'Machiavellian' philosophy that the end justifies the means—however they may conflict with civil, social, and canonic laws. Some evidence for Friar Laurence as a comical figure may be discerned by observing precisely what alterations the dramatist made from his immediate source.

When Shakespeare took up Arthur Brooke's didactic poem, *Romeus and Juliet* (pr. 1562),[18] he found a Friar Laurence who was more sympathetically treated than the playwright elected to depict him, and this in spite of Brooke's Protestant denunciation of friars and their devious ways in the introductory 'To the Reader'.[19] For while Brooke's introduction abhors both friar and lovers for 'abusing the honorable name of lawful marriage to cloak the shame of stolen contracts,' the friar of the poem hardly merits Brooke's invective. The reader sees him first as an ordinary mendicant, 'barefoot' and wearing 'grayish weed'. Robert Stevenson's examination[20] of Shakespeare's alterations from the source suggests certain points that should be considered. Among them is the observation that unlike most of the Franciscan order, Brooke's friar is a 'doctor of divinity' (line 568) who had won his degree at a university.[21] What is more important, however, is that Brooke's friar is not merely a popular confessor but a revered and chosen counsellor of the Prince. Apparently it is his 'bounty' and 'wisdom' more than his easy penance which brings him general esteem in Verona.

The friar, however, is partial to Romeus, perhaps exceeding that professional relationship of 'ghostly sire' (spiritual guardian) to his youthful charge:

The friar eke of Verone youth aye likéd Romeus best.   (584)

But when 'with weeping eyes' Romeus asks him to perform the clandestine marriage, Friar Laurence hesitates with 'a thousand doubts' and discloses 'a thousand dangers like to come' (597–8). Vainly advising the lovers to wait 'a week or twain', he is at last won over 'by earnest suit' while professing the worthy motive of reconciling Capulet and Montague. When the nurse brings news to Juliet that she should go to shrift on Saturday, Brooke's anti-Romanist bias becomes more apparent in the nurse's comment than in anything the friar says:

An easy thing it is with cloak of holiness
To mock the seely mother, that suspecteth nothing less.
(639–40)

Following the pronouncement of banishment from Verona, Friar Laurence gives aid and comfort to Romeus and volunteers to act as liaison between the separated pair. And when Juliet is contracted to the County Paris, the friar considers his part in the plot and hesitates to proceed:

His conscience one while condemns it for a sin
To let her take Paris to spouse, since he himself had bin
The chiefest cause, that she unknown to father or mother,
Not five months past, in that self place was wedded to another.
(2049–52)

He further hesitates to suggest the sleeping potion to Juliet , not from a prick of conscience, but because of his fear that she will fail and

the matter published,
Both she and Romeus were undone, himself eke punishéd.
(2059–60)

Finally, he considers that it would be preferable to hazard his fame 'than suffer such adultery'—particularly since Romeus is his friend. With a reminder to Juliet that his 'fame or shame' rests upon her reticence, Friar Laurence proceeds to reveal the plan for further deception with a sleeping potion. Who knows, he muses, but that if the plan succeeds, he will reveal 'these secrets' himself, 'both to my praise' and to the 'parents' joy' (2170–1). When the ingenious plan fails, Friar Laurence flees 'in fear' from the tomb in order to avoid discovery; but after returning he confesses with repentance his part in the catastrophe: 'the sinfull'st wretch of all this mighty press' (2850). For penance the old friar voluntarily exiles himself for five years, while the nurse, for her part in not revealing the clandestine marriage to Juliet's parents, is banished forever.

But Shakespeare makes of Friar Laurence a more complex and problematic figure. He reduces him from 'doctor of divinity' and Prince's counsellor to a mere popular confessor. Romeo is still his favorite, and when the distraught lover visits the cell at dawn, the exchange indicates mutual friendship:

F. Our Romeo hath not been in bed tonight.
R. That last is true. the sweeter rest was mine.
F. God pardon sin! Wast thou with Rosaline?
R. With Rosaline, my ghostly father? No. (II.iii.42–5)

The friar's response seems indulgent on the surface, perhaps as though he believes a night with Rosaline were not really sinful. If so, Romeo senses the friar's carnal assumption; for addressing his friend as 'my ghostly father' has the effect of chiding the old cleric for a false and, in this case, unworthy conclusion.

If the friar is consistently the voice of wisdom and moderation in the play, he seems slow in giving good counsel to his pupil. For when Romeo asks him to perform the marriage rites, Friar Laurence consents immediately with none of the 'thousand doubts' and thoughts of 'a thousand dangers like to come' which caused Brooke's friar to urge delay. The famous warning in the drama,

These violent delights have violent ends, (II.vi.9)

is not spoken until after Friar Laurence has consented to the clandestine marriage in an earlier scene; and it is prompted by Romeo's urging for a brief ceremony. Apparently lacking the prudent wisdom of his original, the friar in the drama embarks readily upon a 'Machiavellian' course of action, the end of which is to reconcile the feuding houses:

For this alliance may so happy prove,
To turn your households' rancor to pure love. (II.iii.91–2)

It is only later that same day that Friar Laurence implies some possible doubt about his easy consent:

So smile the Heavens upon this holy act
That afterhours with sorrow chide us not! (II.vi.1–2)

He recognizes, as did the Renaissance generally, that violent, heated passion is dangerous: long love must be moderate. But this sound advice comes at the wrong time—too late—for Juliet is already at the door of his cell awaiting the rites. Upon her approach the friar seems perhaps to forget his holy office and instead becomes the man when he comments:

Oh, so light a foot
Will ne'er wear out the everlasting flint.   (II.vi. 16–17)

One could wonder about the psychological inference of vicarious indulgence when he responds to Juliet's greeting:

J. Good even to my ghostly confessor.
F. Romeo shall thank thee, daughter, for us both.   (II.vi.21–2)

Could something of Pandarus' delight enter into his response? The friar, recognizing their burning passion and afraid perhaps to leave them alone because of it, proceeds with brief rites:

Come, come with me, and we will make short work,
For, by your leaves, you shall not stay alone
Till Holy Church incorporate two in one.   (II.vi.34–6)

It is interesting to note, moreover, that unlike Brooke's friar who had heard from each of the lovers their free consent to marry before counselling:

at length the wife what was her due,
His duty eke by ghostly talk the youthful husband knew,
                                                     (763–4)

Shakespeare's friar grants no premarital advice, nor does he explain the obligations attendant upon the sacrament of marriage. It is rather, as he says, 'short work'.

If it is as an ecclesiastic that Friar Laurence's problematic character becomes most evident, it follows that his final judgment must be by the standards of canon low to which he is necessarily committed by irrevocable vows. In this regard a primary consideration should be the friar's apparent disregard of canon law forbidding clandestine marriages. Robert Stevenson points out that during the sixteenth century both Anglican and Roman Catholic canons forbade the clergy to perform secret marriages.[22] And, he states, to marry minors without parental knowledge or consent was considered a serious offence, incurring a penalty of suspension from clerical duties up to three years.[23] According to Stevenson, Brooke softened the offence by making Juliet sixteen years old, 'an age considered the minimum suitable one if we are to trust the most popular of the marriage manuals published in England by any of the Tudor printers'.[24] In Roman Catholic countries the minimum legal age with parental consent was early set by canon law at fourteen for males and twelve for females.[25] Gradually, however, legislators enacted marriage regulations apart from canon law. Henry II of France, for example, decreed in 1556 that marriage contracted by a minor without parental consent was null and void.[26] Yet while Luigi da Porto's *novella* (pub. 1535) made Guilietta eighteen and Brooke's poem made Juliet sixteen, Shakespeare—and this may be not without significance—deliberately reduces the age of his tragic female to not quite fourteen, over two years younger than the minimum legal age.[27] That Shakespeare probably accepted sixteen as a minimum age may be inferred from Capulet's own words to Paris early in the play:

> My child is yet a stranger in the world—
> She hath not seen the change of fourteen years.
> Let two more summers wither in their pride
> Ere we may think her ripe to be a bride. (I.ii.8–11)

Nevertheless, Friar Laurence agrees to marry the lovers in the play without parental knowledge or consent and apparently in defiance of canon law forbidding clandestine marriage.

Before one can maintain that the 'sweet old man' was consistently the voice of wisdom in the drama, it may be a helpful corrective to recall that Brooke's friar was no obvious prevaricator: he merely told Juliet to take the potion home and drink it secretly. Shakespeare's Friar Laurence, however, causes Juliet to utter a deliberate lie in order to deceive her parents:

> Hold, then, go home, be merry, give consent
> To marry Paris. (IV.i. 89–90)

Moreover, the friar further deviates from what one would expect of the religious by becoming himself a prevaricator when he offers 'consolation' at Juliet's apparent death. Friar Laurence counsels the grieving parents not to mourn, for Juliet has 'advanced Above the clouds, as high as Heaven itself'.[28] One would expect that the function of the true is to speak truth. Indeed, in view of his questionable conduct in deviating from spiritual ideals, it would seem that only a romantic and sentimental argument can exonerate Friar Laurence from obvious deceit, hypocritical posing, and prevarication. It appears, rather, that like Fra Timoteo of the *commedia erudita*, Shakespeare's friar has adopted a 'Machiavellian' policy by employing wrong means to

engender a good end. Understood in this way, Friar Laurence
remains somewhat consistently in the tradition of the Italian stage
friars—'sly and tricky'. This aspect of the friar's character at least
occurs to Juliet before consuming the mysterious potion:

> What if it be poison which the Friar
> Subtly hath ministered to have me dead,
> Lest in this marriage he should be dishonored
> Because he married me before to Romeo?   (IV.iii.24–7)

Here Juliet recognizes that the friar's part in the grand deception
would be enough to 'dishonor' him publicly. This fact, together
with the stage tradition of no great trust in friars, would help to
justify her natural fear.

But when Friar Laurence's good intentions miscarry,
Shakespeare seems to strip the old man of his priestly role and
make of him little more than a coward, totally unlike his original.
That is, in Brooke's poem the friar's consolation at Juliet's
catastrophic discovery of Romeo in the tomb is well delivered:

> And then persuaded her with patience to abide
> This sudden great mischance, and saith, that he will soon
>   provide
> In some religious house for her a quiet place,
> Where she may spend the rest of life . . .
> And unto her tormented soul call back exiléd rest.
>   (2715–18, 2720)

But Shakespeare's friar, offering no spiritual consolation and in
great fear of being discovered at the scene, attempts to hasten
Juliet away, even before she has become fully aware of the cosmic
irony which lay Romeo at her bier. His apparent concern is for
his own safety:

> Come, come away.
> Thy husband in thy bosom there lies dead,
> And Paris too. Come, I'll dispose of thee
> Among a sisterhood of holy nuns.
> Stay not to question, for the watch is coming.
> Come, go, good Juliet, I dare no longer stay.   (V.iii. 154–9)

When Juliet refuses to leave the tomb, Friar Laurence flees from
the scene. One can only wonder at the friar's behavior at this
point; for if his former acts of deception can be softened upon the

basis of poor judgment, this stroke of apparent cowardice cannot. Moreover, since his equivocation intended a greater good, one would hopefully expect him to remain at Juliet's side in order to explain his part in the catastrophe. It is interesting, too, that in Bandello (1554) and in da Porto, Fra Lorenzo does not run away but remains in the tomb until taken captive. Dramatically speaking, Shakespeare's friar at this crucial part of the scene could raise serious questions concerning his intention in fleeing: Would he flee Verona without explanation for his part in the tragedy of his friend? Did he suspect that 'too desperate' Juliet would take her own life as she had earlier threatened, in which case his deceit would go undetected? The alternative seems to be that his sense of guilt makes him desperate to the degree that he forgets his spiritual function. The main difficulty with this alternative, however, is that the friar seems to suffer no sense of guilt under interrogation by the Prince. What seems likely is that he reverts to the baser quality of his temporal clay by leaving Juliet uncomforted and unconsoled in the tomb. At least the effect of his course of action seems to vitiate whatever worthy motives he presumed earlier; for whether judged as a mere man or as a cleric in this scene he fails utterly. When his escape is frustrated he is returned a captive, and with an apt announcement from the watch the friar's problematic character is complete:

Here is a friar that trembles, sighs, and weeps.   (V.iii.184)

At the last Friar Laurence undergoes interrogation by the Prince, but he utters only slight public acknowledgment for his guilt. In the poem, however, the friar explains that his willingness to marry the lovers was based on 'nobleness, age, riches, and degree' with an aim of reconciling the feuding houses. Yet though innocent of the murders of which he is initially suspected, he is aware that his sin is against Providence:

Although before the face of God, I do confess
Myself to be sinfull'st wretch of all this mighty press. (2849–50)

In the play, Friar Laurence seems to justify his action without apparent realization of his poor judgment. One does not detect the tone of 'the sinfull'st wretch' in his protestations, but rather that of a blameless cleric:

I am the greatest, able to do least,
Yet most suspected, as the time and place
Doth make against me, of this direful murder.
And here I stand, both to impeach and purge
Myself condemned and myself excused.   (V.iii.223–7)

After confessing his course of action to the assembly, he again implies inculpation:

And if in ought of this
Miscarried by my fault, let my old life
Be sacrificed some hour before his time
Unto the rigor of severest law.   (V.iii.266–9)

Moreover, unlike Brooke's friar who repented and exiled himself for five years, Shakespeare's friar apparently professes no such guilt and consequently undergoes no penance. Not even the orthodox Prince finds him culpable:

We still have known thee for a holy man.   (V.iii.270)

In view of the evidence it becomes difficult to insist upon the traditional interpretation of Shakespeare's friar as 'grave, wise, patient'. And Elizabethan audiences may have recognized in him the vestige of stage friars from the Middle Ages whose disparity between holy ideals and worldly actions were the substance of comic ridicule. This is not to suggest that Friar Laurence is the coarse comic figure of some of his fictional contemporaries, but the portrait we have of him often recalls some of those secular foibles and human weaknesses of which friars in literature were traditionally suspect—deceit, whim, carnality, or hypocrisy. Moreover, it is likely that a highly anti-Roman Catholic audience in 1594 would have viewed Friar Laurence's meddlesome activity in a secular love affair with less sympathy than would later audiences more distant from pervasive religious animosity. For although modern readers are inclined to pardon the friar upon the basis of his personal appeal, his good intentions, and primarily because he favors the young lovers, those perhaps less romantic must pass final judgment upon him as a cleric of dubious conduct. As such he appears not wise but impulsive, meddlesome in secular love affairs, deceitful to Juliet's parents, an equivocator, an instigator of prevarication, and apparently unfaithful to his canonical vows. Shakespeare makes him less the obvious stereotype of comical friars, but by discrediting his holy function in the drama the ultimate effect is similar: he is open in either case to ridicule. As a man he is inconstant and cowardly; as a cleric he is untrue to what his habit professes. It is significant, too, that some later Roman Catholics apparently recognized the problematic nature of Friar Laurence. For, as Stevenson suggests, the unsatisfactory characterization of Shakespeare's friar may have moved nineteenth-century librettists of Italian opera to replace Fra Lorenzo with a Lorenzo who was either a physician or a mere notary. For example, in operas sung at Madrid in 1828 (*Julieta y Romeo*) and at Mexico City in 1863 (*Romeo y Julieta*), Lorenzo is a physician and not a friar.[29]

It is possible, then, that Friar Laurence is best understood as a part of the traditional comic spirit of the passionate love story which ends unhappily. His intentions are good but his hasty consent to unite the lovers in clandestine marriage and his poor judgment and problematic behavior in attempting to maintain the deception are at least partly responsible for the tragic consequences from which good intentions alone cannot exonerate him as a cleric. But with a callous disregard for the lovers, one can say that the friar's end to reconcile Capulet and Montague has been successful, although at great cost. Moreover, since Shakespeare seems in some ways to discredit the cleric's ideal function by questionable conduct and doubtful means, one must consider the possibility that Friar Laurence's character in the drama is at least problematic and probably a mild derogation of friars in general according to commonplace Renaissance attitudes toward Roman Catholic clerics during the last decade of the sixteenth century. By understanding him in this way, Friar Laurence becomes in some significant ways the stereotype of the sly and meddlesome friar of the medieval literary tradition. That Shakespeare seemed to have something of this ancient tradition in mind can be inferred by his otherwise puzzling alterations of the friar from Brooke's poem. For, as it has been suggested earlier, Shakespeare's friar is less admirable, in some ways, and weaker than Brooke's. He is still real enough and sympathetically treated to a point, but he is seemingly deprived of those qualities one expects either in an admirable man or a dedicated clergyman. The result is a problematic figure who merits more than casual acceptance by traditional standards.

NOTES

1. George Ian Duthie, 'Introduction', *Romeo and Juliet*, ed. J. Dover Wilson (Cambridge, 1955), pp. xix–xx.

2. *Shakespeare The Complete Works*, ed. G .B. Harrison (New York, 1952), p. 6. Passages cited will be from this edition.

3. Theodor Sträter wrote of Friar Laurence: 'In his [Shakespeare's] hands the kind Italian monk becomes a large-minded ecclesiastic, a wise natural philosopher, a shrewd politician, who, in the full freedom of an enlightened mind, stands high above the turmoil of the passions and gives his help the worthiest aims', *Die Komposition von Shakespeares 'Romeo and Julia'* (Bonn, 1861), as quoted in *A New Variorum Edition of Shakespeare: Romeo and Juliet*, ed. Horace Howard Furness (New York, 1963), p. 461.

4. Heinrich Mutschmann and K. Wentersdorf, *Shakespeare and Catholicism* (New York, 1952), p. 267.

5. Muriel St. Clare Byrne, *Elizabethan Life in Town and Country*, 7th ed., rev. (London, 1954), p. 159. Roman Catholics in England during the last decade of the sixteenth century were generally regarded as 'a politically disruptive element, as well as a religious sect' (p. 170).

6. Kenneth Myrick, 'The Theme of Damnation in Shakespearean Tragedy', *SP* XXXVIII (1941), 222.

7. See Joseph S. Kennard, *The Friar in Fiction* (New York, 1923), p. 96.

8. Kennard, pp. 102, 105.

9. Franklin M. Dickey, *Not Wisely But Too Well* (San Marino, Calif., 1957), p. 5.

10. Dickey, p. 64.

11. Dickey, p. 66.

12. Dickey, p. 5. Shakespeare sees that 'love is folly, even if delicious folly' (p. 64).

13. R. Warwick Bond lists some of the borrowings in *The Two Gentlemen of Verona* (London, 1925), p. xxviii.

14. Dickey, p. 66.

15. Marvin T. Herrick, *Italian Comedy in the Renaissance* (Urbana, Ill., 1966), p. 8.

16. Herrick, p. 16.

17. Herrick, p. 84. Liguris, the parasite, says to Nicia: 'These friars are subtle, crafty and understandably so, because they know both our sins and their own'.

18. Passages cited are from *Brooke's 'Romeus and Juliet' Being the Original of Shakespeare's 'Romeo and Juliet'*, ed. J. J. Munro (London, 1908).

19. Brooke seems to echo the Injunctions of Elizabeth in denouncing 'superstitious friars' as 'the naturally fit instruments of unchastity'. He also charges the young lovers with 'lust', 'using auricular confession, the key of whoredom and treason for furtherance of their purpose' (p. lxvi).

20. Robert Stevenson, *Shakespeare's Religious Frontier* (The Hague, 1958).

21. Stevenson, p. 31. He may be misleading here, for other Franciscans were university men of considerable reputation, e.g. Roger Bacon and Robert Grosseteste.

22. Stevenson, p. 32. He cites for reference (as a 'fully documented discussion of clandestine marriage and its penalties') the *Encyclopédie Théologique*, IX (Paris, 1844), pp. 507–15.

23. Stevenson, p. 32. See *Constitutions and Canons 1604*, ed. H. A. Wilson (Oxford, 1923), Canon LXII, fol. L_2.

24. Stevenson, p. 32. His reference is to Henry Bullinger, *The Christen state of Matrymone*, trans. Miles Coverdale (London, 1552), fol. 16^v. 'In ch. 5 he stated that any marriage without parental consent was void, founding his case on Scripture and the "Imperyall lawe". Bullinger's treatise was nine times reprinted before 1575. John Stockwood in 1589 published a 100-page treatise proving all marriages without parental consent to be null and void' (p. 49, n. 47).

25. Edward Westermarck, *The History of Human Marriage*, Vol. I (New York, 1922), p. 387. In the 'Schwabenspiegel' the German Catholics could marry without parental consent at fourteen and twelve; and although the people generally opposed the canon law it was upheld at the Council of Trent. See II, 340. See also for an interesting and helpful documentary on Tudor marriages Frederick J. Furnival's *Child-Marriages, Divorces, and Ratifications* (London, 1897).

26. Westermarck, II, 340. 'According to the "Code Civil", a son under twenty-five and a daughter under twenty-one could not, until 1907 [in France], marry without parental consent' (p. 341).

27. In view of Lady Capulet's determination to obey her husband's will, one must read with caution her testimony that ladies of esteem in Verona (younger than Juliet's thirteen years) were already mothers, and that Lady Capulet herself was 'by my count' Juliet's mother 'much upon these years' (I.iii.69–74).

28. In Brooke's poem the friar is not present at the 'death' scene of Juliet.

29. Stevenson, pp. 36–7.

Coppélia Kahn

Coming of Age in Verona

I

Romeo and Juliet is about a pair of adolescents trying to grow up. Growing up requires that they separate themselves from their parents by forming with a member of the opposite sex an intimate bond which supersedes filial bonds. This, broadly, is an essential task of adolescence, in Renaissance England and Italy as in America today, and the play is particularly concerned with the social milieu in which these adolescent lovers grow up—a patriarchal milieu as English as it is Italian. I shall argue that the feud in a realistic social sense is the primary tragic force in the play—not the feud as agent of fate,[1] but the feud as an extreme and peculiar expression of patriarchal society, which Shakespeare shows to be tragically self-destructive.[2] The feud is the deadly *rite de passage* that promotes masculinity at the price of life. Undeniably, the feud is bound up with a pervasive *sense* of fatedness, but that sense finds its objective correlative in the dynamics of the feud and of the society in which it is embedded. As Harold Goddard says, ". . . the fathers are the stars and the stars are the fathers in the sense that the fathers stand for the accumulated experience of the past, for tradition, for authority, and hence for the two most potent forces that mold and so impart 'density' to the child's life . . . heredity and training. . . . The hatred of the hostile houses in *Romeo and Juliet* is an inheritance that every member of these families is born into as truly as he is born with the name Capulet or Montague."[3]

Originally published in *Modern Language Studies* 8, No. 1 (Spring 1978), 171–193. Reprinted by permission of *Modern Language Studies*.

That inheritance makes Romeo and Juliet tragic figures because it denies their natural needs and desires as youth. Of course, they also display the faults of youth: its self-absorption and reckless extremism, its headlong surrender to eros. But it is the feud which fosters the rash, choleric impulsiveness typical of youth by offering a permanent invitation to and outlet for violence. The feud is first referred to in the play as "their parents' strife and their parents' rage" and it is clear that the parents, not their children, are responsible for its continuance. Instead of providing social channels and moral guidance by which the energies of youth can be rendered beneficial to themselves and society, the Montagues and the Capulets make weak gestures toward civil peace while participating emotionally in the feud as much as their children do. While they fail to exercise authority over the younger generation in the streets, they wield it selfishly and stubbornly in the home. So many of the faults of character which critics have found in Romeo and Juliet are shared by their parents that the play cannot be viewed as a tragedy of character in the Aristotelian sense, in which tragedy results because the hero and heroine fail to "love moderately."[4] Rather, the feud's ambiance of hot temper permeates age as well as youth; viewed from the standpoint of Prince Escalus, who embodies the law, it is Montague and Capulet who are childishly refractory.

In the course of the action, Romeo and Juliet create and try to preserve new identities as adults apart from the feud, but it blocks their every attempt. Metaphorically, it devours them in the "detestable maw" of the Capulets' monument, a symbol of the patriarchy's destructive power over its children. Thus both the structure and the texture of the play suggest a critique of the patriarchal attitudes expressed through the feud, which makes "tragic scapegoats" of Romeo and Juliet.[5]

Specifically, for the sons and daughters of Verona the feud constitutes socialization into patriarchal roles in two ways. First, it reinforces their identities as sons and daughters by allying them with their paternal household against another paternal household, thus polarizing all their social relations, particularly their marital choices, in terms of filial allegiance. They are constantly called upon to define themselves in terms of their families and to defend their families. Second, the feud provides a "psycho-sexual moratorium" for the sons,[6] an activity in which they prove themselves men by phallic violence on behalf of their fathers, instead of by the courtship and sexual experimentation that would lead toward marriage and separation from the paternal house. It fosters in the sons fear and scorn of women, associating women with effeminacy and emasculation, while it links sexual intercourse with aggression and violence against women, rather than with pleasure and love. Structurally, the play's design reflects the prominence of the feud. It erupts in three scenes at the beginning, middle, and end (I.i, III.i, v.iii) that deliberately echo each other, and the *peripeteia*, at which Romeo's and Juliet's fortunes change decisively for the worse, occurs exactly in the middle when Romeo in killing Tybalt faces the two conflicting definitions of manhood between which he must make his tragic choice.

It has been noted that *Romeo and Juliet* is a domestic tragedy but not that its milieu is distinctly patriarchal as well as domestic. Much of it takes place within the Capulet household, and Capulet's role as *paterfamilias* is apparent from the first scene, in which his servants behave as members of his extended family. That household is a charming place: protected and spacious, plentiful with servants, food, light, and heat, bustling with festivity, intimate and informal even on great occasions, with a cosy familiarity between master and servant. In nice contrast to it stands the play's other dominant milieu, the streets of Verona. It is there that those fighting the feud are defined as men, in contrast to those who would rather love than fight, who in terms of the feud are less than men. Gregory and Sampson ape the machismo of their masters, seeking insults on the slightest pretext so that they may prove their valor. In their blind adherence to a groundless "ancient grudge," they are parodies of the feuding gentry. But in Shakespeare's day, as servants they would be regarded as their master's "children" in more than a figurative sense, owing not just work but loyalty and obedience to their employers as legitimate members of the household ranking immediately below its children.[7] As male servants their position resembles that of the sons bound by their honor to fight for their families' names. Most important, their obvious phallic competitiveness in being quick to anger at an insult to their status or manhood, and quick to draw their swords and fight, shades into competitiveness in sex as well: "I strike quickly, being moved. . . . A dog of the house of Montague moves me. . . . Therefore, I will push Montague's men from the wall and thrust his maids to the wall. . . . Me they shall feel while I am able to stand" (I.i.7, 9, 18–20, 30).[8] In this scene and elsewhere, the many puns on "stand" as standing one's ground in fighting and as erection attest that fighting in the feud demonstrates virility as well as valor. Sampson and Gregory also imply that they consider it their prerogative as men to take women by force as a way of demonstrating their superiority to the Montagues: ". . . women, being the weaker vessels, are ever thrust to the wall. Therefore I will push Montague's men from the wall and thrust his maids to the wall. . . . When I have fought with the men, I will be civil with the maids—I will cut off their heads . . . the heads of the maids or their maidenheads. Take it in what sense thou wilt" (16–20, 24–25, 27–28). As the fighting escalates, Capulet and Montague finally become involved themselves, Capulet calling for a sword he is too infirm to wield effectively, merely because Montague, he claims, "flourishes his blade in spite of me." With the neat twist of making the masters parody the men who have been parodying them, the fighting ends as the Prince enters. At the cost of civil peace, all have asserted their claims to manhood through the feud.

Tybalt makes a memorable entrance in his first scene. Refusing to believe Benvolio's assertion that his sword is drawn only to separate the fighting servants, he immediately dares him to defend himself. To Tybalt, a sword can only mean a challenge to fight, and peace is just a word:

> What, drawn, and talk of peace? I hate the word
> As I hate hell, all Montagues, and thee.
> Have at thee, coward!   (I.i.72–74)

In the first two acts, Shakespeare contrasts Tybalt and Romeo in terms of their responses to the feud so as to intensify the conflict Romeo faces in Act III when he must choose between being a man in the sanctioned public way, by drawing a sword upon an insult, or being a man in a novel and private way, by reposing an inner confidence in his secret identity as Juliet's husband.

In Act III, the fight begins when Tybalt is effectively baited by Mercutio's punning insults; from Mercutio's opening badinage with Benvolio, it is evident that he too is spoiling for a fight, though he is content to let the weapons be words. But words on the hot midday streets of Verona are effectively the same as blows that must be answered by the drawing of a sword. When Romeo arrives, Tybalt calls him "my man," "a villain," and "boy," all terms which simultaneously impugn his birth and honor as well as his manhood. Mercutio made words blows, but Romeo tries to do just the opposite, by oblique protestations of love to Tybalt, which must seem quite mysterious to him if he listens to them at all: "And so, good Capulet, whose name I tender/ As dearly as mine own, be satisfied" (III.i.72–73). Romeo's puns of peacemaking fail where Mercutio's puns of hostility succeeded all too well. Only one kind of rigid, simple language is understood in the feud, a language based on the stark polarities Capulet-Montague, man-boy. No wonder Mercutio terms Romeo's response a "calm, dishonorable, vile submission" and draws on Tybalt: Romeo has allowed a Capulet to insult his name, his paternal heritage, his manhood, without fighting for them. Like Tybalt, Romeo owes a duty to "the stock and honor of his kin." When Mercutio in effect fights for him and dies, Romeo is overcome by the shame of having allowed his friend to answer the challenge which by the code of manly honor he should have answered himself. He momentarily turns against Juliet, the source of his new identity, and sees her as Mercutio sees all women:

> O sweet Juliet,
> Thy beauty hath made me effeminate,
> And in my temper soft'ned valor's steel!   (III.i.115–17)

In that moment, caught between his radically new identity as Juliet's husband, which has made him responsible (he thinks) for his friend's death, and his previous traditional identity as the scion of the house of Montague, he resumes the latter and murders Tybalt. As Ruth Nevo remarks, "Romeo's challenge of Tybalt is not merely an instance . . . of a rashness which fatally flaws his character. . . . On the contrary, it is an action first avoided, then deliberately undertaken, and it is entirely expected of him by his society's code."[9] As much as we want the love of Romeo and Juliet to prosper, we also want the volatile enmity of Tybalt punished and the death of Mercutio, that spirit of vital gaiety, revenged, even at the cost of continuing the feud. Romeo's hard choice is also ours. Though the play is constantly critical of the feud as the medium through which criteria of patriarchally oriented masculinity are voiced, it is just as constantly sensitive to the association of those criteria with more humane principles of loyalty to family and friends, courage, and personal dignity.

Among the young bloods serving as foils for Romeo, Benvolio represents the total sublimation of virile energy into peacemaking,

agape instead of eros; Tybalt, such energy channeled directly
and exclusively into aggression; and Mercutio, its attempted
sublimation into fancy and wit. (Romeo and Paris seek manhood
through love rather than through fighting, but are finally impelled
by the feud to fight each other.) That Mercutio pursues the feud
though he is neither Montague nor Capulet suggests that feuding
has become the normal social pursuit for young men in Verona.
Through his abundant risqué wit, he suggests its psychological
function for them, as a definition of manhood. Love is only manly,
he hints, if it is aggressive and violent and consists of subjugating
women, rather than being subjugated by them:

If love be rough with you, be rough with love;
Prick love for pricking, and you beat love down.   (I.iv.27–28)

Alas, poor Romeo, he is already dead: stabbed with a white
wench's black eye; run through the ear with a love-song:
the very pin of his heart cleft with the blind bow-boy's
butt-shaft; and is he a man to encounter Tybalt?   (II.iv.14–18)

The conflict between his conception of manhood and the one
which Romeo learns is deftly and tellingly suggested in Romeo's
line, "He jests at scars that never felt a wound" (II.i.1). Juliet is a
Capulet, and Romeo risks death to love her; the trite metaphor of
the wound of love has real significance for him. Mercutio
considers love mere folly unworthy of a real man and respects
only the wounds suffered in combat. Ironically, Mercutio will
die of a real wound occasioned partly by Romeo's love, while
Romeo, no less a man, will die not of a wound but of the poison
he voluntarily takes for love.

Mercutio mocks not merely the futile, enfeebling kind of love
Romeo feels for Rosaline, but all love. Moreover, his volley of
sexual innuendo serves as the equivalent of both fighting and
love. In its playful way, his speech is as aggressive as fighting,
and while speech establishes his claim to virility, at the same
time it marks his distance from women. As Romeo says, Mercutio
is "A gentleman . . . that loves to hear himself talk and will speak
more in a minute than he will stand to in a month" (II.iv.153–55).
Mercutio would rather fight than talk, but he would rather talk
than love, which brings us to his justly famed utterance, the
Queen Mab speech. Like so much in this play, it incorporates
opposites. While it is surely an isolated set piece, it is also highly

characteristic of Mercutio, in its luxuriant repleteness of images and rippling mockery. While it purports to belittle dreamers for the shallowness of the wishes their dreams fulfill, it sketches the dreamers' world with loving accuracy, sweetmeats, tithe pigs, horses' manes and all. In service to the purest fancy, it portrays Mab's coach and accoutrements with workmanlike precision. It pretends to tell us dreams are "nothing but vain fantasy" but this pose is belied by the speaker's intense awareness that real people do dream of real things.[10] In short, Mercutio's defense against dreams gives evidence of his own urge to dream, but it also reveals his fear of giving in to the seething nighttime world of unconscious desires associated with the feminine; he prefers the broad daylight world of men fighting and jesting. Significantly, his catalogue of dreamers ends with a reference to the feminine mystery of birth, with an implied analogy between the birth of children from the womb and the birth of dreams from "an idle brain." He would like to think that women's powers, and desires for women, are as bodiless and inconsequential as the dreams to which they give rise, and to make us also think so he concludes his whole speech with the mock-drama of a courtship between the winds. For him the perfect image of nothingness is unresponsive and inconstant love between two bodies of air. But Mercutio protests too much; the same defensiveness underlies his fancy as his bawdry. Puns and wordplay, the staple of his bawdry, figure prominently in dreams, as Freud so amply shows; relying on an accidental similarity of sound, they disguise a repressed impulse while giving voice to it.[11]

II

In the feud, names (the signs of patriarchal authority and allegiance) are calls to arms, and words are blows. As Romeo and Juliet struggle to free themselves from the feud, their effort at first takes the form of creating new names for themselves to reflect their new identities. When they learn each other's names, they attend only to surnames, which signify the social constraints under which their love must exist. Romeo says, "Is she a Capulet?/O dear Account! My life is my foe's debt" (I.v.119–20), and the Nurse tells Juliet, "His name is Romeo, and a Montague,/ The only son of your great enemy" (I.v.138–39). Juliet's extended

meditation on Romeo's name in the balcony scene begins with
her recognition that for Romeo to refuse his name—to separate
himself from the feud—he would have to deny his father (II.233–
34); she moves from this unlikely alternative to a fanciful effort
to detach the man from the name, and their love from the social
reality in which it is embedded: "'Tis but thy name that is my
enemy./Thou art thyself, though not a Montague" (II.i.238–39).
Through the irony of Juliet's casual "but thy name," Shakespeare
suggests both that it is impossible for Romeo to separate himself
from his public identity as a Montague and that his public identity
is nonetheless extraneous and accidental, no part of what he really
is. The Romeo already transfigured by his love for Juliet is a
different person and his name should reflect it. The exchange
which Juliet proposes hints at this:

> Romeo, doff thy name;
> And for thy name, which is no part of thee,
> Take all myself.   (II.ii.47–49)

In fact, his new identity as a man is to be based on his allegiance
to her as her husband and not on his allegiance to his father. In
the wedding scene, Romeo says with his desperate faith, "It is
enough I may but call her mine" (II.vi.8), an ironic allusion to the
fact that though she now has taken his surname in marriage, all
he really can do is "call" her his, for the feud will not allow their
new identities as husband and wife to become publicly known,
as is all too apparent when Romeo's veiled references to Tybalt's
name as one which he tenders as dearly as his own go
uncomprehended in Act III.

Later, in Friar Lawrence's cell bemoaning his banishment,
Romeo curses his name and offers literally to cut it out of his
body as though it were merely physical and its hateful
consequences could be amputated. Symbolically, he is trying to
castrate himself; as a consequence of the feud he cannot happily
be a man either by fighting for his name and family or by loving
Juliet. Banished and apart from her, he will have no identity and
nothing to live for. His obsession with his name at this point
recalls Juliet's "'Tis but thy name that is my enemy." In the early
moments of their love, both of them seek to mold social reality to
their changed perceptions and desires by manipulating the verbal
signifiers of that reality. But between Romeo's banishment and
their deaths, both learn in different ways that not the word but

the spirit can change reality. Juliet becomes a woman and Romeo a man not through changing a name but by action undertaken in a transformed sense of the self, requiring courage and independence.

Unmanned in the friar's cell by the thought of life without Juliet, Romeo hurls himself to the floor in tears and petulantly refuses to rise. The significance of this posture is emphasized by the Nurse's exclamation, "O, he is even in my mistress' case,/ Just in her case!" (iii.iii.84–85). Echoing the sexual innuendo of the play's first scene in a significantly different context, the Nurse urges him vigorously,

> Stand up, stand up! Stand, and you be a man.
> For Juliet's sake, for her sake, rise and stand!
> Why should you fall into so deep an O? (iii.iii.88–90)

Friar Lawrence's ensuing philosophical speech is really only an elaboration of the Nurse's simple, earthy rebuke. The well-meaning friar reminds Romeo that he must now base his sense of himself as a man not on his socially sanctioned identity as a son of Montague, but on his love for Juliet, in direct conflict with that identity—a situation which the friar sees as only temporary. But this conflict between manhood as aggression on behalf of the father, and manhood as loving a woman, is at the bottom of the tragedy, and not to be overcome.

In patriarchal Verona, men bear names and stand to fight for them; women, "the weaker vessels," bear children and "fall backward" to conceive them, as the Nurse's husband once told the young Juliet. It is appropriate that Juliet's growing up is hastened and intensified by having to resist the marriage arranged for her by her father, while Romeo's is precipitated by having to fight for the honor of his father's house. Unlike its sons, Verona's daughters have, in effect, no adolescence, no sanctioned period of experiment with adult identities or activities. Lady Capulet regards motherhood as the proper termination of childhood for a girl, for she says to Juliet,

> Younger than you,
> Here in Verona, ladies of esteem,
> Are made already mothers. (i.iii.69–71)

and recalls that she herself was a mother when she was about her daughter's age. Capulet is more cautious at first: "Too soon marred are those so early made" (I.ii.13), he says, perhaps meaning that pregnancies are more likely to be difficult for women in early adolescence than for those even slightly older. But the pun in the succeeding lines reveals another concern besides this one:

Earth hath swallowèd all my hopes but she;
She is the hopeful lady of my earth.   (I.ii.14–15)

Fille de terre is the French term for heiress, and Capulet wants to be sure that his daughter will not only survive motherhood, but produce healthy heirs for him as well.

Capulet's sudden determination to marry Juliet to Paris comes partly from a heightened sense of mortality which, when it is introduced in the first act, mellows his character attractively:

Welcome, gentleman! I have seen the day
That I have worn a visor and could tell
A whispering tale in a fair lady's ear,
Such as would please. 'Tis gone, 'tis gone, 'tis gone. (I.v.23–26)

But he cannot give up his claim on youth so easily as these words imply. When he meets with Paris again after Tybalt's death, it is he who calls the young man back, with a "desperate tender" inspired by the thought that he, no less than his young nephew, was "born to die." Better to insure the safe passage of his property to an heir now, while he lives, than in an uncertain future. Even though decorum suggests but "half a dozen friends" as wedding guests so hard upon a kinsman's death, he hires "twenty cunning cooks" to prepare a feast, and stays up all night himself "to play the housewife for this once," insisting against his wife's better judgment that the wedding be celebrated not a day later. For him, the wedding constitutes the promise that his line will continue, though his own time end soon. Shakespeare depicts Capulet's motives for forcing the hasty marriage with broad sympathy in this regard, but he spares the anxious old man no tolerance in the scene in which Juliet refuses to marry Paris.

In Shakespeare's source, Arthur Brooke's versification of an Italian novella, the idea of marriage with Paris isn't introduced until after Romeo's banishment. In the play, Paris broaches his suit (evidently not for the first time) in the second scene and receives a temperate answer from Capulet, who at this point is a model of fatherly tenderness and concern:

> My child is yet a stranger in the world,
> She hath not seen the change of fourteen years;
> Let two more summers wither in their pride
> Ere we may think her ripe to be a bride.
> . . . .
> But woo her, gentle Paris, get her heart;
> My will to her consent is but a part.
> And she agreed, within her scope of choice
> Lies my consent and fair according voice.   (I.ii.8–11, 16–19)

Significantly, though, this scene begins with Capulet acting not only as a father but also as the head of a clan; alluding to the recent eruption of the feud and the Prince's warning, he says lightly, ". . . 'tis not hard, I think,/For men so old as we to keep the peace." Only when his failure to exert effective authority over the inflammatory Tybalt results in Tybalt's death, an insult to the clan, does Capulet decide to exert it over his daughter, with compensatory strictness. Thus Shakespeare, by introducing the arranged marriage at the beginning and by making Capulet change his mind about it, shows us how capricious patriarchal rule can be, and how the feud changes fatherly mildness to what Hartley Coleridge called "paternal despotism."[12] After Tybalt's death, the marriage which before required her consent is now his "decree," and his anger at her opposition mounts steadily from an astonished testiness to brutal threats:

> And you be mine, I'll give you to my friend;
> And you be not, hang, beg, starve, die in the streets,
> For, by my soul, I'll ne'er acknowledge thee,
> Nor what is mine shall never do thee good.   (III.v.193–96)

Perhaps Shakespeare got the inspiration for these lines from Brooke's poem, where Capulet cites Roman law allowing fathers to "pledge, alienate, and sell" their children, and even to kill them if they rebel.[13] At any rate, it is clear that Capulet's anger is as violent and unreflective as Tybalt's, though he draws no sword against Juliet, and that the emotional likeness between age and youth in this instance is fostered by different aspects of the same system of patriarchal order.

Romeo finds a surrogate father outside that system, in Friar Lawrence, and in fact never appears onstage with his parents. Juliet, on the other hand, always appears within her parents' household until the last scene in the tomb. Lodged in the bosom of the family, she has two mothers, the Nurse as well as her real one. For Juliet, the Nurse is the opposite of what the Friar is for Romeo; she is a surrogate mother within the patriarchal family, but one who is, finally, of little help in assisting Juliet in her passage from child to woman. She embodies the female self molded devotedly to the female's family role. The only history she knows is that of birth, suckling , weaning, and marriage; for her, earthquakes are less cataclysmic than these turning points of growth. She and Juliet enter the play simultaneously in a scene in which she has almost all the lines and Juliet less than ten, a disproportion which might be considered representative of the force of tradition weighing on the heroine.

The Nurse's longest speech ends with the telling of an anecdote (I.iii.35–48) which she subsequently repeats twice. It is perfectly in character: trivial, conventional, full of good humor but lacking in wit. And yet it epitomizes the way in which, in the patriarchal setting, woman's subjugation to her role as wife and mother is made to seem integral with nature itself:

> And then my husband (God be with his soul!
> 'A was a merry man) took up the child.
> "Yea," quoth he, "dost fall upon thy face?
> Thou wilt fall backward when thou hast more wit;
> Wilt thou not, Jule?" and by my holidam,
> The pretty wretch left crying and said, "Ay."   (I.iii.39–44)

The story is placed between the Nurse's recollections of Juliet's weaning and Lady Capulet's statements that girls younger than Juliet are already mothers, as she herself was at Juliet's age. This collocation gives the impression of an uninterrupted cycle of birth and nurturance carried on from mother to daughter, under the approving eyes of fathers and husbands. The Nurse's husband, harmlessly amusing himself with a slightly risqué joke at Juliet's expense, gets more than he bargains for in the child's innocent reply. The Nurse finds the point of the story in the idea that even as a child, Juliet had the "wit" to assent to her sexual "fall"; she takes her "Ay" as confirmation of Juliet's precocious fitness for "falling" and "bearing." But in a larger sense than the Nurse is meant to see, "bearing" implies that it will be Juliet's fate to "bear" her father's will and the tragic consequences of her attempt to circumvent it. And in a larger sense still, all women, by virtue of their powers of bearing, are regarded as mysteriously close to the Earth, which, as Friar Lawrence says, is "Nature's mother," while men, lacking these powers, and intended to rule over the earth, rule over women also. As the Nurse says, "Women grow by men" (I.iii.95).

Against this conception of femininity, in which women are married too young to understand their sexuality as anything but passive participation through childbearing in a vast biological cycle, Shakespeare places Juliet's unconventional, fully conscious and willed giving of herself to Romeo. Harry Levin has pointed out how the lovers move from conventional formality to a simple, organic expressiveness that is contrasted with the rigid, arbitrary polarization of language and life in Verona.[14] Juliet initiates this departure in the balcony scene by answering Romeo's conceits, "love's light wings" and "night's cloak," with a directness highly original in the context:

> Dost thou love me? I know thou wilt say "Ay";
> And I will take thy word.   (II.ii.90–91)

Free from the accepted forms in more than a stylistic sense, she pledges her love, discourages Romeo from stereotyped love-vows, and spurs him to make arrangements for their wedding. As she awaits the consummation of their marriage, the terms in which she envisions losing her virginity parody the terms of male competition, the sense of love as a contest in which men must beat down women or be beaten by them:

> Come, civil night,
> Thou sober-suited matron all in black,
> And learn me how to lose a winning match,
> Played for a pair of stainless maidenhoods.   (III.ii.10–13)

She knows and values her "affections and warm youthful blood," but she has yet to learn the cost of such blithe individuality in the tradition-bound world of Verona. When the Nurse tells her that Romeo has killed Tybalt, she falls suddenly into a rant, condemning him in the same kind of trite oxymorons characteristic of Romeo's speech before they met (see especially I.i.178–86); such language in this context reflects the automatic thinking of the feud, which puts everything in terms of a Capulet-Montague dichotomy. But she drops this theme when a word from the Nurse reminds her that she now owes her loyalty to Romeo rather than to the house of Capulet:

NURSE. Will you speak well of him that killed your cousin?
JULIET. Shall I speak ill of him that is my husband?
Ah, poor my lord, what tongue shall smooth thy name,
When I, thy three-hours' wife, have mangled it?   (III.ii.96–99)

Romeo's "name" in the sense of his identity as well as his reputation now rests not on his loyalty to the Montagues but on Juliet's loyalty to him and their reciprocal identities as husband and wife apart from either house.

Juliet's next scene (III.v), in which she no sooner bids farewell to Romeo than learns that she is expected to marry Paris, depicts another crucial development in her ability to use language creatively to support her increasing independence. As the scene opens, it is Juliet who would use words as a pretty refuge from harsh reality, renaming the lark a nightingale, the sunrise a meteor, as though words could stop time from passing, and it is Romeo who gently insists that they accept their painful separation for what it is. But when her mother enters with bitter expressions of hatred toward Romeo, Juliet practices a skillful equivocation that allows her to appear a loyal Capulet while also speaking her heart about Romeo.

When her father's rage erupts moments later, however, Juliet is unable to say more than a few words on her own behalf. Seeking comfort and counsel from the Nurse, the only advice she receives is for expediency. The Nurse is so traditionally subservient to her master that she cannot comprehend a loyalty to Romeo that would involve opposing Capulet, and she has no idea of Juliet's growing independence of her father and commitment to Romeo. Juliet's disbelieving "Speak'st thou from thy heart?" and the Nurse's assuring reply underscore the difference between them as women. The Nurse has no "heart" in the sense that she has no self-defined conception of who she is or to whom she owes her fidelity; for her, affection and submission have always been one. As Coleridge said, she is characterized by a "happy, humble ducking under."[15] On the other hand, Juliet, now inwardly placing fidelity to Romeo above obedience to her father and thus implicitly denying all that family, society, and the feud have taught her, utters a lie in perfect calm to end her conversation with the Nurse. There is no way for her to speak the truth of her heart in her father's household, so she may as well lie. Though she will again employ equivocation in her stilted, stichomythic conversation with Paris later, her closing line, "If all else fails, myself have power to die," bespeaks a self-confidence, courage, and strength no longer dependent on verbal manipulations.

III

In this play ordered by antitheses on so many levels, the all-embracing opposition of Eros and Thanatos seems to drive the plot along.[16] The lovers want to live in union; the death-dealing feud opposes their desire. The tragic conclusion, however, effects a complete turnabout in this clear-cut opposition between love and death, for in the lovers' suicides love and death merge. Romeo and Juliet die as an act of love, in a spiritualized acting out of the ancient pun. Furthermore, the final scene plays off against each other two opposing views of the lovers' deaths: that they are consumed and destroyed by the feud, and that they rise above it, united in death. The ambivalence of this conclusion is worth exploring to see how it reflects the play's concern with coming of age in the patriarchal family.

It cannot be denied that, through the many references to fate, Shakespeare wished to create a feeling of inevitability, of a mysterious force stronger than individuals shaping their courses even against their will and culminating in the lovers' deaths. Yet it is also true that, as Gordon Ross Smith says, the play employs fate not as an external power, but "as a subjective feeling on the parts of the two lovers."[17] And this subjective feeling springs understandably from the objective social conditions of life in Verona. The first mention of fate, in the Prologue's phrase "fatal loins," punningly connects fate with feud and anticipates the rhyme uttered by Friar Lawrence, which might stand as a summary of the play's action:

The earth that's Nature's mother is her tomb,
What is her burying grave, that is her womb. . . .   (II.iii.9–10)

The loins of the Montagues and the Capulets are fatal because the two families have established a state of affairs whereby their children are bound, for the sake of family honor, to kill each other. It is hardly necessary to recall how Romeo's first sight of Juliet is accompanied by Tybalt's "Fetch me my rapier, boy" or how (as I have shown) their very names denote the fatal risk they take in loving each other. Romeo's premonition, as he sets off for the Capulets' ball, that he will have "an untimely death," or Juliet's, as his banishment begins, that she will see him next in a tomb, are not hints from the beyond, but expressions of fear eminently realistic under the circumstances.

The setting and action of the final scene are meant to remind us of the hostile social climate in which the lovers have had to act. It begins on a bittersweet note as the dull and proper Paris approaches to perform his mangled rites, recapitulating wedding in funeral with the flowers so easily symbolic of a young and beautiful maiden, and symbolic of her expected defloration in marriage. By paralleling the successive entrances of Paris and Romeo, one who has had no part in the feud, the other who has paid so much for resisting it, both of whom love Juliet, Shakespeare suggests the feud's indifferent power over youth. Each character comes in with the properties appropriate to his task and enjoins the servant accompanying him to "stand aloof." Their ensuing sword-fight is subtly designed to recall the previous eruptions of the feud and to suggest that it is a man-made cycle of recurrent violence. Paris's challenge to Romeo,

> Stop thy unhallowèd toil, vile Montague!
> Can vengeance be pursued farther than death?
> Condemnèd villain, I do apprehend thee.
> Obey, and go with me; for thou must die.   (v.iii.54–57)

recalls Tybalt's behavior at the Capulets' ball, when he assumed Romeo's very presence to be an insult, and in Act III, when he deliberately sought Romeo out to get satisfaction for that insult. Romeo responds to Paris as he did to Tybalt, first by hinting cryptically at his true purpose in phrases echoing those he spoke in Act III:

> By heaven, I love thee better than myself,
> For I come hither armed against myself.   (v.iii.64–65)

Then once more he gives in to "fire-eyed fury" when Paris continues to provoke him and, in a gesture all too familiar by now, draws his sword.

Shakespeare prepares us well before this final scene for its grim variations on the Friar's association of womb and tomb. Juliet's moving soliloquy on her fears of waking alone in the family monument amplifies its fitness as a symbol of the power of the family, inheritance, and tradition over her and Romeo. She ponders "the terror of the place—"

> . . . a vault, an ancient receptacle
> Where for many hundred years the bones
> Of all my buried ancestors are packed. (iv.iii.38–41)

In a "dismal scene" indeed, she envisions herself first driven mad by fear, desecrating these bones by playing with them, and then using the bones against herself to dash her brains out. This waking dream, like all the dreams recounted in this play, holds psychological truth; it bespeaks both Juliet's knowledge that in loving Romeo she has broken a taboo as forceful as that against harming the sacred relics of her ancestors, and her fear of being punished for the offense by the ancestors themselves—with their very bones.

As Romeo forces his way into the monument, he pictures it both as a monstrous mouth devouring Juliet and himself and as a womb:

> Thou detestable maw, thou womb of death,
> Gorged with the dearest morsel of the earth,
> Thus I enforce thy rotten jaws to open,
> And in despite I'll cram thee with more food. (v.iii.45–49)

When the Friar hastens toward the monument a few minutes later, his exclamation further extends the meanings connected with it:

> Alack, alack, what blood is this, which stains
> The stony entrance to this sepulcher? (v.iii.140–41)

The blood-spattered entrance to this tomb that has been figured as a womb recalls both a defloration or initiation into sexuality, and a birth. Juliet's wedding bed is her grave, as premonitions had warned her, and three young men, two of them her bridegrooms, all killed as a result of the feud, share it with her. The birth that takes place in this "womb" is perversely a birth into death, a stifling return to the tomb of the fathers, not the second birth of adolescence, the birth of an adult self, which the lovers strove for.[18]

But the second part of the scene, comprising Romeo's death speech, the Friar's entrance and hasty departure, and Juliet's death speech, offers a different interpretation. Imagery and action combine to assert that death is a transcendent form of sexual consummation, and further, that it is rebirth into a higher stage of existence—the counterpart of an adulthood never fully achieved in life. That Shakespeare will have it both ways at once is perfectly in keeping with a play about adolescence in that it reflects the typical conflict of that period, which Bruno Bettelheim describes as "the striving for independence and self-assertion, and the opposite tendency, to remain safely at home, tied to the parents."[19] It is also similar to the ambivalent ending of *Venus and Adonis*, another work about youth and love, in which Venus's long-striven-for possession of Adonis takes the form of the total absorption of each person in the other, at the price of Adonis's death.[20]

It might be argued that Romeo and Juliet will their love-deaths in simple error caused by the mere chance of Brother John's failure to reach Romeo with the news of Juliet's feigned death and that chance is fate's instrument. But the poetic consistency and force with which their belief in death as consummation is carried out, by means of the extended play of words and actions on dying as orgasm, outweighs the sense of chance or of fate. The equation of loving with dying is introduced early; frequently, dying is linked to the feud, for instance in Juliet's reference to grave and wedding bed in Act I, scene v, restated in the wedding scene. Romeo's banishment produces an explosion of remarks linking wedding bed with tomb and the bridegroom Romeo with death.[21] The Friar's potion inducing a simulated death on the day of Juliet's wedding with Paris titillates us further with ironic conjunctions of death and marriage. But when Romeo declares, the instant after he learns of Juliet's supposed death, "Is it e'en so? Then I defy you, stars!" (v.i.24),[22] the context in which we have been led to understand and expect the lovers' death is transformed. Romeo no longer conceives his course of action as a way of circumventing the feud, which now has no importance for him. Rather, he wills his death as a means to permanent union with Juliet. When he says, in the same tone of desperate but unshakable resolve, "Well, Juliet, I will lie with thee tonight," as her lover and bridegroom he assumes his role in the love-death so amply foreshadowed, but that love-death is not merely fated; it is willed. It is the lovers' triumphant assertion over the impoverished and destructive world which has kept them apart. Romeo's ensuing conversation with the apothecary is full of contempt for a merely material world, and his confidence that he alone possesses Juliet in death is so serene that he indulges in the mordantly erotic fantasy that amorous Death keeps Juliet in the tomb "to be his paramour" (v.iii.102–5), recalling and dismissing the earlier conception of death as Juliet's bridegroom. Shakespeare fills Romeo's last speech with the imagery of life's richness: the gloomy vault is "a feasting presence full of light," and Juliet's lips and cheeks are crimson with vitality. His last lines, "O true apothecary!/Thy drugs are quick. Thus with a kiss I die" (v.iii.120), bring together the idea of death as sexual consummation and as rebirth. Similarly, Juliet kisses the poison on his lips and calls it "a restorative." They have come of age by a means different from the rites of passage—phallic violence and adolescent motherhood—typical for youth in Verona. Romeo's death in the tomb of the Capulets rather than in that of his own fathers reverses the traditional passage of the female over to the male house in marriage and betokens his refusal to follow the code of his fathers. And it is Juliet, not Romeo, who boldly uses his dagger, against herself.[23]

NOTES

1. A long-standing interpretation of *Romeo and Juliet* holds that it is a tragedy of fate. F. S. Boas, *Shakespeare and His Predecessors* (London: J. Murray, 1896), p. 214; E. K. Chambers, *Shakespeare: A Survey* (London: Sidgwick and Jackson, 1925), pp. 70–71; E. E. Stoll, *Shakespeare's Young Lovers* (London: Oxford University Press, 1937), pp. 4–5; and G. L. Kittredge, ed., *Sixteen Plays of Shakespeare* (New York: Ginn, 1946), p. 674, are the most prominent of the many critics who have shared this view. Stopford Brooke, *On Ten Plays of Shakespeare* (London: Constable, 1905, pp. 36, 65), thinks that the quarrel between the houses is the cause of the tragedy, but sees it in moral rather than social terms as an expression of "long-continued evil." More recently, H. B. Charlton, "Experiment and Interregnum," *Shakespearian Tragedy* (Cambridge, Eng.: Cambridge University Press, 1948), pp. 49–63, calls the feud the means by which fate acts, but objects to it as such on the grounds that it lacks convincing force and implacability in the play. For an orthodox Freudian interpretation of the feud as a regressive, intrafamilial, narcissistic force that prevents Romeo and Juliet from seeking properly non-incestuous love objects, see M. D. Faber, "The Adolescent Suicides of Romeo and Juliet," *Psychoanalytical Review*, 59 (1972–73), 169–81.

2. As usual, Shakespeare portrays the milieu of his source in terms with which he and his audience are familiar; he is not at pains to distinguish the Italian family from the English. Here I accept Lawrence Stone's definition of the patriarchal family: "This sixteenth-century aristocratic family was patrilinear, primogenitural, and patriarchal: patrilinear in that it was the male line whose ancestry was traced so diligently by the genealogists and heralds, and in almost all cases via the male line that titles were inherited; primogenitural in that most of the property went to the eldest son, the younger brothers being dispatched into the world with little more than a modest annuity or life interest in a small estate to keep them afloat; and patriarchal in that the husband and father lorded it over his wife and children with the quasi-absolute authority of a despot." Stone, *The Crisis of the Aristocracy: 1558–1641*, abridged ed. (London: Oxford University Press, 1971), p. 271.

3. Harold C. Goddard, *The Meaning of Shakespeare*, 2 vols. (Chicago: University of Chicago Press, 1951), I, 119.

4. This is a more recent critical tendency than that referred to in note 1, and is represented by Donald A. Stauffer, *Shakespeare's World of Images* (New York: Norton, 1949), pp. 56–57; Franklin M. Dickey, *Not Wisely But Too Well* (San Marino: Huntington Library, 1957), pp. 63–117; and Roy W. Battenhouse, *Shakespearean Tragedy: Its Art and Its Christian Premises* (Bloomington: University of Indiana Press, 1969), pp. 102–30. However, Dickey in his book and Paul N. Siegel in "Christianity and the Religion of Love in *Romeo and Juliet,*" *Shakespeare Quarterly* 12 (1961), 383, see the lovers' passion, flawed though it is, as the means by which divine order based on love is restored to Verona.

5. Siegel, "Christianity and the Religion of Love," p. 387, uses this phrase, but in a moral rather than social context; he sees them as scapegoats through whom their parents expiate their sins of hate and vengefulness.

6. The term is Erik Erikson's, as used in "The Problem of Ego Identity," *Psychological Issues*, No. 1 (1959), 103–5. He defines it partly through a description of George Bernard Shaw's self-imposed "prolongation of the interval between youth and adulthood" in his early twenties. His comments on "the social play of adolescents" further explain the purpose of such a moratorium and raise the questions I am raising with regard to the social function of the feud: "Children and adolescents in their presocieties provide for one another a sanctioned moratorium and joint support for free experimentation with inner and outer dangers (including those emanating from adult world). Whether

or not a given adolescent's newly acquired capacities are drawn back into infantile conflict depends to a significant extent on the quality of the opportunities and rewards available to him in his peer clique, as well as on the more formal ways in which society at large invites a transition from social play to work experimentation, and from rituals of transit to final commitments ..." (p. 118).

7. See Gordon Schochet, "Patriarchalism, Politics, and Mass Attitudes in Stuart England," *The Historical Journal* 12 (1969), 413–41.

8. This quotation and subsequent ones are from *The Complete Signet Classic Shakespeare*, ed. Sylvan Barnet (New York: Harcourt Brace Jovanovich, 1963, 1972). Where relevant I have noted variant readings.

9. Ruth Nevo, "Tragic Form in *Romeo and Juliet*," *Studies in English Literature* 9 (1969), 245.

10. Robert O. Evans, *The Osier Cage: Rhetorical Devices in Romeo and Juliet* (Lexington: University of Kentucky Press, 1966), argues that the Queen Mab speech deals with the real subjects of the play— money and place, the main reasons for marriage—and in the extended treatment of the soldier which concludes its catalogue of Mab's victims "presents what in the milieu of *Romeo and Juliet* was a principal destructive force—violence" (p. 79).

11. Norman Holland, "Mercutio, Mine Own Son the Dentist," in *Essays on Shakespeare*, ed. Gordon Ross Smith (University Park: Pennsylvania State University Press, 1965), pp. 3–14, comments suggestively on the contrast between Mercutio and Romeo in this respect: "He jests at scars that fears to feel a wound—a certain kind of wound, the kind that comes from real love that would lay him low, make him undergo a submission like Romeo's. Mercutio's bawdry serves to keep him a noncombatant in the wars of love. . . . Not for Mercutio is that entrance into the tomb or womb or maw which is Romeo's dark, sexual fate" (pp. 11–12).

12. Quoted in *Romeo and Juliet: A New Variorum Edition*, ed. Horace Howard Furness (Philadelphia: Lippincott, 1871), p. 200n.

13. Arthur Brooke, *The Tragicall Historye of Romeus and Juliet* in *Narrative and Dramatic Sources of Shakespeare*, ed. Geoffrey Bullough, (London: Routledge & Kegan Paul, 1957), I , 336, lines 1951–60.

14. Harry Levin, "Form and Formality in *Romeo and Juliet*," in *Twentieth Century Interpretations of Romeo and Juliet*, ed. Douglas Cole (Englewood Cliffs, N.J.: Prentice-Hall, 1970), 85–95.

15. *Coleridge's Writings on Shakespeare,* ed. Terence Hawkes (New York: Capricorn Books, 1959), p. 118. Coleridge adds to this phrase "yet resurgence against the check," but he is referring to the Nurse's garrulity in the first scene, when she persists in repeating her story against Lady Capulet's wishes.

16. This formulation is Levin's ("Form and Formality," p. 90), but he does not develop it. In a richly illuminating chapter of *Shakespeare and the Common Understanding* (New York: Free Press, 1967) titled "Eros and Death," Norman Rabkin treats *Venus and Adonis, Romeo and Juliet,* and *Antony and Cleopatra* as works which link "love, the most intense manifestation of the urge to life" with "the self-destructive yearning for annihilation that we recognize as the death wish" (p. 151). Rabkin finds this death wish inherent in the love of Romeo and Juliet itself; I find its source in the feud, seeing the lovers impelled to seek consummation in death only because the feud makes it impossible in life.

17. Gordon Ross Smith, "The Balance of Themes in *Romeo and Juliet,*" *Essays on Shakespeare,* ed. Gordon Ross Smith (University Park: Pennsylvania State University Press, 1965), p. 39.

18. In "The 'Uncanny,'" Freud remarks that the fantasy of being buried alive while appearing to be dead is one of intrauterine existence (*Standard Edition,* trans. and ed. James Strachey [London: Hogarth Press, 1961, 1964], XVII, 244). The conflation of womb and tomb, birth and death throughout the play lends weight to this interpretation of the deaths and their setting.

19. Bruno Bettelheim, *The Uses of Enchantment: The Meaning and Importance of Fairy Tales* (New York: Knopf, 1976), p. 91.

20. See my article, "Self and Eros in *Venus and Adonis,*" in *The Centennial Review* 20 (1976), 351–71.

21. See III.ii.136–37; III.v.94–95, 141, 201–3.

22. The second quarto prints ". . . then I denie you starres," which, though it offers a different shade of meaning, still expresses Romeo's belief that he acts independently from fate.

23. In an interesting essay which stresses the importance of the family, "Shakespeare's Earliest Tragedies: *Titus Andronicus* and *Romeo and Juliet,*" *Shakespeare Survey* 27 (1974), 1–9, G. K. Hunter offers a different though related interpretation: "It is entirely appropriate that the 'public' wedding-bed of Romeo and Juliet (as against their previous private bedding) should be placed in the Capulet tomb, for it is there that Romeo may be most effectively seen to have joined his wife's clan, where their corporate identity is most unequivocally established" (p. 8).

Marianne Novy

Violence, Love, and Gender
in *Romeo and Juliet*

... When we leave the comic world Shakespeare's plays show societies with a much more rigid sense of gender distinctions. However, it is not always the male character's desire to monopolize the role of actor and his suspicion of female pretense that enforce these distinctions. In three of Shakespeare's plays, female and male characters share the title. These plays all deviate from the male-actor–female-audience pattern that dominates in *Hamlet, Lear, Macbeth,* and *Othello* and resemble the comedies in other ways as well. In *Romeo and Juliet* and *Troilus and Cressida,* as in *Antony and Cleopatra,* the lovers begin as admiring audiences to each other. Juliet learns to pretend to protect her love of Romeo, and while her pretense fails, Romeo never distrusts her as the other heroes distrust women. Cressida pretends from the very beginning, and in the climactic scene Troilus is an audience to her infidelity with Diomedes. One hero lacks distrust of women, the other seems to learn it by painful experience (though we can find imagery suggestive of such distrust in his language earlier); unlike Lady Macbeth, Ophelia, or Desdemona, but more like the women of comedy, the women maintain or increase their ability to act throughout the play.

In these plays, then, suspicion of women's acting cannot be the cause of the disaster. But issues of gender politics are still important. . . . Unlike the romantic comedies, these plays all include war or blood feud that calls on men to define their

From *Love's Argument: Gender Relations in Shakespeare,* by Marianne L. Novy. © 1984 Chapel Hill: Universty of North Carolina Press, pp. 99–109. Reprinted by permission.

masculinity by violence.[1] In their private world, the lovers may achieve a mutuality in which both are active and genders are not polarized. But in the external world, masculinity is identified with violence and femininity with weakness. . . . Romeo and Juliet establish a role-transcending private world of mutuality in love. But this world is destroyed, partly by Romeo's entanglement in the feud, partly by Juliet's continued life in her parents' house concealing her marriage. In *Troilus and Cressida*, the private world of the lovers contrasts with the military world less than usual in Shakespeare because both are so satirically treated. In both worlds we see self-centeredness, competition, mercantile values, appetite.[2] The war has stopped in the first part of the play, and the idleness of the soldiers and the "open" sexuality of the women, both satirized, make the genders less polarized than usual. But when the war revives and Cressida is exchanged, she submits with the weakness expected of her, while Troilus responds to her infidelity with a savage determination to define his masculinity by violence.[3]

The minor characters in *Romeo and Juliet* establish a background of common beliefs current in both plays: "women, being the weaker vessels, are ever thrust to the wall" (1.1.14–15) while men glory in their "naked weapon" (1.1.32). In the Nurse's view, there are compensations not found in *Troilus*—"women grow by men" (1.3.95)—but she assents to her husband's equation of female sexuality with falling backward.

Two different conventional images of this society link sex and violence. First, sexual intercourse is seen as the success of male attack.[4] For example, Benvolio consoles Romeo in his lovesickness for Rosaline by saying, "A right fair mark, fair coz, is soonest hit" (1.1.205). Romeo describes the futility of his courtship of her thus: "She will not stay the siege of loving terms/ Nor bide th'encounter of assailing eyes" (1.1.210–11). Romeo has assayed this siege because he has already been hit with a different kind of violence—from "Cupid's arrow" (1.1.207). As Mercutio will later put it, he is "stabbed with a white wench's black eye; run through the ear with a love song; the very pin of his heart cleft within the blind bow-boy's butt-shaft" (2.4.14–16). Rosaline does not feel the same way, and thus "from Love's weak childish bow she lives unharmed" (1.1.209). Romeo's imagery conflates his sexual desire for Rosaline and his consequent desire that she fall in love with him—imagery of his attacking her and of love's attacking her.

When Romeo meets Juliet, he gives up using such violent imagery about sexual intercourse; when he uses it about falling in love, summing up to Friar Laurence in riddles, his emphasis is on the reciprocity of their feelings:

I have been feasting with mine enemy,
Where on a sudden one hath wounded me
That's by me wounded. (2.3.49–51)

Alternatively, he follows the image with a conceit that makes Juliet, if accepting, his protection:

Alack, there lies more peril in thine eye
Than twenty of their swords! Look thou but sweet,
And I am proof against their enmity. (2.2.71–73)

In general, with Juliet he gives up images of himself as violent aggressor. He speaks more of wanting to touch her than to conquer her, even if this means wishing away his own identity: "O that I were a glove upon that hand,/That I might touch that cheek. . . ./ I would I were thy bird" (2.2.24–25, 183).[5] Romeo is the only Shakespearean tragic hero who could offer to give up his name, who could say, "Had I it written, I would tear the word" (2.2.57). The strange nineteenth-century stage tradition of casting women as Romeo as well as Juliet may have been in part a response to his lack of violent imagery—except toward his own name—in their love scenes.

Nevertheless, lack of violence in the imagery does not mean a lack of sexual energy and attraction, and Shakespeare's dialogue sensitively suggests the power of their developing relationship. The openness and directness of Romeo and Juliet stand out against the background of the romantic comedies, which celebrate the gradual triumph of love over the inhibitions and defenses of the lovers. Only in *The Merchant of Venice* do two lovers (Portia and Bassanio) talk readily and without disguise at their first meeting. While the lovers in the comedies echo each other's language and imagery as their affinity grows behind their disguises, Romeo and Juliet at once match their shared imagery with more emotional openness.[6]

Throughout this first meeting, Romeo takes the initiative; but at the same time, his language puts aggression at a distance. He speaks humbly about his "unworthiest hand" (1.5.93); if his touch is sin, it is "gentle" (1.5.94); if it is too rough, he would prefer "a tender kiss" (1.5.96). Thus his initiative is that of a pilgrim to a saint and claims to imply the dominance of the woman, not the man. But his saint does not simply stand motionless on her pedestal; she talks back, picking up his imagery and quatrain form, and accepts his hand as showing "mannerly devotion" (1.5.98). Even when she claims that "Saints do not move" (1.5.105), she is still showing her willingness for the kiss that climaxes the sonnet their interchange has become:

> *Juliet.* Saints do not move, though grant for prayers' sake.
> *Romeo.* Then move not while my prayer's effect I take.
>
> (1.5.105–6)

After the kiss, Juliet gives up the imagery of sainthood: "Then have my lips the sin that they have took" (1.5.108). She insists on her sharing of his humanity.

The next time they meet, they share the initiative as well. In the balcony scene, Shakespeare uses the soliloquy convention to show each of them in fantasy speaking to the other first, but breaks that convention by showing Romeo as the audience who responds to become actor along with Juliet. Each speech sets the beloved outside the social framework: Romeo compares Juliet to the sun, her eyes to the stars; Juliet more consciously imagines removing him from society: "Deny thy father and refuse thy name" (2.2.34). It is when she makes a direct offer to her fantasy Romeo that the real one breaks in, and proposes a love that will create a private world between the two of them:[7]

> *Juliet.*   Romeo, doff thy name;
> And for thy name, which is no part of thee,
> Take all myself.
> *Romeo.*   I take thee at thy word.
> Call me but love, and I'll be new baptized;
> Henceforth I never will be Romeo.   (2.2.47–51)

Like a dreamer startled to find a dream materialize, Juliet is taken aback at Romeo's response. She breaks the fantasy of renaming—"What man art thou. . . ? . . . Art thou not Romeo?" (2.2.52, 60)—and momentarily appears to withdraw in fear. Thus the emphasis shifts from shared feeling to male persuasion, as Romeo speaks of the power and value of love, until Juliet responds and acknowledges to the real Romeo what she has said to the fantasy one—"Farewell compliment!" (2.2.89). When the interplay of caution and persuasion begins again, Juliet's anxiety oddly focuses on Romeo's oaths, as if his faith could be guaranteed by his *not* swearing. The unreality of her expressions of distrust adds to the charm of this exchange: there are no hints that she finds men untrustworthy, or that Romeo finds women untrustworthy, or even that the family feud leads either of them to doubts about the other (as distinguished from awareness of the practical difficulties). It is as if the only force working against their trust at this point is the feeling that their love is too good to be true. Romeo suggests this as he momentarily, in Juliet's absence, takes over the verbal caution:

> I am afeard,
> Being in night, all this is but a dream,
> Too flattering-sweet to be substantial.   (2.2.139–41)

By this time Juliet has given up her hesitation; her avowal evokes the self-renewing power of their mutuality but at the same time grounds it in her own autonomy:

> My bounty is a boundless as the sea,
> My love as deep; the more I give to thee,
> The more I have, for both are infinite.   (2.2.133–35)

And as she has been more concerned with the external world in pointing out dangers, she takes the initiative in turning their love from shared fantasy and passion to social institution: "If that thy bent of love be honorable,/Thy purpose marriage, send me word tomorrow" (2.2.143–44).

As the movement of their scenes combines mutuality and male persuasion, the words they use about their love can imply both mutuality and patriarchy. "It is my lady" (2.2.10), says Romeo of Juliet at the beginning of the balcony scene, and near the end she promises that if they marry "all my fortunes at thy foot I'll lay/And follow thee my lord throughout the world" (2.2.147–48). This could reflect either reciprocity of service or a conventional shift from female power in courtship to male power in marriage.

Similarly, when Juliet anticipates her secret wedding night with Romeo, the imagery of female subordination is balanced by imagery of sharing. She speaks of losing her virginity as losing a game, but then it becomes a victory, and her virginity parallel to Romeo's, as she prays to Night, "Learn me how to lose a winning match,/Played for a pair of stainless maidenhoods" (3.2.12–13).

Here and elsewhere, financial imagery turns Juliet into property more directly than it does Romeo: when she speaks of herself as possessing, the object is less Romeo than love:

> O, I have bought the mansion of a love,
> But not possessed it; and though I am sold,
> Not yet enjoyed.   (3.2.26–28)

Similarly, Romeo calls her "merchandise" for which he would adventure "as far/As that vast shore washed with the farthest sea" (2.2.82–83), while Juliet says "my true love is grown to such excess/I cannot sum up sum of half my wealth" (2.6.33–34).

Romeo and Juliet use the image of woman as property in a way that transcends its source in female social subordination; both of them are far from the financial interest that Lady Capulet suggests in her praise of Paris and the Nurse in her observation that Juliet's husband "shall have the chinks" (1.5.117). Nevertheless, the asymmetry in their use of financial imagery coheres with the asymmetrical demands that the male code of violence will make on Romeo and the female code of docility on Juliet.

Their use of other images is more symmetrical. Both lovers speak in words at once sensuously descriptive of beauty and celestially idealizing. Juliet, says Romeo,

> hangs upon the cheek of night
> As a rich jewel in an Ethiop's ear. . . .
> So shows a snowy dove trooping with crows.   (1.5.45–46, 48)

Romeo, according to Juliet, "will lie upon the wings of night/Whiter than new snow upon a raven's back" (3.2.18–19). Romeo has imagined Juliet as the sun and her eyes as stars. Juliet overgoes Romeo's praise in saying that, transformed into stars,

> he will make the face of heaven so fine
> That all the world will be in love with night
> And pay no worship to the garish sun.   (3.2.23–25)

Unlike some of Shakespeare's more solipsistic early lovers, such as Berowne and Proteus, Romeo understands the value of reciprocity in love. He wants its ritual—"Th'exchange of thy love's faithful vow for mine" (2.2.127)—and explains to Friar Laurence, "She whom I love now/Doth grace for grace and love for love allow" (2.3.85-86); he speaks of "the imagined happiness that both/Receive in either by this dear encounter" (2.6.28–29). All this is far from the identification of sex and violence that the imagery of the servants and Mercutio suggests is more usual in Verona.

Why do Romeo and Juliet keep their love secret not only from their parents but also from their peers? Romeo never tells Benvolio or Mercutio of his love for Juliet, though neither one is so committed to the Montagues that they would necessarily be hostile. (Benvolio had no objection to Rosaline as a Capulet; Mercutio belongs to neither house.) This secrecy helps make Mercutio's fight with Tybalt inevitable. Romeo's exclusion of Mercutio from his confidence suggests that his love of Juliet is not only a challenge to the feud but also a challenge to associations of masculinity and sexuality with violence. How can Romeo talk of Juliet to someone whose advice is "If love be rough with you, be rough with love,/Prick love for pricking, and you beat love down" (1.4.27–28)?

It is in part because of the difference between their experience of love and Verona's expected distortion of it that Romeo and Juliet try to keep their relationship private. Yet this secrecy is avoidance of a problem that they cannot ultimately escape.[8] When Romeo tries to act according to his secret love of Juliet instead of according to the feud, Tybalt and Mercutio insist on fighting. And when Romeo's intervention—to stop the fight—results in Mercutio's death, it is clear that Verona's definition of masculinity by violence is partly Romeo's definition as well. "O sweet Juliet," he says, "Thy beauty hath made me effeminate" (3.1.111–12), as he prepares for the fight to the death that causes his banishment.

Just before their crucial fight, Tybalt and Mercutio, speaking of Romeo, quibble on the point that "man," a word so important as an ideal, has from the opening scene the less honorific meaning of "manservant."

> *Tybalt.* Well, peace be with you, sir. Here comes my man.
> *Mercutio.* But I'll be hanged, sir, if he wear your livery.
>
> (3.1.55–56)

This pun is an analogue of the irony that it is precisely in his "manly" vengeance for Mercutio's death that Romeo most decisively loses control of his own fate and becomes, as he says, "fortune's fool" (3.1.134). In a sense, as Mercutio's elaboration of his pun suggests without his awareness, a commitment to proving manhood by violence makes one easily manipulated by whoever offers a challenge. "Marry, go before to field, he'll be your follower!/Your worship in that sense may call him man" (3.1.57–58). In the larger sense, the code of violence that promises to make Romeo a man actually makes him its man—its pawn.

If Romeo shares Mercutio's belief in the manhood of violence, he also shares the Friar's wish for reconciliation. But the Friar has his own version of gender polarization that also contributes to the disaster. He repeatedly uses "womanish" as a synonym for "weak" when speaking to both Juliet (4.1.119) and Romeo (3.3.110), and, more crucially for the plot, encourages Juliet to pretend obedience and death through his potion rather than helping her escape to Romeo (though she has expressed willingness to leap "From off the battlements of any tower,/Or walk in thievish ways"—4.1.78–79). His image of manhood (desirable as an ideal for both sexes) is emotional control: he chides Romeo for his fury and grief at banishment by calling him "Unseemly woman in a seeming man!/And ill beseeming beast in seeming both!" (3.3.112–13). The Friar distrusts passionate love, and, like much of the conventional imagery of the play, identifies passionate love with violence: "These violent delights have violent ends" (2.6.9). It is consistent that he should not encourage Juliet to elopement but rather hopes to stage their reunion in a context of family reconciliation.

Juliet's confidante, the Nurse, has a more positive attitude toward sexuality, but she too underestimates the lovers' intense commitment to each other. Like the Friar, too, she keeps the love secret and encourages Juliet to appear docile to her parents, and finally to marry Paris, since Romeo, she says, "is dead—or 'twere as good he were/As living here and you no use of him" (3.5.226–27). Thus she is counseling Juliet to a conventional acceptance of the husband chosen by her parents. While Juliet refuses this advice, she follows the counsel of pretense that she receives from nurse and friar. The controlled stichomythia of her dialogue with Paris is a sad contrast to her spontaneous participation in Romeo's sonnet. Juliet's acceptance of their advice of pretense and mock death is the point analogous to Romeo's duel with Tybalt where failure to transcend the gender polarization of their society makes disaster inevitable.

Yet before their deaths, Romeo and Juliet can transcend the aggressions and stereotypes of the outside in their secret world. Fulfilling the promise of the balcony scene, they rename each other "love" in their aubade scene, and their imagery suggests the creation of a private world with a technique oddly similar to that of the crucial scene in *The Taming of the Shrew*. To keep Romeo with her longer, Juliet transforms the lark into the nightingale and then transforms the sun into "some meteor that the sun exhales/To be to thee this night a torchbearer" (3.5.13–14). Romeo, after initially contradicting her, showing the caution that was primarily hers in the balcony scene, goes along with the game and accepts her transformation, with awareness of the likely cost:

Let me ta'en, let me be put to death.
I am content, so thou wilt have it so.
I'll say yon grey is not the morning's eye,
'Tis but the pale reflex of Cynthia's brow.   (3.5.17–20)

The scene in which Kate joins in Petruchio's transformation of the sun into the moon and old Vincentio into a young girl is of course quite different in tone. Kate and Petruchio have been engaged in a farcical combat of wills; they are now returning to Kate's father's house, accompanied by Petruchio's friend Hortensio, rather than in a romantic solitude, and they are under no sentence of death or banishment. But both scenes use a verbal transformation of the world—a creation of private world through words—as a metaphor for a relationship. Such a private world is crucial to *Shrew*'s mediation between ideologies of patriarchy and companionship in marriage, as well as to the attempt that Romeo and Juliet make to love each other tenderly in a world of violence. The secrecy of their love heightens at once its purity and intensity and its vulnerability. When the private world is established it is already threatened. As soon as Romeo accepts the pretense "It is not day" (3.5.25), Juliet resumes her caution and returns them to the real world, where Romeo must flee. Nevertheless, they have an absolute trust in each other; on their departure there is no questioning of each other's truths such as . . . in *Troilus and Cressida*.[9] Presciently, they imagine death as the only possible obstacle to their reunion.

Shakespeare changed his source to reduce the age of the lovers, and historical evidence suggests that he also made them much younger than the typical age of marriage for Elizabethan aristocrats (twenty for women, twenty-one for men), who married still younger than other classes (median age twenty-four for women, twenty-six for men).[10] However young the members of Shakespeare's original audiences were—probably a high proportion were in their late teens or early twenties—Romeo and Juliet were still younger than almost all of them. The extreme youth of the lovers emphasizes their innocence and inexperience. Anyone who has lived longer than Romeo and Juliet—anyone who has given up a first love—has made more compromises than they have. It is their extreme purity that gives their love its special tragedy. The play expresses both the appeal and the danger of a love in which two people become the whole world to each other. This little world precariously remedies the defects of the larger one—its coldness, its hierarchies, its violence—but the lovers cannot negotiate recognition by the outer world except by their deaths because of their residual commitment to the outer world and its gender ideals.

NOTES

1. See Coppélia Kahn, *Man's Estate* (Berkeley: University of California Press, 1981), pp. 82–103.

2. See, especially, Raymond Southall, "*Troilus and Cressida* and the Spirit of Capitalism," in *Shakespeare in a Changing World*, ed. Arnold Kettle (New York: International Publishers, 1964), pp. 217–33.

3. See Gayle Greene, "Shakespeare's Cressida: 'A kind of self,'" in *The Woman's Part: Feminist Criticism of Shakespeare*, ed. Carolyn Ruth Swift Lenz, Gayle Greene, and Carol Thomas Neely (Urbana: University of Illinois Press, 1980), pp. 133–49.

4. See Madelon Gohlke, " 'I wooed thee with my sword': Shakespeare's Tragic Paradigms," in Lenz, Greene, and Neely, eds., *The Woman's Part*, pp. 150–52, and cf. M. M. Mahood, *Shakespeare's Wordplay* (New York: Methuen, 1957), p. 60.

5. Cf. Kirby Farrell, *Shakespeare's Creation: The Language of Magic and Play* (Amherst: University of Massachusetts Press, 1975), p. 126.

6. See Harry Levin, "Form and Formality in *Romeo and Juliet*," *Shakespeare Quarterly* 11 (Winter 1960), 9; reprinted in *Modern Shakespearean Criticism*, ed. Alvin B. Kernan (New York: Harcourt, Brace, 1965), p. 287; and Roger Stilling, *Love and Death in Renaissance Tragedy* (Baton Rouge: Louisiana State University Press, 1976), pp. 77–78.

7. Cf. James Calderwood, *Shakespearean Metadrama* (Minneapolis: University of Minnesota Press, 1971), pp. 85–119; and Farrell, *Shakespeare's Creation*, pp. 125–26.

8. Cf. Farrell, *Shakespeare's Creation*, p. 128.

9. This contrast is emphasized by Stilling, *Love and Death*, p. 130.

10. See Lawrence Stone, *The Family, Sex, and Marriage in England, 1500–1800* (New York: Harper and Row, 1977), pp. 46–50; Peter Laslett, *The World We Have Lost*, 2d ed. (New York: Charles Scribner's Sons, 1973), pp. 85–86; and Ann Jennalie Cook, "The Mode of Marriage in Shakespeare's England," *Southern Humanities Review* 11 (1977): 126–32. On the age of the audience, see Alfred Harbage, *Shakespeare's Audience* (New York: Columbia University Press, 1941), pp. 79–80.

Edward Snow

Language and
Sexual Difference
in *Romeo and Juliet*

Romeo and Juliet is about an experience that transcends "a common bound." The play emphasizes the opposition between the imaginative vision its protagonists bear witness to in love and the truth of a world whose order must be enforced at passion's expense. And though events bring Romeo and Juliet together in this experience, language suggests how radically they share it. When they first meet "palm to palm" at the Capulets' ball, for instance, their antiphonal responses generate a perfectly formed sonnet. The moment is emblematic of the erotic relationship as the play views it: two exposed, vulnerably embodied selves reaching out tentatively across sexual difference and social opposition, while their imaginations mingle in an intersubjective privacy that weaves its boundaries protectively around them. And later, when Romeo is admiring Juliet from below her balcony, still hidden from her view, her first words appear inside one of his lines of blank verse, as if his imaginative response to her were the generative matrix from which her own desiring self emerges:

> *Romeo.* See how she leans her cheek upon her hand!
> O that I were a glove upon that hand,
> That I might touch that cheek!

Excerpt from *Shakespeare's Rough Magic*, ed. Peter Erickson and Coppélia Kahn. Newark: University of Delaware Press, 1985, pp. 168–92. Reprinted with permission of Associated University Presses.

Juliet.   Ay me!
Romeo.   She speaks!
       O, speak again, bright ange l . . .   (2.2.23–26)[1]

Juliet's language, in turn, once it acquires a momentum of its own, conjures up Romeo's actual physical presence, even though she herself is absorbed in purely subjective imaginings:

Juliet. What's in a name? That which we call a rose
By any other word would smell as sweet;
So Romeo would, were he not Romeo call'd,
Retain that dear perfection which he owes
Without that title. Romeo, doff thy name,
And for thy name, which is no part of thee,
Take all myself.
Romeo. (appearing to her) I take thee at thy word.
Call me but love, and I'll be new baptiz'd;
Henceforth I never will be Romeo.   (2.2.43–51)

The play is full of tricks like these that make Romeo and Juliet's language seem like a medium in which their relationship takes form as well as an instrument for brining it about. The most pervasive of these devices are the elaborately matched images and turns of phrase that link their separate speeches. Romeo tells Juliet that he has "night's cloak" to hide him from her kinsmen (2.2.75); a few moments later she informs him that "the mask of night" is on her face (2.2.85). The effect is of two imaginations working in the same idiom, in touch not so much with each other as with similar experiences of self and world. Juliet's "Come, night, come, Romeo, come, thou day in night" (3.2.17) communicates with Romeo's "It is the east, and Juliet is the sun" (2.2.3) at a purely transcendental level: both responses are spoken in isolation, yet they are tuned to the same imaginative frequency, and imply the existence of a single world of desire encompassing the two lovers' separate longings. This sense of communication taking place at a level beyond conscious awareness, and bridging distances that desire itself is helpless to overcome, is especially powerful in the final scene, where the phrases of Juliet's grief for Romeo echo and uncannily transform those of his for her.

These subliminal correspondences do more, I think, to convince us that Romeo and Juliet are appropriately fitted to each other than anything which passes directly between them.

Yet the matched speeches that create this sense of fit also measure the differences it subsumes. The very devices which implicate Romeo and Juliet in a shared experience, that is, also focus our attention on a difference in the way each experiences that experience. The boundary between Romeo and the cloak of night he draws around him to hide himself from men's eyes is not the same as the one between Juliet and the mask of night she looks out from in a spirit of uninhibited self-disclosure: the shared metaphoric experience embraces two very different habits of being. In one sense, these differences are purely idiosyncratic: they are what make Romeo Romeo and Juliet Juliet. But they also have to do with what makes one male and the other female. Such, at least, is what I hope to suggest in this study of the separate worlds of desire that appear within the union between Romeo and Juliet. Though I will be dwelling in what follows on differences, I don't mean by doing so to call the relationship itself into question; indeed, it seems to me that the more acutely we become aware of them, the less vulnerable the play's romanticism becomes to the charges of sentimentality, immaturity, or rhetorical superficiality that are often brought against it. And though I will be claiming that these differences consistently favor Juliet's imaginative world, I don't mean to suggest that the critical perspective they imply belittles Romeo: on the contrary, his experience in love now seems to me poignant and phenomenologically complex where once it seemed merely facile and self-indulgent. What I *would* like to suggest, however, is that the language of *Romeo and Juliet* is most intricately concerned not with the opposition between passion and the social order but with the difference between the sexes: and that its subtler affirmations have to do not with romantic love but female ontology.

I

The imaginative universe generated by Romeo's desire is dominated by eyesight, and remains subject to greater rational control than Juliet's. His metaphors assemble reality "out there," and provide access to it through perspectives that tend to make him an onlooker rather than a participant. There is a kind of metonymic fascination in his language with parts and extremities, especially when viewed from a distance, against a backdrop that heightens the sensation of outline and boundary. Juliet "hangs upon the cheek of night/As a rich jewel in an Ethiop's ear" (1.5.45–46); he swears "by yonder blessed moon . . . That tips with silver all these fruit-tree tops" (2.2.107–8); a leader of rope will convey him to "the high topgallant" of his joy (2.4.190); he looks out of Juliet's window to see that "jocund day/Stands tiptoe on the misty mountain tops" (3.5.9–10). Contact with Juliet tends to be a matter of reaching out, and gently touching, while the idea of union with her generates imagery of parts securely fitted to each other rather than wholes merging and boundaries dissolving: "See how she leans her cheek upon her hand!/O that I were a glove upon that hand,/That I might touch that cheek!" His imagination fixes objects in stable Euclidean space, and keeps them separate and distinct, even when entertaining fantasies of metamorphosis. In the world it generates, change can occur when two things exchange places, or when one thing displaces another, but places and things themselves do not seem to be subject to alteration: "Two of the fairest stars in all the heaven,/Having some business, do entreat her eyes/To twinkle in their spheres till they return./What if her eyes were there, they in her head?" (2.2.15-18). The sense this metaphor betrays of transformation as something temporary and provisional haunts Romeo's world, and makes (as we shall see) the growth he experiences in love problematical in a way that Juliet's is not.

Direct apprehensions of process are thus difficult to come by in the world of Romeo's metaphors. If Juliet appears to be alive in the tomb, it is because "beauty's ensign yet/Is crimson in thy lips and in thy cheeks,/And death's pale flag is not advanced there" (5.3.94–96). "Poeticizing" beauty and death in this way keeps them separate and masks the erotic and generative links between them. It also transforms them from realities known in the flesh to "ensigns" that signal conventionally encoded meanings to a distant viewer. Romeo tends to hypostatize feelings in much the same way. When he does imagine himself in the world rather than "looking on" (1.4.38), it is usually by picturing himself as an object in space that is "moved" by external forces. At one point he may "sink" under love's heavy burden (1.4.22), and at another "o'erperch" walls with the help of "love's light wings" (2.2.66), but in both instances the metaphors make him an object that remains separate from and unchanged by disembodied emotional forces acting on him from without. Even time becomes in his language a spatial dimension he moves through as an essentially unchanging object. His favorite metaphor is the sea-journey, with himself more often the ship than the pilot ("He that hath the steerage of my course,/Direct my sail" [1.4.112–13]; "Thou desperate pilot, now at once run on/The dashing rocks thy sea-sick weary bark" [5.3.117–18]). Time can move him from place to place, bring him near his goal or buffet him about, but (so at least his language implies) it rarely works any inner transformation on him, and it remains (again, in his language) the enemy rather than the element of his will.

This is not to deny that Romeo changes during the course of the play, nor that he has several positive experiences of time along the way. The issue here is not so much what happens to him as the way in which his language admits what does happen to him into consciousness. One thing that haunts Romeo throughout the play is a certain disjunction between life and the forms in which he is able to make it present to himself. Thus while his language tends to make him an onlooker to the world, the plot and *mis-en-scène* stress his kinetic involvement in it— leaping and climbing the Capulet walls, fighting with Tybalt, making love to Juliet, riding back and forth between Verona and Mantua, forcing his way into Juliet's tomb, and always, it seems, on his way to or from somewhere when we encounter him.[2] (With Juliet, as we shall see, it is just the opposite: her freedom of movement in the actual world is severely restricted, yet her imagination places her at the center of a dynamic, expanding universe, and seizes uninhibitedly on the sources of gratification that come within reach.) His dream of Juliet—one of his "happiest" temporal experiences—is an example of how the present-at-hand is changed into something remote and elusive when his language reaches out to possess it:

If I may trust the flattering truth of sleep,
My dreams presage some joyful news at hand.
My bosom's lord sits lightly in his throne,
And all this day an unaccustom'd spirit
Lifts me above the ground with cheerful thoughts.
I dreamt my lady came and found me dead—
Strange dream, that gives a dead man leave to think!—
And breath'd such life with kisses in my lips
That I reviv'd and was an emperor.

Ah me, how sweet is love itself possess'd,
When but love's shadows are so rich in joy!   (5.1.1–11)

In reflecting on a present happiness, Romeo translates it into an anticipation of future joy. (Juliet does exactly the opposite: when she anticipates the future—most notably while awaiting Romeo and before drinking the Friar's potion—her imagination makes it present, and she rushes in to fill it.) A change he experiences in the here and now becomes imaginatively intelligible to him as the harbinger of something still "at hand" in a future mystified by desire. His interpretation of the dream's content repeats this process. The dream itself is a beautiful expression of the revivification Romeo has already undergone in his relationship with Juliet. But he interprets it as an auspicious "sign" of what the future holds in store for him. And projecting it out of the present into the imminent future transforms it from a metaphor of the consummated relationship into an ironic foreshadowing of its tragic conclusion ("I will kiss thy lips,/Haply some poison yet doth hang on them,/To make me die with a restorative" [5.3.164–66]).[3]

Even when Romeo embraces the happiness which the presentness of Juliet's love bestows on him, he does so in terms of a potentially tragic future: "but come what sorrow can,/It cannot countervail the exchange of joy/That one short minute gives me in her sight./Do thou but close our hands with holy words,/Then love-devouring death do what he dare, It is enough I may but call her mine" (2.6.3–8). This tendency to think of love as moments of satisfaction rather than a process of growth, and hence to experience happiness within it against a backdrop of apocalyptic loss, is something Romeo shares with the male protagonists in Shakespeare's darkest treatments of love and sexual desire. Compare, for instance, Othello's joy at being reunited with Desdemona on Cyprus, especially in the light of her reaction to his expression of it:

Othello.   If it were now to die,
'Twere now to be most happy; for I fear
My soul hath her content so absolute
That not another comfort like to this
Succeeds in unknown fate.
Desdemona.   The heavens forbid
But that our loves and comforts should increase
Even as our days do grow!   (2.1.189–94)

It doesn't follow from the similarity that Romeo's love for Juliet is just another manifestation of the masculine pathology Othello acts out in his marriage with Desdemona: indeed, the example of Othello should make us appreciate all the more the positive significance of Romeo's unthreatened responsiveness to the energies sexual desire releases in Juliet, and his continued devotion to her after their relationship has been consummated. But there *is* a suggestion that Romeo is a "carrier" of attitudes that are agents of tragedy in Shakespeare, and that Juliet's love only partially redeems him from them.

II

Juliet, however, is the locus of affirmative energies that can't be contained within a tragic frame of reference. Her imaginative universe, in contrast to Romeo's, is generated by all the senses, and by a unity of feeling that is more than just the sum of their parts. Her desire generates images of whole, embodied selves, and extravagant gestures of giving and taking: "Romeo, doff thy name,/And for thy name, which is no part of thee,/Take all myself" (2.2.47–49); "That runaways' eyes may wink, and Romeo/ Leap to these arms untalk'd of and unseen!" (3.2.6–7). She manages to be both subject and object in love without inner conflict or contradiction: "O, I have bought the mansion of a love,/But not possess'd it, and though I am sold,/Not yet enjoy'd" (3.2.26–28). The imagination that formulates desire this way tends to produce images of inwardness and depth rather than distance ("My bounty is as boundless as the sea,/My love as deep" [2.2.133–34]). Thus where Romeo tells her to "look" out her window at the "envious streaks" that "lace the severing clouds in yonder east," she in turn tries to convince him it is the nightingale that "pierc'd the fearful hollow" of his ear (3.5.1–10).[4]

Juliet's sensations tend in general to be more "piercing" and ontologically dangerous than Romeo's. Her imagination inhabits a Blakean universe, where perceptual experience spontaneously invades and emanates from the self, instead of becoming the structuring activity it is for Romeo, even when he is most enraptured. Even vision is for her an armed faculty that penetrates the field of perception instead of gazing into it from a wistful distance: "But no more deep will I endart mine eye/Than your

consent gives strength to make it fly" (1.3.98–99). One of the
things that makes Juliet so formidable is the almost eager
willingness with which she is able to give herself over to the
dynamic, shelterless force-field of emotions and sensations into
which desire plunges her, and experience herself as both the
object and the generative source of its metamorphic energies. (In
this she is the opposite of Blake's Thel.) Submission to its
imperatives becomes for her a "prodigious" coming-into-selfhood:
"My only love sprung from my only hate!/Too early seen
unknown, and known too late!/Prodigious birth of love it is to
me/That I must love a loathed enemy" (1.5.138–41). Out of the
self experienced as object ("Prodigious birth of love it is to *me*")
an "I" springs, impelled by the necessity that is also its motive
force. (In the Nurse's recollection of Juliet's weaning, she is
similarly an "it" from which an "I" emerges, again through an
assent to sexual necessity. The generative imagery is, as we shall
see, a defining characteristic of Juliet's world.) Her language
makes love and hate particularized emotions that both possess
and are possessed by her ("*my* only love," "*my* only hate"), and
characterizes the relation between them as an irreversible
transformation that locates the place where the self gives birth.
In Romeo's parallel utterance, however, they remain abstract
tokens that can be manipulated from a distance in conventional
Petrarchan fashion: "Here's much to do with hate, but more with
love./Why then, O brawling love! O loving hate!/O any thing,
of nothing first create!/O heavy lightness, serious vanity,/. . ./
This love feel I, that feel no love in this" (1.1.176–82). The result
is a kind of objectified "I," adrift in an experience its language
can't specify (". . . that feel no love *in this*"), and lacking the
imperative that moves Juliet.

    In a sense this comparison is unfair to Romeo, since his speech
occurs before he has fallen in love with Juliet. Yet the counterpoint
between the passages seems to insist on it. The Petrarchan side
of Romeo it emphasizes, morever, never entirely disappears from
the play. His response to the revelation that Juliet is a Capulet
contrasts similarly to hers that he is a Montague: "Is she a
Capulet?/O dear account! my life is my foe's debt" (1.5.117–18).
His language of reckoning counterpoints her generative imagery;
she speaks of imperatives springing from within while he refers
to a life held in thrall. Even at the end of the play it is still
basically his old self that grieves for Juliet, though with a depth
of feeling he would have been incapable of before falling in love

with her. His language there, as we have seen, manipulates the opposition between death and beauty in much the same way it did the one between love and hate earlier. And there is the same note (though more poignantly sounded) of a self adrift in experience, partially baffled in its attempts to make received ideas and conventional language express what it is feeling: "How oft when men are at the point of death/Have they been merry, which their keepers call/A lightning before death! O how may I/Call this a lightning?" (5.3.88–91).

Romeo's and Juliet's "I"s are in fact elaborately contrasted in the course of the play, largely through a series of matched passages that explore the relationship between vision, will, and instinct. In the opening scene Romeo and Benvolio together bemoan (as if it were a shared male attitude) the fact that desire is not subject to rational, visual control, and that the actual experience of love involves a turmoil and violence at odds with one's views of it:

> *Benvolio.* Alas that love, so gentle in his view,
> Should be so tyrannous and rough in proof!
> *Romeo.* Alas that love, whose view is muffled still,
> Should, without eyes, see pathways to his will!   (1.1.169–72)

Romeo tends in general to regard vision as an instrument controlled by the conscious will, and hence as the faculty that locates the place of the "I" ("When the devout religion of mine eye/Maintains such falsehood, then turn tears to fires" [1.2.88–89]; "Eyes, look your last!" [5.3.112]). His language tends to make perceptions into possessions and assertions of will: "I'll go along no such sight to be shown,/But to rejoice in splendor of mine own" (1.2.100–101). At the same time it allegorizes instinctual promptings so that they become external to the self—either a blind, alien will or a friendly "counsellor" to whom Romeo lends his own eyes (2.2.80–81).

Juliet's "I," however, is linked more closely by the play of the text with a capacity for assent than with the organs Othello will later term the "speculative and offic'd instruments" of rational will:

> *Nurse.* "Yea," quoth my husband, "fallst upon thy face?
> Thou wilt fall backward when thou comest to age,
> Wilt thou not, Jule?" It stinted and said "Ay."
> *Juliet.* And stint thou too, I pray thee, nurse, say I.   (1.3.55–58)

As Juliet's character unfolds, it becomes evident that this capacity to say "Ay" to necessity involves more than just a woman's learning to "bear" male oppression (1.4.93). It also signals a willingness to surrender the conscious self to the impersonal forces that stir within it. Her "falling backward" will likewise involve a kind of ontological trust in sexual experience and the world which opens with its relinquishments. Against connotations of guilt, subjection, and tragic punishment, it poses the idea of a fall backward into innocence, the reversal or undoing of an original fall.

Juliet's capacity to answer to imperatives that address her from realms beyond the reach of the individual will is central to Shakespeare's conception of her. The motif is asserted in her first entrance: "How now, who calls?" "Madam, I am here,/What is your will?" (1.3.5–6). On the surface she expresses a deference to parental will that her own erotic willfulness will replace, and hence provides us with a touchstone for measuring her growth during the course of the play. But her words also suggest a capacity to hear the forces that call to the self from beyond it, and paradoxically to become *manifest* in answering to their demands. Even when Juliet aligns herself obediently with her parent's wishes, her words manage to articulate a more enigmatic relation between self and will: "I'll look to like, if looking liking move" (1.3.97). It hardly matters whether looking moves liking or liking moves looking in this elusive reply: it seems to regard the willing self as a spontaneous interaction between rational, premeditated intentions and instinctual reactions, rather than associating it with one or the other. (In Blake's terms, she looks *through* her eyes, while Romeo looks *with* his.) As a result she is less susceptible to the conflict Romeo articulates between what is experienced *in* love and what is known *as* love. She is able to accept the blindness of love as proper to its element ("if love be blind,/It best agrees with night" [3.2.9–10]), and welcome and disruptive energies in which it engulfs the self. Her apostrophe to night, with its intense anticipation of the sexual act, is addressed as much to the impersonal force of Eros as it is Romeo: "Come, gentle night, come, loving, black-brow'd night,/ Give me my Romeo" (3.2.20–21). This capacity to embrace sexual experience in all its strangeness (cf. 3.2.15), and still admit it into the self as something intimate and gentle, makes Juliet not only a potentially redemptive figure for Romeo but a touchstone for

Shakespeare's subsequent explorations of the polarities of erotic love.

Juliet's desire, then, functions as an *erotic* reality-principle that counteracts a wistfulness ingrained in Romeo. The images generated by Romeo's desire tend to wind up in a subjunctive, conditional space ("What if her eyes were there, they in her head?"; "O that I were a glove upon that hand,/That I might touch that cheek"), and a part of him always seems more interested in entertaining them as figures of the imagination than in realizing them. Juliet's images, however, exist in an urgently desired future, and are charged with an erotic energy that makes the experience they invoke present and actual in her imagination. It seems no paradox that the desire for Romeo she expresses in her apostrophe to night should culminate in an image that sublimates an experience of orgasm, even though she is anticipating her first sexual encounter: "Come, gentle night, come loving black-brow'd night,/Give me my Romeo, and, when I[5] shall die,/Take him and cut him out in little stars" (3.2.20–22).[6]

Even when Juliet's language seems to place her in the same imaginative world with Romeo, there is often a contrast between the tendency of his metaphors to keep love distant and remote, and hers to bring it up close, and make it possible.[7] Romeo's preoccupation with the light of beauty, for instance, isolates the object of his desire, and mystifies the distance that separates him from it ("It seems she hangs upon the cheek of night," "What light through yonder window breaks?"). When Juliet has recourse to the idea, however, beauty's light becomes an enabling force that emanates from the consummated relationship: "Lovers can see to do their amorous rites/By their own beauties" (3.2.8–9). Their matching images of black-white contrasts differ in much the same way. Romeo's evokes a purely visual experience—a stable figure-ground relationship that again defines an *object* of desire, and isolates it in the distance: "Beauty too rich for use, for earth too dear!/So shows a snowy dove trooping with crows,/As yonder lady o'er her fellows shows" (1.5.47–49). Juliet's, on the other hand, is a sensually experienced image, and it sublimates the physical contact of an achieved sexual relationship: "Come, night, come, Romeo, come, thou day in night,/For thou wilt lie upon the wings of night,/Whiter than new snow upon a raven's back" (3.2.17–19).

Finally, as this last example suggests, Juliet's language of desire is more extravagantly metamorphic than Romeo's. Even when Romeo's imagination plays with the idea of cosmological change, it operates within the grid of the mundane world, and according to its logic: "It is the east, and Juliet is the sun" (2.2.3). Juliet's images, however, loosen the boundaries that fix the rational universe in place, and draw it into a state of continual flux: Romeo is both night and day in night, she both waits for him in the night as he wings his way toward her and is herself the winged night on whose back he lies like new snow—all in the space of two lines. The boundaries between self and world, subject and object, active and passive, male and female become similarly fluid in her imagination, as we shall see in more detail later in this essay. Her figures also (to use a Nietzschean term) transvalue the world more radically than Romeo's. When he places Juliet's eyes in the vacancies left in the heavens by two truant stars, he imagines that they "Would through the airy region stream so bright/That birds would sing and think it were not night" (2.2.21–22). The reversal effected within this characteristically subjunctive fantasy is temporary, and grounded in illusion: the birds sing in the night not because Juliet's brightness has caused them to change allegiances but because it deceives them into thinking night is day, and in doing so triggers their normal routine. In Juliet's companion image, however, the world is permanently transfigured, and the inversion of values that accompanies the change is a matter of conscious erotic commitment: "Give me my Romeo, and when I shall die,/Take him and cut him out in little stars,/And he will make the face of heaven so fine/That all the world will be in love with night,/And pay no worship to the garish sun" (3.2.21–25).

III

The impression, then, is of two distinct modes of desire—one reaching out, the other unfolding—exquisitely fitted to each other, but rarely meeting in the same phenomenological universe. Wherever the language the two lovers exchange most emphatically suggests a sharing of experience, close inspection reveals difference and often, in Romeo's case, poignant estrangement. Always, it seems, there is a lack in Romeo that corresponds to an overflowing in Juliet. Consider the parting remarks that Shakespeare has so carefully fitted together across separate moments near the end of the balcony scene:

> *Juliet.* Good night, good night! as sweet repose and rest
> Come to thy heart as that within my breast.　　　(2.2.123–24)
>
> *Romeo.* Sleep dwell upon thine eyes, peace in thy breast!
> Would I were sleep and peace, so sweet to rest!　　(2.2.186–87)

Juliet wishes for Romeo (as both the lover who desires him and the "saint" who intercedes for him) out of her own sense of well-being—with an intuition, perhaps, that what is "within" her must somehow "come to" him. When she parts from Romeo, she takes with her a love that is a source of "sweet repose and rest," and her instinct is to wish for him the same inner experience in her absence. Romeo, however, can only take this as being left "unsatisfied" (2.2.125). Superficially this may be a joke by the Mercutio in Shakespeare: it suggests that Romeo's idealized romanticism masks ordinary sexual desire. But in a deeper sense Romeo really doesn't seem to know what he wants, and when pressed by Juliet to specify what *would* satisfy him, has to fall back on the notion of an exchange of "vows." His desire seems to originate in a need that is prior to Juliet, and it has to be sustained in language rather than in some burgeoning inner place. In Juliet's case, however, love intrudes into a waiting latency of self and will ("I am here,/What is your will?"; "I'll look to like if looking liking move"), and she experiences it as a "prodigious birth" that once engendered grows of its own accord, and thrives as much on Romeo's absence as on his presence. When she prepares to part from Romeo before her first exit in the balcony scene, her images evoke the generative rhythms of nature ("This bud of love, by summer's ripening breath,/May prove a beauteous flow'r when next we meet" [2.2.121–22]); they anticipate not "satisfaction" but the flowering of what will have been gestating during the interim. Shakespeare suggests just how prodigious this birth in Juliet is going to be by having her "next meet" Romeo only three lines later, when she returns to inform him of feelings that have already grown from images of ripening buds and beauteous flowers into a desire for marriage conceived as a radically *human* form of commitment and risk-taking:

> Three words, dear Romeo, and good night indeed,
> If that thy bent of love be honorable,

Thy purpose marriage, send me word to-morrow,
By one that I'll procure to come to thee,
Where and what time thou wilt perform the rite,
And all my fortunes at thy foot I'll lay,
And follow thee my lord throughout the world.   (2.2.142–48)

But where Juliet experiences genesis and gestation, Romeo is haunted by a sense of emptiness and unreality. While Juliet's love is ripening offstage, Romeo stands alone, anxiously luxuriating in the dreamlikeness of what is happening to him: "O blessed, blessed night! I am afeard,/Being in night, all this is but a dream,/Too flattering-sweet to be substantial" (2.2.139–41). And when Juliet exits again after sharing with him "their" plans for marriage, he again becomes "one too many by [his] weary self":[8]

Juliet. A thousand times good night! (*Exit*)
Romeo. A thousand times the worse, to want thy light.
Love goes toward love as schoolboys from their books,
But love from love, toward school with heavy looks.
                                                      (2.2.154–57)

His metaphor describes love as relief from a state of boredom and oppression that returns when the loved object is "withdrawn" (2.2.130). Unlike Juliet's passion for Romeo, which becomes a reality-principle of its own capable of generating value and direction, Romeo's for Juliet remains to some extent an attempt to escape from a reality he finds oppressive, and it is attended (so, at least, his language here would suggest) by feelings of truancy as well as resolve.

It is thus characteristic of Romeo that his attempt to wish Juliet the kind of "good night" she earlier wished him should turn into a longing to be where she is (ontologically as well as physically) that simultaneously expresses his own unrest ("Would I were sleep and peace, so sweet to rest"). In the process he turns one phenomenological universe into something very like its opposite. Her world of whole selves and embodied feelings ("as sweet repose and rest/Come to thy heart as that within my breast") becomes in his language a realm of personifications and part objects that he gazes into from a wistful distance. More importantly, the "repose and rest" that Juliet experiences *within*, as the very condition of her desire for Romeo, becomes a state of quiescence lying passively "upon" her. Juliet's own imagination later adapts itself to this transformation as she anticipates their sexual union: "Come night, come, Romeo, come, thou day in night,/For thou wilt lie upon the wings of night/Whiter than new snow upon a raven's back" (3.2.17–21). But in doing so she activates Romeo's images: concrete, tactile sensations take the place of personified abstractions, and his quietly fitted surfaces are drawn into a ceaselessly metamorphic flux. The death Juliet inflicts upon herself is likewise a violently erotic consummation of his wish to "rest" quiescently in her breast: "O happy dagger,/ This is thy sheath; there rest,⁹ and let me die" (5.2.169–70). This last transformation is, as we shall see, paradigmatic of the exchange of loves that takes place between Romeo and Juliet: his gentle desire to be "pillowed for ever" (to use Keats' Romeo-like language) on a breast he associates as much with maternal comfort as sexual desire becomes "in" her a violent thrust aimed at the quick of being.

These differences are present in every scene between Romeo and Juliet, and culminate in their separate, elaborately linked deaths. When Romeo forces his way into Juliet's tomb, he is still seeking through union with her the "rest" that eludes him: "Here, here, will I remain/With worms that are thy chambermaids; O, here/Will I set up my everlasting rest" (5.3-108–10). This conjuring with the word "here" echoes his complaint at the beginning of the play of being "out" of the place where he is "in" love: "I have lost myself; I am not here;/This is not Romeo, he's some other where" (1.1.197–98). It also recalls his decision after leaving the Capulets' ball to "turn back" to Juliet in order to "find out" the "centre" of his "dull earth" (2.1.2). His language in the tomb is like a final incantation designed to overcome whatever it is that enforces this distance from himself as well as Juliet. He seems to want to conjure up with words the experience of being in place, the simple "I am here" (1.3.5) that Juliet begins with, and Romeo instinctively associates with her.

Juliet, however, emerges from the experience Romeo wishes to arrive at. (Weaning structures her desire in the same figurative way that search for the peace-giving breast does Romeo's.) By the time she returns to consciousness in the tomb, her initial "I am here" has grown through time into something fuller and more complex: "I do remember well where I should be,/And there I am" (5.3.149–50). And though she wakes effortlessly into the experience of self-coincidence Romeo labors to attain in death, her voice locates it not "here" but "there." She is already "some other where," though in a very different sense than Romeo. Her awakening in the tomb is one of the rare instances, in fact, when her words "turn back" toward their center. Usually the "here" is for her imagination a backing for ventures outward, into the world and across ontological thresholds—not, as it is for Romeo, a goal in which to "set up" an "everlasting rest." Her similarly self-referential "there" when she kills herself a few moments later—"O happy dagger,/This is thy sheath; there rest, and let me die"—unlooses the voice that says "me" from the body that houses it (like a final weaning), and launches it toward an altogether mysterious silence. When she does use "here" in the final scene, the word refers not to where she is but to what's "out there": "What's here? A cup clos'd in my true love's hand?/ Poison, I see, hath been his timeless end" (5.3.161–62). It thus becomes an index of both her openness to the present-at-hand and her access to things that happen in her absence.

Romeo can never quite manage to make Juliet and the situation in which he finds her "here" in this way during the final scene, in spite of his conjurings with the word. He remains incapable of the kind of seeing that *grasps* things as hers does. He is too self-conscious in his grief, and too anxious (in both senses of the word) to materialize in language a death that feels "unsubstantial" to him, to risk the spontaneous responsiveness that comes naturally to her: "Eyes, look your last!/Arms, take your last embrace! and lips, O you/The doors of breath, seal with a righteous kiss/A dateless bargain to engrossing death!" (5.3.112–15). Juliet, on the contrary, merely says "I will kiss thy lips," and then does so (a far cry from her initial "What is your will?"), and registers her surprise with "Thy lips are warm"—a simple tactile observation that goes straight to the heart of grief.

IV

Juliet's "I do remember well where I should be,/And there I am" is a response to an immediate dramatic situation; but the total fabric of the play's language, concerned as it is with constitutive interchanges between the speaking self and the world in which it finds itself, lends the utterance an epigrammatic clarity and resonance.[10] Like a combination of the Cartesian *cogito* and the Freudian *wo es war, soll ich werden*, it articulates an experience of self-coincidence that is both arrival and return—in the present moment, to the body—from a realm closed to consciousness. And the pattern of motifs that it consummates suggests that it is something Juliet grows into during the course of the play. We have already seen how it complicates her initial "Here I am"; it also expands the "Ay me" she first utters in the balcony scene. There she is an unelaborated self (and self-affirmation) on the brink of the experience of sexual desire that will cause it to flower. By the final scene it has been filled out by a "remembering well" that enables her to venture over the threshold between life and death, consciousness and unconsciousness, the self and the non-self, and find herself where she "should be" when she returns.[11] (Cleopatra's "I have/Immortal longings in me" is another "I me" filled out with temporal experience that allows it to cross over and internalize this threshold.)

Though it is Romeo who triggers this flowering in Juliet—the Nurse tells her in their first scene together that "women grow bigger by men" (1.3.95)—echoes in the language of the play suggest that this "remembering well" is an ability she inherits from the Nurse herself: "That shall she, marry, I remember it well . . . I never shall forget it . . . I warrant, and I should live a thousand years, I never should forget it"(1.3.22–47). It involves what seems in *Romeo and Juliet* a uniquely female capacity to "grow bigger" in the element of time—to assimilate, nurture, and in Juliet's case prodigiously transform the happenings of life. The repetitions of the Nurse's reverie about Juliet's weaning issue from an involuntary memory conceived in female rather than male terms—not a chamber of sealed vessels inaccessible to consciousness (this Proustian notion of the past is congruent with Romeo's sense of life as a series of "encounters" [cf. 2.5.29] that pass him by) but a vast interconnectedness in which the self peacefully dwells. Her recollections circle around a natural cataclysm and around human separation and loss—an earthquake, Juliet's weaning, the deaths of "Susan" and her husband—yet they open on an interior space where no real harm can come to the self or the things it cherishes. (Its opposite is the partially repressed realm of phallic violence that haunts the soldier's dream and Mercutio's reverie: "Sometime she driveth o'er a soldier's neck,/And then dreams he of cutting foreign throats,/Of breaches, ambuscadoes, Spanish blades,/Of healths five fadom deep; and then anon/Drums in his ear, at which he starts and wakes,/And being thus frighted, swears a prayer or two,/And sleeps again"

[1.4.82–88].) Her daughter and her husband are alive in her memory, not mourned but loved. The tremors of an earthquake survive as the shaking of a dove-house wall, bidding her to "trudge." Juliet's "fall" becomes an occasion for merriment, and though the crude male jest is at her expense ("Thou wilt fall backward when thou comest to age"), the man who makes it "takes her up," and tenderly reassures her.[12]

The Nurse's memory weaves[13] all this eventfulness into a matrix of primary female experience (birth, lactation, weaning, marriage, maidenheads and their loss) from which Juliet emerges, standing high-lone and saying "Ay." Juliet will be weaned again in the course of the play, this time from the fate the Nurse holds out to her as a woman as well as the one Lady Capulet urges upon her as a wife.[14] Her initial weaning ushers her into a world of "day" the Nurse seems to think of as hers and Juliet's privileged domain, even though she happily acknowledges the presence of her husband and Juliet's parents at its periphery, the latter away at Mantua, the former there to take up Juliet when she falls.[15] The Nurse's reverie conjures up the idea of a woman's life as a vast biological cycle, a succession of archetypal experiences so intimately in touch with natural, generative time ("Sitting *in* the sun under the dove-house wall") that it really does seem plausible to think of living a thousand years. Sexuality is for her a source of pleasure, and the thought of it presides over her happy acquiescence to this realm and the woman's lot Verona prescribes for her. But for Juliet it becomes a *passion*—the source of a willfulness and a metaphysical desire that from the point of view of society and perhaps even nature are essentially transgressive. Her element will prove to be the night, and she herself the epitome of things violent and brief. Yet we are made to feel, I think, that Juliet's link with the primary realm of the Nurse continues unimpaired beneath her movement away from it during the course of the play. The Nurse's temporal rootedness and uncomplicated belief in the *goodness* of sexual experience are incorporated by Juliet's radical will as a voice prompting and giving its blessing to her ventures into the unknown: "Go, girl, seek happy nights to happy days" (1.3.105).[16]

Indeed, the notion of a "voice within" that summons and directs Juliet develops into a full-scale motif during the course of the play, and the Nurse is intricately associated with it. The Nurse first "calls her forth" from offstage, and when she appears, asking "Who calls?" the Nurse replies, "Your mother." Later, at the end of the Capulet ball, when Juliet and the Nurse remain alone together onstage, an anonymous offstage voice calls Juliet's name (Q2's stage direction reads, "One calls within, 'Juliet'"), and it is the Nurse who answers with "Anon, anon!" By the time of the balcony scene, the original situation has come full circle: Juliet, alone onstage with Romeo, hears the Nurse's voice summoning her from offstage, and refers to it as "some voice within" that *she* now says "anon" to. (Later in the scene this offstage summons and Juliet's response break into her address to Romeo, and are in turn assimilated by it.) This sequence appears to establish the Nurse as the generative "mother" of Juliet, and as a transmitter of the voices that call to her both from "within" and "beyond."[17] It also implies an identification or symbiosis between them that Juliet is in the process of growing away from. Its severance appears to be complete when Juliet dismisses the Nurse from *her* breast ("Thou and my bosom henceforth shall be twain"), and then fails to respond to her voice as it attempts to wake her for her marriage with Paris. (The Nurse's increasingly panicky address is a medley of all the calls Juliet has previously answered: "Mistress! . . . Juliet! . . . Why, lamb! why, lady! . . . Why, love, I say! madam! . . . I needs must waken her. . . .") Yet there are suggestions that this apparent repudiation of the Nurse is really a sign that her mediating function of waking Juliet to the voices within has been fulfilled. Thus Juliet, abandoned to her own resources when the Friar deserts her in the tomb, is able to hear the offstage "noise" that frightens him away as if it were personally calling to her,[18] and answers "Yea" (rather than "anon") to it—another convergence of obedience and affirmation in her that issues in an impulsive act of will.

Juliet thus seems to enjoy a smooth passage from the realm of the "good Nurse" (2.5.21, 28, 54) directly into the strangeness of sexual experience. The Nurse's free associations, her husband's jest, and the play of coincidences combine to weave a background for her in which sex is connected with weaning and saying "I." And sexuality does seem a matter of individuation for Juliet— individuation that is instinctively connected with affirmation. She *emerges into* sexual desire (in her two balcony scenes, literally standing "high-lone"), and experiences it as a means of action and a source of bounty, not, as it tends to be for Romeo, the longing for a lost self or distant object.

Needless to say, this is not how the patriarchal order that urges marriage on Juliet intends things to turn out. Marriage for a woman, as Lady Capulet's presence throughout the Nurse's reverie reminds us, is supposed to be a passage from daughter to wife and maid to mother that elides the realm of autonomous female sexuality and the powers associated with it. The notion of the sexual initiation legitimized by the institution of marriage as an unsexing of women is punningly suggested by a series of remarks about the "making" and "marring" of mothers and maids;[19] it is blatantly underscored by Sampson's equation of deflowering and capital punishment: "'Tis all one; I will show myself a tyrant: When I have fought with the men, I will be civil with the maids; I will cut off their heads." Some editors follow Q4 in emending Q2/F's "civil" to "cruel," on the grounds that the act of violence Sampson describes is scarcely a civil one. But the same male logic that makes the taking of a woman's maidenhead a beheading makes it the civil act *par excellence* (as we see in the case of Desdemona): by it her autonomy and her sexual will are taken from her, and she is positioned within the social order, subject to her husband and the rules of married chastity.

The Nurse's and Lady Capulet's counsels come from opposite realms, then, one where women grow by men, the other where a woman is marred by being "made" matron and maid at once. (Lady Macbeth, in taking upon herself her husband's ambitions, makes herself into a diabolical version of what Lady Capulet represents by negating in herself what the Nurse embodies: "Come, you spirits/That tend on mortal thoughts, unsex me here,/. . . Come to my woman's breasts,/And take my milk for gall . . ."). Yet both counsel the same thing, and there is a sense of collusion between them as they do so. Their very presence together before Juliet is emblematic of a social arrangement that contrives to divorce the sexual aspect of motherhood from the figure of the wife, and confine it to a domestic sphere where it will serve rather than threaten the male order that depends on it. But precisely because the female "knowledge" the Nurse embodies is excluded from the realm of male power, there is a sense that Juliet can inherit it in some magically direct way ("were not I thine only nurse,/I would say thou hadst suck'd wisdom from thy teat" [1.3.67–68]), free of the divisions which found that realm and the repressions that maintain it. Her sexuality seems to issue spontaneously from a core of primary identifications, and in a form more potentially disruptive to the male order of things than the anxious phallic assertiveness ("My naked weapon is out") which produces "rebellious subjects" (1.1.81) within it.

Romeo and Juliet is full of a sense of how social prerogatives based on the oppression of women place the men who enjoy them at a disadvantage in the realm of primary experience. Sampson reasons that since "women, being the weaker vessels, are ever thrust to the wall," he will "push Montague's men from the wall, and thrust his maids to the wall" (1.1.15–18), even though he himself has just admitted that the place nearest the wall is the superior position. And the image of the maid thrust against the wall by Sampson's gross assaults, the object not even of sexual lust but deflected male rivalry, is somehow balanced by that of the Nurse "Sitting in the sun under the dove-house wall," alone with Juliet in the world of women, enjoying there the backing of an elemental realm whose existence Sampson, with his insecure phallic readiness to give and take offence, will never even remotely intuit. Mercutio, for whom the "sociable" is an antidote to "groaning for love" (2.4.88–89), likewise perceives woman's position in love as analogous to her position in the civil order, and the sexual act as a means of subduing her to it: "This is the hag, when maids lie on their backs,/That presses them and learns them first to bear,/Making them women of good carriage" (1.4.92–94). Yet the bearing women are expected to endure in society is matched in the realm of ontological experience by a *power* to bear, and bear fruit, that men are denied by a code that regards submission as "dishonorable [and] vile" (as Mercutio terms Romeo's "calm" reaction to Tybalt's challenge), and defines freedom as a matter of keeping one's neck "out of collar" (1.1.4–5). Juliet's apostrophe to night suggests, moreover, that woman's sexual place is where the imagination thrives. The climax of her speech sublimates an intoxicating sensation of floating weightlessly in a void that encompasses the sexual act, while at the same time being oneself its ground and bearing the whole of it ("For thou wilt lie upon the wings of night/Whiter than new snow upon a raven's back"), that seems accessible only from beneath. She is the one in a position to take in sexual experience, and witness the epiphany that occurs at the moment of relinquishment: "Give me my Romeo, and, when I shall die,/Take him and cut him out in little stars,/And he will make the face of heaven so fine . . ." Romeo's imagination, by contrast, does not seem open to the sexual act in the way Juliet's is, and though his experience in love can't be reduced to Mercutio's travesty of it as "a great natural that runs lolling up and down to hide his bauble in a hole" (2.4.91–93), its horizons do seem limited by his desire to rest in Juliet's breast.

Similar ironies govern the socially instituted discrepancy between Romeo's and Juliet's approaches to love. We first encounter Romeo not being addressed by the "intergenerational"[20] will of the Montague family (as we might expect had Shakespeare wished either to portray the love relationship as symmetrical or explore it primarily within the division between the two families),[21] but adrift in the unsupervised realm of male adolescence. Yet the liberty to "inquire" he enjoys there has resulted in a mind full of knowledge about love (obviously acquired, as Juliet remarks, "by th' book") that betrays the absence of any felt connection with the source of instinctual wisdom Juliet draws from. He also enjoys a freedom of movement and the company and support of friends, while she is confined within the family places (hall, bedroom, tomb) and isolated from anyone with whom she might share her experiences as a young woman. But as a result she is the one who seems most capable and at home in the solitude that is love's element ("My dismal scene I needs must act alone"), and the one who provides the impetus and inner direction of their relationship once Romeo initiates it. His social advantages also create transitional conflicts that Juliet is spared. The male bonds that form in adolescence involve phallic allegiances against women and the threats of impotence, emasculation, and effeminacy posed by the actual sexual relation—hence Mercutio's almost compulsive eagerness to generate collective sexual ridicule of the Nurse, and his mockery of a "fishified" Romeo ("without his roe, like a dried herring") who is only "Romeo" (Mercutio insists) when he is "sociable" and not "groaning for love." These attitudes persist, moreover— as the opening scene makes clear—in the adult world, and hence make the conflict Mercutio articulates between social identity and sexual relatedness not just a passing adolescent stage but a permanent male dilemma.[22] Romeo is of all Shakespeare's romantic or tragic heroes the one least inhibited by these male bonds and the cultural values that reinforce them. When the play opens he is already disaffected with society, and too narcissistically self-absorbed to fell the *pull* of friendship. And when he falls in love with Juliet, he positively relishes the submissive role of fitting himself to her will. Yet Mercutio has to die (so the plot seems to tell us) before Romeo and Juliet's relationship can be sexually consummated, and Mercutio himself blames his death on Romeo's betrayal—for "coming between" Mercutio and Tybalt, to be sure, but also, one feels, for allowing something to come between the two of them. Shakespeare thus manages to make the presence of a bad conscience about sexual love that is endemic to masculinity felt in the background of Romeo's experience, and the one short moment that Romeo falls back into it plunges him and the entire play into tragedy: "O sweet Juliet,/Thy beauty hath made me effeminate,/And in my temper soft'ned valor's steel" (3.1.113–15).

V

It is not surprising, then, that Romeo lacks Juliet's temporal and positional assurance (Mercutio's "Where the devil should this Romeo be?" matches her "I do remember well where I should be,/And there I am"), considering what his male background provides for him. Even the Friar, whose place in Romeo's life corresponds to that of the Nurse in Juliet's, can only provide the counsel of someone who has abdicated from the flow of human experience and the disruptions that mark it. His presence as a "ghostly confessor" (2.6.21) introduces into the background of Romeo's love the idea of male celibacy, with its reservations about the legitimacy of sexuality ("So smile the heavens upon this holy act,/That afterhours with sorrow chide us not!" [2.6.1–2]), and its attempt to avoid the alternations of love and grief and attachment and separation which the Nurse's memory transforms into a steady state of well-being. The Nurse, remembering "Sitting in the sun under the dove-house wall," evokes a nature in which earthquakes and weanings magically correspond; the Friar speaks from his "cell" of a nature permanently arrested at the maternal breast, and elides all the "partings" through which life passes on its way from birth to death: "The earth that's nature's mother is her tomb;/What is her burying grave, that is her womb;/And from her womb children of divers kind/We sucking on her natural bosom find" (2.3.9–12). The Nurse's reverie evokes the feeling of being immersed in temporal process, and suggests an ability to communicate with the impersonal forces that dictate the "times" of human life ("Shake, quoth the dovehouse; twas no need, I trow,/To bid me trudge"). The Friar, on the other hand, thinks of time as the "plot" of an unknowable, otherworldly will, and his actions embody a half-guilty attempt to manipulate its "accidents" ("A greater power than we can contradict/Hath thwarted our intents").[23]

Romeo and Juliet mirror these differences, in death as well as life. The noise that frightens the Friar from the tomb triggers, as we have seen, Juliet's final "Yea": it seems to signal her to "be brief" much as the earthquake bid the Nurse to "trudge." Romeo, however, resolves to "defy" the "stars" when he hears of Juliet's death, and must force an unwilling death to take him: "Thou detestable maw, thou womb of death,/Gorg'd with the dearest morsel of the earth,/Thus I enforce thy rotten jaws to open,/And in despite I'll cram thee with more food" (5.3.45–48). Buried in these metaphors of grief is a fantasy of oral retaliation against the withdrawn, depriving maternal breast. It does not so much enter Romeo's psyche as take its place in the haunted male background which the gentleness of his own love stands out against but never entirely exorcises. When he enters the tomb, he similarly leaves behind him troubled images of sexual experience like those that will later possess Othello's deranged imagination: "Alack, alack, what blood is this, which stains/The stony entrance of this sepulchre?/What mean these masterless and gory swords/To lie discolor'd by this place of peace?" (5.3.140–43). Once inside the tomb, where a few moments later Juliet will wake into a remembering well, Romeo grows forgetful, and reality begins to feel dreamlike to him: "What said my man, when my betossed soul/Did not attend him as we rode? I think/He told me Paris should have married Juliet./Said he not so? Or did I dream it so?/Or am I mad, hearing him talk of Juliet,/To think it was so?" (5.3.76–81). Grief may be the immediate cause of this distraction, but the feeling of being adrift in a temporal element that undermines the will and robs consciousness of its experience is deeply characteristic of Romeo. Even when he is happiest in love he tends to regard what is happening to him as a series of winged, half-unreal moments, and reaches out for them with language in an attempt to hold and lengthen them. For Juliet, however, time is a metamorphic principle that animates her from within. The goals Romeo aims for as havens from temporal flux and the "weariness" it causes are for her charged thresholds of being. Even her impatience for their love's future is that of the bud for the flower, not, as it is for Romeo, that of a schoolboy for recess.[24]

These differences are especially pointed in the images with which Romeo and Juliet conjure up ideas of the life-in-death that persists in the tomb. His personifications of the "state" of death are a denial of time, process, and substance: death becomes a jealous lover (or would-be lover) who "keeps" Juliet in thrall, while worms attend on her as chambermaids. The unhappy imagination that creates this image is, in spite of the love that charges it, an enemy of the will in Juliet that tells Romeo's "happy" dagger to "there rest, and let me die." Juliet, on the contrary, anticipating the future into which the Friar's potion will cause her to wake, thinks of the tomb as a place of real, historical time, where physical process continues in the absence of life: "an ancient receptacle,/Where for this many hundred years the bones/Of all my buried ancestors are pack'd,/Where bloody Tybalt, yet but green in earth,/Lies fest'ring in his shroud" (4.3.39–43). Her imagination then proceeds to enliven this place with a scenario that makes crossing over into it all the more urgent: "O, look! methinks I see my cousin's ghost/Seeking out Romeo, that did spit his body/Upon a rapier's point. Stay, Tybalt, stay!/Romeo, Romeo, Romeo! Here's drink—I drink to thee" (4.3.55–58). Romeo's subsequent "Here's to my love!" (5.3.119) is, by contrast, nostalgic, not directional. It is a static gesture with which he fixes himself in the scene of his own death, not a crossing over to Juliet.

The language of the final scene measures these differences in minute detail. Romeo's resolve to "remain" in the tomb ("here, here will I remain,/With worms that are thy chambermaids") is, again, an attempt to conjure up the scene of his death, and prolong it into eternity; Juliet's is an active refusal to "come away" with the Friar, who "dare[s] no longer stay." And Romeo's emphasis on *staying* with Juliet ("I still will stay with thee,/And never from this palace of dim night/Depart again") is undercut when a few moments later she tenderly chides him for having left no poison to help her "after." He thinks of death as an "everlasting rest," but she perceives it as a "timeless end," and resolves in her own death to "be brief." In these last instances, especially, Juliet's language is both more realistic and metaphysically resonant than Romeo's. "Timeless end" is a ruthless tautology spoken by someone for whom life *is* time; yet it simultaneously evokes an afterlife more mysterious and sublime than the eternity Romeo's consciousness is equipped to understand. "After" is a spatio-temporal pun: it refers both to Juliet's crossing-over to Romeo and the situation in which he has "left" her. Both meanings gently underscore the limits of Romeo's imagination: able only to die into the scene of consciousness, not cross over or escape by extinguishing it, and unable to make room or provision there for a *live* Juliet, in spite of his concern for her. His desire to *remain* forever and hers to *be* brief epitomizes the difference between them, a difference that in spite of their fit assigns them separate meanings and destinations. The gold statues erected at the end of the play might almost be symbolic realizations of the state Romeo aspires to in death, but they fail utterly to capture Juliet. Though he sees her in the end as a beauty that makes the tomb "a feasting presence full of light," she associates herself in death with the sudden illumination of the lightning, that active principle "which doth cease to be/Ere one can say it lightens." Romeo leaves behind a letter that acknowledges the audience present at the scene of his death, and its attempt to avoid being misunderstood evokes the problematical, compromised endings of such characters as Lucrece, Hamlet, and Othello. Juliet, however, is content, regardless of how we measure her, to "measure [us] a measure and be gone" (1.4.10). In doing so she becomes a rare unquestioned center of value in the otherwise turbulent world of Shakespeare's tragedies.

NOTES

1. All quotations are from *The Riverside Shakespeare*, ed. G. B. Evans et al. (Boston, 1974).

2. For an acute discussion of the kinesthetic dimension in *Romeo and Juliet*, and on bodies in general in Shakespeare, see Michael Goldman, *Shakespeare and the Energies of Drama* (Princeton, 1972).

3. Other critics have interpreted this dream differently. Norman Holland offers a traditional psychoanalytic reading that stresses the mechanism of "reversal" in "Romeo's Dream and the Paradox of Literary Realism," *Literature and Psychology* 13 (1963), 97–103; for a summary see his *Psychoanalysis and Shakespeare* (New York, 1964), pp. 265–67. Majorie Garber discusses an evolution within the dream from simple prediction to metaphorical or mythic truth in *Dream in Shakespeare: From Metaphor to Metamorphosis* (New Haven, 1974), pp. 44–47. Both critics, like Romeo, interpret the dream by referring it to future events.

4. Here, as elsewhere in this texture of contrasts, a difference between distant objects and inner depths also involves a difference between seeing and hearing. Even the larger dramatic structures that shape the plot contribute to the impression of different hierarchies of the senses operating in the two central characters. Thus in both their first two encounters, at the Capulet ball and in the balcony scene, Juliet is for Romeo first an *object* that then speaks, while he is for her first a *voice* that then becomes manifest.

5. Although Q2 and F both read "when *I* shall die," many editors substitute Q4's "when *he* shall die," usually on the grounds that "I" makes Juliet sound inappropriately selfish. But "he" deprives the image of its orgasmic connotations (which are anything but egocentric), and in doing so eliminates the climax toward which the erotic energy of the entire speech builds. The Q4 reading is actually more like something we would expect from Romeo than Juliet: it absents Juliet from the final image, and fixes Romeo in a spectacular but lonely "Roman" apotheosis. (The New Arden *Romeo and Juliet* alludes to the climax of Ovid's *Metamorphoses*, where Caesar is transformed into a "goody shining starre.") In the Q2/F reading, however, Juliet "takes" Romeo with her in her "death." (There is an analogous difference in the final scene, as we shall see, between Romeo's desire to fix himself in a static, "everlasting" death, and Juliet's to follow him or take him with her into mortality.) She identifies what she experiences at the moment of sexual climax as *his* transformation, and hence posits at the extreme limit of privacy ("when I shall die") a paradoxical sharing of experience. The orgasmic connotations of the Q2/F reading, moreover, allow Juliet a kind of survival with Romeo in the afterlife of the final image, as the pantheistic "all the world" into which her erotic feelings for him burst. This merging of self and object in the feeling of desire is at once the most intense selfishness and the most extreme selflessness: whatever ethical discomfort it may arouse, it is truer to the paradoxes of Juliet's desire than Q4's more conventional mythic altruism.

6. Here again Romeo's imaginative impulses are at odds with his physical actions. In the events of the play, it is he rather than Juliet who most often acts to close the physical distance between them—approaching her at the ball and touching her hand, returning to the Capulet house and climbing the garden wall outside her balcony, scaling a ladder of rope to consummate their marriage in her bedroom, riding back to Verona when he hears of her death, and breaking open her tomb to be with her there.

7. Lady Macbeth, whose invocation to Night is a twisted recollection of Juliet's, operates similarly *within* her husband's mental universe:

pressing for the realization of the deed his imagination conjures up as a *possibility*, and dwells on at arm's length in compulsively subjunctive terms.

8. This is Benvolio's description of the feeling of his own by which he "measured" the "affections" of a solitary, retiring Romeo (1.1.128). The behavior that introduces us to Romeo's idiosyncracies, then, is something by which one adolescent male recognizes himself in another.

9. I have departed from the Riverside text which, following Q2 and F, reads "There *rust*, and let me die." Q1 has "Rest in my bosom. "Rust" makes a kind of sense, and is even consistent—as we shall see—with Juliet's ruthlessly materialist imagination. But in spite of Q1's inferior authority, internal evidence (such as Mercutio's description of Tybalt as a duelist who "rests him minim rests, one, two, and the third in your bosom") overwhelmingly favors "rest," and makes it by far the more resonant reading. Romeo commits suicide resolving to achieve his "everlasting rest" with Juliet, and the Friar tells her just before he runs away that "Thy husband in thy bosom there lies dead" (5.3.155). From the beginning the play's language develops the idea of a restless, unhoused male principle ("My naked weapon is out"; "this drivelling love is like a great natural that runs lolling up and down to hide his bauble in a hole") and a corresponding inner state of narcissistic oppression ("Griefs of mine own lie heavy in my breast,/Which thou wilt propagate to have it pressed with more of thine") that both become "happy" in Juliet's breast when they find their way there through the paradoxes of sexual exchange. "There rest" consummates this theme beautifully, while "rust" bitterly negates it. "Rust" also tends to confirm the male anxieties of Romeo's "O sweet Juliet,/Thy beauty hath made me effeminate,/And in my temper soft'ned valor's steel" (and look forward to their development in Othello's "Keep up your bright swords, for the dew will rust them"), while "rest" grants them a reprise.

10. A gnomic quality tends to attach to the language of location and self-assertion in other plays by Shakespeare more or less directly concerned with ontological "world" and its possession/dispossession. *King Lear*, especially, is insistent in its epigrammatic use of such language: cf. France's "Thou losest here, a better where to find" (addressed to Cordelia), Edmund's "The wheel has come full circle, I am here," and Cordelia's own "And so I am; I am," followed immediately by her gnomic "No cause, no cause."

11. In doing so she passes effortlessly from the subjunctive realm where Romeo's imagination characteristically languishes ("should be") into the present indicative where hers flourishes ("There I am").

12. See Barbara Everett's beautiful essay, "*Romeo and Juliet*: The Nurse's Story," *Critical Quarterly* 14 (1972), 129–39.

13. I use the term "weaves" advisedly. The Nurse's reverie allows us to observe what a Jungian would call "the anima" at work processing the raw material of life, creating from an inchoate jumble of events the illusion of a continuous fabric of experience. Even at the level of language itself there is an impulse to take compounds apart in order to weave them more securely into the ongoing flow: "I'll lay fourteen of my teeth—/And yet, to my teen be it spoken, I have but four—/She's not fourteen" (1.3.12–14). Mercutio's Queen Mab speech, which is in so many ways a complement of the Nurse's reverie, exhibits a similar delight in creating wholes out of disparate components, yet its fragile constructions exist in a "Time out a' mind," and cannot altogether conceal the authorial presence of a destructive, arbitrarily malicious "animus": "Her waggon-spokes made of long spinner's legs,/The cover of the wings of grasshoppers,/Her traces of the smallest spider web . . ." (1.4.62–64).

14. The language of the play suggests, in fact, that it is the Nurse who has to be weaned from Juliet: "Go, counsellor,/Thou and my bosom henceforth shall be twain" (3.5.239–40).

15. Juliet assimilates this beneficent "taking up" as a kind of ontological constant in the background of her own essentially anti-tragic capacity for risk-taking. Romeo, on the other hand, knows it only as an "unaccustomed" feeling brought on by dreams and implemented by "thoughts": "If I may trust the flattering truth of sleep,/My dreams presage some joyful news at hand./My bosom's lord sits lightly on his throne,/And all this day an unaccustom'd spirit/Lifts me above the ground with cheerful thoughts." Here, especially, the difference doesn't so much criticize Romeo as underscore the poignancy of his situation: having to invent and sustain at the level of fantasy and consciousness what is given to Juliet as the stable ground of experience.

16. This discussion of the Nurse's and Juliet's connectedness owes much to the current feminist appropriation of psychoanalytic object-relations theory: Nancy Chodorow's *The Reproduction of Mothering* (Berkeley and Los Angeles, 1978), especially, should be felt in the background of my argument. It must be added, however, that although this perspective provides a rich context within which to understand what Juliet assimilates from the Nurse, it has

practically nothing to tell us about the forces that propel Juliet *away* from the Nurse, into individuality and the undomesticatable "strangeness" of the erotic. Indeed, Shakespeare's portrayal of Juliet brings into focus the limitations of both sides of the current argument within psychoanalytic theory between models of the psyche that privilege object-relations and libido respectively.

17. The convergence of the two "withins"—the one beyond the world of the stage and the one beneath the conscious self—in Juliet's experience, and their manifestation to her as *voice*, suggest the nature of her extraordinary strength of will. (One might contrast Hamlet's equally auspicious summons from these two realms, and the confusion that the Ghost's offstage voice generates from "beneath.") Romeo, on the other hand, must *suppose* controlling forces whose transcendent will remains silent and undisclosed ("But He who hath the steerage of my course,/Direct my sail").

18. The Nurse's own voice, first trying to wake Juliet and then calling for help upon discovering that she is "dead," had earlier prompted Lady Capulet to inquire, "What *noise* is here?" (4.5.17).

19. Cf. Lady Capulet: "younger than you . . . Are made already mothers. By my count,/I was your mother much upon these years/That you are now a maid" (1.3.69–73); also Paris, "Younger than she are happy mothers made ," answered by Capulet, "And too soon marr'd are those so early made" (1.2.12–13). The spoken language here labors to insinuate an *identity* of "mother" and "maid" (through the agency of a "making" that is also a "marring")—as if by being "made" a mother a woman were "made" into a "maid."

20. The term is from Nancy Chodorow, "Family Structure and Feminine Personality," in *Women, Culture, & Society*, ed. Michelle Zimbalist Rosaldo and Louise Lamphere (Stanford, 1974), p. 57.

21. Such assumptions (or conclusions) govern most criticism of the play's alleged dramatic immaturity or limitations. James L. Calderwood, for instance, attributes the play's less-than-total success to a "concentration on, almost celebration of, dramatic form [that] imparts to the play a highly rigid structure based on the division between Montagues and Capulets and lovers and society" (*Shakespearean Metadrama* [Minneapolis, 1971], p. 116), while Sigurd Burckhardt finds it limited by "a symmetry which, even though it is a symmetry of conflict, is comforting" (*Shakespearean Meanings* [Princeton, 1968], p. 264). It has been the contention of this essay, on the contrary, that Shakespeare establishes these conventional dramatic symmetries (in the opening prologue, for instance), only to move within and beyond them to asymmetries that are the "true ground" (5.3.180) not only

of the play's "woe" but its generative energies as well. The story of the two "star-cross'd lovers" we are introduced to in the beginning has by the end become that of "Juliet and her Romeo."

22. See Coppélia Kahn, *Man's Estate: Masculine Identity in Shakespeare* (Berkeley and Los Angeles, 1981), for a seminal discussion of the importance of this conflict throughout Shakespeare's work.

23. For a related distinction between the Nurse and the Friar as "mediators," see Richard Fly, *Shakespeare's Mediated World* (Amherst, 1976), p. 19.

24. I am indebted to Howard Tharsing for this formulation of Romeo and Juliet's temporal differences.

John F. Andrews

Falling in Love: The Tragedy of *Romeo and Juliet*

What happens in *Romeo and Juliet*?[1] What did a dramatist of the 1590s want the "judicious" members of his contemporary audiences to see and hear, and how did he expect them to feel, as they attended the play[2] a later age would laud as the most lyrical of all love tragedies? Before I hazard a response to what is admittedly an unanswerable question, I should make it clear that what I'm really posing is a query about the "action"[3] of Shakespeare's drama, and more specifically about the effect such an action might have been intended to have on a receptive Elizabethan playgoer.[4]

As the late O. B. Hardison emphasizes in the commentary that accompanies Leon Golden's 1968 translation of Aristotle's *Poetics*,[5] there is much to be said for interpreting the earliest technical term for tragic effect, *catharsis*, as a word that means "clarification," and for conceiving of the experience it describes as one that takes place, not in the characters of a dramatic work, but in the audience that participates vicariously in those characters' thoughts, emotions, and interchanges. Hardison reminds us that Aristotle defines tragedy as that category of imitation (*mimesis*) which produces pleasure through a cogent representation of fearful and pitiable incidents. He and Golden stress the passage in which the great philosopher observes that realistic renderings of even the most displeasing subjects delight the viewer by assisting perception and eliciting insight. And they infer that when the father of dramatic theory speaks of the purgation that results from a tragedy, he is focusing primarily on the learning any coherently constructed work of art fosters: the sorting out, the clearing away of confusion or temporary misapprehension, that occurs as a responsive spectator notices, and appreciates, an aesthetically satisfying pattern of logical connections. When Aristotle refers to the catharsis that derives from a well-devised imitation of fearful and pitiable incidents, then, Hardison and Golden deduce that he is probably thinking of the enlightenment—the sense of mental relief, psychic release, and spiritual insight—that a member of the audience enjoys when he or she is able to make sense of a sequence of happenings that initially strike an onlooker as disparate and disorderly.

When we bring this concept of catharsis to bear upon the various species of tragedy, we discover that in some instances the intellectual, emotional, and ethical clarification attained by an attentive theatergoer parallels the hard-earned wisdom of a character who has arrived at self-knowledge through a siege of suffering. In tragic actions which feature this kind of recognition (*anagnorisis*) the central figure is divested of any impurities of mind or heart that impede "Clearer Reason" (*The Tempest*, V.i.68), and he or she acquires a degree of awareness that approximates the comprehension a perceptive member of the audience obtains by tracing and assessing the character's fortunes.[6]

In some instances the clarity a tragic figure realizes is a judgment that amounts to self-condemnation, as happens in *Richard III* and *Macbeth*. In these dramatic sequences the protagonists acknowledge their own guilt and wretchedness in ways an audience can endorse. In other instances the down-cast hero goes beyond an accurate mental evaluation of himself to a remorse that penetrates the conscience, as with the title characters of *Othello* and *King Lear*. Here the protagonists feel sorrow for what they perceive themselves to have done, and in the second case if not the first the audience may be led to conclude that the hero has gone a step further—from remorse to repentance, to a resolve to do whatever is required to make amends for the pain he has inflicted on others and cleanse his own soul.

In rare instances a tragic protagonist proceeds all the way to a complete reconciliation with himself, with those he has injured, and with the Heavens. In these sequences the protagonist arrives at a sense of "at-one-ment" that signifies redemption. In dramatic actions in which this kind of conversion occurs the central figure wins deliverance through an epiphany that transports him or her past the point where even the most sage of witnesses can hope to follow. In Sophocles' *Oedipus at Colonus*, for example, or in Milton's *Samson Agonistes*, the central character is granted a culminating vision in which death is swallowed up in a kind of victory. The hero completes his mission nobly, and as he expires he crosses the threshold to a mysterious but presumably more exalted realm on the unseen side of this world's veil of tears. Here the clarification that takes place in the protagonist surpasses the apprehension of the viewer, and the catharsis that issues in the well-tuned playgoer is akin to ecstatic rapture: a "calm of mind"[7] that accompanies the "wonder"[8] evoked by powers that move us to awe.

In most tragic actions the audience's catharsis is something that can be more aptly described as a sense of "woe" or "pity"[9] for a character whose grasp on reality is shown to be in some way deficient. As we watch a misguided protagonist come to grief under the lamentable circumstances that tragedies usually depict, we feel a wrenching disparity between our own observations and those of the focal figure. If we receive the kind of catharsis the usual tragedy is designed to provide, in other words, we emerge with an understanding that is both broader and more lucid than the impaired perception of the lost hero or heroine.

So what do we find when we turn our attention to *Romeo and Juliet*? As we watch this play do we sense that the protagonists share our view of what undoes them? Do we feel that in the end they transcend our vantage to claim a better world elsewhere? Or do we finally conclude that they fail in some manner, and lack the insight to assess their failure with the acuity an alert audience acquires by contemplating their "misadventur'd piteous Overthrows" (Prologue.7)?

Adherents can be found for all of these interpretations and more. There are many who accept the title characters at their own estimate, perceiving them as helpless pawns of conditions they have no means of countering. There are some who react to them with admiration, even reverence, canonizing them as pure "Sacrifices" of their families' "Enmity" (V.iii.304). And there are a few who blame them for intemperance and hold them responsible not only for their own tragedies but for the untimely deaths of several other characters.

Perhaps the best way to enter the world of the play is to take note of its cosmic imagery, its all-pervasive references to Fortune, Fate, and the Stars. If we hope to recapture something of the experience *Romeo and Juliet* provided its original audience, we need to come away from the tragedy with a conception of what it would have meant in Shakespeare's time to be a victim of "fatal Loins," to feel like "Fortune's Fool," and to seize upon the extremest of measures to "shake the Yoke of inauspicious Stars" (Prologue.5, III.i.144, V.iii.111).

The most important locus for medieval and Renaissance thinking about Fortune and Fate was Boethius' *Consolation of Philosophy*, a Latin dialogue that had probably been written in A.D. 524. Chaucer had used the *Consolation* extensively in the fourteenth century, and it remained so popular in the late sixteenth century that it was translated into Elizabethan English by no less a personage than the Queen herself. When Shakespeare alluded to the *Consolation*, then, he would no doubt have assumed that any literate member of his audience would be nearly as familiar with this masterwork as with the Bible and the Book of Common Prayer.

Any playgoer who had read Boethius would have known that the *Consolation*[10] involves a conversation between Lady Philosophy and a statesman who has fallen into disfavor and now awaits death. The imprisoned political leader is the author himself, and he calls upon a personification of Wisdom to explain why Fortune has treated him so cruelly. During the exchanges that ensue, Lady Philosophy points out that "Fortune" is properly to be regarded as a fictional abstraction, a symbolic embodiment of the role of mutability in human affairs. To those who view her aright, Dame Fortune is nothing more than a convenient name for the fickle and seemingly irrational "Goddess" who bestows and withdraws such worldly gifts as riches, honors, political office, fame, and pleasure. Lady Philosophy acknowledges that many mistakenly believe that happiness is to be found in the possession of goods that are subject to Fortune's caprices. But she insists that those who examine their lives carefully will eventually realize that the only felicity which lasts and is free from anxiety is that which is fixed on a Supreme Good higher than, and unaffected by, the vicissitudes of Fortune. Lady Philosophy doesn't deny that Misfortune is painful, but she insists that if we take it in the right spirit it provides a salutary reminder that everything in this life is fleeting. In the process it encourages us to focus our sights on Heaven, where, according to an even more authoritative spiritual guide, "neither moth nor rust doth corrupt, and where thieves do not break through nor steal" (Matthew 6:20).[11]

Many writers used the terms "Fortune" and "Fate" interchangeably, but Boethius drew a subtle distinction between them. For him "Fortune" was a name for Mutability itself, for what we now refer to as blind Chance. "Fate," on the other hand, was his term for a higher authority that presided over Fortune's seeming arbitrariness. For Boethius, and for subsequent Christian philosophers, Fate (or Destiny, as it was often called) was actually a pagan disguise for Providence, and the author of the *Consolation* saw it as a cosmic principle that was ultimately benign, though forever shrouded in obscurity.

Boethius was valued in Renaissance England for the way he had adapted Christianity to a quasi-Stoic frame of reference. In similar fashion, Saint Augustine was revered for the way he'd made Christianity fit a quasi-Platonic framework two centuries earlier. Augustine's treatise *On Christian Doctrine*[12] and his monumental discourse on the *City of God* were both familiar to educated Elizabethans, and Shakespeare's contemporaries would have seen the author of these two works as a theologian whose writings were fully compatible with Boethius' philosophy. Boethius' dichotomy between those pursuits directed to the Supreme Good (which is immutable) and those directed to all lesser goods (which are mutable) would have been accepted, then, as merely another means of expressing Augustine's distinction between those pursuits that lead to the supreme felicity of the City of God (Jerusalem) and those that leave one mired in the confusion and frustration of the City of Man (Babylon).

According to Augustine, all movement of the soul is prompted by the Will, and that which moves the Will is Love. Love, then, is the basic motivating force in human behavior, and it falls into two categories: (a) Sacred Love, or *caritas* (charity), which urges the Will in the direction of eternal life, and (b) Profane Love, or *cupiditas* (cupidity), which pulls the Will in the direction of temporal life. From Augustine's viewpoint, the sole purpose of religion and ethics is to teach believers what things are to be loved and enjoyed in and of themselves and what things are to be employed in the service of true Love. In his system the proper relation to things (loving and enjoying only the things of God, and using the things of this world solely in obedience to God) is *caritas*; the improper relation to things (loving and enjoying the things of this world, and abusing the things of God for the sake of temporal things) is *cupiditas*.

The cohesion between Augustine's theology and Boethius' philosophy becomes evident as soon we note that only those things which are temporal are subject to Fortune. To be under the sway of Fortune, then—to seek happiness by setting one's heart on those goods that are subject to Fortune's bestowal and removal—is to be guilty of *cupiditas* (misplaced or inordinate love). On the other hand, to rise above Fortune's sphere by aspiring to the immutable Supreme Good—to seek happiness through union with that which lies beyond the realm of Fortune— is to live in accordance with *caritas* (well-placed and duly ordered love).

But what about the Stars? How did they relate to Boethian and Augustinian thought? According to most medieval and Renaissance thinkers, "the Stars" (the Sun, the Moon, the Planets, and the constellations of the Zodiac) exercised a degree of influence on Earth, and this influence conditioned the general and particular destinies of human beings. But it was commonly believed that the Stars could directly affect only the material and corporeal levels of existence. Since Will and Reason were regarded as spiritual rather than physical (material or corporeal) in nature, it followed that these faculties of the human soul could not be influenced directly by the Stars. Will and Reason could be affected by the lower parts of the soul (the Senses and the Passions), however, if they did not maintain proper control over these earthbound dominions; and the lower nature (since it was corporeal in composition) could, in turn, be influenced by the Stars. If the Will or the Reason allowed themselves to be usurped by the Senses or the Passions, then, they became subject to indirect astrological influence and thus to Fortune.[13]

Let us sum up. As we've observed, Fortune, Fate, and the Stars were perceived in Shakespeare's time as interwoven concepts, and all three were integral to a system of ethics that drew heavily on the writings of Boethius and Augustine. Through these concepts, errant behavior could be depicted by any of several interchangeable means of expression: as unfortunate behavior caused by the influence of the Stars, as irrational behavior caused by the whims of Fortune, as improper and intemperate behavior caused by Reason or Will's subjection to the Senses or the Passions, or as disobedient, sinful behavior caused by misplaced or inordinate Love. For an alert Elizabethan, the name one applied to wrongheaded behavior was of little moment; the only thing that mattered was that sooner or later a person recognize it as a course that would result in disaster if it continued unchecked.

We should now be in a position to return to the questions posed at the outset. What "happens" in *Romeo and Juliet*? Do the lovers succumb to forces beyond their control? Do they somehow triumph over the circumstances arrayed against them and emerge as martyrs, as unblemished agents of redemption? Or do they "fall in love" in some ethical and theological sense that would have been meaningful to an audience familiar with Augustine and Boethius?

Suppose we begin our scrutiny of the action by reviewing some of the perspectives the play offers on the protagonists' romantic attachment. The Chorus who speaks the Prologue to Act II describes Romeo's sudden infatuation with Juliet as "Young Affection" gaping to be the "Heir" of "Old Desire" (lines 1–2); he goes on to suggest that the only reason Juliet has replaced Rosaline in Romeo's heart is that this time Romeo's feelings are requited (line 5). From the Chorus' point of view, then, what draws Romeo to Juliet is no different in kind from what attracted him to Rosaline. The young hero is simply shifting his attention to a more receptive subject as he responds to the erotic spurring implicit in his name.[14]

Friar Lawrence's initial response to Romeo's news about "the fair Daughter of rich Capulet" (II.iii.58, 66–68) echoes the Chorus' sentiments:

Is Rosaline, that thou didst love so dear,
So soon forsaken? Young Men's Love then lies
Not truly in their Hearts but in their Eyes.

In a way that recalls Mercutio, who refers to his friend as "Humours! Madman! Passion! Lover!" (II.i.7), and Benvolio, who comments that "Blind is his Love, and best befits the Dark" (II.i.32), Friar Lawrence appears to feel that, notwithstanding its intensity, Romeo's zeal for Juliet is as likely to be a manifestation of "Rude Will" as of "Grace" (II.iii.28). Hence the old man's admonition to "love moderately" (II.iv.14).

Despite his solemn advice, however, the Friar does nothing to impede the "wanton Blood" (II.v.71) that he and Juliet's Nurse both see in their eager charges. Before he even speaks with Romeo's betrothed, Friar Lawrence agrees to channel the youths' ardor into a clandestine marriage. With the Church's sanction, then, they consummate their vows within twenty-four hours of their initial encounter. So much for moving "Wisely and slow" (II.iii.94).[15]

There can be no question that what draws Romeo and Juliet to each other at the outset is physical attraction. But would it be just to assert that their union is based on nothing more elevated than erotic desire? I think not. The poetry with which they declare their feelings makes it well nigh impossible for us to conceive of any situation in which the protagonists could ever again be severed, let alone drift apart. After all, to preserve herself for the husband to whom she has plighted troth, Juliet defies and deceives her parents, evades a match that would advance both her own fortunes and her family's, dismisses the Nurse when the old retainer's pragmatism becomes the voice of "Ancient Damnation" (III.v.235), and drinks a potion she fears may be lethal. Meanwhile, for his part, Romeo proves more than willing to "give and hazard all" (*The Merchant of Venice*, II.vii.16) to uphold his pledge to Juliet. As we see the lovers increasingly isolated by events and, more importantly, by the folly of their elders and the insensitivity of even their closest confidants, we cannot help responding with sympathy for their predicament and admiration for the courage their consecration to each other inspires. By the end of the play it is patent that no one in their society really understands them; they're left completely alone in a world that seems at best indifferent, at worst hostile. In soul-trying times their loyalty to each other is severely tested, and it never falters.

But if the tie that binds Romeo and Juliet is the most precious thing the setting of Shakespeare's tragedy affords, does it follow that we are meant to regard the lovers' "extreme Sweet" (II.Chorus.14) as a delicacy that supersedes all other treasures? Are we to join our hearts and minds with the protagonists' fathers and erect statues of "pure Gold" (V.iii.299) to honor the title characters' fidelity to each other and to Love?

Perhaps so, but I find it difficult to locate a lot to celebrate in the events with which the play concludes. Old Capulet and Old Mountague clasp hands at long last, and if only by default a feud that has wrought untold devastation appears to be history. But at what cost? According to the city's sovereign, the only thing that remains when all is said and done is "A glooming Peace"— that and the Prince's haunting pronouncement that "All are punish'd" (V.iii.305, 295).

So what are we to make of the mood with which the final scene draws to a close? Is it possible that Shakespeare expected his audience to include the lovers themselves in the Prince's stern accounting of Verona's "Woe" (V.iii.309)? Can it be that a relationship so rare that it has become proverbial, a bond that appears indissoluble, was meant to be viewed as in some way defective? The answer, I submit, is yes. I think it more than likely that the playwright intended to have his earliest theatergoers see Romeo and Juliet as protagonists whose tragic flaw derives from the same source as their strength and beauty: the very fact that their devotion to each other is so all-consuming that it eliminates everything else from consideration.[16]

At their first greeting Romeo bows before Juliet as if she were a "holy Shrine" and he a "Pilgrim"; Juliet accepts this description of their venue and grants Romeo's "Pray'r" "lest Faith turn to Despair" (I.v.96, 99, 104, 106). In the Balcony Scene, the next time the protagonists meet, Romeo describes Juliet successively as "the Sun," as "bright Angel," and as "dear Saint," and he tells her "Call me but Love, and I'll be new baptiz'd" (II.ii.3, 26, 56, 50). Juliet responds in kind and declares Romeo's "gracious Self" to be "the God of my Idolatry" (II.ii.114, 115). What this imagery implies is that Romeo and Juliet are forswearing an old creed in favor of a new; their professions, accordingly, are to be understood as the religious vows of converts to a faith that differs from that of their fathers.

In Act III, having just learned of his banishment, Romeo says "'Tis Torture and not Mercy! Heav'n is here/Where Juliet lives" (III.iii.29–30). To be exiled from Juliet's presence is, for Romeo, to be condemned to outer darkness. A few hours later, as the lovers are saying farewell on the morning that ends their one night together, their aubade suggests that their lives are now fundamentally "out of Tune" (III.v.27) with the lark, the daylight, and other manifestations of a harmonious natural order. It is thus apropos that after Romeo's departure Juliet asks "Is there no Pity sitting in the Clouds/That sees into the Bottom of my Grief?" (III.v.198–99). Shortly thereafter she cries "Alack, alack, that Heav'n should practice Stratagems/Upon so soft a Subject as my self" (III.v.211–12).

From these and numerous other passages it is demonstrable that the relationship between Romeo and Juliet is a species, however refined, of *cupiditas*—a form of pseudo-worship in which one's deity is a creature rather than the Creator. Each lover views the other as the Supreme Good. Each accords the other a degree of adoration that Augustine (and innumerable later theologians) had defined as properly directed only to God. Their love becomes a universe unto itself, and when they are deprived of it each of the protagonists concludes that there is nothing left to live for.

But of course if Romeo and Juliet fall victim to idolatry, it is because they also succumb to passion. By indulging the senses and emotions, they allow first the concupiscible (pleasure-driven) and later the irascible (wrath-driven) divisions of the lower, sensible soul to gain hegemony over the rational soul (the Reason).

At the beginning Romeo is subject to the melancholy of a frustrated suitor. He keeps to himself, and when he is sighted by even his closest friend he slips into a "Grove of Sycamour" (I.i.125). Romeo is himself a "sick-amour," a youth afflicted with love-sickness, and his father observes that

> Black and portendous must this Humour prove
> Unless Good Counsel may the Cause remove.   (I.i.145–46)

Romeo's Reason emits warnings, both in the dream to which he several times refers in I.iv and in the misgivings he expresses at the end of that scene (I.iv.106–11), but the protagonist allows Mercutio's set-piece about Queen Mab to convince him, against his better judgment, to put his fear of "Consequence" out of mind. As the title character consents to attend the Capulet ball, his pivotal comment makes it obvious that what his intellect tells him is being suppressed by an act of will: "he that hath the Stirrage of my Course/Direct my Suit" (I.iv.112–13).[17]

From this point on, the hero plunges headlong into action. At his first glimpse of Juliet his senses are so entranced that he is oblivious to the threat posed by Tybalt. Later, in the Balcony Scene, it is Juliet, not Romeo, who expresses apprehensions; he declares "thy Kinsmen are no stop to me" (II.ii.70) and defines himself as a bold mariner (II.ii.83–85). Disregarding her instinctive caution, Juliet allows herself to be seduced by such bravado and agrees, against *her* better judgment, to become the partner of her suitor's rash ventures.

Up to this juncture the concupiscible passions have dominated the behavior of both lovers. Following Romeo and Juliet's hasty marriage, however, the irascible passions begin asserting themselves. Almost as soon as he departs from his wedding Romeo comes upon an incipient quarrel between Mercutio and Tybalt. The fresh bridegroom is not yet ready to reveal his new kinship with the Capulets, and as a result his conciliatory reply to a challenge Tybalt thrusts at him is misinterpreted by Mercutio as an expression of "calm, dishonorable, vile Submission" (III.i.76). Romeo's hotheaded friend steps in to defend the honor he assumes a lethargic and cowardly Mountague is incapable of maintaining for himself. In an urgent attempt to prevent needless conflict, Romeo lunges between the two duelers. Unfortunately the protagonist's efforts at peacemaking prove fatal to Mercutio, and Romeo's ally dies cursing the house of Mountague as vehemently as he had earlier scorned the Capulets.

To this moment in the scene Romeo has "thought all for the best." For the first time in the play, he has acted with judgment, restraint, and genuine valor. But now he finds himself in an unaccustomed position. By turning the other cheek and trying to comport himself as an honorable gentleman, he has unwittingly made himself appear dishonorable and contributed to a calamity. After a too-brief pause for reflection, he reacts to the "Plague" in his ears by accepting Mercutio's erroneous judgment on measured behavior that the audience will have recognized as anything *but* "Effeminate" (III.i.112, 114, 122). Casting aside his momentary self-control and rationality and yielding to an idolatrous concern for the kind of male "Reputation" that demands vengeance,[18] Romeo spurns "respective Lenity" to make room for "Fire-ey'd Fury" (III.i.119, 131–32). He disregards the Prince's prohibition against further bloodshed and takes the enactment of "Justice" into his own hands (III.i.189–91).[19]

The slaying of Tybalt functions as the turning-point in the action. Before this development there has been at least a possibility of success for Romeo and Juliet. Their fathers have both shown a willingness to end the feud, and there has thus been some basis for the Friar's optimism that the marriage of a Capulet to a Mountague might bridge the way to a more harmonious future. With the deaths of Mercutio and Tybalt, however, the hostility between the two factions is rekindled, and the Prince can see only one way to prevent further carnage: by removing Romeo from "fair Verona" before more "Civil Blood" makes more "Civil Hands unclean" (Prologue.2–4).

By the time Romeo arrives at the Friar's cell in III.iii he is practically beside himself. Upon learning that he has been banished, he falls to the ground, his abject posture symbolizing the topsy-turvy state of a soul no longer led by Reason. In this condition he draws a dagger, and only the Friar's intervention forestalls an instant suicide:

> Hold thy desperate Hand!
> Art thou a Man? Thy Form cries out thou art!
> Thy Tears are Womanish; thy wild Acts
> Denote th' unreasonable Fury of a Beast!
>
> . . . .
>
> Hast thou slain Tybalt? Wilt thou slay thy self?
> And slay thy Lady that in thy Life lives
> By doing damned Hate upon thy Self?   (III.iii.107–17)

The answer to the Friar's last two questions will turn out to be affirmative. And the questions and answers that precede them explain why.

In IV.i Juliet comes to the Friar's cell, like Romeo with a knife, and like Romeo determined to take her own life. Seeing in her "the strength of will to slay [her] self" (line 72), the Friar suggests a less desperate remedy for her difficulties. He then gives her a potion that will suspend her bodily functions for enough time to allow her to be mourned and entombed. Meanwhile he sends a message to Juliet's husband. Due to unforeseen difficulties Romeo fails to receive it, and a day later he has no way of knowing that there is literal truth in his servingman's euphemistic report that the heroine is "well" and "sleeps in Capel's Monument" (V.i.17–18).

Now the protagonist descends into an even deeper depression. Purchasing poison from an Apothecary whose appearance resembles that of Despair in Spenser's *Faerie Queene*,[20] he makes his way to Juliet's tomb. Upon his arrival, as he dismisses his man Balthasar, Romeo depicts himself in language that summons up memories of the Friar's rebuke in III.iii.107–17:

> The Time and my Intents are savage wild,
> More fierce and more inexorable far
> Than empty Tigers, or the roaring Sea.   (V.iii.37–39)

The pertinence of these words is almost immediately borne out when the desperate title character is provoked by an uncomprehending Paris and kills him. Moments later Romeo's portrayal of his "Intents" is illustrated yet again when he downs the liquid he has brought with him to the cemetery:

> Come, bitter Conduct; come, unsavory Guide.
> Thou desp'rate Pilot, now at once run on
> The dashing Rocks thy seasick, weary Bark.   (V.iii.116–18)

Within seconds Juliet awakens to find her dead husband, and his example inspires her to plunge his dagger into her own breast. Thus does Romeo "slay" his "Lady" by "doing damned Hate" upon himself (III.i.116–17). And thus does Shakespeare emblematize the fatal consummation of a union forged in unregimented idealism.

We should now be in a position to comment on the roles of Fortune, Fate, and the Stars in *Romeo and Juliet*. As we have observed, the protagonists are prompted by their concupiscible passions into an idolatrous relationship that makes them vulnerable to forces beyond their ken. As chance would have it, these forces combine to unleash the irascible passions that destroy Mercutio, Tybalt, Paris, and eventually Romeo and Juliet themselves. To put it another way, by forfeiting rational governance over their own behavior, the lovers subject themselves to the waywardness of happenstance. They become Fortune's fools (III.i.144). In a sense that they don't recognize, they become "fated."

In the process, by reducing themselves to menial servants of emotional and astral influences that would have had no power to manipulate them if they had kept their souls under the guidance of Reason, they become "Star-cross'd" (Prologue.6). Ironically and sadly, at no point in the action are the "Stars" more securely in command than at the moment when a tragically misled Romeo commits a mortal sin in a futile effort to "shake" their "Yoke" from his "World-wearied Flesh" (V.iii.111–12).

It should not escape our notice, of course, that most of the play's other characters are also culpable victims of Fortune, Fate, and the Stars. The Capulets have sought to rise in worldly status, using their daughter as an unwilling instrument to that end, and that is one of the reasons we cannot bring ourselves to place much blame on Juliet for disobeying her unfeeling parents. It seems altogether apt that the Capulets' "ordained Festival" turns to "black Funeral"; they learn by bitter trial that on the Wheel of Fortune "all things change them to the contrary" (IV.v.84–85, 90). Meanwhile Mercutio, Tybalt, and Paris all submit in their own ways to Fortune's turns and suffer the consequences.

Even the sententious Friar can be seen as Fortune's plaything. For a man of the cloth he seems inordinately preoccupied with his worldly standing (hence his well-intended but ill-advised efforts to use unauthorized means to end the city's feuding, and hence his frantic scurrying about to cover his traces and avoid

Romeo and Juliet

being caught at the graveyard in Act V), and many of his error-prone judgments and makeshift expedients presuppose an improvident reliance on Fortune's notoriously unreliable cooperation.

In many respects the play's society as a whole is shown to be at the mercy of Fortune, Fate, and the Stars. The setting for Shakespeare's tragedy is, after all, a microcosm of postlapsarian humanity. And in this context the fates of Romeo and Juliet turn out to be a "Scourge" (V.iii.292), a divine judgment, in senses that exceed the meaning intended by the Prince.

But how should all of this affect an audience experiencing the drama? Ultimately, like most of Shakespeare's tragedies, *Romeo and Juliet* appears designed to leave us with an enhanced appreciation of what it means, in Christian terms, to be human. If we've profited as we ought to from the action, we will know the protagonists better than they know themselves. And we will understand—alas, in a way they do not—what brought their story to its grievous denouement.

And how will we appraise the "Death-mark'd Love" (Prologue.9) of these beautiful and pitiable youths? If we have attended to what we have seen and heard, our sentiments will echo the humility and compassion implicit in a sixteenth-century cleric's prayer of thanksgiving. As he witnessed a small company of wrongdoers being carted off to their dooms, he said "But for the grace of God, there goes John Bradford."[21]

NOTES

1. I realize, of course, that "What happens in *Romeo and Juliet*" varies each time the tragedy is performed; this was no less true of productions in the playwright's own lifetime than of those that have occurred in "After-hours" (II.vi.2). For a provocative discussion of the impossibility—if not indeed the undesirability—of "definitive" realizations of a dramatic script, see Jonathan Miller's *Subsequent Performances* (New York: Viking, 1986). For a thoughtful application of Miller's principles to recent interpretations of Shakespeare's most famous love-drama, see Barbara Hodgdon's "Absent Bodies, Present Voices: Performance Work and the Close of Romeo and Juliet's Golden Story," in *Theatre Journal*, 41:3 (October 1989), 341–59.

2. I am acutely conscious of oversimplification when I refer to "the play" as if there were a single rendering of *Romeo and Juliet* (or of any of Shakespeare's works) that can answer to such a term. What a given person sees or hears on a particular occasion depends not only on the sensibility he or she brings to the encounter but also on what text of the drama is presented and how that text is treated by those who present it.

In 1597 and 1599, respectively, two versions of *Romeo and Juliet* appeared in quarto printings. The later version is less crude and appears to be more directly related to an authorial manuscript than the earlier; it advertises itself as "Newly corrected, augmented, and amended," and (appropriately, in my view) it constitutes the control text for modern editions of the title. Because the Second Quarto is itself flawed in places, however, it too is usually "corrected, augmented, and amended" by modern editors, frequently with material spliced in from the comparatively corrupt First Quarto and less frequently with material drawn from the derivative later quartos—Q3 (1609), Q4 (undated but evidently issued around 1622), and Q5 (1637)—and from the 1623 First Folio (whose *Romeo and Juliet* appears to have been set from the Third Quarto). An inevitable consequence of the plethora of options afforded the post-Elizabethan editor, director, and commentator is that no two *Romeo and Juliet*s are exactly the same.

In this article all quotations from the plays and poems are referenced to *The Guild Shakespeare* (New York: GuildAmerica Books, 1989–92), a 19-volume annotated edition I've recently completed for the Doubleday Book & Music Clubs.

3. For Shakespeare's own use of the terms "judicious" and "action," see *Hamlet*, III.ii.1–52.

4. I would underscore the word *might* in this sentence. We have very little information about how Elizabethan playgoers responded to Shakespeare's tragedies, and much of what we do have is subject to debate.

5. See *Aristotle's Poetics: A Translation and Commentary for Students of Literature* (Englewood Cliffs, N.J.: Prentice-Hall, 1968), particularly pages 115–20. My thinking on catharsis in Shakespeare has also been richly informed by Hardison's "Three Types of Renaissance Catharsis" in *Renaissance Drama*, n.s. 2 (1969), 3–22, and by the writings of the late Virgil K. Whitaker, especially in *The Mirror Up to Nature* (San Marino: The Huntington Library, 1965), and Roy Battenhouse, above all in *Shakespearean Tragedy: Its Art and Its Christian Premises* (Bloomington: Indiana University Press, 1969).

6. The situation I describe here is the norm for Shakespearean comedy and romance, where catharsis ("dis-illusionment") must

occur in the central characters in order to bring about the resolution that constitutes a happy ending. I've written in more detail about the relationships between tragedy and comedy in "Ethical and Theological Questions in Shakespeare," an article in Volume II of *William Shakespeare: His World, His Work, His Influence*, edited by John F. Andrews (New York: Scribners, 1985). For further comment on the relationship between "disillusionment" and catharsis in Shakespearean tragedy, see the Editor's Introduction to Volume 4 (*Julius Caesar* and *Antony and Cleopatra*) of *The Guild Shakespeare*.

7. *Samson Agonistes*, line 1758.

8. *Hamlet*, V.ii.375. Among Shakespeare's tragedies, the only one that strikes me as approaching this kind of denouement is *King Lear*, where (depending on how the final moments of the play are staged) a long-suffering protagonist can be construed either as dying in despair or as departing from "this tough World" with a glimmer of faith and hope that promises to "redeem all Sorrows" (V.ii.311, 264). There are some who see *Hamlet* and *Antony and Cleopatra* as tragedies that also carry us to the verge of "divine comedy." I can find some basis for this reading of the Prince of Denmark's final moments, but up to the point where Hamlet and Laertes exchange forgiveness I see little reason to take at face value the allusions to Providence that are usually interpreted as indicating a "sweet Prince" with his heart in the right place. In *Antony and Cleopatra* I discern no textual warrant for the view that an audience is to be persuaded by the protagonists' grandiloquent assessments of themselves or by the "New Heaven, New Earth" they claim to win by disavowing the "dungy" clay kingdoms they cede at last to Caesar (I.i.17, 35). I discuss Milton's appropriation of tragic form in "'Dearly Bought Revenge': *Samson Agonistes, Hamlet*, and Elizabethan Revenge Tragedy," *Milton Studies*, 11 (1979), 81–108. For a fascinating new analysis of the different types of Christian tragedy, I recommend "Religious Patterning in Shakespeare's Major Tragedies" by Sherman H. Hawkins in *Transactions of the Connecticut Academy of Arts and Sciences* 50 (June 1991), 151–88.

9. See *Hamlet*, V.ii.375, and *King Lear*, V.iii.231–32.

10. The edition of *The Consolation of Philosophy* that I have used is the translation and commentary by Richard Green (Indianapolis: Bobbs-Merrill, 1962).

11. Friar Lawrence invokes "Philosophy" in III.iii.55–56 of *Romeo and Juliet* when he explains to a desperate Romeo that he should welcome "Adversity's sweet Milk." Both here and later in the play (see V.v.65–83), the Friar calls attention to Lady Philosophy's

teaching that "bad" fortune is actually better for us than what we incorrectly think of as good fortune. In *As You Like It*, II.i.1–17, Duke Senior sounds a Boethian note when he observes that "Sweet are the Uses of Adversity." And in *King Lear*, IV.i.19–21, Gloster speaks similarly when he says that "Full oft 'tis seen/Our Means secure us, and our mere Defects/Prove our Commodities."

12. I am indebted to the translation and commentary by D. W. Robertson, Jr. (New York: Liberal Arts Press, 1958). Robertson also discusses *On Christian Doctrine* extensively in *A Preface to Chaucer* (Princeton: Princeton University Press, 1962).

13. For a more detailed exposition of the relationship between astrology and medieval and Renaissance psychology, see Walter Clyde Curry's "Destiny in *Troilus and Criseyde*" in *Chaucer and the Medieval Sciences* (New York: Oxford University Press, 1926). Also see John W. Draper, "Shakespeare's Star-Crossed Lovers," *Review of English Studies* 15 (1939), 16–34; Douglas L. Peterson, "Romeo and Juliet and the Art of Moral Navigation," pp. 33–46 in *Pacific Coast Studies in Shakespeare*, edited by Waldo F. McNeir and Thelma N. Greenfield (Eugene: University of Oregon Books, 1966), and James L. Calderwood, "*Romeo and Juliet*: A Formal Dwelling," in *Shakespearean Metadrama* (Minneapolis: University of Minnesota Press, 1971).

14. Romeo's surname in all the original texts is spelled "Mountague." Given Shakespeare's wordplay on "ague" (fever) in "Sir Andrew Ague-cheek" (as the name of the foolish suitor is rendered in the First Folio text of *Twelfth Night*), it seems reasonable to assume that the playwright was fully aware of the symbolic potential in "Mount-ague." See *Love's Labor's Lost*, IV.i.1–4, for related play on "Mounting," and compare the aptness of such additional Shakespearean names as *Launcelet* ("small lance") in *The Merchant of Venice* and *Fortinbrasse* (a rendering of the French *Fortinbras*—"strong in arms"—that picks up on "Brazen" and "Mettle" when the name is introduced in I.i.65–102) in the Second Quarto of *Hamlet*. In V.iii.159 of *All's Well That Ends Well*, we learn that Diana, the maiden Bertram believes himself to have mounted, derives from "the ancient Capilet," an Italian family whose surname can be translated "small horse." What's in a name then? Quite a lot, particularly if we disregard modern editors' "corrections" of Shakespeare's spelling and retain the designations the playwright himself provided. See *The Guild Shakespeare*, Volume 16, page 468, for a note on "Doctor Buts" and other symbolic nomenclature in *Henry VIII*.

15. See James C. Bryant, "The Problematic Friar in *Romeo and Juliet*," *English Studies* 55 (1974), 340–50, for background that might have

been pertinent to an Elizabethan audience's perception of the Friar and his role in the events that lead to tragedy.

16. A. C. Bradley is seldom recalled nowadays, but one of the wisest and most memorable observations ever uttered about Shakespearean tragedy is his remark that "[i]n the circumstances where we see the hero placed, his tragic trait, which is also his greatness, is fatal to him." In my view, Romeo and Juliet illustrate both this and another of Bradley's generalizations about Shakespeare's tragic protagonists: "In almost all we observe a marked one-sidedness, a predisposition in some particular direction; a total incapacity, in certain circumstances, of resisting the force which draws in this direction; a fatal tendency to identify the whole being with one interest, object, passion, or habit of mind." See *Shakespearean Tragedy* (London: Macmillan & Co., 1904), pp. 26–27.

17. Here I retain the Second Quarto spelling *Stirrage*, which plays on *stir* (compare I.i.9, where Gregory observes that "To move is to stir") and reminds us that Romeo's "Steerage" will prove that "Love" can be considerably more "rough" (I.iv.27) than the jesting Mercutio suspects. Romeo's nautical imagery anticipates what he will say to Juliet in II.ii.83–85 ("I am no Pylat, yet wert thou as far/As that vast Shore wash'd with the farthest Sea,/I should adventure for such Marchandise") and what he will say just before he expires in V.iii.116–18. The *Pylat* spelling in II.ii.83 may be an authorial allusion to Pontius Pilate; if so, it casts an ironic light on the sacrificial imagery in Capulet's benediction at V.iii.304.

18. We sometimes forget that an excessive love of "Reputation" was regarded as a form of idolatry in the Renaissance. For a consideration of this theme in another Shakespearean love tragedy, see David L. Jeffrey and J. Patrick Grant's "Reputation in *Othello*" in *Shakespeare Studies* 6 (1970), 197–208. Meanwhile, for perceptive observations about the part gender plays in male codes of behavior, see Coppélia Kahn's "Coming of Age in Verona," in *Modern Language Studies* 8 (Spring 1978), 171–193; Marianne Novy's *Love's Argument* (Chapel Hill: University of North Carolina Press, 1984); Edward Snow's "Language and Sexual Difference in *Romeo and Juliet*," in *Shakespeare's Rough Magic*, edited by Peter Erickson and Coppélia Kahn (Newark: University of Delaware Press, 1985); and Eve Kosofsky Sedgwick's *Between Men: English Literature and Male Homosocial Desire* (New York: Columbia University Press, 1985).

19. In doing so, of course, he disregards the teaching Elizabethans would have been familiar with from the homily *Of Obedience* (1547) and the later homily *Against Disobedience and Willful Rebellion*

(1574), both of which drew on the Apostle Paul's Epistle to the Romans (12:17–13:7) to remind subjects that they should "Recompense to no man evil for evil," instead leaving to God and his ordained "powers that be" the judging and punishing of crimes. The popularity of revenge tragedy in the Elizabethan and Jacobean theater was an implicit acknowledgment that men who prized their honor (their self-respect and their social standing) frequently found it difficult, if not impossible, to submit themselves to passive, longsuffering forbearance, even though they recognized that the code duello was explicitly condemned by the Lord they claimed to worship (see the Sermon on the Mount, especially Matthew 5:38–44). For a fuller discussion of the ethical, social, and political tensions that resulted from this disparity between supposedly "masculine" and "feminine" approaches to the resolution of conflict, see Fredson Bowers' *Elizabethan Revenge Tragedy, 1587–1642* (Princeton: Princeton University Press, 1940) and Eleanor Prosser's *Hamlet and Revenge*, revised edition (Stanford: Stanford University Press, 1971).

20. See Book I, Canto ix, stanzas xxvii–liv. I owe this observation to Professor Joan Hartwig of the University of Kentucky, who shared it with me in 1971 when we were both teaching at Florida State University.

21. An earlier version of this essay, "The Catharsis of *Romeo and Juliet*," appeared in *Contributi dell'Istituto di Filologia Moderna* (Milan, 1974), pp. 142–75. I am grateful to the editor of that volume, Professor Sergio Rossi of the University of Turin, for permission to publish a revision of the original article. I also wish to acknowledge the degree to which my thinking about *Romeo and Juliet* has benefited from the writings of others not previously cited in these notes, among them Ralph Berry, *Romeo and Juliet: The Sonnet-World of Verona*," in *The Shakespearean Metaphor* (London: Macmillan, 1978); James Black, "The Visual Artistry of *Romeo and Juliet*," in *Studies in English Literature* 15 (1975), 245–56; Franklin M. Dickey, *Not Wisely But Too Well: Shakepeare's Love Tragedies* (San Marino: Huntington Library, 1957); Harley Granville-Barker, *Prefaces to Shakespeare*, IV (Princeton: Princeton University Press, 1946); Jack J. Jorgens, "Franco Zeffirelli's *Romeo and Juliet*," in *Shakespeare on Film* (Bloomington: Indiana University Press, 1977); Harry Levin, "Form and Formality in *Romeo and Juliet*," *Shakespeare Quarterly* 11 (1960), 3–11; M. M. Mahood, *Shakespeare's Wordplay* (London: Methuen, 1957); Thomas E. Moisan, "Rhetoric and the Rehearsal of Death: The 'Lamentations' Scene in *Romeo and Juliet*," *Shakespeare Quarterly* 34 (1983), 389–404; Norman Rabkin, "Eros and Death" in *Shakespeare and the Common Understanding* (New York: Free Press, 1967); Susan

Snyder, "*Romeo and Juliet*: Comedy into Tragedy," *Essays in Criticism* 20 (1970), 391–402; and Stanley Wells, "Juliet's Nurse: The Uses of Inconsequentiality," in *Shakespeare's Styles*, edited by Philip Edwards, Inga-Stina Ewbank, and G. K. Hunter (Cambridge: Cambridge University Press, 1980).

Bibliography

Andrews, John F. "Falling in Love: The Tragedy of *Romeo and Juliet*" (revision of an essay first published in 1974).

Ashcroft, Dame Peggy. "Romeo and Juliet." *Shakespeare in Perspective.* Volume I. Ed. Roger Sales. London: Ariel Books, 1982.

Berry, Ralph. "*Romeo and Juliet*: The Sonnet-World of Verona." *The Shakespearean Metaphor.* London: Macmillan, 1978, pp. 37–47.

Black, James. "The Visual Artistry of *Romeo and Juliet*," *Studies in English Literature*, 15 (1975), 245–56.

Bruce, Brenda. "Nurse in *Romeo and Juliet*." *Players of Shakespeare.* Ed. Philip Brockbank. Cambridge: Cambridge University Press, 1985, pp. 91–102.

Bryant, James C. "The Problematic Friar in *Romeo and Juliet*," *English Studies*, 55 (1974), 340–50.

Calderwood, James L. "*Romeo and Juliet*: A Formal Dwelling," in *Shakespearean Metadrama.* Minneapolis: University of Minnesota Press, 1971, pp. 85–119.

Dickey, Franklin M. *Not Wisely But Too Well: Shakespeare's Love Tragedies.* San Marino, California: Huntington Library, 1957, pp. 102–17.

Draper, John W. "Shakespeare's 'Star-Crossed Lovers,'" *Review of English Studies*, 15 (1939), 16–34.

Garber, Marjorie. "*Romeo and Juliet*: Patterns and Paradigms," in *The Shakespeare Plays: A Study Guide*. La Jolla: University of California at San Diego, 1979, pp. 50–63.

Hapgood, Robert. "*West Side Story* and the Modern Appeal of *Romeo and Juliet*," *Shakespeare Jahrbuch* (Heidelberg), 8 (1972), 99–112.

Harris, Julie. "Foreword to *Romeo and Juliet*." *The Guild Shakespeare*, Vol. 2. New York: GuildAmerica Books, 1989, pp. vii–x.

Hodgdon, Barbara. "Absent Bodies, Present Voices: Performance Work and the Close of Romeo and Juliet's Golden Story," *Theatre Journal*, 41:3 (October, 1989), 341–59.

Jorgens, Jack. *Shakespeare on Film*. Bloomington: Indiana University Press, 1977, pp. 79–91.

Kahn, Coppélia. "Coming of Age in Verona," *Modern Language Studies*, 8, No. 1 (Spring 1978), 171–193.

Levin, Harry. "Form and Formality in *Romeo and Juliet*," *Shakespeare Quarterly*, 11 (Winter 1960), 3–11.

Mahood, M. M. "Romeo and Juliet." *Shakespeare's Wordplay*. London: Methuen, 1957, pp. 56–72.

McGuire, Philip. "On the Dancing in *Romeo and Juliet*," *Renaissance and Reformation*, n.s. 5 No. 2 (1981), 87–97.

Novy, Marianne. "Violence, Love, and Gender in *Romeo and Juliet*." *Love's Argument: Relations in Shakespeare*. Chapel Hill: University of North Carolina Press, 1984, pp. 99–109.

Peterson, Douglas L. "*Romeo and Juliet* and the Art of Moral Navigation." *Pacific Coast Studies in Shakespeare*. Ed. Waldo F. McNeir and Thelma N. Greenfield. Eugene: University of Oregon Books, 1966, pp. 33–46.

Snow, Edward. "Language and Sexual Difference in *Romeo and Juliet*." *Shakespeare's Rough Magic*. Ed. Peter Erickson and Coppélia Kahn. Newark: University of Delaware Press, 1985.

Snyder, Susan. "*Romeo and Juliet:* Comedy into Tragedy," *Essays in Criticism*, 20 (1970), 391–402.

Traversi, D. A. *An Approach to Shakespeare*. New York: Doubleday, 1956, pp. 110–38.

Van Doren, Mark. "Romeo and Juliet." *Shakespeare*. New York: Henry Holt, 1939, pp. 63–75.

Wells, Stanley. "Juliet's Nurse: The Uses of Inconsequentiality." *Shakespeare's Styles*. Ed. Philip Edwards, Inga-Stina Ewbank, and G.K. Hunter. Cambridge: Cambridge University Press, 1980, pp. 51–66.